Wealth and Disaster

WEALTH and DISASTER

Atlantic Migrations from a Pyrenean Town in the Eighteenth and Nineteenth Centuries

Pierre Force

Johns Hopkins University Press   *Baltimore*

© 2016 Johns Hopkins University Press
All rights reserved. Published 2016
Printed in the United States of America on acid-free paper
2 4 6 8 9 7 5 3 1

Johns Hopkins University Press
2715 North Charles Street
Baltimore, Maryland 21218-4363
www.press.jhu.edu

Library of Congress Cataloging-in-Publication Data

Names: Force, Pierre, author.
Title: Wealth and disaster : Atlantic migrations from a Pyrenean town in the eighteenth and nineteenth centuries / Pierre Force.
Description: Baltimore : Johns Hopkins University Press, 2016. | Includes bibliographical references and index.
Identifiers: LCCN 2016007277 | ISBN 9781421421285 (hardcover : acid-free paper) | ISBN 1421421283 (hardcover : acid-free paper) | ISBN 9781421421292 (electronic)
Subjects: LCSH: Lamerenx, Marc-Antoine, 1710-1771 or 1772—Family. | Mouscardy, Jean, approximately 1720-1797—Family. | French—Haiti—Cap-Français Region—Biography. | Immigrants—Haiti—Cap-Français Region—Biography. | Coffee growers—Haiti—Cap-Français Region—Biography. | Labastide-Clairence (France)—Biography. | France—Emigration and immigration—History. | Pyrenees—Emigration and immigration—History. | Haiti—Emigration and immigration—History. | Caribbean Area—Emigration and immigration—History. | BISAC: HISTORY / United States / General. | HISTORY / Europe / France. | HISTORY / Caribbean & West Indies / General. | HISTORY / Modern / 18th Century. | HISTORY / Modern / 19th Century.
Classification: LCC F1929.C3 F67 2016 | DDC 972.9—dc23
LC record available at https://lccn.loc.gov/2016007277

A catalog record for this book is available from the British Library.

Special discounts are available for bulk purchases of this book. For more information, please contact Special Sales at 410-516-6936 or specialsales@press.jhu.edu.

Johns Hopkins University Press uses environmentally friendly book materials, including recycled text paper that is composed of at least 30 percent post-consumer waste, whenever possible.

Hapette trinketaren orhoitari

CONTENTS

Preface ix
Acknowledgments xvii
*Note on Geographical Names, Measurement Units,
and Currency Units* xix

1 Origins of a Migration Network   1

2 The Coffee Boom and the Jealousy of Trade   29

3 House-Based Societies and Emigration   62

4 War and Property Rights   88

5 Nation, Citizenship, and Atlantic Migrations   117

6 Conclusion   155

Appendix A. Genealogical Table: House of Uhart-Juzon   *161*
Appendix B. Genealogical Table: House of Berrio   *166*
Appendix C. Genealogical Table: House of Mouscardy   *169*
Notes   *173*
Bibliography   *209*
Index   *223*

PREFACE

La passion de l'histoire m'a dominé toute ma vie. J'ai souvent entretenu des correspondances sur des faits qui n'intéressent personne: je me plais, par exemple, à savoir comment s'appelle un champ que j'ai vu sur le bord d'un chemin, qui possédait jadis ce champ, comment il est parvenu au propriétaire actuel; je m'attache de même à découvrir ce que sont devenus des cadets disparus vers telle ou telle époque.

My entire life, I have been led by a passion for history. I've often corresponded on topics that are of interest to no one else: for instance, I like to learn the name of a field I pass along a road, who owned it in the past, and how it came to the current proprietor. I seek even to discover what became of younger sons who, excluded from inheritance, disappeared around this or that time.

Chateaubriand, Mémoires d'outre-tombe, 1850

Il te faudrait élever les Pyrénées au standing international. Parfaitement. Elles n'ont pas la classe. On ne les prend pas au sérieux. Elles manquent de poids, de gravité.

You should elevate the Pyrenees to international consideration. Absolutely. They're not classy. They fail to be taken seriously. They have little weight, little gravitas.

Henri Lefebvre, Pyrénées, 1965

On March 14, 1826, a musical comedy by Eugène Scribe entitled *L'oncle d'Amérique* (The American uncle) was performed for the first time in Paris. It told the story of a young woman who wants to get married but has no dowry. Her suitor persuades a coachman to pretend to be her uncle from America: a Saint-Domingue plantation owner entitled to the famous indemnity that the Haitian government has just committed to paying in exchange for France's recognition of the island's independence. In the following excerpt, the impostor, named Bonnichon, introduces himself to Louise, the young woman whose uncle he claims to be:

> BONNICHON: Yes, my lovely child. I am a landowner in America, in Saint-Domingue. It's far away, isn't it? You can't get there by post coaches.
> *To the tune of "Foursome"*
> Among the most honest traders,
> I am famous there for my plantations
> I have fields there, houses, and negroes
> Around two millions' worth.

LOUISE: Eh what? Blacks?
BONNICHON: A magnificent product!
   Hey, but the color makes no difference, my child:
   Whether it came from Europe or America,
   Money is always white.[1]

This passage shows clearly that for French audiences in 1826, *America* did not yet mean the United States and was still identified with the former colony of Saint-Domingue, which had won de facto independence in 1804 and formal recognition in 1825. It also shows that Saint-Domingue was seen as a land where enormous fortunes had been made, and the connection between these fortunes and slavery was clearly understood: the metaphorical syllepsis ("money is always white") unites in a single word the literal meaning (the white color of money, specifically silver coins) and the figurative sense (the white color of the race). The passage also suggests that there was skepticism about the reality of those fortunes. In the play, the wealthy American is an impostor. In France in the 1820s, refugees from Saint-Domingue who had been displaced by the Haitian Revolution were viewed with a mix of admiration and contempt, as former slave owners who were perhaps rich or perhaps ruined and came from a world that no longer existed.

Such ambivalence in fact predated the demise of the colony. Stanislas de Wimpffen, a French traveler who visited Saint-Domingue in the late 1780s and wrote a rather cynical account of his journey, mentioned the popular prejudice in continental France that equated Saint-Domingue with unlimited wealth: "It is well established, especially among the inhabitants of metropolitan France, that one only needs to breathe the air of the colonies to get as rich as Cresus. Overlooking what happened to those who killed themselves working, one is satisfied with the occasional sight of someone who was especially lucky and made a fortune. Thus the prejudice acquires the strength of a mathematical demonstration."[2] As a result, according to Wimpffen, "*American* and *millionaire* will remain synonymous in France for a long time."[3] In Wimpffen's opinion, this was in many ways an illusion. The conspicuous displays of wealth by "Americans" who returned home to France for short visits were not a reflection of their actual economic circumstances: "Do not be fooled by the childish and laughable splendor that some colonists display temporarily in Paris or in coastal cities. I know the secret of those charlatans. The carriage in which Mr. American struts so awkwardly, the wardrobe reminiscent of the Marquis de Mascarille, the diamonds that shine on his black hand, have cost him several years' worth of income and the sale of part of his plantation."[4]

When they were in France, these visitors presented Saint-Domingue as an Eldorado. Back in Saint-Domingue, they privately complained that the island was hell on earth: "I have never seen an American in France who did not rehearse, with more exaggeration than truth, the charms of living in Saint-Domingue. Since I have been here, I have not met one, not even one, who did not curse Saint-Domingue and the recurring impediments that caused him, year in, year out, to stay longer in such hell."[5]

The figure of the American uncle conjured up a coincidence of opposites: an image of wealth and disaster. I would like to argue that this ambivalence was tied to specific historical circumstances, and I propose to understand its roots by reconstructing the experience of a few emigrants who left the western French Pyrenees in the eighteenth century and established coffee plantations in northern Saint-Domingue. I will tell the story of two families: the Lamerenx family, whose first emigrant sailed to Saint-Domingue in 1729, and the Mouscardy family, whose first emigrant left France sometime before 1750. Both families came from the same Pyrenean town, La Bastide Clairence, approximately fifteen miles inland from the port city of Bayonne, and settled in the same town in Saint-Domingue, Saint-Martin-du-Dondon, approximately twenty miles south of Cap-Français. I will follow each family over three generations. After the Haitian Revolution, most of the Lamerenx descendants resettled in Cuba and started coffee plantations there. The Mouscardy descendants remained in Haiti and took part in the building of the new nation.

If *American* conjured up an idea of wealth, *uncle* implied kinship. A big part of this story is about the kinship dimensions of emigration and colonization. In the cases under study here it was generally the younger sons who left, while the firstborn, male or female, inherited the estate. There is, however, one prominent counterexample of a firstborn and heir who chose emigration. I try to understand the meaning of this exception to the rule, and I ask what the exception tells us about the meaning of the rule itself.[6]

Why the western French Pyrenees? First, because the number emigrating to Saint-Domingue from that region was significant: the historian Jacques de Cauna estimates that up to 40 percent of the white population of Saint-Domingue in the eighteenth century came from southwestern France (the area south of Bordeaux and west of Toulouse, down to the Spanish border).[7] The main ports of emigration were Bordeaux and Bayonne. Traffic from Bordeaux was much greater, but if we focus on Bayonne, which was the port of choice for emigrants from the western Pyrenees in the strict sense (the small area closest to the Spanish border), we find that it produced approximately twelve hundred emigrants to Saint-Domingue between 1749 and 1777 (the only period for which we have detailed records).[8] That is a significant number if one recalls that the entire white population in Saint-Domingue in 1789 was only about thirty thousand. Also, the Pyrenean communities that produced the emigrants whose stories are told in this book happen to have a long pedigree as objects of social-scientific study. Several concepts in sociology and anthropology are associated with case studies conducted in the western French Pyrenees, including Frédéric Le Play's "Pyrenean stem family,"[9] Pierre Bourdieu's "matrimonial strategies,"[10] Henri Lefebvre's "rural communities,"[11] and Claude Lévi-Strauss's "house-based societies."[12] I draw on this rich body of ethnographic and theoretical work (which is especially meaningful, albeit potentially problematic, in the case of Bourdieu and Lefebvre, who had indigenous knowledge of the subject matter).[13]

In standard accounts of Atlantic history, the violence and instability that characterized the Atlantic world are acknowledged, but the emphasis is on the overall stability of exchanges that one finds if one considers the Atlantic system as a whole. According to the historian Bernard Bailyn, "Information as well as trade and people moved in stable routes."[14] As to the mercantilist policies of imperial powers, which depended on exclusive trading zones, Bailyn observes that they were undercut by massive smuggling to the point of becoming irrelevant: "Despite all the commercial hostilities between rival nations and competitive interests, the pan-oceanic commercial webs that developed as the Atlantic world matured were interwoven, complex and multitudinous."[15]

Microhistorical observation reveals a different picture, however, one of discontinuities and severed links. It shows how chaotic the lives of these emigrants were: they got rich, then poor, then rich again; they fought wars and switched sides more than once during those wars; they lost touch with relatives or associates for decades; they pledged allegiance to one sovereign, then to the enemy of that sovereign. I contend that the chaotic nature of these lives was a consequence of the instability of the colonial trade system itself. Wealth generation was predicated on the military enforcement of exclusive trading zones, which were under constant attack by commercial rivals who were also enemies. There was no practical or conceptual distinction between a competitor and an enemy.

This connection between trade and warfare was self-evident in the eighteenth century, but it is harder to grasp now because free traders have long won the battle of ideas that Adam Smith started with his attack on mercantilism in *The Wealth of Nations*.[16] However, as the intellectual historian István Hont argues, mercantilism was not merely a flawed economic doctrine.[17] It was the modern form of statecraft practiced by all the major European powers. Surprisingly, Hont has little to say about colonial commerce, even though it was a key component of the mercantile system.[18] For an account of colonial commerce and its role in pursuing the political and military objectives of European powers, we have to go back to much older scholarship, such as Eli Heckscher's classic study of mercantilism[19] or Richard Pares's masterful *War and Trade in the West Indies*.[20] One could also mention Albert Hirschman's first book, *National Power and the Structure of Foreign Trade*, written during World War II, which showed the similarities between classic mercantilism and the use of trade by Nazi Germany in the

1930s to wield political influence in southern and eastern Europe.[21] Historical work is always a product of its time. Atlantic history became a dominant paradigm during the 1980s and 1990s, a period of growing optimism about free trade and globalization. Mercantilism was a major object of study during the 1930s, a period of intense "jealousy of trade," to use an expression that Hont borrowed from Hume.

One may ask why I chose to write about people who made fortunes thanks to slave labor and who kept lamenting the loss of their properties after they were dislodged by the Haitian Revolution. Two years after the beginning of the slave insurrection, which caused many French colonists to take refuge in the United States, Thomas Jefferson wrote to James Monroe, a fellow slave owner, that "the situation of the St. Domingo fugitives (aristocrats as they are) calls aloud for pity & charity. Never was so deep a tragedy presented to the feelings of man."[22] The plight of the Saint-Domingue refugees no longer elicits such sympathy. (I should note that Jefferson's own feelings on the matter were mixed: a few weeks before he wrote to Monroe, he facetiously suggested in a letter to his daughter Martha that the Saint-Domingue refugees should be sent to live "among the Indians, who could teach them lessons of liberty & equality.")[23] One may also wonder about the use of the word *disaster* in my title. In the grand scale of human suffering the disasters these emigrants experienced cannot be compared to the extermination of the natives of Hispaniola or the mass displacement of Africans caused by the Atlantic slave trade. The characters I follow had many unappealing traits. On the one hand, they were entrepreneurial, resourceful, hard-working, adventurous, and accomplished practitioners of intercultural negotiation. On the other hand, they were greedy, suspicious, despotic, occasionally callous, and consistently litigious. There was mistrust even within the family sphere, as siblings sued one another over the control of family assets.

I would invoke two authorities in support of my choice of subject matter. In *The Kingdom of This World*, the great Cuban novelist Alejo Carpentier tells the story of a Saint-Domingue plantation owner who takes refuge in Cuba following the Haitian Revolution.[24] The story is told from the point of view of a slave named Ti Noël, who follows his owner into exile and subsequently leaves him to return to Haiti. Carpentier's choice of narrator is a literary device that the conventions of historical scholarship do not allow. Yet the choice I made of following two families over several generations results in a narrative arc that is fairly similar to the one found in Carpentier's novel. By following the Lamerenx family, we move from Saint-Domingue to Cuba. With the Mouscardy family we return to Haiti. In the process, we cross national and racial boundaries several times. I would submit that if Carpentier found enough material there for an epic novel, there should be plenty for an interesting microhistory. As to the nastiness and litigiousness of the people I study, I would say that it is a boon to the historian, who can count on an extensive legal record. I would also invoke the opinion of Pierre Bourdieu, who hailed from a village not far from La Bastide Clairence and liked to claim that in Pyrenean societies "the question of the economic basis of domestic power" was approached "more realistically than in other societies." What Pyrenean inheritance customs can teach us, according to Bourdieu, is that "the sociology of the family, which is so often depicted as based on sentiment, might be no more than a particular case of political sociology."[25]

In the past twenty years there has been an outpouring of research on the Haitian Revolution, colonial slavery, the plantation economy, and the Atlantic world. My own path to these issues was a circuitous one. It started with an interest in the archives of rural areas that initially seemed to have no connection to the Atlantic world. In that sense it was similar to the path taken several decades ago by the colonial historian Gabriel Debien, whose Atlantic journey started with an exploration of private archives from the Poitou region.[26] I began this research in 2008 following a conversation with the mayor of La Bastide Clairence about a house that had just become municipal property. The house seemed to have historical significance because an old indoor tennis court (*jeu de paume*) was attached to it. Little was known about it, however. I volunteered to research the ownership history of the house in the Archives départementales, thinking it would take only a day or two. I found that in 1899 the house had been owned by a shoemaker who lived in Montevideo, Uruguay, and leased it to an inhabitant of La Bastide Clairence. That was interesting but not entirely surprising, as I knew about Basque emigration to South America in the nineteenth century. As I went further back in time, I found that in 1818 the house had been the property of a family whose members were scattered across the Atlantic: some lived in a neighboring town in France, some lived in various places in Cuba, and one lived in New Orleans. The family name, Lamerenx, and the house name, Berrio, were entirely unfamiliar to me, even though I thought I had a good knowledge of the history of the town of La Bastide Clairence. Finding evidence of emigration to the Caribbean in a rural area that seemed to have few connections to the wider world piqued my curiosity. I then discovered that the Lamerenx family was one of several families from La Bastide Clairence that produced emigrants to Saint-Domingue in the eighteenth century. I reconstructed their itineraries by following the archival trail across the Atlantic. Because trying to tell the story of several families would have resulted in an unmanageable cast of characters, I decided to limit myself to the Lamerenx and Mouscardy families, who had the earliest emigrants and therefore the richest histories and also provide an opportunity for comparison and contrast, one being noble, the other being a peasant family.

The work of reference on southwestern French emigration to the Caribbean in the eighteenth century is *L'Eldorado des Aquitains*, by Jacques de Cauna. While building on Cauna's findings, I explore issues that a macrohistorical approach cannot address, such as individual decisions to emigrate. Like Emma Rothschild in *The Inner Life of Empires*,[27] I borrow from the genre of prosopography, and I take each individual as a monad offering a vista of the world as a whole. However, my subjects are more obscure than hers and did not leave an extensive correspondence. Their trajectories have to be reconstructed mainly from legal and administrative documents, as Linda Colley did in *The Ordeal of Elizabeth Marsh*.[28] Rothschild's subjects had eventful and complicated lives, but they operated for the most part within the comparatively safe confines of the British Empire. Being often on the losing side of wars, my subjects experienced catastrophic disruptions.

Methodologically this book has a good deal in common with the work of Rebecca Scott and Jean Hébrard, who have studied the peregrinations of an Atlantic creole family over several generations.[29] The questions I ask of the material are different, however. Scott and Hébrard focus on one family's struggle to secure their status and rights as free persons. I focus on the pursuit of economic opportunity in chaotic circumstances. Aside from these microhistories, which stand out methodologically, I make use of the recent and very rich production on colonial Saint-Domingue, the Haitian Revolution, and Caribbean history in general. By observing the comings and goings of a few individuals between the western French Pyrenees and the Caribbean, I am able to show how these two worlds became interconnected (something that recent histories of the Caribbean often fail to do): who emigrated and how depended on one's position in the Pyrenean house-based system; capital accumulation in Saint-Domingue relied on Pyrenean networks; in turn, wealth earned in America changed the rules of the game back home.

Thus an investigation that started a few years ago in the Archives départementales des Pyrénées-Atlantiques with a limited purpose morphed into something much more ambitious. The initial goal was not forgotten, however. The house of Berrio and its tennis court, known to today's inhabitants of La Bastide Clairence as *le trinquet Hapette*, were added to the register of historic places by a French governmental decree on September 8, 2011.[30]

For all quotations from primary sources, I give the original language (French, Spanish, or Gascon, with modernized spelling) in the notes.

ACKNOWLEDGMENTS

I thank Léopold Darritchon, who was mayor of La Bastide Clairence at the time of my research, for giving me unfettered access to the municipal archives. Thanks are also due to Véronique Sallaberry-Auzi, deputy mayor for cultural affairs, to Marianne Simpson, town secretary, and to the team of volunteers (especially Geneviève Sallaberry) who catalogued the archives and indexed the minutes of the deliberations of the municipal council from 1680 to 1950. Professional archivists could not have done a better job. Warmest thanks as well to Denis Dufourcq and François Dufourcq for giving me access to their family papers, including documents collected in La Bastide Clairence by their late father, Pierre Dufourcq.

At Johns Hopkins University Press, Elizabeth Demers was an enthusiastic supporter of the project from the beginning. I am grateful to her and to the three anonymous readers for helping to make this a better book.

Christina Schutt, a lawyer in Port-au-Prince and a descendant of Jean Mouscardy, kindly shared the results of her extensive genealogical research. Dr. Maite de Lamerens and her cousin Paul de Lamerens generously provided information about the more recent history of the Lamerenx family. Alina Arce, a civil engineer in Havana and a Lamerenx descendant, made a major contribution to this research by identifying and retrieving key documents in the Cuban National Archives.

This book was written during a year I spent at Princeton University as a fellow of the Shelby Cullom Davis Center for Historical Studies (2014–15). I had stimulating conversations with each of the other fellows: Nicole Archambeau, Pamela Ballinger, David Barnes, Jennifer Foray, Atina Grossmann, and Rebecca Nedostup. Thanks to David Bell for encouraging me to apply. I am grateful to Philip Nord, who served as director of the center; with Matthew Karp, he fostered an atmosphere of vigorous intellectual exchange and mutual supportiveness.

From 2011 to 2014 I served as dean of humanities at Columbia University, reporting first to Nicholas Dirks, now chancellor of the University of California, Berkeley, then to David Madigan, executive vice president for arts and sciences. I thank both for supporting the notion that the administrator need not extinguish the scholar and for allowing me to spare a few hours a week for my own research, while carrying out very demanding duties. I am also grateful to Margaret Edsall, associate vice president for academic affairs, for making my job easier and more enjoyable than it would otherwise have been.

Many people, at Columbia University and beyond, helped by giving advice or by reading early drafts of this work. Special thanks are due to Jeremy Adelman, Jacques de Cauna, and Emmanuelle Saada. Many thanks as well to Christopher L. Brown, Paul Cheney, Maryse Condé, Nicholas Cronk, Vincent Debaene, Christiane Demeulenaere-Douyère, Daniel Desormeaux, Souleymane Bachir Diagne, Mamadou Diouf, Madeleine Dobie, Eric Foner, my daughter Charlotte Force, Jean Hébrard, Timothy Jenkins, Antoine Lilti, Florence Olivier, Jean-Baptiste Orpustan, Jesús Rodríguez Velasco, Rebecca Scott, Pamela Smith, Jérôme Luther Viret, and Wendy Warren.

Parts of chapters 1 and 3 were initially published in an earlier form in an article entitled "Eighteenth-Century Matrimonial Strategies and Emigration to the Americas: The House of Berrio in La Bastide Clairence," published in *Annales. Histoire, Sciences Sociales* (English edition) 68:1 (2013), 75–106 (translated from the French by John Angell). Elements of chapter 5 initially appeared in previous form in "The House on Bayou Road: Atlantic Creole Networks in the Eighteenth and Nineteenth Centuries," *Journal of American History* 100:1 (2013), 21–45.

NOTE ON GEOGRAPHICAL NAMES, MEASUREMENT UNITS, AND CURRENCY UNITS

Lower Navarre in the eighteenth century was nominally a kingdom, ruled by the king of France, who was also king of Navarre and had claims on Upper Navarre, the part of the kingdom south of the Pyrenees, which had been under Spanish rule since 1512. The Parliament of Navarre, located in Pau, had jurisdiction over Lower Navarre as well as the province of Béarn. In 1790 Lower Navarre became a part of the Basses-Pyrénées department, which was renamed Pyrénées-Atlantiques in 1969.

The monetary unit in eighteenth-century France was the livre (0.011 ounces of gold or 0.16 ounces of silver). The colonial livre used in Saint-Domingue was worth two-thirds of the metropolitan livre. The livre was the accounting unit in recorded transactions. The currency in circulation comprised mainly Spanish and Portuguese coins.

One livre was worth 20 sols or 240 deniers.

The French franc used after 1803 was worth roughly one *ancien régime* livre.

The Spanish dollar (*peso de ocho* in Spanish, *piastre forte* or *gourde* in French) was used in Cuba and the rest of the Spanish Empire. The US dollar was based on the Spanish dollar. One Spanish or US dollar was worth approximately 5.5 metropolitan livres, or 8.25 colonial livres.

In Saint-Domingue the Portuguese gold coin (*la Portugaise d'or* in French) minted in Brazil was also used. It was worth 8 Spanish dollars, or approximately 66 colonial livres.

The area unit for land transactions in Saint-Domingue (still used as a customary unit in Haiti today) was the *carreau*, defined as a square with sides of 100 paces. One *carreau* was approximately 1.3 hectares or 3.2 acres. In Cuba the land-transaction unit was the *caballería*. One *caballería* was approximately 10 *carreaux*, or 13 hectares, or 33 acres.

The area unit for land transactions in France before the adoption of the metric system was the arpent. One arpent was 0.84 acres or 0.34 hectares.

The weight unit for coffee in Saint-Domingue was the millier. One millier was one thousand pounds of coffee.

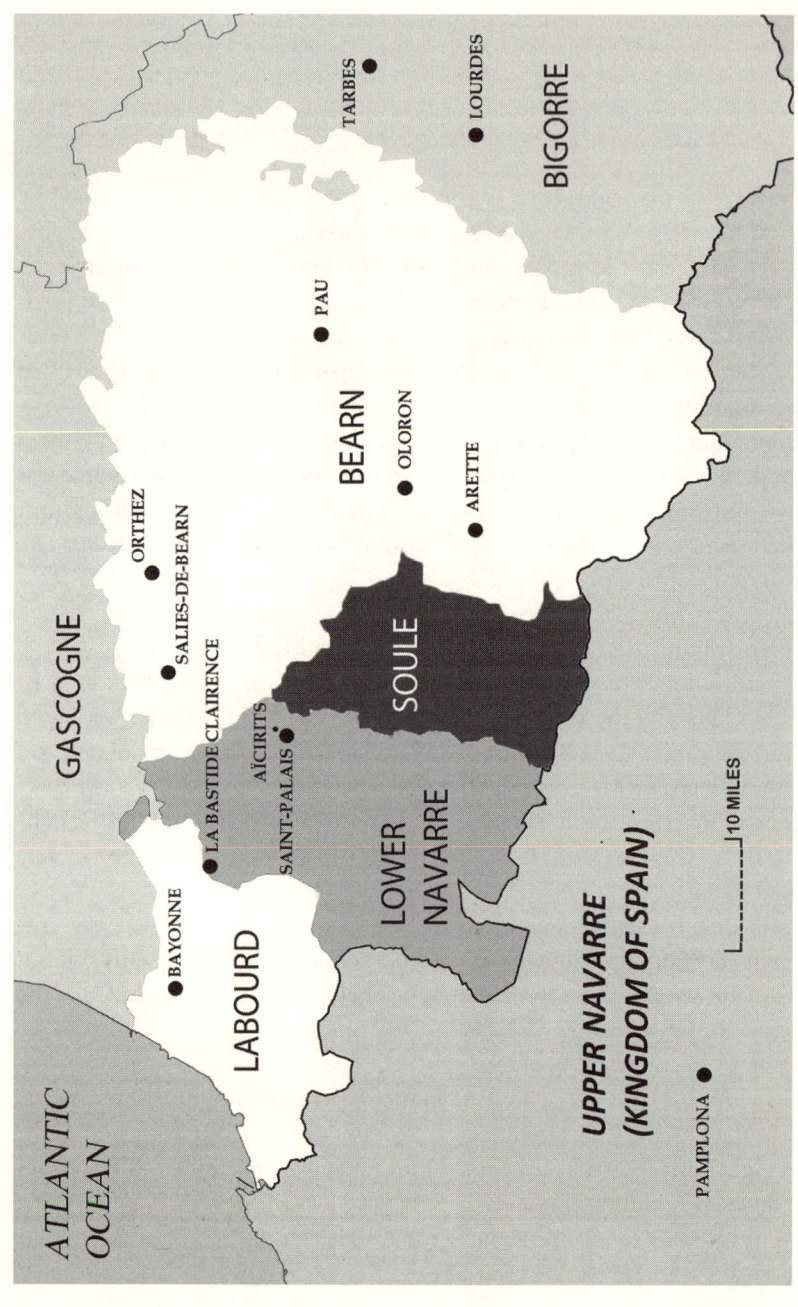

Lower Navarre and Béarn in the eighteenth century. The Parliament of Navarre, located in Pau, had jurisdiction over Béarn, Soule, and Lower Navarre. The Estates General of Navarre generally met in Saint-Palais. Map by the author.

Wealth and Disaster

CHAPTER ONE

Origins of a Migration Network

Je n'ai, mon fils, à vous donner que quinze écus, mon cheval et les conseils que vous venez d'entendre.

I have nothing to give you, my son, but fifteen crowns, my horse, and the counsels you have just heard.

Alexandre Dumas, *Les trois mousquetaires*, 1844

In a lecture at the Sorbonne in 1983 entitled "History and Ethnology," Claude Lévi-Strauss offered an example of the connection between these two disciplines that was based on his work on "house-based societies," which compared eleventh-century Japan, the Fiji Islands, and medieval Europe.[1] This stood in contrast to earlier work in which he had categorized kinship systems by using combinations of binary opposites such as patrilineal versus matrilineal and exogamous versus endogamous. Close examination of how the great European "houses" of the premodern period were transmitted across generations reveals that both men and women could inherit. It also shows that marriages at times involved closely related families but could also be formed between families that had not been related previously. According to Lévi-Strauss, the "house" is a social unit distinct from the family in that it does not necessarily correspond to agnatic lineage and may "occasionally even lack any biological basis." Instead of constituting a transgenerational biological bond, a "house" represents "a material and spiritual heritage that incorporates dignity, origins, kinship, names and symbols, position, power, and wealth."[2]

As the anthropologist Timothy Jenkins has observed, Pierre Bourdieu's studies of peasant society in Béarn, collected in the 2002 volume *The Bachelors' Ball*, address an issue that, while seemingly unrelated, is highly relevant to this question.[3] Bourdieu (who had indigenous knowledge of the subject matter, being himself from a Bearnese rural family)[4] analyzed the traditional organization of Bearnese agricultural estates into "houses," concluding that celibacy among male heirs was symptomatic of a poor fit between the modern world and local customs governing alliance and succession among the peasantry. Bourdieu's studies also echo those of Frédéric Le Play, an antimodern sociologist who invented the

"Pyrenean stem-family," a concept based on his fieldwork in Cauterets in 1856.[5] Le Play distinguished the "stem-family" from two other broad systems of family organization, the "patriarchal family" and the "unstable family." One of the principal characteristics of the "stem-family" was its emphasis on the preservation and transfer of the "house," a process protected by customs that included the stipulation that a single descendant in each generation be designated the sole heir. According to Le Play, the "stem-family" and its related hereditary customs were widely distributed throughout Europe, including Scandinavia, Holstein, Bavaria, Tyrol, Northern Italy, and the French and Spanish Pyrenees. Le Play interpreted the constitution of the feudal order, whose cardinal rule was the integral transfer of fiefdoms, as evidence that the seignorial class had adopted the "stem-family" model.

Because of the rule requiring the integral transfer of assets and property, one sibling—in theory the eldest—inherited everything, and the remaining descendants were obliged to make do with very little. Under the *ancien régime*, these customs produced figures such as the young Gascon nobleman (*cadet de Gascogne*) later popularized by Alexandre Dumas in *The Three Musketeers* and Edmond Rostand in *Cyrano de Bergerac*, as well as the lesser-known type of the younger son of a Norman noble family (*cadet de Normandie*). A recent treatment of the theme is a film entitled *Cadets de Gascogne*, produced for the Arte television channel in Europe in 2003. The screenplay is a fictional adaption of Pierre Bourdieu's ethnographic work by his younger son Emmanuel Bourdieu.[6] According to the script, a young Gascon nobleman would leave the country of his birth to seek his fortune elsewhere in France or Europe. Beginning in the late seventeenth century, the possible destinations also included the "American islands" (primarily Saint-Domingue, as the historian Jacques de Cauna has shown).[7]

Although this pattern of emigration has been remarked upon, its causes have rarely been explored in any depth in previous scholarship.[8] In Bourdieu's work, emigration to the Americas, which was massive in Béarn beginning in the latter half of the nineteenth century, is framed as a necessity among younger siblings who risked poverty: "There were many departures during the bad years between 1884 and 1892."[9] According to the historian Marie-Pierre Arrizabalaga, however, Basque emigration in the nineteenth century was weakly correlated with economic cycles.[10] Further, as Adrián Blázquez has contended, emigration demanded relatively significant resources and was therefore not an option open to the poor.[11] The relationship between primogeniture and the emigration of younger siblings has an obviousness that is perhaps misleading. The legal historian Jérôme Viret has illustrated that hereditary customs in the Perche region of France, which experienced a wave of migration to Canada in the seventeenth century, were indeed relatively egalitarian.[12] In any case, although younger siblings represented a high proportion of Basco-Bearnese emigrants, it remains true that emigration represented only one of a number of options, and the reasons behind the decision to emigrate merit further investigation.

Historical anthropology like that presented by Lévi-Strauss in his 1983 lecture can contribute to an understanding of the factors surrounding the decision to emigrate. To illustrate what may have been the matrimonial strategies of the nobility under the *ancien régime* from the perspective of those who conceived and executed them, Lévi-Strauss quoted Saint-Simon's *Mémoires*, in particular remarks regarding his own marriage. In concluding, he proposed that a better understanding of the concept of the "house" could be reached by closely examining sources that social historians have long despised, such as the Gotha Almanach and the d'Hozier genealogies, and he suggested that such studies could provide a natural complement to the use of parish records and notarial archives in historical scholarship.[13]

The present chapter is written in this spirit. It opens a large case study of the emigration patterns among members of an eighteenth-century family belonging to the lesser nobility from the French Basque country to Saint-Domingue. The alliance strategies of this particular house will be examined, revealing the options available to the older and younger siblings while attempting to explain the reasons behind emigration decisions from the emigrants' own points of view. In-depth investigation enabled me to gather a good deal of documentation regarding this family's history in the Basque country, Saint-Domingue, Cuba, and New Orleans. The obvious advantage of working on a noble family is the greater abundance of documents, although as Lévi-Strauss suggested, "the clever matrimonial combinations conceived by Blanche of Castile" closely resembled "those that peasant families continued to build until well into the nineteenth century."[14] This parallelism between the matrimonial practices of noble "houses" and peasant families may allow a degree of generalization of the findings of this case study to other social strata. In the following chapters, I also discuss the emigration of a peasant family whose trajectory I was able to reconstruct in some detail. They came from the same parish as the noble family and settled in the same area in Saint-Domingue.

The Trajectory of a First Emigrant: Marc-Antoine Lamerenx

Work by the geographer Torsten Hägerstrand has demonstrated that the single most important predictor of migratory flows was earlier migrations. In fact, Hägerstrand found that maps of Swedish migratory fields from 1940 were nearly identical to those of 1785.[15] Hence the concept of the "first emigrant,"[16] to whom all emigrants of a particular area are connected. Hägerstrand did not speculate extensively on how these connections worked at the microlevel. The concept of chain migrations, developed by a different group of social scientists, is a useful complement to Hägerstrand's observations. In their classic article, John S. MacDonald and Leatrice D. MacDonald showed that Italian immigrants in the United States in the early twentieth century clustered according to their areas of origin. For instance, most of the Italians of Stamford, Connecticut, came from just two towns, Avigliano (Potenza) and S. Mango sul Calore (Campania). Similarly, most Italians in Norristown, Pennsylvania, came from the town of Sciacca in Girgenti Province, Sicily.[17] Family networks and patronage systems were behind this clustering.

In this book I show the existence of a multigenerational network of emigrants who were all connected to one emigrant, Marc-Antoine Lamerenx, who set sail for Saint-Domingue in 1729. Marc-Antoine has a special status in this story not only because he was the first emigrant. He stands out because he was the only one in the chain of generations under study who did not experience financial ruin, as well as the only one in his family whose inheritance pattern fits the textbook case. A younger son, he migrated to America, as his elder brother had inherited the family estate. He made a fortune using slave labor to grow coffee and died a rich man. His children and nephews, however, were displaced by the Haitian Revolution and tried to rebuild their lives with various degrees of success. As to his father, Jean Lamerenx, he was the youngest in a large group of siblings. Under normal circumstances, he would not have inherited the family estate. However, the presumptive heir, Pierre Lamerenx, had migrated to Holland and joined the Dutch East India Company (VOC). A Calvinist like the rest of his family, he refused a forced conversion to Catholicism following the revocation of the Edict of Nantes by Louis XIV. The younger son Jean converted, inherited the estate, and had several children, including Marc-Antoine. Now let us turn to the exact circumstances of Marc-Antoine's migration to America. To do so, we must begin with an event that took place much later in his life.

In 1769, Marc-Antoine Lamerenx, a wealthy coffee planter from Saint-Domingue, traveled to Versailles with his son, Jean-François, to press a matter that was important to the family. Marc-Antoine wanted his son to join the light cavalry of the King's Guards (*chevau-légers de la garde du roi*). What Marc-Antoine was seeking for his son was a very prestigious assignment. The *chevau-légers* belonged to the royal household, and in addition to regular military duties, they took part in the personal protection of the king. Since only noblemen were allowed to join this particular regiment, proofs of nobility had to be presented. An extensive bureaucratic process had been undertaken with the royal genealogists the year before, and Marc-Antoine traveled to the court to plead his case in person. Just before his return home, he attached a long memorandum to a letter requesting that he be awarded the Saint-Louis Cross.[18] This document, along with the dossier compiled by the court genealogists, enables us to reconstruct his career and the circumstances of his emigration with some precision.

Born in 1710, Marc-Antoine Lamerenx was the second son of Jean Lamerenx (c. 1670–1750) and Suzanne de Lespade, *sieur* and *dame* of Uhart-Juzon, a noble estate located in Aïcirits, on the outskirts of Saint-Palais in Lower Navarre. Thus when he set sail to America in 1729 Marc-Antoine was a subject of Louis XV in his capacity as king of Navarre, not king of France. Navarre, a small trans-Pyrenean kingdom, had been independent until its southern portion was annexed by Aragon and Castile in 1512. The ruling dynasty took refuge in its possessions north of the Pyrenees (Lower Navarre and Béarn), which retained nominal independence as the Kingdom of Navarre under French protection. In 1589, when King Henry III of Navarre became King Henry IV of France, Navarre became de facto a part of France, a relationship formalized in 1620 when Louis XIII proclaimed the reunion of Navarre to the French crown. Until 1789, however, Navarrese judicial authorities held that the reunion was illegal because it had not been ratified by the Estates General of Navarre. They strenuously objected to the term *province* to designate Navarre and kept affirming the existence of a Kingdom of Navarre separate from the Kingdom of France;[19] thus the expression *this kingdom* in pre-1789 notarial records is to be understood as referring to the Kingdom of Navarre.

Marc-Antoine had an elder brother, Mathieu, who inherited the entire estate of Uhart-Juzon. The integral transgenerational transfer of a house was made possible by an array of legal mechanisms and was the prevailing custom in the Basque country, in Béarn, and in certain parts of Bigorre. Bourdieu, who conducted fieldwork in Béarn in the 1960s, noted that the practice was in the process of disappearing and was a reflection of "traditional peasant society."[20] Le Play, who described the practice in Bigorre in 1856, expressed concern about its imminent disappearance, which he viewed as a necessary result of the egalitarianism in matters of succession that was inscribed in the Civil Code. Jenkins's book, which is based on fieldwork conducted in Béarn thirty years after Bourdieu, emphasizes the persistence of the practice, however. The "house" represented a living trust that was transferred to a single member of each generation. A distinction was made between *biens propres* (entailed property) and *biens acquêts* (assets acquired through the industry of the master of the house); after an asset had been owned for three generations, it was considered entailed and became inalienable. The master or mistress of the house had the right to dispose only of *biens acquêts*, that is, assets that he or she had earned, and he or she was therefore not the full proprietor of the *biens propres*, which belonged to subsequent generations.

This system was not unique in Europe. In England, it existed under the name *fee tail*,[21] and as *mayorazgo* it governed the great noble and bourgeois fortunes starting in 1505 in Castile.[22] Introduced in France under the First Empire as *majorat*, it sought to protect great fortunes from the "redistributive" influence of the Civil Code. (Ultimately abolished in 1848, the practice of *majorat* is a central feature of the plot of Balzac's short story *The Marriage Contract*.) A quotation from Karl Marx used by Bourdieu as an epigraph to his article on matrimonial strategies in Béarn very succinctly encapsulates the essence of the system: "The beneficiary of the entail, the eldest son, belongs to the land. The land inherits him."[23] The particularity of the practice in the Pyrenees was that the entail was in effect the default system and applied to all agricultural properties, large or small, noble or non-noble (unlike in other parts of France, where different rules applied to noble and commoner estates). Primogeniture was a key feature of the system, but the range of possible local interpretations was governed by a single, overarching imperative: the integral transfer of entailed property and assets to the next generation. In Lower Navarre and in the Lavedan region (valleys upstream from the city of Lourdes), this meant absolute cognatic primogeniture, in which the firstborn child, whether son or daughter, was the sole heir. In Béarn, the heir was preferably a boy, but in the absence of a male heir, eldest daughters could inherit (male-preference cognatic primogeniture), the crucial question being the intact transfer of the "house." According to Bourdieu, primogeniture "is but the expression in genealogical terms of the absolute priority given to the principle of impartible inheritance."[24]

When Marc-Antoine filed an application with the royal genealogists in 1769 to prove his nobility, he submitted a chart summarizing the transfer of the Uhart-Juzon estate over four generations. The chart made it clear that in the second generation the estate had been transmitted through a female heir (Fig. 1.1). The original owner of the estate, Jean de la Forcade, baron de Gouze and *sieur* d'Uhart-Juzon, had three sons and a daughter who died without issue and two daughters, Marthe and Rachel, who both had children. Marthe, who inherited the Uhart-Juzon estate because she was the older sibling, married into the Doat family. Rachel married into the Lamerenx family, with a dowry but no rights to the Uhart-Juzon estate. Subsequently Marthe's son sold the Uhart-Juzon estate to Rachel's son, Jean Lamerenx, making him *sieur* d'Uhart-Juzon, with all the privileges attached to the name, including its coat of arms. Such transmission was consistent with the Custom of Navarre.

An important feature of the house-based system, as Lévi-Strauss noted, was its disconnection from biological lineage. Efforts were made to "keep the house in the family," but if those efforts failed, the house could be sold and the symbolic capital attached to the estate transferred to the new owners.[25] Nobility itself could be bought and sold, as it was entirely predicated on the possession of a noble estate. That had been the experience of the Lamerenx family in previous generations. Marc-Antoine's grandfather Isaac Lamerenx, a commoner, had been a successful barrister with the Parliament of Navarre. In 1663 he had purchased the noble estate of Domec de Precilhon, near the city of Oloron, and he

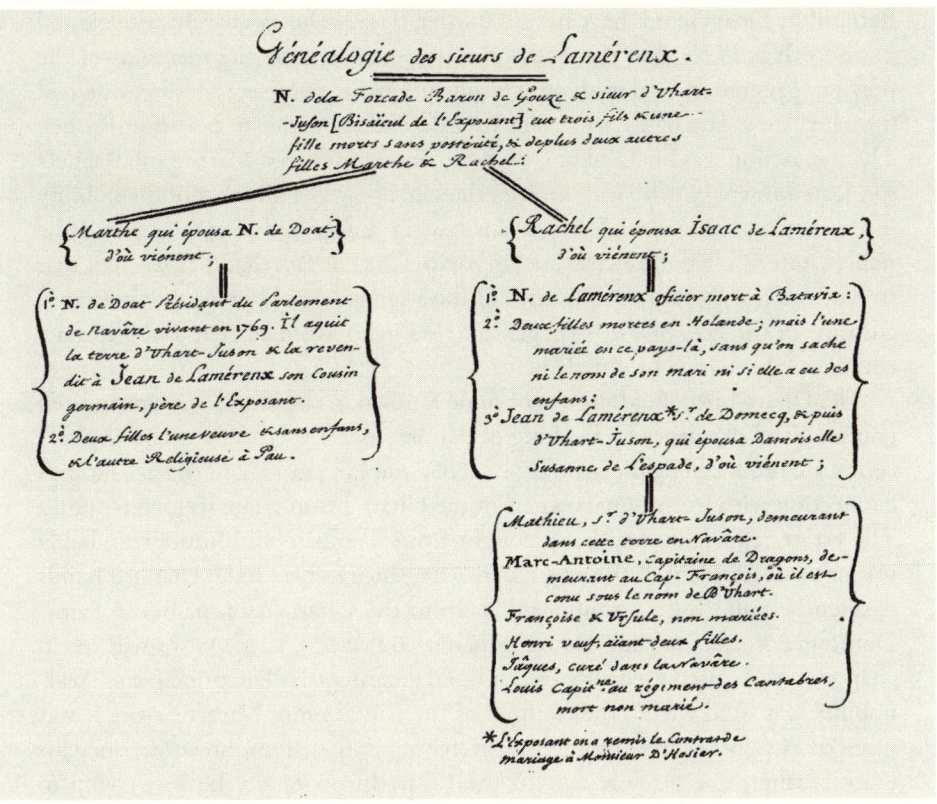

Fig. 1.1. Genealogical chart summarizing the transmission of the Uhart-Juzon estate. BnF, Nouveau-d'Hozier 201-4482.

was received the same year as a member of the nobility in the Estates General of Navarre. Some years later Marc-Antoine's father, Jean Lamerenx, sold the estate of Precilhon and purchased the estate of Uhart-Juzon, which belonged to his first cousin Jean-Bernard de Doat.

This, at least, is what the royal genealogists reported. However, if we look at the sources closely, we must conclude that the transaction cannot have happened between the two cousins. The royal genealogists did not indicate the exact date of the purchase of the Uhart-Juzon estate by the Lamerenx family. The lack of a precise record may be owing to the fact that the transaction took place during a time of turmoil, when part of the family migrated to Holland and those who stayed behind converted to Catholicism. It can be ascertained that the transaction was initiated between 1690, when Isaac Lamerenx was still living on his estate of Precilhon, and 1696, when Isaac had died and his wife Rachel was designated as the possessor of the Uhart-Juzon estate in a notarial deed.[26] Jean-

Bernard de Doat cannot have been the seller, because he was barely one year old in 1690. It is likely that the transaction was arranged by the members of the previous generation, and more specifically its female members: Marthe, who had inherited the estate of Uhart-Juzon from her father, sold it to her sister Rachel. The transaction was finalized in 1704 by a contract between Marthe and Rachel's son Jean Lamerenx, who was received the same year as a member of the nobility in the Estates General of Navarre "for having purely and simply acquired the noble estate of Uhart-Juzon located in Aïcirits."[27] The fact that d'Hozier got that part of the story wrong is indicative of the strangeness of Pyrenean inheritance customs in the eyes of the royal genealogists, who assumed that a noble estate could only be owned by a male heir.

The Uhart-Juzon fiefdom was of some renown in the kingdom, having been granted fiscal privileges by the king of Navarre as early as 1429, according to a certificate produced by the fiscal tribunal of Pamplona in 1766.[28] Marc-Antoine's connection with the original owners of the Uhart-Juzon estate seemed tenuous. The estate reportedly had been bought from a cousin who himself probably was not a descendant of the original owners, since noble estates changed hands frequently. Still, Marc-Antoine laid claim to the Uhart-Juzon name. In Saint-Domingue he was not known as Lamerenx but as d'Uhart. As we will see in chapter 3, this raised eyebrows among royal genealogists. The principle of "real" nobility was valid within the confines of the Kingdom of Navarre, since it was received custom. Marc-Antoine was stretching that custom, however: since his elder brother, not he, was heir to the Uhart-Juzon estate, he was trying to convert "real" nobility, based on real estate, into "personal" nobility, based on lineage.

In the memorandum summarizing his career, Marc-Antoine Lamerenx explained that he had sailed from Europe in 1729 "recommended to Monsieur de Nolivos, then governor of Petit-Goâve, who selected him to be his aide-de-camp in 1732."[29] In 1736 Marc-Antoine moved to Dondon, a mountainous and very sparsely populated district in the northern part of Saint-Domingue, on the border with the Spanish part of the island (Fig. 1.2).

In 1737 Marc-Antoine became a noncommissioned militia officer in the cavalry of Dondon. He took a long trip back home in 1741. (One piece of evidence for his presence in Lower Navarre is that he fathered a child with a peasant girl from Arhansus, a village near the Uhart-Juzon estate.)[30] Back in Saint-Domingue, in 1742 he married Elizabeth Le Jeune, the daughter of prosperous colonists from Grande Rivière, a neighboring parish.[31] The couple started cultivating coffee on a large piece of forest that had been granted by the governor of Saint-Domingue to Elizabeth Le Jeune before her marriage.[32] They received another major land grant in 1747,[33] and Marc-Antoine rose in the hierarchy of the colonial militia. He became a lieutenant in the cavalry of Dondon in 1756 and was

Fig. 1.2. Map of the northern part of the island of Saint-Domingue by Louis Élie Moreau de Saint-Méry, 1796. The town of Dondon is near the border with the Spanish part of the island. From Moreau de Saint-Méry, *Description de la partie française* (1797), vol. 1.

promoted to reformed captain in 1760 and full captain in 1764. In his memorandum he indicated that "he was not able to accept sooner the commission of officer he was offered more than once upon his arrival in the colony" because "he could not afford to provide for the soldiers who cannot support themselves when they have to go out on patrols."[34] He explained further that "each colonist, even though he is enlisted, receives no salary and serves at his own expense in the colony."[35] In other words, his ascension in the hierarchy of the colonial militia was slow because he did not make his fortune quickly.

By the time of the Seven Years' War (1756–63), however, his wealth was considerable. In order to protect the island against attacks by the British during the Seven Years' War, the governor, Armand de Belzunce, had ordered barracks and warehouses to be built in Dondon to house up to five battalions that could retreat from the coast and then counterattack (an innovative tactic that was later used with great effectiveness by Toussaint Louverture and by Dessalines during the Haitian War of Independence).[36] Marc-Antoine gave room and board on his plantation to many of the officers and engineers sent for this purpose. He boasted that he was personally close to Governor Belzunce (who, incidentally, was also of Basque descent and served for just six months before dying of illness). Lamerenx hosted Belzunce twice on his plantation, and he took him and his officers on a complete tour of the gorges, canyons, and narrow pathways that marked the border between the French and Spanish parts of Saint-Domingue. When peace came in 1763, the barracks were emptied of soldiers, but the following year they were used to house 242 refugees; some were French settlers expelled by the British from Acadia, and the rest were Germans who had survived the failed attempt to colonize Kourou in French Guiana.[37] Two-thirds died of illness in less than a year.[38]

The Seven Years' War was the only event that Marc-Antoine experienced as a disaster (he called it a "calamity"). However, he and his family were never in immediate physical danger. The British never attempted a land invasion.[39] There were severe shortages of imported flour (in spite of active smuggling from New York via Monte Cristi, on the Spanish side of Hispaniola),[40] leading the local authorities to forbid the use of flour to feed slaves. Native staples like yams and cassava were consumed instead, by slaves and masters alike when shortages were the most acute.[41] There was no starvation, however. The war was a calamity because it was bad for business. According to Marc-Antoine's report, the price of coffee fell to 4 sols per pound (because the British blockade prevented exports to France), while the price of imported goods jumped for the same reasons: one hogshead of wine was worth 600 livres, and a 150-pound barrel of flour sold for 250 livres. In other words, in order to buy one pound of flour to make French-style bread, Marc-Antoine had to sell eight pounds of coffee. This was a dramatic departure from normal market conditions, in which coffee was a luxury good. (After the war the price of coffee increased to 14 sols per pound, the price of the hogshead of wine decreased to 150 livres, and that of the barrel of flour decreased to 45 livres.)[42] Being a good host, Marc-Antoine treated the king's officers to French wine and French-style bread no matter how exorbitant the cost, spending a total of 90,000 livres. Being perceived as a reliable benefactor of the king's men was priceless.

Marc-Antoine's military service was not particularly distinguished. He was involved in a border skirmish with the Spanish in 1754. A few years earlier, in 1746, his company had been sent to rescue a fort in the city of Miragoâne that had been attacked by an English fleet. The fort had been very far from Dondon, however, and by the time of his arrival the English had already departed. This kind of low-intensity warfare was characteristic of the relationship between the three imperial powers that jockeyed for preeminence in the Caribbean in the eighteenth century. Even outside of periods of open war, Saint-Domingue colonists had regular military engagements against the British or the Spanish (sometimes in alliance with one against the other). Having no acts of bravery to brag about, and a relatively short service as a commissioned officer, Marc-Antoine insisted on his munificence in favor of the king's men, which he thought made him worthy of the Saint-Louis Cross.

This attempt to convert economic into symbolic capital was not successful. Marc-Antoine did not obtain the medal he sought, as the awarding of the Saint-Louis Cross had strict seniority rules, and perhaps the quid pro quo was too explicit. He died in 1771 or 1772, shortly after his return from France, and his nephew Jean-Pierre Lamerenx, who had migrated from Lower Navarre in 1764, succeeded him as captain of his colonial militia company in Dondon.[43] The trip to Versailles had been successful regarding its main purpose, however. A certificate of nobility was issued by d'Hozier and signed in the king's name by Gabriel de Choiseul, secretary of state for the navy, on August 4, 1770.[44] Marc-Antoine's son Jean-François was admitted to the light cavalry of the King's Guards on September 20, 1770.[45] There is no record of his subsequent career, and we know from a letter his mother wrote in 1793 that he had died by that time.[46] The regiment, which had originally been brought from Navarre by Henry IV when he became king of France,[47] was disbanded in an effort to trim military budgets in 1787.

Government-Sponsored Migrations

The mention of "Monsieur de Nolivos, Governor of Petit-Goâve," as Marc-Antoine's first sponsor in Saint-Domingue is revealing and helps us understand the patronage system that made his migration possible. A fact that goes unmentioned in the memorandum but would have been obvious to its readers is that Marc-Antoine's protector, Monsieur de Nolivos (c. 1675–1732), was the late father of the current governor of Saint-Domingue, Pierre-Gédéon de Nolivos (1714–1785), an immensely wealthy man who owned several sugar and coffee plantations on the island and a townhouse (*hôtel particulier*) located on rue de la Grange Batelière in Paris. Marc-Antoine was not nearly as rich as the governor, but his own story repeated on a smaller scale the story of the Nolivos family, country squires from Béarn who made a fortune in America. The father of the current governor, also named Pierre-Gédéon, was first sent to Saint-Domingue as a captain in 1707, after taking part in several privateering expeditions.[48] Born in Sauveterre-de-Béarn, he was the younger son of Gédéon de Nolivos, a judge in the Parliament of Navarre. Marc-Antoine himself had close ties to the Bearnese judicial system. His grandfather Isaac Lamerenx had been a barrister with the Parliament of Navarre. His father's first cousin was Jean-Bernard de Doat (1689–1775), president of the Parliament from 1715 to 1748. His maternal uncle and namesake, Marc-Antoine de Lespade, was a barrister with the Parliament.

In referring his younger son, Marc-Antoine, to Pierre-Gédéon de Nolivos in

1729, Jean Lamerenx was appealing to the Bearnese judicial network and calling on professional as well as familial and even religious connections (Protestants bearing biblical forenames who were forcibly converted to Catholicism after the Revocation of the Edict of Nantes). It is difficult to assess the importance of the religious dimension in migration decisions in the early eighteenth century because at that stage everyone who had remained in France was officially Catholic (some continued to practice their faith clandestinely, as did the Marranos in Spain). There are indications, however, that it was very significant. Jacques de Cauna has shown that in the Agenais region, outmigration to Saint-Domingue coincided with historically Protestant population centers (the town of Clairac, for example), and a large proportion of those emigrants came from the upper echelons of society, where Protestants were more likely to be found.[49] While no systematic study has been done for Béarn, it is likely that a similar pattern could be found, especially since both areas had been under the rule of the Calvinist Albret dynasty. In that sense there was continuity between the emigration of Pierre Lamerenx to Holland in 1684 (discussed in greater detail below) and the emigration of his nephew Marc-Antoine Lamerenx to Saint-Domingue in 1729. In both cases emigration relied on a network that was simultaneously professional, familial, and religious.

If we go further up the chain of migrations, we will find that Nolivos owed his own appointment to Charles de Salaberry (1659–1734), *premier commis* (chief clerk) of the Ministry of the Navy responsible for the Levant. Charles de Salaberry adds an interesting twist to this story of regional solidarities. According to official biographies published in the eighteenth century, his family was originally from Saint-Jean-Pied-de-Port in Lower Navarre and had entered the service of the kings of France after the accession of Henry III of Navarre to the French throne.[50] The Navarrese aristocratic connection seems to have been entirely fictional, however, prompting d'Hozier to make some ironic remarks about Salaberry's "vision" in his confidential files.[51] Still, it was widely believed at the time, and Salaberry did go out of his way to favor his imaginary compatriots. Salaberry was the director of the Levant bureau from 1688 to 1709. The navy's worldwide operations came under two divisions: Ponant (the Atlantic fleet) and Levant (the Mediterranean fleet). As director for the Levant, Salaberry was in charge of the ports of Toulon and Marseille, the Levant trade, the consulates of Algiers, Tunis, and Tripoli, the consulates of Italy and Spain, the forests of Burgundy that produced ship masts, the "American islands" (i.e. the French Caribbean), and privateering operations worldwide.[52]

Salaberry reported directly to the secretary of the navy, who reported to the king. This post enabled Salaberry to facilitate the travel of a large number of Basque and Bearnese officers who helped populate the Caribbean colonies. Hailing from a poor, peripheral region that was physically and politically very far from the seat of power, these emigrants took advantage of a few "ethnic" connections (fictional or not) in the upper echelons of government. As a result, they played a major role in the development of the Caribbean colonies. Salaberry's letters to Nolivos notifying him of his appointment as captain and his assignment to Saint-Domingue are couched in the language of personal favors that demand total loyalty in return. On August 31, 1707, Salaberry wrote to Nolivos: "I took the opportunity of a breach of conduct by Monsieur de la Salle, who in fairness should have been appointed ahead of you, to propose to the King that you be given one of the unassigned companies in the island of Saint-Domingue."[53] On September 21, 1707, Salaberry wrote again: "I proposed to the King that you immediately be given a commission as full captain even though you should only be reformed captain, because His Majesty noticed your effectiveness in recruiting soldiers and because I hope this favor will encourage you to serve with greater zeal and to do whatever is needed to maintain your company and to train its soldiers."[54]

The purview of the Levant bureau included commercial, diplomatic, and military matters, as well as emigration, which were inextricably linked and came under Salaberry's sole authority (exerted on behalf of the secretary of the navy). Private interests were confounded with those of the government, particularly during the early phases of French expansion in the Caribbean, when privateering played a major role. Salaberry participated as a financial partner with Louis XIV, himself an investor on a personal basis, in outfitting and arming several privateer ships sailing out to the Caribbean from Toulon.[55]

An exchange of letters between Salaberry and Jean-Pierre Casamajor de Charitte, then interim governor of Saint-Domingue, is indicative of the breadth of Salaberry's authority.[56] Charitte, who hailed from the Basque province of Soule, had sent Salaberry samples of a plant native to Saint-Domingue that he thought was tea. After examining the samples carefully, even making an infusion and tasting it, Salaberry wrote to say that he did not think it was tea, but he reserved judgment because the plant was wild and perhaps could approximate the flavor of genuine tea through cultivation. He added that if the experiment was successful, he would grant Charitte exclusive privileges for the cultivation of tea in Saint-Domingue. Such monopoly on cultivation would result in a de facto monopoly on the market for tea in France, because Charitte's tea would beat teas from China in terms of production costs, and because they would enter France without import duties. Charitte replied that he was interested in pursuing this opportunity. In response, Salaberry reiterated his skepticism, but he approved the experiment, saying that Charitte was surely motivated by the advancement of the public good in addition to his own self-interest.[57] He recommended that Charitte seek advice from a certain Mr. Filgerard, who had recently returned from China and could determine whether it was genuine tea. In the affirmative, the expert could also explain how the cultivation and processing should be arranged. The project never got off the ground, but this small example illustrates the workings of the colonial trade system. The colony was allowed to trade only with the mother country. This monopolistic trade was enforced by military means and regulated directly by the Ministry of the Navy. In the case of Saint-Domingue, the enforcement and the regulation were directed by Salaberry himself, who spotted business opportunities and gave advice to those reporting to him, allowing them to make fortunes quickly thanks to monopolistic conditions.[58]

Another example of what a modern economist would see as bureaucratic meddling with the market is a 1707 edict by André Bourreau-Deslandes, who served as intendant of Saint-Domingue. He issued a long list of regulations specifying the features of good-quality tobacco, and to encourage cultivation he promised that the government would buy the entirety of tobacco crops at fair prices. (Sugar was more profitable, but officials wanted to limit its production to keep prices high.) He prefaced his decision with the following declaration of principle: "Because His Majesty knows that the best way of favoring commerce in a country and to draw a multitude of ships to it is a wide range of manufactures and of goods produced, he has expressly instructed us to incite the inhabitants of Saint-Domingue to resume the cultivation of tobacco."[59] His Majesty's instructions had of course come in the form of a letter from Salaberry. Deslandes added that wealthy colonists could use some of their slaves for this effort, while unmarried and unemployed immigrants (former indentured servants who had come under three-year contracts) could earn a living by growing tobacco themselves and eventually get married once they had accumulated a small capital.[60]

The military aspect was emphasized in a report submitted by Bourreau-Deslandes's successor ten years later. Jean-Jacques Mithon de Senneville, then intendant of the colony, continued Deslandes's efforts to revive the cultivation of tobacco. (Like his predecessor, he failed, as colonists naturally chose the crops that were most profitable.) He concluded his report by stating that commerce was under a dual threat: pirates, who "infect and have seized control of the seas," and English traders, because "it is well known how much their activities harm French commerce."[61] Colonists outfitted three ships at great expense for the naval protection of the island, but the cost was more than the colony could afford. Mithon requested two frigates from the king's navy, and he argued that the operation would almost pay for itself because the frigates could seize the cargo of English traders. (Two frigates were sent three years later, to little avail.)[62] The peroration insisted on the combined political and economic benefits of a strong naval presence. Left to their own devices, the colonists would have less respect for the king's authority, and they might be tempted to do business with English traders. Sending two or three warships would prevent such unfortunate developments:

The purpose of these warships is to show His Majesty's power in these very distant lands, to have it respected by foreigners, and to mark a clear intent to protect the populations, thus keeping them perfectly obedient and respectful of the authority of their superiors. Because warships have been rarely seen ... the populations have felt abandoned, they are slowly losing their strong impression of the greatness of our sovereign master, and the respect and fear they had in their hearts gives way to audacity.[63]

What this correspondence makes clear is that from the point of view of Navy Ministry officials, there was no conceptual or practical distinction between military efforts, settlement efforts, and the development of trade.

Prior Migration History of the Lamerenx Family

When he filed an application with the royal genealogists in 1769, Marc-Antoine declared that establishing his nobility would be unusually challenging because most of the family papers had been lost.[64] Marc-Antoine's paternal uncle, Pierre Lamerenx, the presumptive heir to the family estate, left France following the Revocation of the Edict of Nantes accompanied by two of his sisters. He became a military officer with the Dutch East India Company and died in Batavia. According to Marc-Antoine, unsuccessful attempts were made at the time to retrieve the papers from Pierre's sisters.[65] In 1769 there was no longer any communication with that branch of the family. Both sisters were dead. Word had come that one sister had married, but no one knew her husband's name or whether she had had children.[66] The language of the memorandum suggests faint memories from a relatively distant past, fragmentary information conveyed through oral tradition, and difficult communications between two branches of a family that were split by geography and religion.

Marc-Antoine had undoubtedly lost touch with the émigré Lamerenx. The loss of family papers, however, may have been more of a convenient excuse. When Marc-Antoine's elder brother died in 1783, a complete inventory of his belongings was conducted. Numerous family papers dating from 1615 to 1783 were itemized,[67] suggesting that the documents had been handed over by Rachel de la Forcade, Marc-Antoine's grandmother, to her younger son, Jean, who inherited the estate after the presumptive heir fled to Holland.

Information regarding the exact circumstances of this earlier episode is scarce, but it is important to try to reconstruct it. Although Marc-Antoine was the "first emigrant" with respect to migration to Saint-Domingue, the generation before him also had experienced emigration in the form of a major dislocation. Until the Revocation of the Edict of Nantes the entire Lamerenx family was Protestant. In the Kingdom of Navarre, Calvinism had been the state religion since 1560, when Henry IV's mother, Queen Jeanne III d'Albret, converted from

Catholicism and had the New Testament translated into the languages her subjects spoke, namely, Basque and Bearnese. In Lower Navarre the conversion was resisted by the Catholic Basque population, but in Béarn Calvinism spread, especially in the upper classes of society. In the first half of the seventeenth century, the vast majority of Béarn elites were Protestant, even after the reunion of the Kingdom of Navarre to the French crown. The estate of Uhart-Juzon, purchased by the Lamerenxes in the late seventeenth century, was in Catholic Lower Navarre, but the family was originally from Béarn. Marc-Antoine's father and grandfather had lived in Oloron in Béarn. The first noble estate purchased by the family in 1663, Domec de Precilhon, was near Oloron. An ancestor had been on the government payroll as a Protestant religion teacher in the town of Maslacq, Béarn, in the 1620s.[68] In 1658, Jean de la Forcade, Marc-Antoine's great-grandfather, directed in his will a payment of three hundred livres to the Calvinist minister in the town of Gouze, Béarn.[69]

Before the formal revocation of the Edict of Nantes, a very zealous intendant, Nicolas-Joseph Foucault, was sent to Béarn to persuade the king's Calvinist subjects to convert to Catholicism. Foucault came with a sizeable military force as well as a large group of Jesuit priests charged with explaining Catholic doctrine to heretics. In a letter to Secretary of State Colbert de Croissy attached to an initial list of new converts, Foucault bragged that he would convert two-thirds of Béarn's Calvinists in less than two months without violence or civil disturbance.[70] Indeed, using a mix of implicit and explicit threats, temporary doctrinal accommodations (e.g., distributing French translations of the Latin Mass and restricting the use of images in Catholic churches), and promises of pensions or desirable posts for converts he saw as opinion leaders, he was able to win over the majority of the Béarn elites in just a few months. In the city of Oloron, where the Lamerenxes lived at the time, 361 persons from the most prominent families converted on July 1, 1685, at a ceremony attended by thousands that ended with bonfires and gun salutes.[71] It is likely that Marc-Antoine's father, Jean, and his grandparents Isaac and Rachel converted on that occasion.

A rational-choice theorist *avant la lettre*, Foucault assured Colbert de Croissy that Protestants were unlikely to emigrate, because "they feel greater attachment to their assets than to their religion."[72] Thus, Foucault added, "there is no need to be afraid that they will flee to Spain."[73] Foucault was only partly right. Significant numbers of Bearnese Protestants did emigrate to Holland and England via Spain, and the inhabitants of villages near the Spanish border were ordered to watch the mountain passes and arrest the fugitives.[74] Fines were levied against Catholics to whom Protestants who were about to emigrate consigned their possessions.[75] When a conversion took place, generally the entire family converted, but in the Lamerenx family some converted and some chose to emigrate. The eldest son, Pierre, fled to Holland. The records of the Dutch East India Company show that he enrolled as a midshipman (*adelborst*) and took sail to Batavia from the island of Texel in North Holland on Christmas Eve, 1684.[76] Pierre may have decided to leave at the outset of Foucault's harassment campaign, which began on June 18, 1684, with a decision barring Protestants from access to the legal profession in Béarn.[77] He arrived in Batavia after an eight-month trip that included a two-month stopover in Cape Town.

According to Marc-Antoine, two sisters went to Holland with Pierre and stayed there. Evidence shows that their itineraries were more complicated, however. These two sisters were living in England in 1698, and this fact was known to their mother, Rachel.[78] One of the sisters (the one who stayed unmarried) appears repeatedly on the lists of needy Huguenot refugees receiving aid from the British government. She was listed as "Marthe Lamerin of Béarn, barrister's daughter," living on Frifth Street in London, in 1707.[79] The last mention, in 1728, is of "Marthe de la Merenx, of Béarn, 63 years old," living in Ireland.[80] The other, much younger sister, Jeanne, was indeed residing in Holland in the early eighteenth century. She married a Huguenot refugee from the Poitou region in Amsterdam in 1704 and eventually settled with her husband in Celle (Lower Saxony) under the protection of the Duke of Brunswick-Lüneburg-Zell. She had eight children, four of whom lived to adulthood and became prominent members of the French Reformed Church in Celle. (Marc-Antoine never knew he had several Protestant cousins in Germany.)[81]

Of Rachel's six children, four emigrated and two stayed in Béarn. Those who stayed had no choice but to convert to Catholicism. When the Revocation took place, one older sister who was already married fled to England with her husband (a fact not mentioned in Marc-Antoine's account).[82] The sister who remained married a military officer in a Catholic ceremony in 1702.[83] The youngest male child, Jean (Marc-Antoine's father), married Suzanne de Lespade of Saint-Palais, Lower Navarre, in a Catholic ceremony in 1706.[84]

The details of Pierre Lamerenx's emigration to Holland are scant, but it is likely that it took place within a patronage system that bore some similarities to that of Marc-Antoine's emigration one generation later. There was one prominent Bearnese in the Dutch East Indies in the 1680s, Isaac Lostal de Saint-Martin (c. 1629–1696) (Fig. 1.3), who had a distinguished career with the Dutch East India Company and was appointed commander of the VOC garrison in Batavia in 1679.[85] Lostal's trajectory was especially remarkable because while the VOC employed many nationalities, non-Dutch employees rarely got the top jobs. Isaac Lostal and Pierre Lamerenx came from the same town, Oloron, and the same small milieu, that of Bearnese lawyers. (In the early 1680s there were no more than 200 barristers in the entire Kingdom of Navarre, 150 of whom were Protestants.)[86] Isaac Lostal's brother, Gratian, was a barrister with the Parliament of Navarre and purchased the office of deputy mayor of Oloron in 1703.[87] Their

Fig. 1.3. Portrait of Isaac Lostal de Saint-Martin (c. 1629–1696) attributed to Jan de Baen (1633–1702). Oil on canvas. A member of the Council of the Dutch East Indies and commander of the VOC garrison in Batavia, Lostal was a Protestant émigré from Oloron, Béarn. Rijksmuseum, Amsterdam.

father, Pierre Lostal, was a barrister as well.[88] It is safe to assume that Pierre Lamerenx went to Batavia under the protection of his compatriot Lostal de Saint-Martin or someone close to him.

Comparing the Lostal and Lamerenx families, one notices that in each family group some chose to emigrate and some chose to stay. How does one account for variations in individual choices? As Foucault indicated in his letter to Colbert de Croissy, the choice was between one's conscience and one's assets. As the eldest, Pierre was the presumptive heir to the family estate, and he could accept that role if he converted to Catholicism. Instead he chose emigration, which would almost certainly deprive him of his status as heir. There is no doubt that this decision can be understood as a matter of individual conscience. At the same time, divergent individual decisions can also be understood within the strategy of the family group as a whole. In the mid-1680s the Lamerenx family was faced with a stark choice: on the one hand, loyalty to Calvinism, which had been the family's faith for several generations; on the other hand, the possession of an estate that had conferred nobility on the family. One can conceive of the divergent individual decisions as a hedging strategy that sought to reconcile the family's two incompatible objectives: remaining noble and remaining Protestant. Pierre chose to serve a Protestant state and advance its interests worldwide. Jean chose to serve the interests of the Uhart-Juzon estate, thus upholding the nobility of the Lamerenx family. It is remarkable in that respect that Pierre remained unmarried, a status typical of younger sons who embraced a military career. In deciding to emigrate, the firstborn made himself a *cadet*. He died intestate in Batavia on January 2, 1700.[89] Sometime later, Pierre's mother and sole heir received a bill of exchange in the amount of 1,002 guilders, a sum later transferred to Pierre's younger brother, Jean, and added to the Uhart-Juzon estate.[90] Similarly, when Lostal de Saint-Martin died unmarried in Batavia in 1696, his possessions, including twelve hundred books, went to his brother and sole heir, Gratian, who had stayed in Oloron and converted to Catholicism. Emigration and loyalty to religious faith did not preclude loyalty to the "house."

At the time of decision making, individuals did not necessarily experience their own choices and the choices of their relatives as entirely irreversible. On January 18, 1668, Isaac Lostal de Saint-Martin wrote from Colombo, Ceylon, to his brother, Gratian, in Oloron. He confided that he was homesick and tired after fourteen years of uninterrupted warfare against the Portuguese. As a result, he had requested a discharge. He heaped praise on Louis XIV and insisted that friends and relatives who were making plans to join him in Asia should serve the king of France instead:

> It is very surprising to me that even though you encourage me for many reasons to leave the service, you let our relatives entertain the design of coming here to join me. You have no idea how difficult the trip is and how inconvenient this would be for me. Thus, I expect that they will have been dissuaded from carrying out these plans, and if the opposite happens, this will make me very unhappy. If someone is itching for war, there is nothing more advantageous or glorious than the service of our King, which they can join to seek their fortune or a glorious death.[91]

The discharge was not granted, Lostal was promoted, and it is likely that when the harassment of Protestants began in earnest the migration network was reactivated. (Later that year the number of Protestant churches allowed to operate in Béarn was decreased by royal edict from sixty to twenty.)[92] Back in Lower

Navarre, when Marc-Antoine's grandmother Rachel de la Forcade made a donation to her daughter Jeanne in 1698, she mentioned all her children in the deed, including the firstborn Pierre, and did not indicate that the younger son was the presumptive heir.[93] Her husband, Isaac, having died a few years earlier, Rachel was the sole possessor of the Uhart-Juzon house, and she herself negotiated and signed the sharecropping contract for the estate in 1696.[94] At that point she may have thought there was still a slim chance that the firstborn son would come home. This was not entirely unreasonable: a few years earlier (admittedly, before the Revocation), Jean-Baptiste Colbert had been able to poach a high-ranking Huguenot member of the Dutch East India Company, François Caron (1600–1673), who left his post in Batavia to start the French East India Company.[95] Following Pierre's death in 1700 the choice was clear. In 1704 Rachel arranged for her younger son, Jean, to become master of the Uhart-Juzon estate.

Migration and Impartible Inheritance

The first chapter of Alexandre Dumas's *Three Musketeers* is entitled "The three presents of d'Artagnan the elder." The presents of the father to the son, who is about to seek his fortune in Paris, are a fourteen-year-old Béarn pony, fifteen crowns, and some sage advice. The son also receives a letter of recommendation addressed to Monsieur de Tréville, captain of the king's musketeers. Once in Paris, the younger d'Artagnan cannot join the musketeers, but thanks to Tréville's protection he joins a company of Guards as a cadet. *Cadet* in French was originally a military term, coming from the Bearnese word *capdèt*, which meant "chief."[96] Since many younger sons from southwestern noble families became *cadets* in the military, the word came to designate the order of birth in a family: the *aîné* was the firstborn, the *cadet* was the younger son (sometimes meaning the youngest, sometimes the second born). The main character in Dumas's novel doesn't quite fit the pattern, since he is an only son. The standard story, however, is recounted in Dumas's source, the pseudomemoirs of d'Artagnan, published by Courtilz de Sandras in 1700. Here is how d'Artagnan introduces himself:

> Be this as it may, having been brought up poorly enough, for my mother and father were not rich, directly I attained the age of fifteen I dreamt only of setting out to seek my fortune.
>
> All the "cadets" (younger sons) of Béarn, the province whence I came, were much on the same footing, partly because the people of this district are by nature adventurous, and partly because the sterility of their country holds out small hopes of satisfying all their desires. A third reason, not less potent than the other two, served to strengthen my determination; it had before my time been the cause of many of my neighbors and friends leaving their firesides.
>
> A poor gentleman of our neighborhood had some years previously set out for

Paris with only a small valise upon his back, and had amassed such a large fortune at court, that had he possessed as much subtlety as he did courage there would have been nothing he might not have aspired to. The King had given him command of his "Company of Musketeers."[97]

The main elements of the standard story are the lack of economic opportunities for *cadets* in the province and the hope of succeeding in Paris under the protection of a relative or neighbor who had migrated some years earlier and made his fortune. The phrases *cadet de Gascogne* and *cadet de Normandie* were already proverbial in the early eighteenth century. Saint-Simon in his memoirs mentioned "a younger son from Gascony [*cadet de Gascogne*], who had nothing even though he was from a good house."[98] The same author also mentioned an ambitious officer who sought to get rich because "as a younger son from Normandy [*cadet de Normandie*] he was very poor."[99] It is worth noting in passing that Alexandre Dumas, who popularized the image of the *cadet de Gascogne*, was himself the grandson of a gentleman from Normandy, Antoine Davy de la Pailleterie, who sought his fortune in Saint-Domingue and had children with a slave woman, Marie Cessette, who was the novelist's grandmother. However, the family history doesn't entirely fit the textbook case, because Antoine Davy de la Pailleterie was a firstborn son: he followed in the footsteps of his younger brother, Charles, who emigrated first.[100]

In order to achieve a fuller understanding of Marc-Antoine's decision to emigrate, we must compare his trajectory with those of his brothers and sisters and see how each child was treated in the father's will. Here are brief profiles of the children, in the order of their birth:

Mathieu (c. 1706–1783), heir to the Uhart-Juzon estate, was received as a member of the nobility in the Estates General of Navarre on September 1, 1730.[101] He married Anne de Marmont, heiress to the house of Berrio in La Bastide Clairence, Lower Navarre, on March 13, 1741. Eight children.

Françoise (c. 1707–1785), unmarried, lived with her elder brother, Mathieu, on the Uhart-Juzon estate.

Marc-Antoine (c. 1710–c. 1771) migrated to Saint-Domingue in 1729. He married Elizabeth Le Jeune, daughter of plantation owners, on November 24, 1742.[102] Three children.

Jacques was the parish priest of Hosta (1754), Aïcirits (1760), and Arbouet-Sussaute (1764), Lower Navarre.

Marie-Ursule (c. 1720–1787), unmarried, lived with her elder brother Mathieu on the Uhart-Juzon estate.

Henri (c. 1721–1791), an employee of the *régie de tabac* (state monopoly for tobacco), married Gratianne Harriet, heiress to the (commoner) house of Aguiabehere in Hélette, Lower Navarre, on February 5, 1755. Four children.

Louis (after 1721–before 1769), a captain in the Cantabre Volunteers regiment, Bayonne, recruited an infantry company when the regiment was created in 1745; took part in the battles of Fontenoy and Rocoux during the War of the Austrian Succession;[103] migrated to Saint-Domingue on the ship *La Société*, outfitted for departure from Bayonne on February 15, 1755; and died without issue.

When the father, Jean Lamerenx, dictated his last will in 1749, he indicated that he had a spouse, five sons, and two daughters. His spouse received fifteen hundred livres. His son Jacques, a priest, had already received a "clerical title" (a sort of ecclesiastical dowry) of two thousand livres. This title provided a lifetime annuity of twenty livres (with the capital to return to the elder branch on the beneficiary's death). The testator expected Jacques to be able, with this very small income, to "maintain himself and consider himself paid his paternal and maternal legitime, which is all the more reasonable since the testator has expended considerable sums to arrange the promotion of Jacques to the order of the priesthood."[104] (*Legitime* was a term from Roman law designating the share of inheritance mandated by law.) Marc-Antoine, married in Saint-Domingue, was, "as regards word that has arrived to the testator, in a good state of honest fortune, and because he cost him to equip him and for two voyages, he wants him to accept the sum of 800 livres for all of his rights to the paternal and maternal legitime."[105] The two unmarried daughters, Françoise and Ursule, each received 600 livres. One son, Henri, was allotted 400 livres, while the last son, Louis, got nothing. Mathieu, the eldest son, was declared universal heir and received everything not left to the others. At first glance, there seems to have been a deliberate intention of favoring certain younger siblings (Jacques and Marc-Antoine) over the others, who are also treated unequally. In fact, the will specifies that the oldest brother, acting on the counsel of *proches* (trusted neighbors and relatives), will be responsible on the death of the testator for paying the legitime to Françoise, Ursule, Henri, and Louis but not to Jacques and Marc-Antoine, who are considered to have already received their allotment and thus have no further rights beyond what is specified in the will.

As Anne Zink and Bernard Derouet have shown, the use of vocabulary derived from Roman law such as "universal heir" and "rights to the legitime" can easily lend itself to confusion.[106] In Roman law, the entirety of the parents' assets and properties was to be inherited, and each heir received a share. But the Navarrese logic was not that of children's "rights" over the property owned by the previous generation. The "house" was transmitted to a single heir, in this case to Mathieu, the eldest son. One revealing fact in this connection is that wills that adhered to the Custom of Navarre never included an appraisal or even a list of the testator's property and assets. *Biens propres* that belonged outright to the estate automatically were transferred to an heir, with no need for an evaluation or inventory. As Derouet has observed, inheritance was more closely related to identity than to property. It represented only the moment at which the eldest child became the master or mistress of the house, in the same way as royal successions, when *le mort saisit le vif* (the transfer of sovereignty is instantaneous). It was the parents' duty, however, to provide for the younger children, a duty that was transferred to the eldest child upon the parents' death. The criterion was not a minimal share of the inheritance, as the legitime would have been defined in Roman law. In Navarrese customary law, the legitime was defined simply as an adequate sum for the younger siblings to establish themselves. Marc-Antoine began his own career with the assistance of his father, who paid to outfit him and financed his voyages to Saint-Domingue. He went on to make his own fortune, and because he had no need of his parents' money, he was obliged to settle for a very modest share of the paternal and maternal inheritance. A larger share of the inheritance would be reserved for the remaining younger siblings because they were not yet established.

A notable hierarchy was implicit in the manner in which the younger siblings established themselves that roughly corresponded to their birth order. The eldest, Mathieu, inherited the entire house. Marc-Antoine, the second son, emigrated to Saint-Domingue, a choice that in 1729 must have seemed more desirable than the army or clergy. The third son, Jacques, became a priest. The fourth, Henri, became an employee of the state agency that regulated tobacco, and in 1755 he married the (commoner) heiress of an agricultural estate, with whom he had several children. The fifth son, Louis, became an officer in a regiment based in Bayonne before also leaving for Saint-Domingue in 1755 to join his brother Marc-Antoine and eventually died without heirs. The two daughters, Françoise and Ursule, remained unmarried and lived in the Lamerenx house at Aïcirits, whose master was their elder brother Mathieu, until their deaths. Within the house-based system, the unmarried child continued to be identified with the house and remained under the protection of the parents and later of the heir. In their implicit hierarchy, the Lamerenx siblings' itineraries represent, in descending order, the range of available options at the time: heirship, emigration, the priesthood, marriage to an heiress, a military career, and remaining single while residing in the familial house.

It is tempting to suggest generalizations concerning the relationship between certain types of hereditary customs and particular emigration patterns and practices. Le Play made a parallel between younger sons in Gascony and Normandy, suggesting that Norman emigration to Canada in the seventeenth century could be explained by unequal rules governing inheritance.[107] Indeed, the Pays de Caux (the only part of Normandy that possessed truly inegalitarian hereditary practices) experienced a wave of migration to Canada as well as Saint-Domingue during the eighteenth century (Alexandre Dumas's grandfather was from the Pays de Caux).[108] But there is a certain level of generality at which these similarities lose their meaning. For example, discussions of German emigration to America in the nineteenth century typically emphasize instead the relationship between emigration and hereditary egalitarianism, with the idea that the excessive subdivision of agricultural properties contributed to emigration. According to Simone Wegge, however, emigration was even more widely practiced in regions with greater degrees of hereditary inequality.[109]

In fact, as Derouet has demonstrated, posing the problem solely in terms of hereditary equality or inequality obscures the most important point. In Roman law, the legator could divide his properties among his heirs as he saw fit, on the condition that no share fell below a minimum threshold. Under the customs that prevailed in western France, the goal was to "preserve properties within the family"; as a result, property was automatically transferred—without the possibility of the legator appointing a privileged successor—to the entire next generation of a family group. Derouet remarks that the automaticity of inheritance was also a fundamental characteristic of Pyrenean house-based societies, with one important difference: instead of being transferred to the entire next generation, the properties were inherited by a single representative of the successors, in such a way as to ensure that "the same logic is ultimately used in the service of the property itself and not of a group of relatives."[110] Derouet adds that a common characteristic of these customs-based systems was the exclusion of dowried children. This rule was explicitly formulated in the Custom of Navarre (Fig. 1.4): "If the children following the first born are married and dowried by their parents, they will not be allowed to claim any supplement to their legitime from the entailed property."[111] Children who received a sum to allow them to establish themselves elsewhere were excluded from the inheritance, which was reserved for "true" heirs, meaning those who had stayed at home. In this sense, dowried children were no longer considered members of the "family."

This partly corroborates Jérôme Viret's observations regarding emigration from the Perche region to Canada in the seventeenth century. Viret notes that because the Perche was a region with egalitarian customs, emigrants did not leave because they were "excluded," in the legal sense, from the inheritance. Instead, these were "liberatory migrations" by which emigrants who had received funding to settle elsewhere voluntarily excluded themselves from the family unit. In the case of the "first emigrant," Marc-Antoine de Lamerenx, it is obvious that as a younger brother, he did not leave for the colonies because he had received nothing. On the contrary, he left because he had received a sum that enabled him to create a life for himself elsewhere. His father financed two trips, the first in 1729 and the second in 1741, just before his marriage in Saint-Domingue to Elizabeth Le Jeune, the daughter of colonial settlers. It is probable that when he

Fig. 1.4. Title page of the 1722 edition of *Los fors et costumas deu Royaume de Navarre deça ports, avec l'estil et aranzel deudit Royaume* (The Privileges and Customs of the Cis-Pyrenean Kingdom of Navarre, with the Procedures and Fiscal Regulations of Said Kingdom). The Custom of Navarre was originally published in 1611.

returned to Saint-Domingue in 1741, Marc-Antoine took with him some *pacotille* (trade goods carried by passengers duty-free and resold to finance settlement costs in the colonies), whose sale would have provided an adequate, if modest, sum that made it possible for him to marry.

The dowry played a crucial role in the Pyrenean house-based system, as Zink has shown. The heir to the house endowed the younger son or daughter, who would become the "adventitious" master or mistress of another house (the equivalent of a prince or queen consort in royal dynasties). The dowry was rarely paid in cash, becoming a credit extended by the "emitting" house to the "receiving" house. The situation was complicated by the fact that the receiving house was required to reimburse the dowry to the emitting house in the event of a childless marriage. This "right of return" (*tournedot*) was guaranteed by a mortgage on the property of the receiving house. Consequently, "dowries that were agreed upon but unpaid, of sisters, brothers, uncles, aunts, were added to the legitimes, which were never set, and to the adventitious dowries of extinguished branches of the family, which the house was obliged to pay." These mortgages became a threat to the integrity of the houses, "because these are privileged debts for which one could be compelled to sell one's lands," but at the same time they guaranteed the integrity of the houses, because no house would benefit from forcing another house to sell its lands, at the risk of triggering a chain of sales and the collapse of the system. According to Zink, "These mortgages and long delays represent a kind of fiduciary circulation; on the one hand, they enabled younger siblings to establish themselves, not independently of any consideration of fortune, but without regard to cash flow. Because it could commit itself over very long periods of time, the original house freed itself of debt little by little by devoting its annual profits in cash or livestock . . . or better yet, it was freed when a new marriage occurred or the return of a dowry triggered a new marriage or a substitution in the chain of credits." This was thus a credit-based and hence deferred-payment-based system. Such deferred payments "rendered both useless and impossible the alienation of land and constituted, based on legitimes that might appear to present the greatest danger to the houses' integrity, the most important guarantors of such integrity by providing, in addition to bans and limitations, the security of an entire system."[112]

We can see here that emigration played an ambiguous role in the circulation of dowries. To Jean Lamerenx, his younger son's emigration to Saint-Domingue must have appeared advantageous for several reasons. Marc-Antoine should in theory have married a noble heiress, but that would have meant providing a dowry for him that matched the level of the new wife's fortune. Jean Lamerenx must have calculated that so significant a dowry, even if not paid up front, would represent too great an expense for the house and thus it would be preferable to finance the travel costs of his younger son, while the costs of the second trip were covered by the dowry received when Mathieu, his oldest son, married. Indeed, Marc-Antoine's second voyage in 1741 coincides precisely with Mathieu's ascension to the role of master of the estate of Uhart-Juzon, an event that was triggered by the presumptive heir's marriage (March 13, 1741). The younger son was thus established on the strength of the dowry received when the eldest married. There was a specific rule in the Custom of Navarre providing for this: "The parents who own the property will use the dowry to buy back those parts of the estate that have previously been sold, to pay off creditors, to marry off their children . . . and they may use the rest in a prudent and responsible fashion."[113]

Using the dowry of one child to marry off another child came third in the list of allowed priorities, after making the entail whole and paying off privileged creditors. Similarly, the youngest son, Louis, set sail to Saint-Domingue on February 15, 1755,[114] two weeks after he was a witness at his brother Henri's wedding, which took place in Hélette on February 5, 1755. It is safe to conclude from this co-occurrence that their older brother Mathieu had paid their legitimes to them a few months earlier in settlement of the inheritance of their father, who had died in 1750. (In a 1751 arrangement Mathieu pledged 1,565 livres to all the siblings except Marc-Antoine.)[115] Paying for the voyage of a younger sibling was, in any event, less expensive than paying a dowry, and the younger sibling who made a fortune in America would need nothing at the time of an inheritance. Funding the trip of an emigrant disturbed the credit system in two ways, however: first, the travel costs and start-up funds needed to set oneself up in the colonies had to be paid in cash, which could necessitate selling land; second, the emigrant's "dowry" evaded the reciprocal credit system between houses and became the property of its receiver, who invested it "in the islands" and was therefore not available to pay to the in-laws of the younger son, married off with the right of return (*tournedot*) to the emitting house in the event that the marriage was childless.

As seen above, according to Zink's analysis, the system of dowry circulation enabled younger children to become established "on credit." Zink adds that unlike in other regions of France, the specificity of the Pyrenees "did not reside in the fact of only marrying a single child of the house, nor in a concern for keeping the family estate intact." Under the *ancien régime* in France, despite the great variety of egalitarian and inegalitarian hereditary practices, customs, or written laws, the concern with the estate's integrity was constant. In Zink's view, the uniqueness of the Pyrenees region was "the impossibility for the younger brother to settle near the parental household once he was married." In this sense, "the spirit of Pyrenean customs is the non-multiplication of houses."[116] Lands not privately owned by an individual house were moors or pastures owned collectively by the houses, and no new house could be established in these common areas. A younger son who wanted to settle, even if he had sufficient funds, could acquire neither the lands of an existing house nor any part of the pastures that belonged to the community of houses. In principle, the only options available to a younger brother were to remain single or to marry an heiress, because "there is no other place to which one can take one's legitime and make one's living outside the house system."[117] Emigration was in that sense a new option, opening up a possibility that had not existed before: earning one's living outside the house system.

There was therefore a real connection between Pyrenean houses and emigration, but the nature of the link was less intuitive than it might seem. Strictly speaking, emigration was not the result of unequally distributed estates, because there was no distribution. The entire estate went to a single heir. However (and this goes against the traditional image of the penniless *cadet*), the family group did provide for the establishment of other children. Emigration was originally just one option among others for dowried children who were excluded from sharing in the inheritance. The appeal of this particular option became increasingly great for both parents and children with time, however. From the perspective of the parents, equipping a younger son for Saint-Domingue was less expensive than providing a dowry for him so that he could marry an heiress. From the standpoint of younger sons, being a priest, a military officer, or a government employee would procure a stable income, but bringing even modest start-up funds to the islands offered such a significant return on investment that eventually the eldest children sought to emigrate as well. This was what happened in the generation following Marc-Antoine's, as we will see in chapter 3.

CHAPTER TWO

The Coffee Boom and the Jealousy of Trade

> The King also, having care to make his realm potent, as well by sea as by land, for the better maintenance of the navy, ordained: "That wines and woods from the parts of Gascony and Languedoc, should not be brought but in English bottoms," bowing the ancient policy of this estate, from consideration of plenty to consideration of power.
>
> Francis Bacon, *History of the Reign of King Henry VII*, 1622

Marc-Antoine Lamerenx sailed to Saint-Domingue in 1729 with some symbolic capital (his family's nobility and the protection of a colonial official) but little or no economic capital. When his grandchildren petitioned the French government for their share of the indemnity the Haitian government had agreed to pay in exchange for the recognition of the island's independence, the family's properties were estimated to have been worth a total of 1.3 million francs in 1789.[1] To get a sense of the magnitude of that sum, one should recall that the Louisiana Purchase as a whole amounted to 68 million francs. One family's net worth was about one-fiftieth of the price the US government paid for one-third of the North American continent.

The wealth of France's Caribbean colonies was noted by many contemporary observers. It was even discussed, and analyzed, by the founders of economic science. Adam Smith, in *The Wealth of Nations*,[2] and Jean-Baptiste Say, in his *Treatise on Political Economy*,[3] speculated on the causes of such wealth. They based their speculation on a number of empirical observations that show that they were pretty well informed about the plantation system. Adam Smith observed that Saint-Domingue was "the most important of the sugar colonies of the West Indies, and its produce is said to be greater than that of all the English sugar colonies put together." He also opined that "the prosperity of the sugar colonies of France has been entirely owing to the good conduct of the colonists, which must therefore have had some superiority over that of the English."[4] These works of speculation did not have an exclusively academic audience. There is evidence that some planters read *The Wealth of Nations*. In 1798 a lawyer and former coffee planter from Saint-Domingue, Pierre Joseph Laborie, who sided with the British during the Haitian War of Independence, published a book in

London entitled *The Coffee Planter of Saint Domingo*, in which he discussed Smith's observations about the French Caribbean colonies in some detail.[5] The work was conceived as a handbook for prospective emigrants who might be interested in using French coffee-plantation methods in Jamaica. In 1802, a former plantation manager from Saint-Domingue, S. J. du Coeurjoly, who was trying to earn a living as an author in Paris, published a book entitled *Manuel des habitants de Saint-Domingue* (Saint-Domingue planters' handbook), which was also aimed at prospective emigrants and coincided with Napoleon's attempt to retake the island and to reestablish slavery.[6] The book did not feature quotes from Adam Smith, but it included population and agricultural-production statistics, as well as a treatise on tropical diseases by a medical doctor who had lived on the island.

These discussions in learned as well as semilearned discourse, when combined with microhistorical analysis, can help illuminate the perception and the motives of people on the ground. They give us a sense of perceived opportunities and of the common ways of taking advantage of those opportunities. They also reveal universally shared assumptions about the use of commerce to promote national grandeur and a sense that for imperial powers like Britain and France trade issues and military issues were inextricably linked. Marc-Antoine made his fortune growing coffee. Let us start with the origins of coffee growing in Saint-Domingue, since Marc-Antoine was there at the very beginning.

Origins of Coffee Growing in Saint-Domingue

According to Coeurjoly, in his *Saint-Domingue Planters' Handbook*, the coffee plant was originally grown in Yemen. It was taken to Europe by the Dutch circa 1690 and then to Java, where it was cultivated on a large scale. In 1714, the mayor of Amsterdam sent a coffee plant as a gift to the king of France, and the plant grew in the King's Garden (Jardin des plantes). In 1720, a naval officer named Déclieux took one plant from the King's Garden to Martinique, where coffee began to flourish, replacing the cocoa plantations that had just been devastated by a hurricane. From Martinique, coffee spread to Guadeloupe and Saint-Domingue. In 1787, a citizen of Port-au-Prince proposed a subscription to erect a statue honoring Déclieux, the "father of coffee" in the Antilles. The amount raised was only 4,032 livres from seventeen subscribers. Yet, Coeurjoly adds, "Holland awarded a statue to the citizen who enriched the nation's commerce by discovering the art of salting herrings!"[7] As the historian Steven Topik puts it, "Purveyors of this neat story are unwitting assistants of international traders and mass roasters who had a vested interest in positing a monolithic sort of coffee."[8] For marketing purposes, it was important to indicate that coffees grown in the Americas were legitimate descendants of a single Mocha ancestor. It was also important to show that coffee growing in the colony had its origin in royal patronage. Laborie, the author of the 1798 *Coffee Planter of Saint Domingo*, was less interested in genealogical details, but he too started by mentioning that coffee had been introduced to Saint-Domingue "so early as sixty years ago." Subsequently, it "improved to such a height of increase and perfection, that the annual produce exceeded seventy million of pounds [in 1789]." The coffee grown in Saint-Domingue, "though inferior to that of Mocha, where the tree seems to be indigenous, was no less perfect than that of Martinico; vying even with the coffee of the island of Mauritius or Bourbon."[9]

Regarding the introduction of coffee from Martinique to Saint-Domingue, there were two competing, partly overlapping stories (both reported by Louis Élie Moreau de Saint-Méry). One involved the Jesuits, those indispensable characters in narratives of early globalization. The other involved a character with whom we are already familiar, Monsieur de Nolivos, Marc-Antoine's first sponsor in Saint-Domingue. According to one account, Jesuits took coffee plants from Martinique to Saint-Domingue in the 1720s and experimented in growing coffee on their plantation in Terrier-Rouge, on the northern plain of Saint-Domingue.[10] The other account credited Nolivos with introducing coffee to the island: he was reportedly given some seeds during a stopover in Martinique and started planting coffee on Ester, his estate in Léogane Parish, on the western plain of Saint-Domingue, in 1726. In the 1760s these original coffee trees could still be seen on the Nolivos plantation, as well as on the neighboring plantations of Cassaigne, La Ravine, and Mithon.[11] What the two stories have in common is that the first coffee-growing experiments were conducted in the coastal areas of Saint-Domingue. There is also a consensus that these areas were less than ideal for the cultivation of coffee, which required a cooler climate. According to Moreau de Saint-Méry, in 1738 coffee was introduced to the mountainous parish of Dondon, whose climate proved to be ideal, and the Saint-Domingue coffee boom started there: "It was in Dondon that the first coffee trees brought from the Windward Islands were planted, and some great fortunes were created in that parish thanks to the success of those first manufactures, which are thought to have begun in 1738."[12]

In the memorandum summarizing his career that was discussed in chapter 1, Marc-Antoine indicated that he had moved from the western part of Saint-Domingue to Dondon in 1736 and become a noncommissioned militia officer in the cavalry of Dondon Parish in 1737. As we have seen, he took a trip to France in 1741. On that occasion his parents provided him with a small capital that allowed him to marry Elizabeth Le Jeune, the daughter of colonists from Grande-Rivière, a neighboring parish, the following year. This puts him in the right place at the right time: Marc-Antoine was in Dondon at the start of the coffee boom, and some of the first coffee-growing experiments had been conducted on the plantation of his patron Nolivos in Léogane. Seeing the success of the first coffee plantations, he was able to emulate it quickly thanks to his marriage and his establishment as a planter. Having first-mover advantage, he amassed one of those "great fortunes" Moreau de Saint-Méry described in 1797.

Dondon in the 1730s was still very sparsely populated. It was established as a parish in 1727, but the official limits were not designated until 1742. The place was hard to reach, as it was entirely surrounded by mountains. Moreau de Saint-Méry found the area pleasing to his pre-Romantic taste, judging that "there may not be anywhere in the Colony a site as picturesque as this parish," which was surrounded by "enormous mountains" with "reclining rocks," and "the disorder of these masses is a testimony almost everywhere to the great movements of the earth."[13] The first European settler was reportedly André Minguet, a surgeon and freebooter who took part in the French raid on the Spanish town of Cartagena de Indias in 1697 and obtained a huge land grant from Jean-Baptiste Ducasse, leader of the expedition and governor of Saint-Domingue, in 1698. According to Moreau de Saint-Méry, Minguet's first abode in Dondon was a cave that had been used as a sanctuary by the Taíno people. Now a minor tourist attraction in Haiti, the place was and is still known as the Voûte à Minguet (Minguet's Cave). In the eighteenth century the only remaining signs of Taíno presence were archeological in nature. Moreau de Saint-Méry wrote that "there is every indication that Dondon used to have a large Indian population. Fragments of their vases, as well as statues that evoke their superstitious ideas, can be found everywhere."[14] In Moreau de Saint-Méry's account, the cave was a place of worship that attracted natives, led by their chiefs, from all over the island. The Taíno belief was that the Sun and the Moon had escaped the cave to go illuminate the world. The first humans followed them. In punishment for their temerity, they were metamorphosed into lizards and birds, and the guardians of the caves were changed into stone statues.

Moreau de Saint-Méry's account of the legend was in all likelihood borrowed and freely adapted from the account of Ramón Pané, a Hieronymite priest who was asked by Christopher Columbus to record the religious beliefs of the natives of Hispaniola.[15] Moreau de Saint-Méry, who had read both Voltaire and Rousseau in addition to Father Pané's ethnographic account, contended that "these naked and ignorant men" showed the greatest pride in their beliefs, since they thought they were direct descendants of the first humans. He concluded that "one million of nature's firstborn sons" had been wiped out by "a handful of Spaniards," leaving just a few tokens of their beliefs and the memory of their cruel fate "floating on the ocean of the ages."[16] Adam Smith had written in a similar spirit a few years earlier: "Folly and injustice seem to have been the principles which presided over and directed the first project of establishing those colonies; the folly of hunting after gold and silver mines, and the injustice of coveting the possession of a country whose harmless natives, far from having ever injured the people of Europe, had received the first adventurers with every mark of kindness and hospitality."[17]

Paths to Capital Accumulation: Marc-Antoine Lamerenx and His Sons-in-Law

Coeurjoly's *Saint-Domingue Planters' Handbook* included a remarkable conversation between a "European" and an "American" that was written as a series of frequently asked questions. The European was a prospective emigrant. The American was a colonist who had extensive knowledge of the island of Saint-Domingue. The American painted a uniformly and implausibly rosy picture of the colony, insisting that "if you choose to go, with good conduct, making a fortune there is easy."[18] The conversation is informative nonetheless. Written at the end of the colonial period, as the French were about to lose the war against their former slaves, it described the various ways of getting rich in Saint-Domingue as they were understood at the time. Coeurjoly did not recommend starting a plantation right away. Given the prosperity of the colony, getting into the game at that stage was very expensive, and an immigrant had to accumulate some capital first. Laborie, in his *Coffee Planter of Saint Domingo*, did envisage the possibility of starting a coffee plantation right away, but he insisted that sizeable capital was needed: "I would not advise any man to undertake a settlement, who has not the command of 3 or 4,000 pounds sterling, independent of the land purchased."[19]

The paths to wealth described by Coeurjoly and Laborie correspond to a mature stage in the development of the colony, when available land had become scarce and expensive. For Marc-Antoine in Dondon in the 1740s the situation was different: land was plentiful and free. As we saw in chapter 1, Marc-Antoine insisted that he had not made his fortune quickly. From the time of his arrival in Saint-Domingue in 1729 to his trip to France in 1741 he did not accumulate any significant wealth, since his parents had to pay for his passage and his equipment when he returned to the colony in 1742. Things started to change when he married upon his return. The financial details for Marc-Antoine and his generation are difficult to reconstruct because the notarial records for that period have been lost, but it is likely that Marc-Antoine was able to start a coffee plantation with his wife's dowry and with the small capital provided by the sale of *pacotille* that he took with him on his second trip. Undeveloped land belonged to the king, and the governor of the island had discretionary power in making land grants to colonists. These grants initially were large, typically 225 or 100 or 64 *carreaux* (700 or 300 or 200 acres), usually square-shaped (squares of 1,500 or 1,000 or 800 paces, respectively). Elizabeth Le Jeune brought 64 *carreaux* of

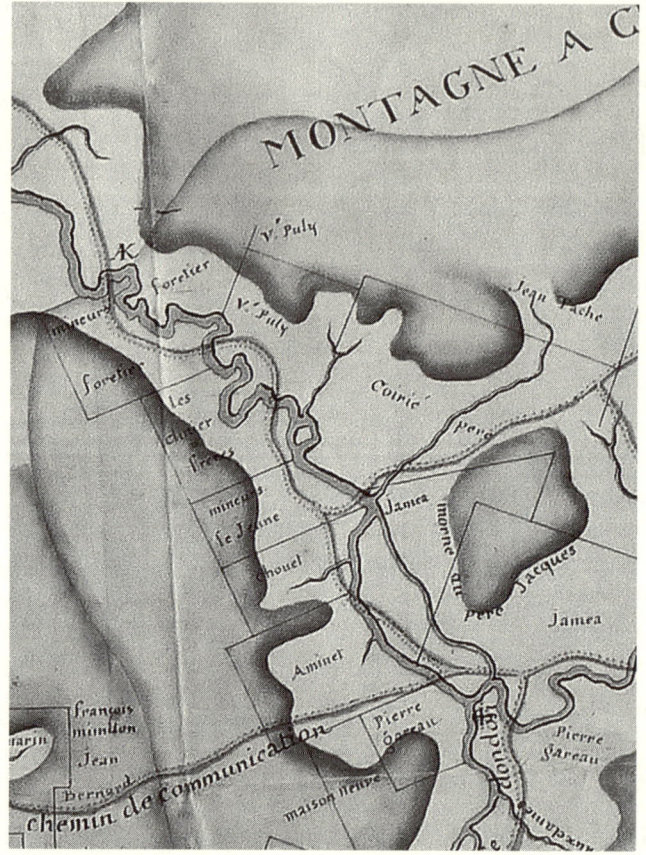

Fig. 2.1. Original land grants in the Matador District of Dondon, c. 1740. Detail of map by Guitière, royal land surveyor (south-up orientation). The letters "AK" mark the Spanish border. Elizabeth Le Jeune's lot is marked as "mineurs Le Jeune" (minor Le Jeune children). ANOM, Fonds ministériels, Dépôt des fortifications des colonies, 1636–1913, DFC, Fonds Moreau de Saint-Méry.

uncultivated land to the marriage. It was located in the area of the parish that was settled first, the Matador District of Dondon, on the border with the Spanish part of the island (Fig. 2.1).

Elizabeth had received the land as a royal grant in 1740, reportedly because she was the granddaughter of one of the soldiers who had asserted French authority over the island during the reign of Louis XIV. We know these details from the record of a protracted dispute about property limits between Elizabeth Le Jeune and one of her neighbors.[20] The lawsuit arose from faulty land surveying that took place in the early 1740s, at the outset of the coffee boom. Elizabeth's lawyer was none other than Moreau de Saint-Méry, who later wrote the famous description of Saint-Domingue. Her opponent's lawyer was Pierre Joseph Laborie, the future author of *The Coffee Planter of Saint Domingo*. The world of coffee planters was a very small one. When Moreau de Saint-Méry published his book in 1797, Elizabeth, known as *la dame Duhart*,[21] was still recorded as the owner of a large coffee plantation in the Matador District of Dondon (the place was still known as *habitation Duhart* in the late nineteenth century).[22]

In addition to the 1740 deed, there is a record of an even larger land grant (225 *carreaux*, or 700 acres) received by Marc-Antoine and Elizabeth in 1747.[23] This lot was in the western part of Dondon, which became a separate parish, Marmelade, in 1773 (Fig. 2.2). While sugar planting was a capital-intensive industry, starting a coffee plantation did not require a large capital investment.[24] According to Laborie, only a dozen slaves were needed at first, and the best results were obtained by growing coffee on newly cleared slopes. When Laborie wrote in the 1790s, the deforestation of the island had reached an advanced stage. In the 1740s it was only beginning. In the first year of operation a dozen slaves were provided with tools (hoe, scraper, axe, and billhook) to clear a small part of the lot by felling trees and burning the underbrush (Fig. 2.3).

Masters and slaves lived in huts at first. Permanent buildings were not erected until after the first few crops had brought in sufficient revenue (Fig. 2.4). According to Adam Smith, this path to capital accumulation distinguished Saint-Domingue from the British Caribbean colonies, in which plantations were started with large capital investments from the mother country: "The stock which has improved and cultivated the sugar colonies of England has, a great part of it, been sent out from England, and has by no means been altogether the produce of the soil and industry of the colonists." As a result, Smith contended, "the prosperity of the English sugar colonies has been, in a great measure, owing to the great riches of England, of which a part has overflowed, if one may say so, upon those colonies."[25] In the French Caribbean colonies, on the other hand, and "particularly the great colony of St. Domingo," there was little capital investment coming from France, and the capital that established plantations was "raised almost entirely from the gradual improvement and cultivation of those colonies."[26]

In Smith's hierarchy of desirable paths to economic development, the Caribbean colonies occupied a middle ground between the agricultural settlements of North America (the best) and the government by merchants of the East India Company (the worst). Smith agreed with the physiocrats that the natural path to economic growth was through the development of agriculture, and he described the commerce-led development that had historically taken place in Europe as unnatural. The development of towns and commerce had eventually lifted agriculture, but this path was "retrograde" (i.e., the reverse of what should

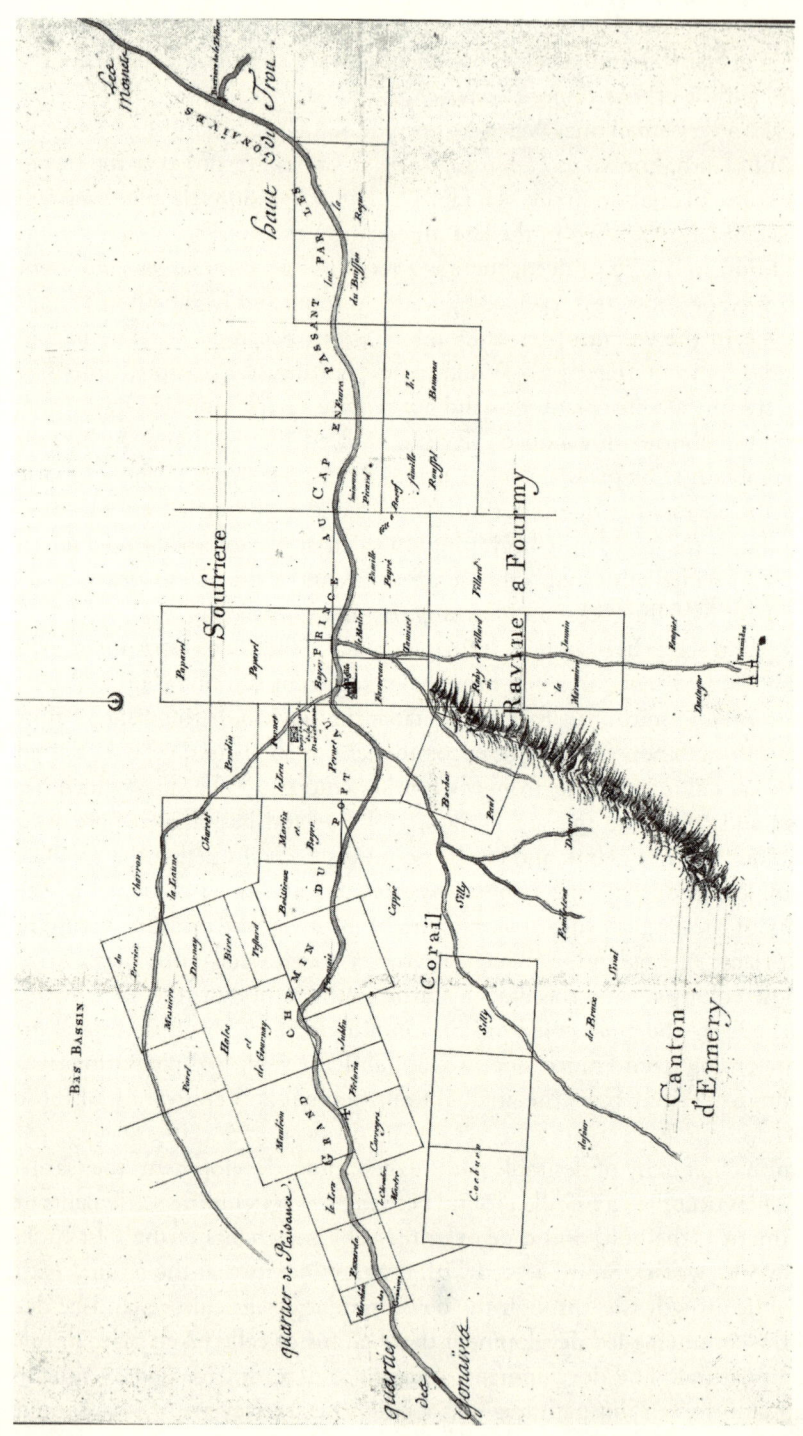

Fig. 2.2. Marmelade in 1779. The Lamerenx–Le Jeune land grant of 1747 (not shown on this map) was in the Soufrière District. ANOM, Fonds ministériels, Dépôt des fortifications des colonies, 1636–1913, 15 DFC 107B.

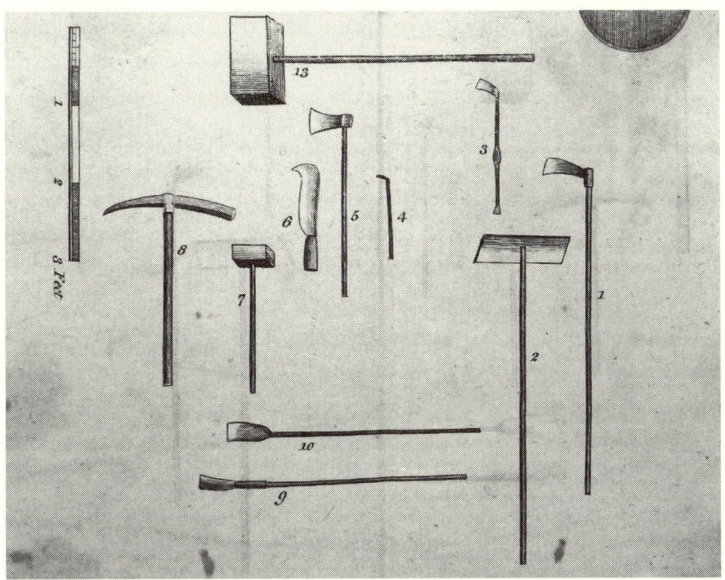

Fig. 2.3. Forest-clearing tools, illustration from Pierre Joseph Laborie's *The Coffee Planter of Saint Domingo*. Even in the heyday of coffee growing, on a typical plantation part of the land remained uncultivated standing wood or savannas (see Fig. 2.4).

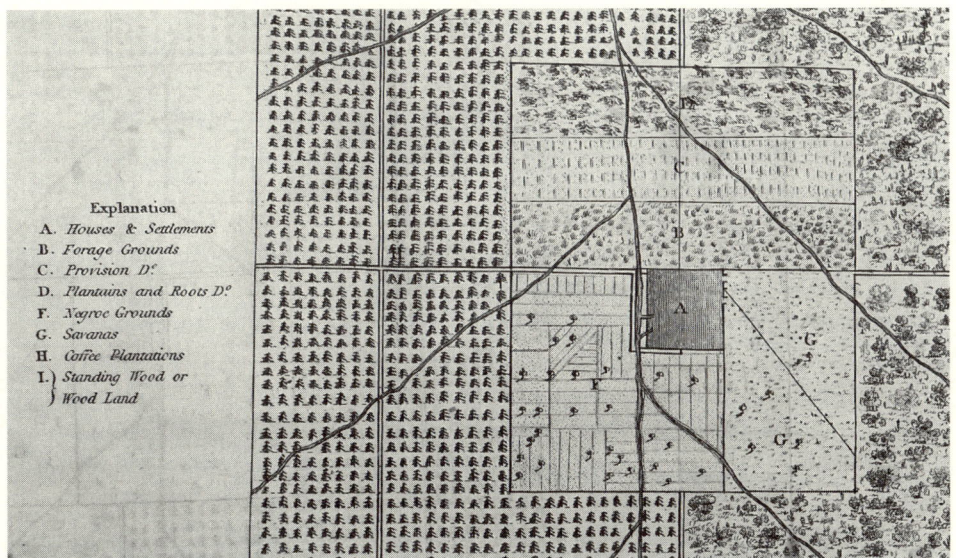

Fig. 2.4. Map of a coffee plantation (detail), from Pierre Joseph Laborie's *The Coffee Planter of Saint Domingo*. The large area to the right (I) is standing wood; the coffee trees (H) are to the left; and slave quarters (F) are in the middle.

have happened naturally): agriculture should have developed before commerce.[27] For Smith, the system of long-distance commerce coupled with slavery that formed the basis for the development of the Caribbean colonies was the epitome of "unnatural" development. Yet colonists had freedom of trade with the mother country—commerce with other countries was prohibited, of course—while in Asia commerce was controlled by a monopolistic trading company. In the Americas, the development of agriculture by free laborers in the continental colonies approximated what Smith deemed to be the "natural" path to economic development.[28] Colonists did not start with large capital investments derived from monopolistic commercial profits. They simply reinvested agricultural profits into further improvement of the land. In Smith's view, this "healthy" aspect of capital accumulation was something Saint-Domingue shared with the British North American colonies and distinguished the French colony from the British sugar islands.

Whether this analysis correctly describes the whole of Saint-Domingue's economy is an open question. Sugar plantations required large capital investments because of the large number of slaves required to operate a plantation and the cost and complexity of the processing plant: the money did at least in part come from France. Nevertheless, Smith's analysis appears to fit an industry that is not explicitly mentioned in *The Wealth of Nations*, namely, coffee production, which required much more modest levels of start-up capital and therefore attracted a wider range of entrepreneurs.

Marc-Antoine's first step toward wealth was his 1742 marriage to Elizabeth Le Jeune. The couple had two daughters (the son, who joined the King's Guards in 1770, died young and without issue). The elder daughter, Marie-Elizabeth, married Charles François Pichot de Kerdisien Trémais (c. 1724–1784) in the early 1770s. Trémais, a commissary of the navy who specialized in financial matters, had earned a reputation as a troubleshooter who could investigate corrupt colonial officials. He was appointed subdelegate general of the intendant of Saint-Domingue in 1763. In 1769 he married a young widow who owned a coffee plantation in Marmelade and inherited the plantation when she died of illness shortly thereafter. Thus he was a widower who already owned a plantation when he married Marie-Elizabeth. The younger daughter of Marc-Antoine and Elizabeth, Marguerite-Françoise, married Charles de Saint-Germain du Houlme (1740–1787) in 1777.[29] Saint-Germain was a captain in the Agenois regiment, which had recently been posted to Saint-Domingue. The marriage contract specified that all property acquired after the marriage by either spouse by purchase or inheritance would become the joint property of the couple. Saint-Germain was the owner of a small fiefdom in Normandy. His patrimony was dwarfed by his wife's wealth, which was potentially half of what Marc-Antoine and Elizabeth had accumulated. The marriage was very profitable for the bridegroom.

This pattern of military officers contracting advantageous marriages in the colony was recorded early on by Jean-Baptiste Labat, a Dominican priest who visited Saint-Domingue in 1701 and published a voluminous account of his voyage to the New World in 1722. In the fifth volume, Labat recounted his visit to the house of Jean-Baptiste Ducasse, the legendary privateer and former governor of Saint-Domingue who had led the French raid on Cartagena in 1697. Labat opined that the splendor of Ducasse's fortune had "attracted to Saint-Domingue many of his Basque compatriots." He added that since Ducasse was "naturally magnificent, generous, and munificent, they did not come away empty-handed, and neither did those many others he promoted, putting them in a position to gratify others, as long as they followed his example."[30] (Ducasse was from Béarn, but as Jacques de Cauna indicates, in Saint-Domingue Basque, Bearnese, and Gascon immigrants were all seen as coming from the same region.)[31]

In Ducasse's house, decorated by a series of portraits of the Spanish governors of Cartagena taken as trophies in the 1697 raid, Labat heard the story of a Gascon officer who had come to Saint-Domingue to seek his fortune and married an aging widow who owned a large plantation. The Gascon officer had come to see Governor Ducasse, who received him very well. The officer had explained that he had spent all his money serving the king and was seeking fortune in the colony. Because, in Labat's words, Gascony was "the country of clever inventions rather than the country of bills of exchange,"[32] the Gascon gentleman had devised the following scheme: each planter in the parish would lend or give him one slave, allowing him to gather the fifty to sixty workers he would need to start his own plantation. Amused by this proposal, Ducasse had feigned to take it seriously and presented it at a town meeting. Predictably, the response had been unenthusiastic. Ducasse had then advised his compatriot that marriage was the shortest path to wealth. The Gascon gentleman had immediately gone hunting for a wife and located an aging widow who had outlived several husbands and was very wealthy. (The lady hailed from Dieppe in the Pays de Caux, a region that produced significant outmigration to Saint-Domingue.) He had courted her assiduously, declared his love, and clubbed a rival who had been courting her for a while. He had pressed her to the point of saying he would not leave the premises until she agreed to marry him. The lady had relented, and a few days later they were married, having signed a marriage contract stipulating a mutual donation of all their assets. "Darn," she had said later, "you see, I had no choice but to marry if I wanted the Gascon gentleman to leave the house: he swore he would not leave otherwise."[33]

This story is a comical version of the matrimonial strategies of Marc-Antoine's sons-in-law and indeed Marc-Antoine himself. When Marc-Antoine married Elizabeth Le Jeune in 1742, he brought a small sum of money to the marriage, but his capital was mainly symbolic: his nobility and his service under a powerful patron. Similarly, when Charles de Saint-Germain married Marie-Elizabeth Lamerenx in 1777, what he brought to the marriage was mainly the prestige of being a captain in the king's army. Shortly after the marriage, his commanding officer, Charles de Cadignan, wrote to the secretary of the navy requesting that Saint-Germain be transferred from the Agenois regiment to the colonial militia with a promotion to the rank of lieutenant colonel.[34] He emphasized the advantageous marriage Saint-Germain had contracted, implying that the promotion would be consistent with his recently improved economic status. Furthermore, this would not be a drain on resources, since militia positions were unpaid. Finally, it was in the government's interest that fine officers like Saint-Germain should decide to settle in Saint-Domingue permanently. The request was denied. Stung by the refusal, Cadignan wrote to the secretary of the navy again, reiterating the request as a personal favor.[35] The secretary replied that he was sorry to have to say no again and promised to keep Saint-Germain in mind for future promotions.[36] When the reply arrived in Saint-Domingue, Cadignan had just died of a tropical disease, and the regiment was taking part in a famous episode of the American War of Independence, the siege of Savannah, under the command of Count d'Estaing.[37] Many died or were wounded in the failed operation. Saint-Germain settled in Marmelade with his wife, Marguerite-Françoise, and officially retired from the service in 1783 without the promotion he had sought but with the Saint-Louis Cross, an honor that had eluded his father-in-law, Marc-Antoine.[38]

As mentioned above, Charles de Trémais was already a plantation owner when he married Marc-Antoine's daughter Marie-Elizabeth, but his wealth was newly acquired. Trémais had had feud with a neighbor named Pierre Cappé (more about this dispute later). One day he had received an unpleasant letter from Cappé reminding him that they were both upstarts (*deux hommes parvenus*).[39] This must have stung Trémais, who came from minor Breton nobility, while Cappé was a commoner. (Trémais made a copy of the letter and forwarded it to the governor of Saint-Domingue as evidence of Cappé's low-bred insolence.) Cappé had added that his own marriage had brought him little and that all his assets had been earned thanks to his own efforts, implying that that had not been the case with Trémais.[40]

The marriage contract between Charles de Saint-Germain and Marguerite-Françoise Lamerenx contained a clause stipulating that the couple would not make any acquisitions in Normandy and that even if they did, the Custom of Paris, rather than the Custom of Normandy, would apply to those assets. The Custom of Paris, which applied to all civil-law matters in Saint-Domingue, was egalitarian. (It formed the basis for the drafting of the Civil Code after the French Revolution.) Its main features included the joint ownership by husband and wife of assets acquired after the marriage and equal shares in the inheritance for all children, male or female. This is how Laborie summarized the rule: "At the death of a parent or progenitor, all the children had an equal right to his or her inheritance, real and personal, without any preference of sex or primogeniture."[41]

According to Adam Smith, the egalitarianism of the Custom of Paris was one of the reasons for the economic dynamism of Saint-Domingue: "The French colonies, indeed, are subject to the custom of Paris, which, in the inheritance of land, is much more favourable to the younger children than the law of England."[42] Smith's notion was that the right of primogeniture and the use of entails, which was in force in many parts of Europe, hindered the development of agriculture:

> In Europe, the law of primogeniture, and perpetuities of different kinds, prevent the division of great estates, and thereby hinder the multiplication of small proprietors. A small proprietor, however, who knows every part of his little territory, who views it with all the affection which property, especially small property, naturally inspires, and who upon that account takes pleasure not only in cultivating but in adorning it, is generally of all improvers the most industrious, the most intelligent, and the most successful.[43]

Inheritance rules limiting the division of estates were counterproductive, as the most efficient improvement of the land came from small proprietors. Primogeniture and entails created an artificial shortage of agricultural land, which kept prices higher than they would have been under normal conditions. As a result, potential improvers of the land were priced out of the market. Egalitarian inheritance customs like the Custom of Paris, however, made it possible for agricultural estates to reach optimal size. Thanks in part to the stipulations of the Custom of Paris, in Saint-Domingue the real-estate market was remarkably liquid, and agricultural land changed hands at a frenetic pace. One consequence of this phenomenon was that land surveying was much more active in Saint-Domingue in the eighteenth century than in continental France. By 1789 most of the island had been systematically surveyed in order to regularize property titles and facilitate real-estate transactions.[44] Such systematic efforts did not begin in continental France until Napoleon established the cadastre in 1807. It took some thirty years to survey the entire country. Aside from the Caribbean colonies, the only French territory that was systematically surveyed in the eighteenth century was Corsica, after it was conquered in 1769.[45] Land surveying was an important component in the assertion of imperial power.

Marc-Antoine came from Lower Navarre, a region that had some of the strongest rules of primogeniture in Europe, as well as a system of entails that applied to all agricultural properties, large and small. The legal environment in Saint-Domingue could not have been more different. Marc-Antoine and his wife, Elizabeth, like the other early settlers, were given large tracts of land in the

1740s. The tracts were so large that they were simply unable to cultivate the entirety of the land they owned. When their daughters married, there was plenty of land they could exploit in partnerships with their husbands, who became co-owners at the time of succession. As Derouet points out, the meaning and use of the dowry was very different in house-based systems than it was in communities governed by egalitarian customs like the Custom of Paris. In house-based systems, dowrying children meant excluding them from the inheritance by giving them a relatively small sum of money or a small property that was of peripheral importance to the patrimony. In contrast, in communities governed by the Custom of Paris the dowry was usually the first in a series of gifts meant to help the children and their spouses to establish themselves. Usually, at the time of succession most of the parents' assets had already been transferred as gifts to the next generation.[46] In addition, Saint-Domingue had few restrictions regarding the sale of real estate. (The Custom of Paris had one rule, the *retrait lignager*, which gave relatives the right to repurchase family properties, but this rule seems to have been seldom followed on the island.)[47]

Thus Marc-Antoine's heirs did not hesitate to sell the land they felt they could not exploit themselves. For instance, in 1778 Charles de Trémais, Marc-Antoine's son-in-law, co-owner with his wife, Marie-Elizabeth Lamerenx, of a large lot in Marmelade, sold 74 *carreaux* (236 acres) of land located in the Soufrière District of the parish.[48] Of the 74 *carreaux*, only 7 were planted in coffee, 5 were used for slave dwellings and subsistence farming, and the remaining 62 were uncultivated savanna. The price was 43,000 livres. The land was only a fraction of the original grant of 225 *carreaux* (700 acres) received by Marc-Antoine Lamerenx and Elizabeth Le Jeune in 1747. The buyer was Jean Mouscardy, himself an early settler, who, like Marc-Antoine, had come from Lower Navarre (more about him later). About one year later, Mouscardy sold part of his acquisition (10 *carreaux*) to a neighbor named François Fauquet.[49]

In 1776, Adam Smith reported that it was possible to start a plantation in North America with as little as 50–60 pounds, making "the purchase and improvement of uncultivated land" a very profitable use of capital. (It was much more profitable than the purchase of a small agricultural property in England, which would have cost between 2,000 and 3,000 pounds.)[50] What would that sum have purchased in Saint-Domingue? Sixty pounds would have been worth approximately 2,000 Saint-Domingue livres. In the 1778 transaction mentioned above, one *carreau* of uncultivated savanna was worth 500 livres, meaning that for 60 pounds one could have purchased 4 *carreaux* (12 acres) of uncultivated land. That would have been a rather small plantation, but it indicates that in the late 1770s the land in Marmelade was still affordable. Of course these valuations did not account for the value of slave labor. In an appraisal that took place ten years later, the uncultivated land belonging to Marc-Antoine's daughter Marie-

Elizabeth was estimated at 600 livres per *carreau* (not significantly different from the 1778 estimation).⁵¹ However, in the cultivated sections, which had been valorized thanks to slave labor, the prices were considerably higher. In the section of the property that had the most productive coffee trees, a mere three *carreaux* of land was worth 5,250 livres, and the coffee trees planted on the lot were worth 21,000 livres. This means that slave labor had multiplied the value of uncultivated land by a factor of 14. Smith's remarks about the use of land in the colonies were a continuation of Locke's speculation that "in the beginning all the world was America."⁵² Both Locke and Smith observed the market for agricultural land in the American colonies and hypothesized that it approximated what had been the emergence of property rights in the state of nature. Having noticed that the value of an acre of uncultivated land in America was close to zero, Locke concluded that "it is *labour* then which *puts the greatest part of value upon land*, without which it would scarcely be worth anything."⁵³

From La Bastide Clairence to Dondon: Jean Mouscardy and Other Bastidots

Marc-Antoine's emigration to Saint-Domingue does not seem to have attracted other migrants from Aïcirits, the village of his birth, except for his younger brother Louis, who emigrated in 1755. As we saw in chapter 1, Marc-Antoine took a trip home in 1741. On that occasion he attended the wedding of his elder brother Mathieu, who married Anne de Marmont, the heiress of a prominent family from La Bastide Clairence, a town approximately halfway between Aïcirits and the Atlantic port of Bayonne. Mathieu and his wife settled in La Bastide Clairence after their marriage. Marc-Antoine's presence must have been noticed at the wedding, and Mathieu must have subsequently relayed news of his brother's good fortune to his neighbors, because over the next thirty years a significant number of Bastidots (as citizens of La Bastide Clairence are called) migrated to the island.

The first emigrant to follow in Marc-Antoine's footsteps was Jean Mouscardy (c. 1720–1797). The exact date of his emigration is not known. The record of departures from the port of Bayonne has been kept only for the 1749–77 period. His name does not appear in this record, meaning that he probably emigrated before 1749. We know from a dossier regarding the sequestering of his colonial properties by the French government in the 1790s that he purchased a large piece of land in the Soufrière District of Dondon in 1750. (The district became a part of Marmelade Parish when it was established in 1773.)⁵⁴ The seller, the widow Paparel, was one of the original settlers of the area. Jean Mouscardy's exact date of birth also is not known, because the baptism records for La Bastide Clairence in the 1720s are incomplete. What is certain is that Jean Mouscardy was the younger son of a couple of landowning farmers, Augé Mouscardy and

Marie Labache. In accordance with the Custom of Navarre, the firstborn child, Jeanne Mouscardy (c. 1715–1795), inherited the family farm (referred to in notarial documents as the house of Mouscardy). She married a carpenter named Jean Bordenave, who became the "adventitious master" of the house of Mouscardy, while she was the mistress of the house. Jean Mouscardy had two younger siblings: a brother, also called Jean, who worked as a day laborer and married a woman named Jeanne Padouen, also a day laborer; and a sister, Marie, who worked as a governess in a household of merchants (*négociants*) in Bayonne before marrying Jean Thore, a master cooper, in 1750.[55] In chapter 1 we saw the options available and choices made by the children of Jean Lamerenx and Suzanne de Lespade: the firstborn inherited the Uhart-Juzon estate; the other choices included emigration to Saint-Domingue, the army, the clergy, marriage with an heiress, and celibacy on the parental estate. In the case of the Mouscardy family, the choices were not the same, because the family was lower on the socioeconomic ladder, but the pattern was still broadly similar. The firstborn child, in this case a woman, inherited the family farm. The others had to seek salaried employment or emigrate.

Jean Mouscardy took a trip home in 1769–70 to invest some of the money he had earned as a coffee grower. He left funds in custody with a notary in La Bastide Clairence. He acquired a townhouse on rue du Pont-Majour, in Bayonne's business district, for 11,000 livres in cash and made it available to his sister and brother-in-law, Marie Mouscardy and Jean Thore, who probably paid nominal rent.[56] The ground floor was leased to a trimming and button maker. In 1789 the house was still occupied by Jean Mouscardy's widowed brother-in-law, Jean Thore, and two children (Marie had died a few years earlier).[57] After an extended stay in the region of his birth, on December 7, 1770, Jean Mouscardy sailed back to Saint-Domingue from Bordeaux accompanied by a twelve-year-old slave named Jean.[58] Two years later, Jean-Roch Lambert, a notary in La Bastide Clairence, conducted a complex transaction on Mouscardy's behalf.[59] He purchased notes receivable from two different creditors. As a result, Mouscardy became the creditor of a man named Jean Greciet for a total of 3,094 livres. Mouscardy earned interest on the capital, but this was not a randomly chosen investment: Greciet was the owner of a farm next to the Mouscardy estate in La Bastide Clairence, owned at the time by Jean Mouscardy's elder sister, Jeanne. The loan to Greciet was guaranteed by a mortgage on his farm, meaning that the farm could become the property of the Mouscardy family if Greciet failed to make the promised payments. It should be noted that notaries in rural areas, in continental France as well in Saint-Domingue, played a key role in the development of credit markets whose sophistication has only recently been recognized. They arranged borrowing and lending agreements, calculated interest due, wrote up the details of mortgage contracts, and facilitated the purchase and sale of existing debts.[60]

In 1789 Jean Mouscardy was the owner of two contiguous coffee plantations in Marmelade and a house in Cap-Français. The total area of the plantations was 136 *carreaux* (approximately 400 acres). The total estimation of his properties in the *Indemnité de Saint-Domingue* was 552,000 livres, not quite as much as the estimation of properties belonging to Marc-Antoine's widow and children, which came to more than a million livres altogether, but still considerable wealth, especially considering that Jean Mouscardy's starting capital (economic and symbolic) had been quite modest.[61] We can get a sense of the amount of the legitimate Jean Mouscardy took with him to Saint-Domingue by looking at the dowry his younger sister received when she married Jean Thore in 1750.[62] If, as is likely, he received about the same amount as his sister's dowry, he was able to buy approximately 1,000 livres' worth of *pacotille*, which he sold upon arrival at two or three times the purchase price. This would not have been sufficient to buy land and slaves, even though uncultivated land in the mountains was cheap and slaves were not as expensive in the 1740s as they were in the 1780s.[63] Mouscardy may initially have worked as a plantation manager, an occupation that came with 10 percent of the net revenue of the plantation. According to Coeurjoly, this was the most desirable position for those who did not have the funds to establish a coffee plantation immediately. Jean Mouscardy may have managed the plantation that Marc-Antoine Lamerenx and Elizabeth Le Jeune established on the land they received in the Soufrière District in 1747. It is highly likely, in any case, that Marc-Antoine Lamerenx was Jean Mouscardy's patron and protector. He was also his immediate neighbor. The land that Mouscardy purchased in 1750 was adjacent to the Lamerenx–Le Jeune lot in the Soufrière District.

Jean Mouscardy invested a fraction of his earnings in his hometown of La Bastide Clairence and in Bayonne. The purpose of these investments was to support his siblings and possibly to provide himself a place to retire. The greater part of the money was reinvested in Saint-Domingue, where the return on investment was considerably higher than in Europe. In 1778, Jean Mouscardy purchased 74 *carreaux* (200 acres) of land from Marc-Antoine's daughter and son-in-law for a sum of 43,000 livres.[64] This approximately doubled the size of his agricultural landholdings. In 1784 he bought a house located at the corner of rue Neuve and rue de la Fontaine in Cap-Français for 108,000 livres (houses in desirable locations in the colony's largest city fetched very high prices).[65] The house was leased to a commercial tenant.

Jean Mouscardy's prosperity in Saint-Domingue proved to be a magnet for his family. Two of his nephews (sons of his elder sister Jeanne, the mistress of the house of Mouscardy) joined him in the Soufrière District. Jean Bordenave, a cooper by trade, sailed from Bayonne on *La Thérèse Bernard*, which was outfitted for departure on 22 April 1764.⁶⁶ Another nephew, also named Jean (but called Pierre in Saint-Domingue), emigrated twelve years later. He was a carpenter and made the voyage on the snow *La Reyne*, outfitted for departure from Bayonne on July 4, 1776. The older nephew embarked as an *engagé*, while the younger one sailed as a *passager*. Emigrants who did not have the funds necessary to establish themselves in the colony went as indentured servants (*engagés*), with their employers covering the cost of their passage in exchange for a three-year work obligation.⁶⁷ This was how the older nephew emigrated. The younger one, on the other hand, traveled as a *passager*, meaning that he paid about 300 livres for the passage and dined at the captain's table. The system of indentured labor was gradually abandoned, the last *engagé* sailing from Bayonne in 1771.⁶⁸

Both Mouscardy nephews worked as master carpenters in Marmelade. The older one became a building contractor.⁶⁹ Neither of them had sufficient funds to start a coffee plantation, but they earned a good living. As Coeurjoly indicated, skilled workers were in high demand in the colony and commanded high wages: "Carpenters, masons, coopers, smiths, wheelwrights, saddlers, coach builders, watchmakers, goldsmiths, jewelers, tailors, and wigmakers can find employment easily. Skilled labor is very expensive."⁷⁰

Lawyers were in high demand as well. Mathieu Lamerenx and Anne de Marmont, married in La Bastide Clairence since 1741, financed the emigration of Anne's younger brother, Jean-Pierre de Marmont, a law-school graduate. Jean-Pierre de Marmont did not stay in the colony very long. He returned home, married the daughter of a notary, and took over his father-in-law's practice in the town of Saint-Martin-d'Arberoue in Lower Navarre. In 1764, Jean-Pierre Lamerenx, the firstborn son of Mathieu Lamerenx and Anne de Marmont, emigrated as well. The trip was funded by the sale of a meadow that belonged to Anne de Marmont, after a long dispute between husband and wife about the use of family assets. (We will come back to the emigration of Jean-Pierre Lamerenx in chapter 3.)

As I mentioned above, the most desirable occupation for those who did not have the funds to purchase a plantation was to manage a plantation on behalf of the proprietor. This was the occupation of Jean-Pierre Colombots, a citizen of La Bastide Clairence, who in 1770, at the age of eighteen, set sail for Saint-Domingue from Bayonne as an *engagé*.⁷¹ Jean-Pierre Colombots was the illegitimate son of a local nobleman, also named Jean-Pierre, and a woman named Marie Renard. The father did recognize his son and provided for his training as a surgeon, but the son was not sufficiently well off to sail as a passenger. In the late 1770s Colombots was the manager of the Biret coffee plantation in Marmelade, which belonged to a merchant based in Cap-Français.⁷² Jean-Pierre Colombots accumulated significant wealth as a plantation manager, and he invested part of his earnings in slaves, which provided a convenient store of value. In 1779 he signed a leasing agreement with a master carpenter from Marmelade. Four Congo slaves, named Jupiter, Marseille, Larose, and Michel, were to be employed by the carpenter as apprentices for a two-year period. The slaves were estimated to be worth 2,000 livres each, and the annual cost of the lease was 250 livres per slave, payable in cash (a return on assets of 12.5%). All four slaves were stamped with the name Colombots in capital letters.[73]

As Coeurjoly indicated, plantation managers could earn additional money as agents (*fondés de pouvoir*) in transactions on behalf of other absentee owners: "If you like agriculture, you can become an apprentice in this sector; you will become a bookkeeper, then a manager; and the credit you earn in that occupation will help you become an agent in business transactions."[74] For instance, acting on behalf of a merchant from Cap-Français named Jean Larroque, Colombots purchased 100 *carreaux* (300 acres) of agricultural land in 1784 for 27,000 livres. The beneficiaries of the purchase were the six mulatto children of Françoise Alzire, a free woman of color from Marmelade.[75] One of the witnesses was a Bastidot: Pierre Bordenave, the younger of the Mouscardy nephews. For an immigrant from La Bastide Clairence in Dondon or Marmelade, America was a paradoxical combination of the unfamiliar and the familiar, a new world but also a world populated with familiar faces from across the ocean.

One apparently insignificant detail in the deed indicates that there was much more to this transaction than I have just described. Near the end of the document, there is mention of the fact that the transaction was taking place in the house of Jean Mouscardy in the Soufrière District of Marmelade. At first sight, this is simply further confirmation that colonists from La Bastide Clairence congregated in the same area of Saint-Domingue as neighbors, relatives, and business partners. Still, it is not clear why Jean-Pierre Colombots would decide to conduct a business transaction in the home of his compatriot Mouscardy, since Mouscardy was not a party to the transaction. The likely reason is that Mouscardy was in fact a party to the transaction, even though this is not stated anywhere in the deed. Colombots acted on behalf of Jean Larroque, a merchant in Cap-Français, who was the legal guardian of the six minor children of Françoise Alzire. Jean Mouscardy's properties were sequestered during the Revolution. We know from the sequestered-properties dossier that Larroque was Mouscardy's agent, business partner, and close friend.[76] Mouscardy took refuge in Larroque's home in Cap-Français when his plantation was taken over by insurgent slaves in 1791. Among the six mulatto children, one was named Jean-Théodat and another, Bonne. In the memoirs of Démesvar Delorme (1831–1901), a nineteenth-century Haitian statesman and political theorist, there is a passage regarding Delorme's maternal grandmother, Bonne Mouscardy, and her elder brother, Jean-Théodat Mouscardy, who served as a general in the Haitian army. According to

Delorme, the father of Jean-Théodat and Bonne was a white planter named Mouscardy.[77] We can safely infer from these clues that Jean Mouscardy was the father of the six mulatto children named in the 1784 deed.

There is no evidence that Jean Mouscardy ever married in Saint-Domingue. He may have had a child out of wedlock in La Bastide Clairence before migrating to the colony. In 1748 the parish priest in La Bastide Clairence baptized a boy named Pierre. The mother, Marie Portantin, declared that the father was "Jean, younger son of the house of Mouscardy, who promised that he would marry her."[78] One reason for Jean Mouscardy's decision to emigrate, in addition to the usual calculus of younger sons, may have been to get out of this unadvantageous marriage commitment. However, Jean Mouscardy had a younger brother who was also named Jean. It is not certain, therefore, that the delinquent father was our emigrant. It should also be added that out-of-wedlock births were relatively frequent in the region and did not carry quite the stigma that they did later on in the nineteenth century. One important difference was that the priests who wrote out the baptism certificates named the fathers on the basis of the mothers' declarations. After the advent of the Civil Code, the father could be named only if he had explicitly acknowledged his paternity.

What was the nature of the relationship between Jean Mouscardy and Françoise Alzire, the mother of his mulatto children? In the 1784 deed she was referred to as "Françoise dite Alzire négresse libre" (Françoise, a.k.a. Alzire, free negress). The name Alzire was made famous by a play that Voltaire brought to the stage in 1736, *Alzire ou les Américains* (Alzire, or the Americans). The play told the story of a captive Inca princess who loved an Inca prince and was loved by the Spanish governor of Peru.[79] As Christopher Miller points out, Alzire was a popular name for female slaves brought to the French-speaking Caribbean.[80] Françoise Alzire was probably a manumitted slave. The number of her children suggests that she had a long-term relationship with Jean Mouscardy and that she was his *ménagère* (household manager). This type of arrangement was common in Saint-Domingue. The historian John Garrigus describes the position of housekeeper as "the most powerful position an enslaved woman might hold on a plantation. Colonists regarded the *ménagère* as equivalent to a spouse, for she was often the mistress both of the household staff and the proprietor's bed."[81]

If we ask why Jean Mouscardy did not marry, the answer would be that his housekeeper, Françoise Alzire, was in fact his wife. The nature of the relationship was probably obvious to everyone, but the difference between it and a legally sanctioned marriage was that children could not inherit. Some legal stratagems had to be used to transfer property, leading to arrangements like the one discussed here, in which none of the principals (father, mother, or children) signed the agreement. Larroque's serving as the guardian of Mouscardy's mulatto children was a slightly unusual arrangement. The more common practice was for the white father to appoint himself as guardian. Mouscardy may have preferred this arrangement because he had those children late in life and was already in his mid-sixties. He was also apparently in ill health; his shaky handwriting suggests that he may have suffered from a neurological disorder.

At any rate, the size of the gift to his children (100 *carreaux*, or 300 acres of land) indicates that he wished to establish them as coffee growers. The deed mentions that the lot had one slave cabin in a state of disrepair and 3,000 coffee trees. The number of trees means that only 1–2 percent of the lot was cultivated (the average density of coffee trees on a plantation was 5,000 per *carreau*).[82] This explains in part the low price paid for such a large tract of land. Another reason was probably that the land was in the Nouvelle Flandre District of the canton of Ennery in Marmelade, which was the remotest and least developed. The original land grant for the lot had taken place in 1776, just eight years earlier. (Ennery became a separate commune after seceding from Marmelade during the Haitian Revolution.) It seems that Mouscardy was counting on his children's efforts to valorize land that was acquired at a bargain price, thus repeating what had been his own experience in the 1750s. I should add that it was not unusual for free people of color in Saint-Domingue to own plantations and slaves. According to Garrigus, who compiled statistics for the southern part of Saint-Domingue, in the 1780s free people of color were involved in 44 percent of rural-land transactions and 57 percent of slave sales.[83]

In the Mouscardy family tradition as reported by Démesvar Delorme, Françoise Alzire was a *mulâtresse*, a woman of mixed race.[84] The language of the 1784 deed categorized her as a *négresse*, or entirely of African descent. The relevant information carried by the term *mulâtresse* is that Françoise Alzire was free. *Mulâtresse* suggested "free-colored," even though being of mixed race did not necessarily coincide with freedom, and some free people of color were not of mixed race.

The cases of emigration we have seen so far cover most of the occupations of the colonists. According to Coeurjoly, the remaining option was commerce. One would start with the *pacotille* one had brought over from France and complement it with merchandise on consignment from ship captains. The merchant had six months to pay the captain for the full cost of the merchandise on consignment. If the merchant failed to pay, the captain could request that the merchant be imprisoned. (According to the code of commerce, only ship captains had this right.) A successful merchant could become a *négociant*; Jean Larroque, Jean Mouscardy's agent, was a *négociant* in Cap-Français. What distinguished one from the other was the extent of one's credit. A *négociant* was a merchant whose ability and willingness to make future payments could be trusted. The last step on the road to commercial success was becoming a correspondent for one of the large trading houses located in France's Atlantic ports. Coeurjoly concluded his description with a cautionary note: "If you try out commerce, be sure to collect the money that is owed to you, and do not extend credit to the first comer, because in this country everyone is more than willing to buy, but very few are eager to pay."[85]

Of all the Bastidots who set sail for Saint-Domingue in the eighteenth century, only one became a merchant. (Others did try commerce in Cuba and New Orleans after they lost their plantations, as we will see in chapters 4 and 5.) Jean Hiriart (1771–1808) was the son of a couple of landowning farmers, Pierre Hiriart and Jeanne d'Iron.[86] His mother was the mistress of the estate, called the house of Helçart. Jean had an elder brother, Pierre Hiriart (c. 1768–1833), who became master of the estate upon his parents' death. At that point the Civil Code was in force, but the line of succession was still consistent with the Custom of Navarre. In the 1790s Jean Hiriart was established in Fort-Dauphin (now Fort-Liberté), a coastal town near the border with the Spanish part of Hispaniola. He served as commander of a National Guard regiment in Fort-Dauphin. In 1808 he was doing business selling wine and condiments in the city of Santo Domingo, then ruled by a French general with a rump force salvaged from the defeat at the hands of Dessalines's Haitian troops in 1804. Hiriart died of a tropical disease shortly before the city surrendered to Spanish and British troops, putting an end to the last remnant of French rule in Hispaniola. His total assets upon his death were estimated to be worth approximately $4,000. These included his house ($1,600), two slaves ($400), a bill of exchange on a New York merchant named William Doyle ($400), and inventory worth $1,600. Jean Hiriart had paid his dues to the local Masonic Lodge since his arrival in Santo Domingo.[87]

At first sight Hiriart's trajectory does not fit the pattern of chain migrations, because unlike other emigrants from La Bastide Clairence, he did not settle in Dondon or Marmelade. However, his place of origin was an important part of his identity: in Saint-Domingue he was known as Jean Bastidot. It is also clear that he knew fellow Bastidots. Some of them were his neighbors in Santo Domingo in 1808.[88] And Hiriart testified to it himself. Having returned to La Bastide Clairence in 1794 to take care of some business, he was questioned by the local authorities about the whereabouts of a Saint-Domingue colonist from La Bastide Clairence, Jean-Pierre Lamerenx, who was suspected to be counterrevolutionary émigré. He testified that he had indeed known Lamerenx and his family in Saint-Domingue and that according to some reports Lamerenx had fled to the Spanish side of Hispaniola.[89]

Masters and Slaves on a Coffee Plantation

Ten years after Marc-Antoine's visit to Versailles, his son-in-law Charles de Trémais visited the seat of power to advance several matters that were pending. The issue that preoccupied Trémais the most was the long-running dispute he had with one of his neighbors in Marmelade, a retired military officer named Pierre Cappé (who, incidentally, hailed from the western Pyrenees—not Lower Navarre, but Bigorre, a province further east).[90] Trémais addressed his complaint directly to the secretary of the navy because he believed that only an intervention from the highest levels of government would be able to restrain Cappé. The details of the dispute are interesting because slaves were involved on both sides, and we get a sense from Trémais's narrative of the ordinary violence in master-slave relations, in addition to the atrocities committed by Cappé on his own slaves.

Trémais was a former high-ranking official himself, and he had been a planter for only about ten years when he filed the complaint. His perspective on master-slave relations was that of both an insider and an outsider. His superiors in the colonial administration saw him as a man of scrupulous honesty and an exceptionally able financial administrator who had uncovered important cases of corruption and mismanagement. They also described him as an official with an excessive zeal to do the right thing.[91] While serving as deputy to the intendant of the colony, he had commissioned an investigation of the prison facilities in Cap-Français. The commission found that a man had been imprisoned without due process and that all prisoners were kept in squalid conditions. The governor warned Trémais that he had overstepped his authority in ordering this investigation and that he should drop the matter immediately. Trémais complied. When he left the service to establish himself as a planter in Marmelade, he impressed his new neighbors as an enlightened figure who was an early adopter of technological innovations and followed the best practices in growing coffee. He installed a lightning rod on his plantation,[92] and he processed his coffee by washing it in basins, a technique deemed to be the most efficient.

To give a sense of Cappé's character, Trémais started with an anecdote. One day Cappé hired a cooper from the neighboring Trémais plantation to make wood shingles. Slaves had Sundays off and were allowed to work for pay on their free days. After producing a certain quantity of shingles, the slave went to Cappé to request a payment. Cappé told him to come back later. When the slave came back, Cappé, seeing him at a distance, yelled: "What do you want, nigger?" The slave responded: "The money you promised." Cappé, offended that the slave would insist on getting his due, threw a club at his legs and missed him. The slave ran away. Cappé threw stones and missed again. He reached for his gun and would have shot the slave if his wife had not stopped him. Cappé had the slave arrested by the local militia. As Trémais indicated, "The policy in force in the colony is such that when a White man complains about a Negro, he always gets satisfaction."[93] As a result, the slave's punishment was being prepared. However, some unnamed persons who knew about his innocence intervened and obtained his release.

Something much more serious happened a few years later. Cappé complained to Trémais that his slaves were dying at an alarming rate, and he suspected that poison was involved. Cappé arrested the commander of his plantation and questioned him under torture. Commanders played a key role in the plantation system. They were the ones who exerted the day-to-day control of the slaves. They had in-depth knowledge of all technical operations involved in coffee processing but did not take part in the work themselves. They distributed tasks and enforced discipline through corporal punishment. Laborie insisted that "Drivers or Commanders are the soul of a plantation." As such, "they ought to possess fidelity, affection, intelligence, sobriety, discretion, justice, and severity."[94] Coeurjoly had a more cynical view of the qualities required in a commander. His advice to prospective planters was not to rely on the commander's supposed fidelity: "He is often worse than all the other slaves, and it is in your interest to pick him accordingly: because he is meaner he will inspire more fear." Coeurjoly added that the commander "will feign a perfect devotion to you, which will be utterly misleading."[95]

Cappé's assumptions about his commander do seem to have been consistent with Coeurjoly's. Cappé's commander confessed to the poisoning and said that the poison had been provided by the commander of the Trémais plantation. Trémais put his own commander under arrest and went to the Cappé plantation with three witnesses to hear the testimony of Cappé's commander, who had been so brutally tortured that he was on the verge of death. Trémais exhorted Cappé's commander to tell the truth because he was about to die. With great tranquility, interrupted only by surges of physical pain, and ignoring the loud threats uttered by his master, Cappé's commander retracted all his confessions, which he said had been made under duress, and declared: "As I am to appear before God, I don't want to lie." Trémais's commander was thus exonerated, but his master kept him under arrest until Cappé formally notified Trémais that he no longer had quarrel with him, which happened the following day.

Cappé's persecution of Trémais's commander continued nonetheless. Sometime later, the *négresse hospitalière* (slave woman in charge of the infirmary) on the Cappé plantation confessed to having used poison provided by Trémais's commander. Cappé even produced a phial he said contained the poison. The contents were tested on a dog, who survived. Trémais's commander was exonerated again, but the accused woman was given a lifetime sentence to hard labor by the tribunal in Cap-Français.

Cappé eventually got his way. On Christmas Eve, Trémais's commander went to a neighboring plantation to join a dance party attended by a hundred slaves in a coffee warehouse. He danced the *calenda* (the most popular dance among slaves in Saint-Domingue) to the rhythm of calabashes, traditional instruments from Western Africa. At nine in the evening, a patrol from the local militia entered the warehouse under the pretext of curbing excessive noise. They went up to the commander, arrested him, and summarily executed him. Because the head of the militia was a close friend of Cappé's, Trémais strongly suspected Cappé of having ordered the killing.

At the beginning of his memorandum to the secretary of the navy, Trémais mentioned that Cappé was very close to a planter named Cockburn, "whose bloody principles he has adopted regarding the management of Negroes." Trémais characterized Cappé and Cockburn in the following way: "I have them both as neighbors. They are a disaster for the district."[96] Indeed, Cockburn seems to have had a reputation as an especially cruel and violent master. In 1814 the Haitian author Baron de Vastey described Cockburn as a well-known perpetrator of atrocities against slaves, which he spelled out in graphic detail.[97] Trémais mentioned his moral revulsion against Cappé's methods, including the use of torture, which, according to the Code Noir, could only be practiced by the king's representatives. He also said that it was an "abominable policy" for the judicial system to side systematically with the masters regarding disputes between masters and slaves.[98] The legal historian Malick Ghachem has shown that colonial officials were indeed worried that unchecked violence by masters against slaves posed a threat to the long-term viability of the colonial system.[99] According to Trémais's account, his repeated appeals to the colonial authorities had sometimes moderated Cappé's behavior. Cappé was warned by successive governors and kept quiet for some periods of time.

This aspect of French colonial administration was remarked upon by the author of *The Wealth of Nations*. According to Smith, because the French colonies had an essentially military form of government, the royal authority did intervene to some extent in the relations between masters and slaves, and this afforded the slaves a modicum of protection:

> The law, so far as it gives some weak protection to the slave against the violence of his master, is likely to be better executed in a colony where the government is in a great measure arbitrary, than in one where it is altogether free. In every country where the unfortunate law of slavery is established, the magistrate, when he protects the slave, intermeddles in some measure in the management of the private property of the master; and, in a free country, where the master is perhaps either a member of the colony assembly, or an elector of such a member, he dare not do this but with the greatest caution and circumspection.[100]

In that sense, according to Smith, slaves were slightly better off in Saint-Domingue than in the British Caribbean islands, and this was, paradoxically, a consequence of the fact that the French colony was less free politically. Jean-Baptiste Say made an identical assessment: "But there are some extremely rare cases, where interference between the owner and his property is even beneficial to production itself. For example, in all countries that admit the detestable right of slavery, a right standing in hostility to all others, it is found expedient to limit the master's power over his slave."[101]

According to Trémais, however, whatever power the colonial government had to control the behavior of planters was limited by the fact that there was a quick turnover of colonial administrators, and his direct appeal to the secretary of the navy was itself an indication of unsuccessful efforts in that respect. It also seems clear from the exchange of letters between Trémais and Cappé that the latter had stronger local support. "You have no friends in this neighborhood," Cappé wrote to Trémais.[102] As to Smith's assessment of slave management in Saint-Domingue, Laborie, a former planter, appreciated the compliment, but he did not think the French planters were more humane. He agreed that the power of the master was under the control of the governor and the courts; however, he concluded that "though presentments have been brought and prosecuted against masters, in very heinous instances, even so late as in 1787, that check was very seldom put in practice, lest submission should be impaired."[103] Masters worried that their control over slaves would collapse if the judicial system vindicated a slave in a dispute with a master.

A degree of humanity seems to have been present in the Trémais household regarding the management of slaves. Shortly after Trémais's death, four slaves ran away from the plantation: Philippe, a creole slave; Eustache, of the Meserable nation; Crispin, of the Congo nation; and Marguerite, of the Ibo nation. Trémais's widow, Marie-Elizabeth Lamerenx, published a notice in the *Affiches américaines* with the promise of a reward on the express condition that the slaves not be harmed (an unusual clause in such announcements).[104] Yet the absence of cruelty did not alter the intrinsic violence of slavery itself. After Cappé complained to Trémais that slaves and cattle had trespassed on his property, in order to placate his neighbor Trémais told him that he could shoot any slave or any mule, and he promised not to complain about it. Good relations with a troublesome neighbor trumped respect for human (and animal) life. There are also indications that Trémais's widow had grown up on a plantation where slaves were treated in a predictably harsh way. In 1770, when her father, Marc-Antoine was in Versailles trying to get her brother into the King's Guards, a thirty-year-old slave woman named Rosette had escaped. Marie-Elizabeth's mother, Elizabeth Le Jeune, had published a notice in the *Affiches américaines* promising a reward of three hundred livres for the return of the slave, specifying that she was wearing a three-pronged collar shackle and "[had] not yet recovered from the whipping she received not long ago."[105]

The slaves of the Cappé and Trémais plantations were involved in another incident that Moreau de Saint-Méry mentioned in his description of Marmelade.[106] In 1786 four slaves were arrested for organizing large nocturnal assemblies in which slaves from several plantations congregated and possession rituals were performed. One of the accused was a slave named Julien from the Lalanne plantation. A slave named Goma, who belonged to Pierre Cappé, accused Julien of organizing nocturnal meetings on the Trémais plantation. Since the accusation was based on a single testimony, Julien was not convicted. The other three accused slaves were sentenced to death (two fugitives in absentia). Julien was ordered to witness the hanging of the third convict before he was released to his owner.[107]

War, Commerce, and Slavery

The high profitability of sugar and coffee growing in the British and French Caribbean colonies was frequently remarked upon by contemporary observers. In a discussion of sugar planters in an early draft of *The Wealth of Nations*, Adam Smith mentioned the "exorbitancy of their profites."[108] Similarly, Jean-Baptiste Say reported as "a well-known fact" that investors who purchased a plantation in Saint-Domingue would recoup their investment in just six years (a return on assets of about 16%), while in Europe an investment in agricultural land would be recouped in twenty-five to thirty years (a return on assets of 3–4%).[109] In 1791 Trémais's widow wrote to her cousin Prudent-Jean Bruley, an absentee owner who lived in Tours, with an attractive business proposition: she offered him the opportunity to take a 50 percent share in the purchase of a plantation that was worth 1.5 million livres, claiming that the investment would be recouped in less than eight or nine years (a return on assets of more than 12%). Bruley thought highly of his cousin, whom he described as "a Creole woman who was as savvy as she was bright."[110] However, he dithered, and he later congratulated himself on his indecision, as the plantation was burned down when the slaves revolted just a few weeks later.

In Coeurjoly's *Manual*, the European asked: "The planters of this country must be very rich?" The American gave a qualified response. Planters were rich, but they spent too much of their revenue: "Many planters in Saint-Domingue are very rich in appearance; but they are heavily indebted to the merchants, because they do not know how to moderate their spending. Some planters own several plantations and have up to seven or eight hundred Negroes belonging to them."[111] Merchants played a key role in the colonial system.[112] They purchased the sugar and coffee crops from the planters, and they supplied the planters with slaves as well as food and manufactured goods from the mother country. There was competition among merchants, but Saint-Domingue planters were allowed to do business only with merchants established in French ports, and those merchants were allowed to trade only with the French colonies. This kept sugar and coffee prices high, because Saint-Domingue planters did not have to compete with British planters when selling their production. This also raised the price of slaves, food, and manufactured goods brought by the merchants to the colony, leading to endless recriminations between planters and merchants.

We can see an example in a letter by Trémais's widow, Marie-Elizabeth, who continued to correspond with Guillaume de Bellecombe, the governor of Saint-Domingue, after he returned to France. Along with her wishes for the New Year, she informed Bellecombe of the death by tropical illnesses of several of their mutual friends, and she quoted the price of slaves and the price of coffee. "Our coffee sells for 21 sols [per pound]," she wrote, adding that "there is reason to believe this price will hold thanks to bad crops everywhere," and especially in Marmelade and Dondon, where production had dropped by almost two-thirds from normal levels. Under the circumstances, Marie-Elizabeth added, "it is inconceivable that the price of Negroes should increase to the point that they sell on board for up to 2,500 livres."[113]

According to Laborie, "The jealousies and mutual complaints of the planters and of the traders had no end." The planters "lamented the price of importations, and chiefly of negroes, continually increasing." As to the merchants, they "exclaimed against the debts due by the colony, which they pretended to be little short of one hundred millions."[114] The feud between planters and merchants was over their respective shares of the profits generated by monopolistic trading. This explains why Marie-Elizabeth Lamerenx had her eye on just two prices: the price she had to pay for new slaves (and other imports) and the price she was getting for her coffee. These two parameters determined how much of the profits stayed with her and how much went to the merchants. As Adam Smith put it, "It is chiefly in order to purchase European goods, that the colonies part with their own produce. The more, therefore, they pay for the one, the less they really get for the other, and the dearness of the one is the same thing with the cheapness of the other."[115] As to the mutual recriminations between planters and traders, according to Laborie, both groups had benefited from the system. On the one hand, he opined, "it was only by the advances of trade that the colony had been settled and carried to that state of prosperity which it enjoyed in 1789." On the other hand, unpaid debts "had not prevented individuals from accumulating immense fortunes in almost every port of France, entirely resulting from traffic with the colony."[116]

While there was consensus about the high profitability of sugar and coffee growing, the role of slave labor in the generation of profits was a matter of controversy. Smith argued that slave labor was expensive and uneconomic and that its massive use in the Caribbean was a consequence, rather than a cause, of the exorbitant profits made in the sugar islands. He observed that sugar was the most profitable crop in the Americas, while corn was the least profitable. Tobacco was somewhere in between. Sugar planters used many slaves, corn planters used no slaves, and tobacco planters were somewhere in between. Smith reasoned that sugar planters used slaves on a large scale because they could afford it; tobacco planters used some slaves because they could afford it to some extent; and corn planters used no slaves because they could not afford the expense:

> The pride of man makes him love to domineer, and nothing mortifies him so much as to be obliged to condescend to persuade his inferiors. Wherever the law allows it, and the nature of the work can afford it, therefore, he will generally prefer the service of slaves to that of freemen. The planting of sugar and tobacco can afford the expence of slave-cultivation. . . . The profits of a sugar-plantation in any of our West Indian colonies are generally much greater than those of any other cultivation that is known either in Europe or America: And the profits of a tobacco plantation, though inferior to those of sugar, are superior to those of corn, as has already been observed. Both can afford the expence of slave-cultivation, but sugar can afford it still better than tobacco. The number of negroes accordingly is much greater, in proportion to that of whites, in our sugar than in our tobacco colonies.[117]

Smith gave a political and psychological explanation rather than an economic one for the use of slave labor in the Caribbean colonies. According to his account, planters used slaves to satisfy their tyrannical impulses, but the use of slaves was more expensive than the use of free labor, and planters could afford the high cost of slave labor because their profits were kept artificially high by monopolistic trading conditions.

Jean-Baptiste Say, by contrast, argued that slave labor was a key factor in the high profitability of the plantation system. He calculated that the total cost of a slave was less than half the cost of an unskilled free laborer. He reasoned that among free laborers the desire to work more to earn more was offset by the desire for instant gratification, which limited productivity. On the other hand, he argued, "the slave works to satisfy a boundless need: his master's greed."[118] In that sense, the free laborers' desire for instant gratification hampered their productivity, but the same desire among masters increased the productivity of slaves because it made them work as hard as possible. Say concluded his demonstration by observing that colonists were unanimously opposed to the abolition of slavery because they knew, "against the opinion of Steuart, Turgot, and Smith,"[119] that free labor was more expensive. These famous economists had been misled by their desire to find reasons of self-interest for condemning slavery. "Would colonists," Say asked, "be so adamantly attached to this order of things if experience and instinct did not tell them that their profits would decrease and their expenses would increase as a result of a change?"[120] Coeurjoly's assessment was consistent with this remark. Speaking on behalf of the planters and their agents, he noted that the value of a plantation was entirely determined by the number of its slaves: "We assess our revenues exclusively on the basis of the number of Negroes of either sex who are employed in our manufactures."[121]

When a commission was appointed by the French government to distribute the proceeds of the indemnity pledged by Haiti in exchange for the recognition of the island's independence, there were extensive discussions about how to calculate the value of agricultural properties once owned by colonists. The question asked by the commission was what the properties as a whole would be worth if the colonists were to repossess them. The gross value of Haiti's agricultural exports in 1823 was approximately 30 million francs. After production costs were deducted, the net value was about 15 million francs. Furthermore, it was assumed that it took ten years on average to recoup an agricultural investment made in Saint-Domingue. This meant a return on assets of 10 percent, a more conservative figure than the 16 percent mentioned by Jean-Baptiste Say in 1803.[122] This would put the current fair-market value of agricultural properties in Haiti at 150 million francs. Accordingly, the Haitian government agreed to pay an indemnity in the amount of 150 million francs. Another way of looking at the issue was to start with the value of Saint-Domingue's exports prior to the Revolution: about 150 million francs in 1789. Using the same return on assets as in the previous calculation, the total value of agricultural properties in Saint-Domingue would have been 1.5 billion francs in 1789. In that sense, the indemnity covered the 1789 value of agricultural properties with a 90 percent discount.

In order to calculate the value of individual properties, the commission gave the former owners two options. They could document the annual production of their plantations, or they could provide evidence for the number of slaves they owned. The latter method seemed easier from the owners' point of view,[123] but it posed some methodological as well as legal problems. The indemnity was supposed to offset the loss of real estate, not the loss of movable property. Yet according to the Code Noir, slaves were movable property. The members of the commission solved the problem by referring to the consistent practice of notaries, who counted plantation slaves as real property in evaluations of estates.[124] The other issue was the inequity involved in ignoring differences in the fertility and location of the land. The commission settled the issue by establishing two classes for coffee plantations. The first class was defined by easier access to the sea and by an abundance of undeveloped land, which provided growth potential. In the first class, a coffee plantation was estimated to be worth 355 francs per slave. In the second class, a coffee plantation was worth 295 francs per slave.[125] This way of proceeding was of course deeply offensive to the Haitians. In early negotiations between the two governments, President Alexandre Pétion of Haiti had declared that his country would not pay anything for slaves, "because their freedom has been recognized."¹²⁶ Yet in the indemnity agreement there was a tacit recognition by the Haitian side that the value of slaves would indeed be the basis for calculations.

Using these numbers in connection with the amount of the indemnity received by Marc-Antoine's descendants, we can get a sense of how many slaves worked on the coffee plantations of Marc-Antoine's widow and daughters on the eve of the Haitian Revolution. The total indemnity was 126,608.40 francs. The total number of slaves would have ranged from 350 to 430, depending on how the land was rated. This is somewhat below the testimony provided by the mother and daughters themselves when they took refuge on the Spanish side of Hispaniola after the slave insurrection. In a letter to the Spanish governor, Marc-Antoine's widow, Elizabeth Le Jeune, stated that she had 140 slaves. Her daughter Marie-Elizabeth claimed to have 400. Her other daughter, Marguerite-Françoise, said that she had one of the handsomest plantations in the area, but she did not specify how many slaves she had.¹²⁷ It is likely that the women's own testimonies were closer to the mark, as the commission worked with official census counts from the prerevolutionary period, in which planters underreported the number of their slaves in order to minimize the capitation tax.¹²⁸ As to Jean Mouscardy, based on the *Indemnité de Saint-Domingue* numbers, he would have had between 135 and 160 slaves.

In the final analysis, the high profitability of coffee growing in the Caribbean was a consequence of French and British mercantilist policies. In standard accounts of Atlantic history the impact of these policies is generally minimized, on the grounds that smuggling was pervasive, as it was practically impossible for imperial powers to enforce monopolistic regulations. In Bernard Bailyn's words, "Mercantilist theories, national rivalries, and nationalist historiography obscure the degree to which a stable pan-Euro-Afro-American economy developed."¹²⁹ Yet mercantilism was more than a flawed economic policy or theory. István Hont has shown that it was the modern form of statecraft practiced by all major European powers.¹³⁰ According to classic reason-of-state theory, the goal of the prince was to maximize the power of his nation against the power of rival nations. This was done through diplomatic and military means. Commerce and wealth creation were absent from these traditional accounts, as it was assumed that wealth had a corrupting influence on a nation's martial spirit. The new and revised doctrine, which took hold in the mid-seventeenth century, provided a central role for commerce. A nation's power was defined by the size of its commerce, because the wealth provided by commerce was needed to support large military budgets. This led to what Hume called the jealousy of trade: the idea that one nation's commercial prosperity was necessarily a threat to the commercial prosperity and military power of its rivals.

As the historian Paul Cheney noted, colonial expansion is curiously absent from Hont's account of mercantilism (except for the British colonial rule over Ireland), but it was clearly an essential part of the system.[131] The profits generated by long-distance commerce were meant to support large armies and navies. In turn, large military forces were needed to enforce exclusive trading zones against smugglers, pirates, and merchants from competing nations. As the historian Richard Pares put it, "International trade was thought of as warfare."[132] Beyond their own protected national markets, Britain and France were competitors for the supply of colonial goods to European markets. The cheapest and most effective way of increasing market share was to forcibly prevent one's competitor's goods from reaching European ports.[133] Commerce and war were in a tangled relationship. On the one hand, peacetime was favorable to commerce because ships could freely roam the seas. In wartime, commerce was difficult: ships crossed the Atlantic in convoys under military escort, and for significant periods of time commerce was halted altogether.[134] For instance, during the year 1755–56, out of 314 ships that sailed out of Bordeaux to the Antilles, nearly 300 were captured, most of them on their way back.[135] During the long eighteenth century, Saint-Domingue was in a state of open war with Britain and/or Spain about half of the time.

As we saw in chapter 1, during the Seven Years' War, Marc-Antoine Lamerenx had great difficulty selling his coffee: prices fell dramatically because the British blockade made it very difficult to export anything to France. And for the same reason, imports of wine and flour became outrageously expensive. In a microhistorical study of a sugar plantation near Port-au-Prince during the American War of Independence, Paul Cheney has shown that the plantation was on the verge of bankruptcy because sugar prices collapsed and the plantation could not service its debt.[136] Financial conditions for Marc-Antoine Lamerenx or Jean Mouscardy never became so dire, because as first movers they had little or no debt, and coffee required a smaller capital investment than coffee anyway. It was clear in every case that profits were highly vulnerable to war. As Cheney puts it, Saint-Domingue "was deeply integrated into the world economy but in such a manner as left it periodically—and catastrophically—cut off from the metropolitan center."[137] While long-distance commerce was vulnerable to war, the high profits it generated were predicated on the military enforcement of exclusive trading zones, and the profitability of smuggling was itself predicated on such enforcement (as is the case for the trade in illegal drugs today). In addition, the high prices caused by scarcity were an incentive to trade, which resumed energetically when sea lanes opened up again. In that sense, war was both a cause of and a hindrance to commercial profits.

This tangled relationship between war, commerce, and slavery is manifested in the fact that Marc-Antoine's sons-in-law, who became co-owners of the plantations he bequeathed to his daughters, were both veterans of the Seven Years'

War. Charles de Trémais was stationed in Louisbourg, on Cape Breton Island, as a financial controller during the second siege of the fortress by the British, which resulted in surrender by the French on July 26, 1758. The secretary of the navy subsequently sent him to investigate the administration of the intendant of New France in Quebec City. His multiyear investigation, conducted entirely in wartime, uncovered widespread abuse and corruption, and Trémais received a royal pension for his services. He was sent to Saint-Domingue in 1763 on a similar mission.[138] Marc-Antoine's other son-in-law, Charles de Saint-Germain, served in the Agenois regiment throughout the Seven Years' War. The regiment fought in Germany from 1758 to 1762 and was later sent to Saint-Domingue. Saint-Germain sailed from Brest on November 20, 1775, and arrived in Cap-Français in early 1776.[139] He married Marguerite-Françoise Lamerenx less than two years later, on November 12, 1777. A quick look at the biographies of these two sons-in-law illustrates the global nature of eighteenth-century imperial rivalries, as well of personnel management. Trémais went from the northern confines of the French Empire to its large tropical island. Saint-Germain served for many years in the middle of Europe before his regiment was posted to Saint-Domingue.

It was evident to contemporary observers that a large fortune could be amassed quickly in Saint-Domingue. As Jean-Baptiste Say argued, because returns on assets were many times higher in Saint-Domingue than in Europe, emigrants were willing to overlook the island's harsh climate and high mortality. There was also a clear sense that the high profitability of sugar and coffee growing had a dual cause: the use of slave labor and the monopolistic trade between the colony and the mother country. For Jean-Baptiste Say, who provided the most sober assessment of the entire system, this spectacular generation of wealth produced two classes of losers. First, the slaves: "the economies resulting from the slave's work go into the planter's pocket thanks to the quasi-exclusive privilege he has in selling to the mother country." Second, the European consumers, "who would get the goods at a lower price, even if they came from further away, if trade were free."[140] The fact that the system produced a few winners, whose fortunes were dazzling, gave an illusion of prosperity, which led to continuing efforts to protect exclusive trading zones. "And it is for the protection of this imaginary advantage," Say concluded, "that almost all the wars of the eighteenth century have been undertaken, and that the European states have thought themselves obliged to keep up, at a vast expense, civil and judicial, as well as marine and military, establishments, at the opposite extremities of the globe."[141]

CHAPTER THREE

House-Based Societies and Emigration

Je veux bien que bon nombre de cadets émigrants trouvent à se caser dans les familles du pays en épousant des héritières, mais il n'y a qu'une héritière par demeure, et les demeures sont limitées et les cadets sont légion.

Granted, some younger sons may avoid emigration by marrying heiresses and settling locally, but there is only one heiress for each house, and the number of such houses is limited, while the younger sons are many.

Pierre Lhande, *L'émigration basque*, 1910

In chapter 1, I discussed the emigration of Marc-Antoine Lamerenx as one option among the options available to younger sons in the western Pyrenees. In this chapter, I will discuss a case that seems anomalous: the emigration of a firstborn son. Marc-Antoine's success as a coffee grower in Saint-Domingue attracted several relatives and neighbors to the island. All of them were younger sons, with one notable exception. In 1764, Jean-Pierre Lamerenx, the firstborn son of Marc-Antoine's elder brother and the presumptive heir to the Uhart-Juzon house, emigrated to Saint-Domingue and settled next to his uncle Marc-Antoine in Dondon. Why did a firstborn son choose to emigrate? What were the consequences of this choice? This chapter is an attempt to answer these questions.

Marc-Antoine's elder brother, Mathieu Lamerenx, settled in La Bastide Clairence in 1741 after marrying Anne de Marmont, who came from a prominent family of the town. Their eldest child, Jean-Pierre, was born in La Bastide Clairence in 1742. He was baptized by a priest named Jean de Marmont, his maternal great-uncle. His godfather was Jean-Pierre de Lombart, the parish priest of La Bastide Clairence and a cousin on the maternal side. His godmother was Suzanne de Lespade, his paternal grandmother. Nowadays La Bastide Clairence is a village in the Pyrénées-Atlantiques department. The present-day economy of the area is based primarily on agriculture and tourism. The village includes a number of sixteenth- and seventeenth-century half-timbered houses and belongs to an association named France's Most Beautiful Villages. At the time of the *ancien régime*, however, La Bastide Clairence was not merely a village but one of the five chartered *villes*, or towns, of Lower Navarre. In the mid-eighteenth century the population of La Bastide Clairence was approximately two thousand (about twice its current size). The town enjoyed privileges dating from its founding in 1312 by Louis I, who ruled Navarre before being crowned king of France as Louis X le Hutin. Navarre, a small trans-Pyrenean kingdom that was independent until its southern portion was annexed by Spain in 1512, possessed no coastal territory and thus lacked direct maritime access. La Bastide Clairence is about fifteen miles from the ocean and is connected to the port city of Bayonne by a small tributary of the Adour River. From the point of view of Pamplona, the capital of Navarre, the town's location offered distinct military and commercial advantages: it enabled the kingdom's northern reaches to be defended and provided a link to the ocean. Until 1512, when the capital was transferred to Pau following Spanish annexation, La Bastide Clairence was dependent on the capital of Navarre in Pamplona. When Henri III of Navarre was crowned King Henry IV of France in 1589, La Bastide Clairence became a de facto part of France, a relationship formalized in 1620, when Louis XIII decreed the reunion of Navarre to the French crown. Until 1789, however, Navarrese legal authorities held that the reunion was null and void because it had not been endorsed by the Estates General of Navarre. It was only in December 1789 that the citizens of La Bastide Clairence, caught up in the enthusiasm of the Revolution, formally approved the town's incorporation into the Kingdom of France.[1]

Divorce, Navarre Style

In March 1763, an unusual ruling by the Parliament of Navarre, located in Pau, was conveyed to the *jurats* (town officials) of La Bastide Clairence. Two months earlier, Sieur Mathieu Lamerenx and his wife, Dame Anne de Marmont, had appealed to the Parliament to arbitrate in a disagreement involving their household property and assets. Because the couple—who had been married under a rule of separation of property—were deeply in debt, they found themselves compelled to sell some land. Anne de Marmont wanted to sell her husband's lands, and he wanted to sell land belonging to her. The Parliament authorized the principle of the sale, but it declined to rule on the details, ordering that a tribunal of *proches* (family members and neighbors of the spouses) should decide which properties and how many of them would be sold.[2]

Each party had the right to nominate two members of the arbitration panel. Anne de Marmont nominated her cousin Jean-Pierre de Colombots, a nobleman from La Bastide Clairence, and Jacques Ducamp, the town secretary.[3] Mathieu Lamerenx picked his brother Jacques, the parish priest of Aïcirits. Jacques declined the appointment, citing his heavy responsibilities in the parish, and was replaced by another Lamerenx brother, Henri. The other judge nominated by Mathieu Lamerenx was a surgeon from Saint-Palais named d'Abbadie.

The choice of judges highlights an important characteristic of the Marmont-

Lamerenx marriage. The judges picked by Anne de Marmont were prominent people from La Bastide Clairence. Those picked by Mathieu Lamerenx were outsiders to the town. Anne de Marmont's family had resided in La Bastide Clairence for several generations. Her grandfather, Jean de Marmont (1652–1718), was a younger son of a noble family from Orthez in Béarn who had married an heiress from La Bastide Clairence, Marie de Lombart, mistress of the Berrio house (d. 1721). He also purchased the position of "perpetual mayor" of the town in 1693, benefiting from the royal edict of August 1692 regarding the purchase of municipal offices. Furthermore, in keeping with the absolute cognatic primogeniture dictated by Navarrese custom, Anne de Marmont had become the sole proprietor of the family seat, Berrio, and its attendant lands after her father's death in 1739. Her two younger brothers and her younger sister were left only with the legitime, a modest inheritance assigned to the remaining heirs.

Anne de Marmont's husband, Mathieu Lamerenx, Marc-Antoine's elder brother, had been named universal heir by his father in 1749 and by his mother in 1755. On his father's death in 1750, he had assumed ownership of the *salle* (noble house) of Uhart-Juzon in Aïcirits, which was approximately twenty miles from La Bastide Clairence. After Mathieu Lamerenx and Anne de Marmont married in 1741, the couple settled in the Berrio house in La Bastide Clairence. Notarial documents designated them as *sieur et dame de Berrio* but for Mathieu *sieur de Berrio* was only a courtesy title. Legally, Anne de Marmont was the sole proprietor of the Berrio house: she had inherited it two years before her marriage, when she was only fifteen. At the time, her uncle Jean de Marmont had been named administrator of the estate. When he died in 1751, Mathieu Lamerenx became the administrator—but not the owner—of his wife's estate.

During the twenty years that the couple resided in La Bastide Clairence, Anne bore seven children, and Mathieu Lamerenx participated in the town government after being elected *jurat* in 1752.[4] Around 1760, the family left La Bastide and took up residence on the Lamerenx estate in Aïcirits. A severe disagreement erupted between the two spouses around this time, prompting Anne to leave Aïcirits and return to Berrio. By the time the tribunal assigned to arbitrate the dispute was formed in 1763, the spouses were barely on speaking terms—a boon for historians, since the dispute was recorded in a series of separate depositions. The transcripts preserved in the municipal archives of La Bastide Clairence make it possible to see beyond the legal language used by the clerk of court and hear the spouses' "voices," particularly when one converts the reported speech contained in the records into direct discourse (which is not always even necessary, because the clerk occasionally made mistakes and directly reported what was said).

In the first deposition, Mathieu described the "sad situation" of his and Dame de Marmont's properties and the urgency of selling land to settle their debts. He also asserted that while his wife's estate in La Bastide was "commoner" property, the Lamerenx estate in Aïcirits was "noble property."[5] Lamerenx cited this distinction to justify selling his wife's lands, with the understanding that he would then owe the amount of the proceeds of the sale to his wife. His concern with preserving noble property stemmed from a legal peculiarity of Lower Navarre and Béarn in which nobility was considered "real," meaning that merely owning an asset considered to be noble provided access to a noble seat in the Estates General of Navarre. In fact, as we saw in chapter 1, this was how the Lamerenxes, a bourgeois family from Oloron, had initially acquired their noble title a century earlier. In 1663, Isaac Lamerenx, a barrister with the Parliament of Navarre, had purchased the noble house of Précilhon, near Oloron, which was later exchanged for a second noble house, the *salle* of Uhart-Juzon in Aïcirits, along with its attendant lands.[6] It was therefore possible within the "house" system as practiced at the time to assume the name, properties, and coat of arms of a family with which one had no blood ties. Conversely, however, shedding one's noble assets could be interpreted as relinquishing noble status.

In responding to her husband's deposition, Anne de Marmont acknowledged "that it is only too true that the state of her affairs and those of Sieur Mathieu Lamerenx is extremely sad, which is public knowledge." She added that the start of their problems had coincided with the moment her husband became administrator of her estate: he "appropriated money and livestock for himself," "refusing to provide what his family needed." Not only did he use his wife's properties "as if master," "but he also cut wood and made other degradations from which only he profited." Anne de Marmont provided two principal reasons for rejecting the solution her husband recommended. First, her husband's debts were so extensive that even the sale of all of her properties would not cover them. Second, because the spouses had been married under the separation of property, any proceeds from the sale of her lands that were applied to pay his debts would constitute a loan by the wife to her husband. This loan could never be reimbursed, however, because the "estate of Sieur Mathieu Lamerenx was explicitly dowried in the marriage contract between his mother and father."[7] Indeed, as the historian Anne Zink has demonstrated, "whereas in Roman law a dowry lasted for only as long as the marriage, in the Pyrenees, dowried status was transferred to the offspring of the marriage, meaning that the marriage was assumed to last as long as there were descendants."[8] As a result, the dowry was transmitted to the succeeding generation and retained its inalienable character. In other words, because Lamerenx had inherited property from his parents on the explicit condition that it be transferred to his own children, he was not free to dispose of it. The stipulations regarding the dowry were one building block in the legal architecture discussed in chapter 1, which was aimed at ensuring the integral transgenerational transfer of a "house."

Anne de Marmont asserted before the judges that her husband's claims were illegitimate, arguing that she "should be able to enjoy the property that she had inherited peacefully," the Berrio house. She did, however, consent to the sale of some of her assets for one specific purpose: to finance the journey of Jean-Pierre Lamerenx, her eldest son, to Saint-Domingue, where he would join his uncle Marc-Antoine, who had already settled there as a coffee planter. Since this was considered a mutual expense, she was prepared to furnish half of the necessary funds, and her husband would be responsible for the other half.

Her husband's response was that he had already financed her younger brother's travels to Saint-Domingue, advancing "a sum of two thousand livres in clothing and *pacotille*." He considered the argument that dowried inherited property could not be sold "imaginary." His wife replied that the livestock sold to finance her younger brother's passage to the colonies had belonged to the Berrio house. The most important point was that if the Berrio house were sold to clear the debts of the Lamerenx house, only one house would remain. If Anne de Marmont's property were to be "entirely dismantled, sold, and merged" with the Lamerenx estate, Anne de Marmont "would find herself, if that were to occur, with no property and with no assistance." She repeated that she "resisted the sale of her assets in order to confound them with the Lamerenx estate."[9]

Lamerenx replied, "less to criticize his wife's conduct than to inform us, the members of the commission and the *proches*, of the sad situation of the family," that his wife had used and misused his assets: "She sold my grain in my absence," the clerk recorded, neglecting to transpose the statement into reported speech. His wife retorted that she "had had to use that year's crop, and even to divest herself of certain items of furniture, to provide for her own and her eldest son's subsistence. If Sieur Mathieu Lamerenx had behaved as a husband and a father, she would not have been obliged to resort to such extremes." She reiterated that her husband's assets, like her own, were inalienable "with respect to the dowries for which they were responsible and which amounted to 18,000 livres" (probably a reference to her brothers' and sisters' dowries, which were promised but remained unpaid). Anne concluded by rejecting the distinction between noble and non-noble property that formed the basis of her husband's arguments: "Regardless of whether or not the property of Sieur Mathieu Lamerenx is noble, its quality does not at all diminish that of the lady making the deposition, who cherishes her property, even if it is rural, as much and even more than that of Sieur Mathieu because by owning it she will live peacefully and according to her own design."[10]

To the modern ear, these words sound like a vigorous assertion of autonomy. Indeed, absolute, nongendered primogeniture is often presented today as the expression of a kind of Pyrenean protofeminism.[11] Further, Anne de Marmont expresses herself in the language of subjectivity, which is all the more striking when retransposed into direct speech: "Regardless of the reputation of my husband's property and my property, mine is dear to me, and it is the guarantee of my independence." However, Anne de Marmont's "individualism" can also be interpreted as the manifestation of the corporate interests represented by the Berrio house. As Bourdieu puts it, "Identifying the interests of the designated head of the family with those of the patrimony is a more effective way of establishing his or her identification with the patrimony than the application of any expressly stated and explicit norm."[12] In other words, Anne de Marmont's individual interest in simply being able to "live peacefully" was the strongest guarantee of the continuity of the Berrio house.

After the depositions had been recorded, the tribunal withdrew to deliberate, but the difficulty of the case before them was so great that they could not arrive at an agreement. Because of this impasse, they proposed appointing a single mediator, Arnaud de Bordus Darrieux, a gentleman of the town known for his wisdom, a decision that was accepted by both spouses. After consulting two lawyers, and in accordance with the mediator's judgement, the members of the tribunal finally issued an opinion on a number of points. The Lamerenx properties and assets, like those of Anne de Marmont, were dowried and therefore in principle inalienable. Notwithstanding its inalienable status, however, they ruled that the Marmont property would be sold at auction, with 1,200 livres from the proceeds of the sale set aside to outfit the couple's elder son and finance his voyage to Saint-Domingue. After the Marmont debt was settled in full, the remaining balance would be applied to the Lamerenx debts. Since the marriage, 13,500 livres of Marmont assets had been spent, of which the Berrio house was entitled to half based on repossession rights. The final clause commanded Anne de Marmont to either return to the conjugal home or be cloistered in a convent:

> We are of the opinion that Dame Anne Lamerenx should join Sieur Mathieu, her husband, to make their habitation in the Lamerenx house to live there according to the rules of reason and good sense, the aforementioned Sieur Mathieu having suitable regard for the aforementioned Lady. And if they are unable to bear each other's company, we are of the opinion that Dame Anne should be placed in the convent Sainte-Marie d'Oloron in Béarn, to remain cloistered there until it pleases God to inspire her to rejoin her husband, Sieur Mathieu, and her family, without which she can under no pretext leave the convent.[13]

For as long as she resided in the convent, Anne de Marmont would receive a pension of 300 livres per year, to be paid from the proceeds of a gristmill belonging to her husband. If he failed to pay the pension, she would have the right to seize the mill and arrange for it to be managed. At first sight, the decision appears to have sided with the husband, but there was in fact an attempt to reconcile the interests of the two houses. The inalienable character of both houses was confirmed (putting the husband in the wrong on this point). Once affirmed, however, this rule was immediately violated: the Berrio house was to be sold, because preserving one of the houses was preferable to losing both. Financing the eldest son's emigration to Saint-Domingue was given priority over all other considerations. A right to repossession was also acknowledged. Since the marriage, Mathieu Lamerenx had sold 13,500 livres in his wife's assets to underwrite household expenditures. He would be required to return half of this sum to his wife or to her brothers and sisters if the couple were to die without heirs. The most important point, according to the *proches*, was not to decide in favor of one party or the other but, because both houses were imperiled, to focus instead on preserving at least one of them: "The motives that determined our consent to the sale of the Marmont property, in order to procure the liquidation of the debts of the aforementioned house and those of the Lamerenx property, have as their sole purpose the preservation of the latter, which we look upon as the inalienable property of the children of Sieur Mathieu and Dame Lamerenx."[14]

The tribunal concluded by reaffirming the inalienable character of entailed property and forbidding the Lamerenx couple from "undertaking any debt, or mortgaging or alienating the aforementioned assets without the permission of justice."[15] The tribunal's decision, which appears to violate the "rules" regarding the inalienability of entailed property, allows us to understand the meaning and function of such "rules." Bourdieu argues that ethnographers or sociologists who enunciate "rules" based on observed patterns of behavior are usually mistaken, because they take, "according to the old saying of Marx, 'the things of logic for the logic of things.'" Bourdieu prefers to understand the "rules" as "a juridical or quasi-juridical type of principle that is more or less consciously produced by the agents, or a set of objective regularities that must be followed by anyone who enters a game." He compares the agent to an athlete who has "a feel for the game" that comes from education and practice (*habitus*).[16] The good player "is continually doing what needs to be done, what the game demands and requires."[17] In that sense the player's actions are strictly constrained. At the same time, competency "cannot be achieved by mechanical obedience to explicit, codified rules (when they exist)." The sense of the game "is unevenly distributed, in society as well as on a team." When it is in short supply, "one appeals to wise men, who in Kabylia are often poets too. They know how to take liberty with the official rule and thereby save the essential part of what the rule was meant to guarantee."[18] Here, the *proches* (fulfilling the same function as the "wise men" in Kabylia—the other rural region that Bourdieu studied and frequently compared to the western Pyrenees) took liberty with the rules in order to achieve what was understood to be the essential goal. In violation of the principle of impartible inheritance, the ruling recommended selling the Berrio house, but it ultimately did so in the name of this very same principle.

The clause that commanded the wife to return to the conjugal home or be confined to a convent appears to be a brutal affirmation of the patriarchal order, which raises the question whether the ruling was enforced. In fact, Anne de Marmont claimed to be ill when she was summoned to hear the sentence read. Mathieu Lamerenx and the members of the tribunal traveled to the Berrio house. The transcript of the encounter concludes as follows:

> At one o'clock in the afternoon on December 15, 1763, the aforementioned commissioner and *proches*, assisted by Sieur Mathieu Lamerenx, having transported ourselves to the Berrio house, proceeded with the publication of the opinion of the aforementioned *proches* in the presence of Sieur Mathieu and Dame Lamerenx, to which judgment Sieur Mathieu stated that he acquiesced. The aforementioned Lady stated that she did not at all acquiesce and refused to sign when called upon to do so by both the said commissioner and the *proches*.[19]

Anne de Marmont, judging the decision unjust and fully aware of her rights, refused to sign. The arbitration ruling was not binding. The affair was redirected to the Parliament of Navarre, which immediately ruled on one point, in agreement with both parties: a meadow belonging to the Berrio house would be sold to enable the eldest son to travel to Saint-Domingue. Anne de Marmont continued to reside in La Bastide Clairence as owner of the Berrio house and its tenant farms until her death in 1781. Mathieu Lamerenx withdrew to his property in Aïcirits, where he died 1783. There were more iterations of the legal dispute between husband and wife in their old age. In 1771, against her husband's objections, Anne was authorized by the Parliament of Navarre to sell as much land as necessary to settle a debt due to Daniel Mendès, a Jewish merchant from the town of Saint-Esprit, near Bayonne. In addition, up to 1,000 livres from the sale could be used for medical expenses.[20] In virtue of this authorization, in 1779 Anne de Marmont ceded half of the future income from one of her farms to Daniel Mendès.[21] The following year she sold a small trellised vineyard (4 arpents, or 3 acres) to a citizen of La Bastide Clairence for 900 livres.[22] When Anne de Marmont died in 1781, the house of Berrio was diminished but still standing.

In the transcript of the dispute, the husband and wife accused each other of profligacy and carelessness, but Anne de Marmont had further reasons for complaint. Her husband had had several children out of wedlock with peasant women at Aïcirits, a fact not mentioned in the minutes of the tribunal. In 1761 Jacques Lamerenx, the parish priest of Aïcirits and Mathieu's younger brother, had celebrated the marriage of a man named Pierre Lamerenx.[23] The marriage certificate indicated that the bridegroom was the "natural" (i.e., out-of-wedlock) son of Mathieu Lamerenx and Isabelle d'Enauthandi, a farmer's daughter. One of the witnesses was Jean Lamerenx, master of the Urruti house in Aïcirits and in all likelihood also an illegitimate son of Mathieu Lamerenx. When the newly married peasant couple had their first child in 1762, the grandfather, Mathieu Lamerenx, was the godfather and signed the baptism register. This was common practice; the godparents were very frequently the grandparents.[24] The unusual aspect was that an illegitimate line was thus symbolically recognized.

In 1770, a man named Mathieu Lamerenx, son of Jean Lamerenx of the Urruti house, was married in Aïcirits. Mathieu Lamerenx, esquire, master of the Uhart-Juzon house, attended the ceremony and signed the register as a witness.[25] There is no explicit mention of filiation in the record, but it is nearly certain from the coincidence of last names and first names that Mathieu Lamerenx, esquire, attended the wedding of his grandson Mathieu, son of his illegitimate son Jean (children very often bore the name of a grandparent). The evidence suggests that these out-of-wedlock filiations were public knowledge in Aïcirits and that Mathieu protected and advanced his illegitimate children and grandchildren. The clanlike structure that Mathieu created in Aïcirits is very different from the "stem family" that Le Play saw as characteristic of the western Pyrenees. It resembles what Le Play called the "patriarchal family," a large group living together and descended from a single ancestor. Anne de Marmont may have been unaware of the existence of this extended family while she was living in La Bastide Clairence. It is likely that she discovered it when the couple moved to Aïcirits around 1760, and she may have felt humiliated by the fact that her husband's illegitimate family had a quasi-official existence. This may have been the proximate cause of her return to La Bastide Clairence.

A modern-day interpretation would suggest a psychological explanation for the quarrel: a woman decides to separate from her unfaithful, indifferent, or careless husband. However, the deeper reasons for the dispute lie elsewhere. In the language of Pyrenean customs, there were only four possible matrimonial combinations: an heir married a younger sister; an heiress married a younger brother; a younger brother married a younger sister; or an heir married an heiress. The first two cases were preferable in terms of perpetuating the "house." In both instances the younger brother or sister provided a dowry and remained subordinate to the heir or heiress (both men and women could be dowried). According to the expression in common usage in eighteenth-century notarial documents, a younger brother who married the heiress of X house became the "adventitious master of X," with only his wife retaining the right to be called "mistress of X." Marriages involving a younger sibling on both sides were unimportant from this perspective because few assets or properties were at stake: according to a Bearnese expression quoted by Bourdieu, such a marriage was labeled "a marriage between hunger and thirst."[26]

The situation most widely considered problematic and to be avoided whenever possible was marriage between heirs. According to Eugène Cordier, a legal historian who studied Pyrenean customs in the 1850s, marriages between heirs were universally frowned upon. Cordier related an anecdote concerning an arranged marriage between heirs in the province of Soule in which "neither of the two spouses wanted to leave their own house to go to the other's house." Similarly, in Saint-Jean-Pied-de-Port, in Lower Navarre, peasants were "convinced that marrying an heir with an heiress could only bring misfortune to both spouses."[27] A century later, Bourdieu observed a similar situation in Béarn in which two great families were united by marriage and the two heirs continued living on their own estates, causing a neighbor to remark that "one wonders when they ever got together to produce children." Bourdieu contends that the disapproval of marriage between two elder children was always expressed in the same manner: "Take the case of Tr., who married the Da. girl. He keeps going back and forth between the two places. He is always on the road, he is everywhere, and he is never at home. The master should be there."[28]

The quasi prohibition of marriage between heirs had undoubtedly evolved over time. Although few surviving notarial records from earlier periods exist, marriage between heirs did occur among sovereign houses and the upper nobility. When Pamplona was conquered in 1512, Navarre was governed by a king and a queen, Jean d'Albret and Catherine of Navarre, both of whom were heirs. The king who conquered them, Ferdinand of Aragon, had himself been married to a queen, Isabella of Castile, who had died a few years earlier. As Michel Nassiet has observed, in this system, "property that had until that point belonged to two distinct lines was joined in a single, cumulative property. This option allowed territorial growth and a concentration of income or fiscal potential. From one generation to the next, ambitions tended to increase." Nassiet calls this strategy the "hot option." Conversely, "the matrilineal transfer of the name and coat of arms created a new dynasty that replaced the extinguished line for ownership of the same estate. The territory did not increase, and the balance of power did not change. In the face of random demographic changes, this strategy sought to regulate the matching of lineages with property and principalities." Nassiet calls this strategy the "cold option, because its purpose was identical reproduction."[29] In Pyrenean communities, the "cold option" was the norm, its objective being to ensure the continuity of each house by forbidding one house to absorb another and forestalling the possibility of creating a new house.

In the Marmont-Lamerenx dispute, the mutual accusations of profligacy and carelessness were not the essential point. For Anne de Marmont, her husband's greatest failing was that he had treated the assets of the Berrio house "as if master" because they were assets that he administered but did not own. Similarly, Mathieu Lamerenx complained that his wife had sold crops belonging to the Lamerenx house as if they were her own property. Marriage between heirs inevitably created conflict between man and wife about the management of the house, whereas in marriages between heirs and younger siblings the younger sibling was subordinate. In marriages between heirs, the collision between two sovereignties yielded inherently unstable situations. In the words of Lévi-Strauss, house-based societies are characterized by situations in which relationships of superiority and inferiority between individuals or groups "cease to be transitive" because "nothing prevents a position that is superior in certain respects from being inferior in others."[30] While the husband was the master of his house, and the wife was the mistress of hers, no mechanism existed for deciding in favor of one house or the other in the event of a clash. The choice of a residence had a simultaneously practical and symbolic value in terms of the exercise of domestic power. For the first twenty years of their marriage, Mathieu Lamerenx's primary residence had been La Bastide Clairence, where all of his legitimate children were born, but he had often made prolonged visits to his property in Aïcirits (which explains his numerous illegitimate offspring). During that time, the wife had been symbolically superior, because her husband lived "at her house." Conflict erupted when the family moved to Aïcirits around 1760. Anne de Marmont appears to have quickly found the new living situation intolerable, because she left her husband to go "home" in 1763. The conflict even extended to the burial place of family members: one of the couple's young children who died in La Bastide Clairence in 1757 was exhumed and buried in Aïcirits three years later. The conflict had long remained latent, erupting only after the death in 1751 of Anne de Marmont's uncle, who had administered the Berrio house, and the death of Mathieu Lamerenx's mother in 1755, which allowed him to take full possession of the Lamerenx house in Aïcirits.

As Bourdieu stated, "What was at stake in this open or hidden conflict over the place of residence was, again, the predominance of one or the other lineage and the extinction of a 'house' and its name."[31] In the Marmont-Lamerenx conflict, what Anne de Marmont found unacceptable was "the sale of her assets in order to confound them with the Lamerenx estate,"[32] in other words, the dissolution of the Berrio house and the name associated with it. According to Bourdieu, "The question of political authority within the family becomes most acute . . . when an eldest son marries an eldest daughter." The case of Pyrenean families, in which "the question of the economic basis of domestic power . . . is approached more realistically than in other societies," suggests that the "the sociology of the family, which is so often depicted as based on sentiment, might be no more than a particular case of political sociology."[33]

A Firstborn Son Emigrates

In August 1764 Mr. Larradé, the sergeant ordinary and town crier of La Bastide Clairence, assisted by Noël Etchegorry on the drum, announced three times—on August 2, 26, and 30—that the Plaisance meadow belonging to Dame Anne de Marmont would be publicly auctioned, pursuant to a ruling by the Parliament of Navarre on July 2, 1764, stipulating that 1,200 livres from the proceeds of the sale would finance the elder Lamerenx son's voyage to Saint-Domingue. The bidding opened on September 2 at a starting price of 1,200 livres.[34] After several bids were placed, Arnaud de Bordus Darrieux (the mediator in the Marmont-Lamerenx dispute the previous year) placed the winning bid of 1,400 livres. Because the sale was the execution of a judicial ruling, the expenses were assigned to the future traveler under the name "Lamerenx elder son," an indication of his status as presumptive heir, and were duly itemized (see Table 3.1).[35]

Three hundred of the 1,200 livres were spent on travel expenses—*passage en droiture* (i.e., travel directly to America, as opposed to slave-trading expeditions, which stopped in Africa)[36]—with the remainder spent essentially on *pacotille* and clothing: jackets, an overcoat, a morning coat, slippers, silk stockings, and the sword, all of which would enable the young Lamerenx to honorably affirm his status as a gentleman once he arrived in the colonies. There remained 53 livres, 17 sols, and 2 deniers of pocket money. The fabrics that made up the *pacotille* were luxury articles, including *gros de Tours* (silk fabric), *taffetas de Florence* (for lining dresses and hats), *toile de Troyes* (for making handkerchiefs), *batiste* (fine linen cloth), *drap d'Elbœuf* (woolen cloth), and *basin de Hollande* (cotton fabric). Once sold at twice or three times their purchase price, these items would supply the traveler with funds to help him settle in the colony.

The ledgers of the port of Bayonne (Fig. 3.1) show that "Jean-Pierre Lamerenx, esquire, 22 years, average height and brown hair" embarked aboard the snow *La Marianne*, which boarded its passengers on August 23, 1764, in preparation for sailing to Cap-Français in Saint-Domingue.[37] The ship made sail in September, carrying five paying passengers and three *engagés*. The paying passengers included Raymond and Jean-Pierre Bourbon, brothers from Martinique; Jean-Baptiste Diesse, a physician from the town of Mouguerre, near Bayonne; and Jean-Pierre Mora, a blacksmith from Pouillon, in the Dax diocese. The *engagés* were Etienne Despassailler, a cooper from Mugron, in the Aire-sur-Adour diocese; Martin d'Etcheverry, a carpenter from Larressore, in the province of Labourd; and Daniel Bath, a carpenter from Maslacq, in Béarn. All these locations (except Martinique) were within a fifty-mile radius of Bayonne (Fig. 3.2). As a paying passenger, Jean-Pierre dined at the captain's table during the voyage. The routine on board included morning prayer followed by breakfast at eight, dinner at noon, and supper at seven, followed by prayer at eight.[38] Passengers had to bring their own mattresses and pillows. With favorable winds, the crossing took about forty-five days. (Most westward crossings took place in April and September, to take advantage of the trade winds.) Jean-Pierre was welcomed in Saint-Domingue by his paternal uncle Marc-Antoine Lamerenx.

Within a few short years, Jean-Pierre Lamerenx was able to start his own

TABLE 3.1.
Itemized expenses incurred to equip Jean-Pierre Lamerenx of La Bastide Clairence prior to his passage to Saint-Domingue (1764)

August 13	1 half-beaver hat from Paris	15 livres
	1 black taffeta tie	3 livres 10 sols
	1 hair cover	2 livres 5 sols
September 4	10 yards ½ ribbed silk fabric from Tours	49 livres
	6 yards white Florence fabric	28 livres 10 sols
	3½ yards rateen	5 livres 12 sols
	2 yards ¼ Elbeuf-style fabric	28 livres 2 sols 6 deniers
	2 yards thin serge	2 livres 12 sols
	2 pieces Holland-style cotton cloth	42 livres
	13 yards ⅔ rateen	21 livres 17 sols 4 deniers
	36 yards linen cloth from Troyes	108 livres
	1 dozen embroidered wristbands	4 livres
	3 yards fine batiste	39 livres
	4 pairs embroidered cuffs	31 livres 7 deniers
September 5	2 pairs of white silk stockings from Paris	26 livres
	1 sword and knot from Bellas the younger	18 livres
	1 waist-belt	3 livres
	1 hat with gold braid and plume from Bubaton	25 livres
	1 hair cover with ribbon	2 livres 15 sols
	for the making of a complete suit of silk fabric from Tours	15 livres
	for that of seven jackets	24 livres 10 sols
	for that of a riding coat	5 livres
	for two of the same riding-coat buttons	2 livres
	for an account for supplies and sewing and other work done by Marimaïté	91 livres 10 sols
	to Samuel Louis Nounès, Jew, for four pairs of embroidered cuffs	16 livres
	to Mr. Delanc, jeweler, for a small and large pair of buckles	24 livres
	to Miss Castaing for six bonnets of knitted cotton	12 livres
September 6	to Clément Etchemendy of La Bastide Clairence	20 livres 8 sols 6 deniers
	to Mr. Jean Laborde, mattress-maker, for a mattress and pillow	10 livres 10 sols
	to Mr. Esteben Baundola for three pairs of shoes	13 livres 10 sols
	to Messrs. Dubroca brothers for a suit of red camlet	92 livres 11 sols 6 deniers
	to Salles, shoemaker, for another	12 livres
	for minor supplies	51 livres 12 sols
	to Mr. Savigny [for passage to Saint-Domingue]	300 livres
	balance due upon boarding	53 livres 17 sols 2 deniers
	Total	1,200 livres

continued

Original French

13 août	1 chapeau demi-castor de Paris	15 livres
	1 cravate de taffetas noir	3 livres 10 sols
	1 bourse à cheveux	2 livres 5 sols
4 septembre	10 aunes ½ gros de Tours	49 livres
	6 aunes Florence blanc	28 livres 10 sols
	3 ½ aunes ratine	5 livres 12 sols
	2 aunes ¼ drap façon Elbeuf	28 livres 2 sols 6 deniers
	2 aunes sergette	2 livres 12 sols
	2 pièces basin de Hollande	42 livres
	13 aunes ⅔ ratine	21 livres 17 sols 4 deniers
	36 aunes de toile de Troyes	108 livres
	1 douzaine poignets brodés	4 livres
	3 aunes batiste fine	39 livres
	4 paires manchettes brodées	31 livres 7 deniers
5 septembre	2 paires de bas de soie blancs de Paris	26 livres
	1 épée et le nœud de chez Bellas cadet	18 livres
	1 ceinturon	3 livres
	1 chapeau ganse en or avec plumet de chez Bubaton	25 livres
	1 bourse à cheveux avec le ruban	2 livres 15 sols
	pour façon d'un habit complet en gros de Tours	15 livres
	pour celle de sept vestes	24 livres 10 sols
	pour celle d'une redingote	5 livres
	pour deux mêmes gros boutons de redingote	2 livres
	pour un compte des fournitures et coutures et autres ouvrages fournis par Marimaïté	91 livres 10 sols
	à Samuel Louis Nounès Juif pour quatre paires manchettes brodées	16 livres
	à M. Delanc orfèvre pour une paire de boucles grande et petite	24 livres
	à Melle Castaing pour six bonnets de coton tricoté	12 livres
6 septembre	à Clément Etchemendy de La Bastide Clairence	20 livres 8 sols 6 deniers
	au sieur Jean Laborde, matelassier, pour un matelas et un oreiller	10 livres 10 sols
	au sieur Esteben Baundola pour trois paires de souliers	13 livres 10 sols
	à Messieurs Dubroca frères pour un habit de camelot rouge	92 livres 11 sols 6 deniers
	à Salles cordonnier pour un idem	12 livres
	pour diverses menues emplettes	51 livres 12 sols
	à Monsieur Savigny [pour passage à Saint-Domingue]	300 livres
	à l'embarquement argent pour solde	53 livres 17 sols 2 deniers
	Total	1200 livres

Source: Darrieux-Juson family papers, La Bastide Clairence. Courtesy of Denis Dufourcq.

Fig. 3.1. The Port of Bayonne Seen from the Left Bank of the Adour River, 1776. Engraving by Yves Le Gouaz (1742–1816) from a drawing by Nicolas Ozanne (1728–1811).

coffee plantation, which adjoined his uncle's in the Matador District of Dondon. By 1829, when his heirs were granted an indemnity by the Haitian government in exchange for the recognition of Haitian independence by Charles X, his estate was valued at 152,750 francs. (As we saw in chapter 2, the indemnity was meant to cover 10% of the assessed value of the property.)[39] Based on the figures of the government commission discussed in chapter 2, we can estimate that Jean-Pierre Lamerenx's plantation had somewhere between forty and fifty slaves, slightly above the average number for coffee plantations.[40] The plantations of Marc-Antoine Lamerenx and Jean Mouscardy, which had been operating since the beginning of the coffee boom, were considerably larger.

When he first arrived in Saint-Domingue (Fig. 3.3), Jean-Pierre Lamerenx's capital, other than the income from selling his *pacotille*, was primarily symbolic. The clothes and sword that he brought with him from the mainland attested to his social status as a gentleman. He also benefitted from his uncle's protection, which probably facilitated his acquisition of land and slaves (a considerably smaller investment for a coffee plantation than for a sugar plantation, as we saw in chapter 2). His most significant asset, however, was in all likelihood the dowry of his wife, Françoise Silly, who came from a family of early settlers and coffee planters. Françoise, daughter of François Silly and Elizabeth Fleury, had

Fig. 3.2. The General Government of Guyenne and Gascogne, by Jean Covens and Corneille Mortier, Amsterdam, 1742 (detail). La Bastide Clairence is the northernmost town of Lower Navarre, with a fluvial connection to the port city of Bayonne, in the province of Labourd. The Spanish border appears at the lower left. Labourd and Lower Navarre together are designated as "Le Basque" (Basque lands). From David Rumsey Historical Map Collection, www.davidrumsey.com.

Fig. 3.3. View of Cap-Français, Island of Saint-Domingue, Seen from the Road to the Petite Anse Pier, 1791 (detail). Engraving by Nicolas Ponce (1746–1831).

several siblings and cousins who owned coffee plantations in Dondon and Marmelade. Her parents owned a coffee plantation in Marmelade. Her mother was descended from the original settlers of Dondon Parish.[41] In 1777, Elizabeth Fleury, widowed and sole proprietor of her coffee plantation, made a donation to her daughter Françoise and her son-in-law Jean-Pierre Lamerenx to help them develop their own coffee plantation in Dondon.[42] It comprised 4,838 livres in cash and an entire family of slaves valued at 8,000 livres: the father, Gabriel; the mother, Barbe; and five children, Eustache (a.k.a. Mastoquet, "the heavy one"), Clémence, Amelle, Jacob, and Catherine. Here, the meaning and use of the dowry was very different from what it was in Lower Navarre, where a dowried child was no longer a member of the "house" and therefore excluded from the inheritance. As Bernard Derouet explains, in egalitarian systems the dowry was not "compensation" paid by one family to another but rather "help given *to the children themselves* to allow them, in association with—and on an equal basis with—their spouses to build a new family unit."[43] Under the egalitarian Custom of Paris, which was in force in Saint-Domingue, the dowry was usually followed by other gifts from the parents (*avances d'hoirie*). These allowed the children and their spouses to establish themselves, which in the planter class meant starting their own plantations instead of waiting to inherit their parents' properties.

Jean-Pierre's path to wealth was similar to the one taken by his uncle Marc-Antoine. Having arrived with symbolic capital and limited economic capital, he married into a family who had settled in the area when land was free and slaves were relatively inexpensive. This gave Jean-Pierre and his wife, Françoise Silly, an advantage in starting their coffee plantation. However, any expansion of the property had to be undertaken at current market prices. In 1781 Jean-Pierre and Françoise paid 9,000 livres for a modest nine *carreaux* of land planted in coffee, which they purchased from one of Françoise's relatives. They had some difficulty making the payments, which were due in coffee.[44] Like his uncle, Jean-Pierre served in the colonial militia. In 1769, five years after his arrival in the colony, he was a lieutenant in the First Cavalry Company of Dondon Parish (a unit with a total headcount of 52).[45] His uncle Marc-Antoine was captain of the Second Cavalry Company. Overall, the Dondon militia included two white cavalry companies, one white company of riflemen, one free-colored cavalry company, and one squad of free blacks, with a total headcount of 224 in 1769. Following Marc-Antoine's death, Jean-Pierre Lamerenx succeeded his uncle as captain of the Second Cavalry Company in 1772.[46] Within the space of approximately twenty years, Jean-Pierre Lamerenx, whose starting capital was comparatively modest, had made a fortune in America thanks to the considerable profits made possible by slave labor. After his father died intestate in 1783, he returned to the Continent in 1786 to settle the succession, remaining in France for nearly two years.

His return to France, according to testimony gathered twenty years later, "made a big splash and attracted a number of people who were curious to see him."[47]

Marc-Antoine, Jean-Pierre's paternal uncle, was a younger sibling who had moved to Saint-Domingue in 1729. According to the rules of primogeniture, Mathieu Lamerenx, Jean-Pierre's father and the elder brother of Marc-Antoine, had inherited the *salle* of Uhart-Juzon in Aïcirits. It is noteworthy that within the span of a single generation, emigration to Saint-Domingue became an option for more than just younger sons. In view of the symbolic prestige and economic advantages associated with his status as heir, it might appear surprising that Jean-Pierre decided to join his uncle Marc-Antoine in 1764, an anomaly that makes investigating his story interesting. His "case" violates the general rule. Close examination makes it possible to determine whether the exception confirms the rule or the rule should be formulated differently.[48] The record of the dispute between his parents clearly states that Jean-Pierre wanted to emigrate and that this consideration took precedence over all others in the eyes of the tribunal: "It is essential to facilitate the travel of their eldest son, Jean-Pierre Lamerenx, to the Islands of America, where he says he wishes to go."[49] It is also worth noting that the need to help their eldest son travel to America was the only point on which both spouses agreed. It is possible that the parents believed that the indebtedness of both the Lamerenx and Berrio houses would make it difficult for him to marry the younger daughter of another great house. The system of mutual credits granted between houses appears from this perspective to resemble a pyramid scheme that was on the verge of collapsing. Perhaps Jean-Pierre wanted to escape a system that protected estates by rendering assets inalienable but at the same time condemned the master of the house to be endlessly assailed by creditors. This was precisely what occurred on the death of Mathieu Lamerenx in 1783, when a dozen individuals presented themselves to demand that their debts be repaid from the deceased's inventory of assets.

Jean-Pierre went to Saint-Domingue at the invitation of Marc-Antoine, his American uncle. Marc-Antoine undoubtedly offered a shining example of a rapid, accessible way of accumulating wealth, as well as a generally more advantageous economic situation than Jean-Pierre would have had as master of the Lamerenx and Berrio houses. Furthermore, leaving did not mean that Jean-Pierre was abandoning his status as presumptive heir to both houses. Rather, he was hedging his bets. Although, as I will demonstrate, this dual strategy would ultimately prove problematic, at the time of his departure it must have seemed to provide the optimal solution. By emigrating to Saint-Domingue while retaining his status as heir, Jean-Pierre was in fact causing two unrelated logics to enter into conflict. On the one hand, he was placing himself under the protection of his father's brother, a fellow nobleman who shared the same patronymic surname. Since Marc-Antoine had been dowried and excluded from the Lamerenx house when he left for Saint-Domingue, the connection between Jean-Pierre and Marc-Antoine was of a "parental" nature and independent of the house-based system. On the other hand, Jean-Pierre did not renounce his role as heir, as prescribed by Navarrese customs. As Lévi-Strauss remarked, "An individual who is potentially affiliated to numerous groups can keep some affiliations in reserve, lose others, put forward those that he finds most suitable and better his material situation or social status depending on the circumstances, the place, or the time."[50]

In this respect, it should be noted that the Lamerenx family presented different definitions of their nobility inside and outside Lower Navarre. Within, their status as owners of the *salle* of Uhart-Juzon in Aïcirits gave them access to the Estates General of Navarre among the ranks of the nobility. The logic was that of "real" nobility rooted in ownership of a noble property. Outside Navarre, the family put forward a "parental" definition of their nobility. Marc-Antoine's entire argument when he sent his file from Saint-Domingue to the royal genealogists in Versailles was based on the fact that his eldest brother, as well as his father and grandfather, were noblemen.[51] The genealogists greeted the request with skepticism. Marc-Antoine produced a document from the Estates General of Navarre certifying that the Uhart-Juzon house had been a noble and illustrious estate since time immemorial. The employee of the royal services, Jean-Nicolas Beaujon, noted in the file that the Lamerenxes had purchased the house in the 1690s and that the family's nobility was therefore anything but immemorial. Thanks to this acquisition, "the Lamerenx family was grafted onto the Uhart-Juzon family."[52] The Parisian employee's remark was based on a blood-based, genealogical view of nobility. In Navarre, however, nobility was founded on property, and it was legitimate to assume the coat of arms and name of a house without the slightest blood relationship to the previous owners. In fact, Marc-Antoine's application represented an attempt to convert "real" nobility, based on property, into hereditary nobility. The employee, believing that recognizing the Lamerenx family's nobility would set a dangerous precedent for the king's monopoly on granting noble rank but also wanting to satisfy the request, recommended that the king publish an ambiguous declaration that could be read both as granting nobility and as acknowledging it.[53] Ultimately, Jean-Pierre possessed two separate identities, one on each side of the ocean: in Saint-Domingue, he was a Navarrese gentleman; in Lower Navarre, he was the master of the Lamerenx and Berrio houses.

Blood Ties, Residency, and the House-Based System

One possible question raised by the conflict over inheritance rules concerns what became of the Berrio house after Anne de Marmont's death in 1781. In conformity with Navarrese customs, the eldest child, Jean-Pierre Lamerenx, then a coffee planter in Saint-Domingue, became heir to the house. In the fall of 1785, Jean-Pierre crossed the Atlantic to manage his parents' succession and to leave three of his children (two sons and a daughter) to be educated in France in the care of their paternal aunt, Ursule Lamerenx, a widespread practice among Saint-Domingue colonists. The daughter, Marguerite, spent two years in a convent in Bayonne before being left in the care of her aunt in 1788. In 1802, having reached majority, both sons went to join their father, who by that time had settled in Cuba. The year was a propitious window for transatlantic travel because of the Treaty of Amiens between France and Great Britain. Marguerite was married in France in 1804.[54]

The Lamerenx succession clearly must have become rather complex, because Jean-Pierre requested two six-month extensions of his original request for one year's leave from the militia.[55] The notarial archives of the period contain numerous transactions involving Jean-Pierre and the Lamerenx properties. Despite the complexity of these transactions, the records reveal a single strategy. Jean-Pierre sold his mother's properties in La Bastide Clairence and used the proceeds to pay his father's debts and repurchase properties that had previously belonged to his father in Aïcirits. In particular he sold the largest of the tenant farms belonging to the Berrio house in La Bastide Clairence for 9,000 livres.[56] By merging the two houses and accepting the dissolution of the Berrio house in order to ensure the survival of the Lamerenx house, he thus did what his mother had always refused to do. Jean-Pierre Lamerenx did not use money earned in Saint-Domingue to settle debts in Lower Navarre or purchase property there. When he sailed back to Saint-Domingue in 1788, he had paid off most of his parents' creditors and repurchased some of his father's properties, but he still owed 4,284 livres lent to him by a notary from Arudy, in Béarn.[57] He probably calculated that any profits made in Saint-Domingue should be reinvested there, since returns on investments were much higher in the colony. Thirty years later the money was still due.

As shown above, according to the rules of Navarrese custom the heir was not free to dispose of the estate's *biens propres*. Therefore, in principle Jean-Pierre was not free to sell the Berrio house. The law did provide for a portion of the inheritance to be allocated to younger siblings, however, and on June 16, 1787, Jean-Pierre received a notice from the Parliament of Navarre authorizing him to sell his maternal assets and use the proceeds to pay the legitime to his brothers and sisters.[58] On September 7, 1787, he sold the Berrio house to a certain François Barbaste, a merchant in Saint-Palais, for the sum of 1,650 livres.[59] Several weeks later, however, Jean-Pierre's younger brother (whose first name was also Jean-Pierre and who also had returned from Saint-Domingue for the succession, unmarried and known under the name of chevalier de Lamerenx) received the

Berrio house in payment of his rights to the legitime, freeing François Barbaste of his obligation to pay for the property.[60]

By a kind of inertia inherent in hereditary customs, the Berrio house, which had nearly been put up for sale so many times, was returned to the family. The record shows that the chevalier de Lamerenx sailed back to Saint-Domingue from Bordeaux on November 20, 1787,[61] leaving the house in the hands of renters and making no provision for maintenance. In 1790, the town council of La Bastide Clairence noted that the Berrio house was threatening "to imminently become a ruin and that its fall could harm the inhabitants who are obliged to travel down the street on which this house is located."[62] The council ordered the owner's proxy to undertake repairs or the house would face demolition. In 1800 the house was rented to a family of hosiers.[63]

The precise scenario of the next generation's inheritance is not entirely clear. It seems that the chevalier de Lamerenx died relatively young and heirless. Whatever the exact circumstances of the transfer, it was consistent with Navarrese customs, which provided for a "right of return" (*tournedot*), meaning that the dowry or legitime returned to the elder branch of the family in the event that there were no descendants. Because the chevalier de Lamerenx had no offspring, the Berrio house returned to the ownership of his elder brother Jean-Pierre, who had originally ceded title to the building in payment of the legitime. Forced to leave Saint-Domingue by the Haitian Revolution, Jean-Pierre died in Cuba in 1810 after establishing a coffee plantation near the town of Matanzas. When he returned to Saint-Domingue in 1788 after managing his parents' succession, Jean-Pierre Lamerenx named an administrator of his estate, who died a few years later. In 1812 the Saint-Palais court, noting the owner's absence, appointed Jean-Pierre's daughter Marguerite and her husband, Daniel Laborde, administrators of the Lamerenx and Berrio houses.[64]

In December 1817, Jean-Pierre's eldest son, Charles Lamerenx, who was born in Saint-Domingue in 1775, landed in France for the first time, after a turbulent existence that included a conviction for piracy and an extended prison term in Cuba (more about Charles's life in chapter 5).[65] Charles was welcomed by his sister, Marguerite, who had not seen him for exactly thirty-two years. Since the 1812 judgment naming her administrator of the family properties, Marguerite had resided in the Lamerenx house at Aïcirits. As his sister's guest, Charles, armed with a signed document from his mother and the rest of his brothers and sisters (who were living in Cuba), immediately brought suit against her. Since the Civil Code was in effect in 1818, the Berrio house, along with the remaining Lamerenx properties, was considered the joint property of all of the siblings together with the mother. Ruling in favor of Charles and against his sister Marguerite, the tribunal unseated her and appointed him administrator of the family properties.

Everything in the records suggests that he behaved *en maître* (as if master), pursuing the same strategy that his father had pursued thirty years earlier by selling land belonging to his maternal grandmother, Anne de Marmont, to cover debts contracted by Mathieu Lamerenx, his paternal grandfather. On June 29, 1818, the Berrio house and two of its tenant farms were sold for 4,000 francs to a Bayonne merchant, Jacob Gomès (a descendant of the small Jewish community of La Bastide Clairence).[66] Five years later, the house (without the tenant farms) was resold to a hosier, Pierre Cornu Galan, whose grandsons all migrated to Uruguay.[67] The 1818 sale thus signaled the end of the Berrio house as a "house" in terms of Navarrese customs. Indeed, after that date the name Berrio no longer appears in notarial documents and census data, and the house came to be referred to as Garchot or Galan (from the name of the hosier who owned it) or as *maison du jeu de paume* (in reference to an indoor tennis court that adjoined the house). Starting in the early twentieth century, it was called *trinquet Hapette*, after its new owner, Bernardin Hapette,[68] who converted the old-fashioned real tennis court into a court dedicated to Basque pelota.

What conclusions can be reached concerning the relationship between hereditary customs in the Pyrenees region and patterns of emigration? In a study of several Basque villages in the nineteenth century, Marie-Pierre Arrizabalaga contends that absolute cognatic primogeniture, which persisted in regional practices despite the egalitarian impetus of the Civil Code, was the principal cause of emigration.[69] She concurs with the conclusions of Louis Etcheverry, a legal historian and disciple of Le Play.[70] Arrizabalaga supports her argument with several observations, including the fact that common beliefs notwithstanding, emigration was not caused by poverty. Nineteenth-century Pyrenean emigrants were the younger children of mid-sized agricultural estates inherited by eldest sons or daughters, and younger siblings used their shares of the inheritance to pay for their passage and establish themselves as farmers or craftsmen in Argentina or Uruguay. According to Arrizabalaga, emigration became increasingly democratic with the rise of emigration agencies that provided the funding needed for the voyage and for settling in a new country. Until the 1860s, however, emigration for the most part concerned the children of landowners and typically functioned through family networks (e.g., when emigrants joined an uncle or cousin already living in America). This model of emigration was what Le Play called "rich emigration," which he associated with the "stem-family," in contrast to what he termed "poor emigration" tied to the "unstable family."[71]

As we saw in chapter 1, according to Anne Zink, "The spirit of Pyrenean custom is in the non-multiplication of houses."[72] Lands not owned by a particular house were moors and pastures owned collectively by the houses, and no new house could be established on this collective property. Even if he had the requisite funds, a younger son could not establish a new house in the community of his birth, because there was no land for sale. Thus, in principle the only options available to a younger son were to remain single or to marry an heiress. As Zink puts it, "There is no other place to which one can take one's legitime and make one's living outside the house system."[73] But as we have seen, emigration did offer a space for making one's living outside the house system. By taking his legitime with him to Saint-Domingue, Marc-Antoine escaped the system of reciprocal credits that characterized dowries in Lower Navarre. In the next generation, the firstborn son Jean-Pierre Lamerenx chose to join his uncle Marc-Antoine in Saint-Domingue instead of marrying a younger daughter from the region, who would have brought a dowry into the fold. The pressing need to equip their eldest son accentuated the conflict between Jean-Pierre's parents to the point that it became a crisis centered on the use of the household assets. The crisis required legal intervention, and its outcome brought about the gradual dismantling of the Berrio house. Seen from this perspective, emigration was simultaneously a consequence of the system and a phenomenon that contradicted its spirit, because the heirs themselves left, and the departures of younger children or heirs led to land sales that made the real-estate market more liquid, thus contributing to the potential recombination of the houses. Such a turn of events resembles what Nassiet called the "hot option."[74] While the house-based system sought to preserve the status quo, that is, to maintain the estates without growth, the emigration of Jean-Pierre Lamerenx, heir of Berrio and Uhart-Juzon, was undoubtedly consistent with the logic of increasing the houses' property. Jean-Pierre's choice and that of the previous generation were thus contiguous, since, in violation of custom, two houses had been united. A coffee plantation in Saint-Domingue was now added to the Berrio and Lamerenx houses of Lower Navarre, which had been joined by marriage.

The experience of the Mouscardy family was different, but it too shows how emigration opened up options that were not available under the traditional house-based system. In Zink's view, what made the western Pyrenees unique was "the impossibility for the younger brother to settle near the parental household once he was married."[75] Yet in the Mouscardy family a younger brother established himself next to the house of Mouscardy. As we saw in chapter 2, when Jean Mouscardy made a voyage to the region of his birth in 1769–70, he purchased a townhouse in Bayonne, and he left some funds in custody with a notary in La Bastide Clairence. Two years later, acting on his behalf, the notary purchased notes receivable from two different creditors for a total of 3,094 livres. The debtor, a man named Jean Greciet, owned a farm next to the Mouscardy house in La Bastide Clairence, whose proprietor was Jean Mouscardy's elder sister. The debt was guaranteed by a mortgage on the property. Greciet being unable to make the payments, Jean Mouscardy took ownership of the farm, known as the Guillebert house, and he had it managed by his younger brother (also named Jean), who until then had been making a living as a day laborer. When Jean Mouscardy the American died in 1797, he had several mulatto children in Saint-Domingue, who owned a coffee plantation under a deal arranged by their father in 1784. Under French law the mulatto children, being illegitimate, could not inherit, and there were no legitimate children. The designated heirs were Jean Mouscardy's nephews in Bayonne, who received most of their uncle's assets. However, Jean Mouscardy's younger brother inherited his elder brother's property in La Bastide Clairence and became officially the master of the Guillebert house, which stood next to the Mouscardy ancestral house.[76] Such development stood against the spirit of Pyrenean customs: a *cadet* had established his own house next to the parental estate. This could be viewed as a variant of the "hot option." It was not the merger of two houses but the acquisition of two contiguous houses by members of the same family.

Derouet refers to the comparative weight of criteria related to "blood ties" and "residency" in customs that govern succession.[77] He demonstrates that in house-based systems the place of residence counted far more than blood ties in ensuring the legitimacy of an inheritance. The new master or mistress of the house was legitimate because he or she was born in the house, had always known it, and had learned to manage both the house and the various relationships between the house and the community. Traditionally, the eldest sibling fulfilled these criteria, leading to convergence between absolute cognatic primogeniture and the residency rule. But the emigration of the eldest child opened a gap in the system. When his father died in 1783, Jean-Pierre Lamerenx "automatically" became master of the Lamerenx house. Eight days later, his sister Ursule moved to assert her right to become the mistress of the Uhart-Juzon house should the fate of her emigrant brothers remain unknown. Arguing that she was "the ablest person to take up the administration of the estate of her deceased father,"[78] she commissioned a complete inventory of the house, adding that she had had no news of her two brothers who had emigrated to the Caribbean several years earlier and that she was intended to inherit the house in the event of their death without heirs. It was only after the eldest sibling arrived three years later that the inheritance was decided in favor of Jean-Pierre.

Jean-Pierre's hesitation in granting powers of attorney to manage his properties in Lower Navarre suggests how difficult it was to manage assets from afar. Following his mother's death in 1781, Jean-Pierre put his maternal uncle Paul Auguste de Marmont in charge of administering the maternal properties.[79] After his father died in 1783, he revoked the power of attorney he had given to his uncle and put his paternal aunt in charge of administering all paternal and maternal properties.[80] A few months later he changed his mind again. He reestablished Paul Auguste de Marmont as administrator of all family properties.[81] The language of the deed indicates a concern about offending those affected by these abrupt changes. Jean-Pierre professed to trust his uncle and his aunt equally, stating that his intent was only to free his aunt from the burden of administering his affairs.

The subsequent generation faced nearly the same difficulty when Marguerite, Jean-Pierre's daughter, born in Saint-Domingue but raised in France since 1786, was appointed administrator of the Lamerenx house by judicial decision in 1812. Only in 1818 did her older brother, Charles, take possession of the house after bringing suit against her immediately upon arriving from America. Under the house-based system, the eldest shared governance of the house with the parents once he or she was married. If the heir was in America, the house remained in the hands of aging parents, who often were not fully capable of managing it. When they died, the master's place remained empty. When Jean-Pierre's father, Mathieu, died, the inventory of the house revealed the poor condition of the buildings and the inadequate maintenance of the wooded land, trellised vineyards, and orchards, all of which were described as "almost devastated."[82] Emigration created a clash between the criteria of blood ties, expressed through primogeniture, and residency.

Emigration and House-Based Systems in the *Longue Durée*

This chapter has primarily considered the fate of one family belonging to the lower nobility. Its relevance in terms of Pyrenean houses in general, of which only a minority were noble, could be considered limited. However, it appears that under the Pyrenean house-based system, while differences between nobles and commoners were important in some respects, they have little bearing on the questions examined here. On the one hand, the possession of a *salle* provided access to the Estates General of Navarre among the ranks of the nobility. On the other hand, all houses participated in local governments on an equal basis, and the same customs that regulated inheritance applied to both noble and nonnoble houses. The Berrio house was not a noble one, although in terms of "blood ties" Anne de Marmont, who was Berrio's mistress, was noble because of her father, Bernard de Marmont (1686–1739). Her status within the community of La Bastide Clairence, however, was based on her position as "lady of the Berrio house." The ascending genealogy of the *sieurs et dames de Berrio* reveals that the house's alliances had been at times local and at other times distant, sometimes involving noble families and sometimes involving commoners. Anne de Marmont's mother, Anne de Moirie, was the daughter of a banker and *bourgeois* of the city of Bayonne, Michel de Moirie (alliance of the house with a distant commoner).[83] Anne's paternal grandfather, Jean de Marmont, was the younger son of a noble Bearnese house (alliance of the house with a distant noble) who had married the heiress to the Berrio house, Marie de Lombart, herself a member of a commoner family that had resided in La Bastide Clairence for several generations. (Jean de Lombart, Anne de Marmont's great-grandfather and the royal prosecutor of La Bastide Clairence, had been among the drafters of the Aranzel, the document that codified the fiscal regulations of Lower Navarre in 1632.) Symbolic prestige was tied less to nobility in the sense of lineage than it was to the role of master or mistress of the Berrio house, transmitted through either men or women and through either local or distant alliances, in accordance with Lévi-Strauss's definition of "house-based societies."

Arrizabalaga's study of Basque hereditary customs and emigration patterns in the nineteenth century reveals striking continuity of practices between the period discussed here and the period after the introduction of the Civil Code. Indeed, there is little to distinguish the inegalitarian eighteenth century from the ostensibly more egalitarian nineteenth century. In the eighteenth century, integral transfer was softened by the legitime. In the nineteenth century, the Civil Code was applied in such a way as to ensure quasi-integral inheritance. Similar goals were pursued under the two different legal systems. As Bourdieu puts it, "If the Bearnese have managed to keep their successional traditions alive in spite of two centuries of Civil Code, this is because they learned a long time ago to play with the rules of the game."[84] Under the *ancien régime*, emigrants were dowried children who used their legitime to finance their travels and settle in America. In the nineteenth century, at least until around 1860, emigrants were the children of large or middling landowners who used their inheritances for the same purposes. As had been the case under the Old Regime, in the nineteenth century a single heir inherited the house, because the Civil Code was flexible enough to allow unequal partition of the estates. As also had been the case under the Old Regime, emigration flowed through family networks, meaning that it too was unevenly distributed. Villages with the oldest tradition of emigration, in other words, villages whose "first emigrant" had left several generations earlier, had the highest rates of emigration. The principal difference between the Civil Code era and the Old Regime arose when the eldest child emigrated, a relatively common occurrence that meant that the house, instead of having no master, was immediately assigned to a younger brother or sister. Arrizabalaga considers this weakening of primogeniture a "progressive" process of change.[85] Under the house-based system, however, primogeniture was simply the means of pursuing one primary objective: the integral transfer of the house. Naming a younger sibling master or mistress allowed for the perpetuation of the system by adapting to the realities of emigration, which affected the oldest and younger siblings alike.

CHAPTER FOUR

War and Property Rights

> *Un si immense sujet, la révolte des noirs de Saint-Domingue en 1791, lutte de géants, trois mondes intéressés dans la question, l'Europe et l'Afrique pour combattants, l'Amérique pour champ de bataille.*
>
> Such an immense subject, the revolt of blacks in Saint-Domingue in 1791, a struggle of giants, three worlds involved in the issue, Europe and Africa as opponents, America as the battlefield.
>
> Victor Hugo, preface to *Bug-Jargal*, 1832

One of the paradoxes of the Haitian Revolution is that in the midst of chaotic fighting, mass slaughter, and shifting political loyalties there was constant attention paid to property rights. Plantation owners left the island in successive waves throughout the revolution. Their abandoned properties were taken over by the revolutionary government, but legally there was no transfer of ownership. The properties were under sequestration. They were being administered by the government on a temporary basis until a final determination was made about ownership. Properties under sequestration were leased to farmers who paid rent to the government. When French republican rule over the island was consolidated under the authority of Toussaint Louverture in the late 1790s, efforts were made to recall plantation owners, who were encouraged to reclaim their properties and have the sequestrations lifted. Few planters came back, but many did submit the necessary paperwork through agents in the colony to have the sequestration of their properties lifted. The proclamation of Haitian independence in 1804 put an end to the process. One of the articles of the Haitian Constitution forbade land ownership by white foreigners, thus sealing the expropriation of former colonists. That was not the end of the story, however. The recognition of Haiti's independence by France in 1825 was predicated on the payment of an indemnity to compensate colonists for the loss of their property. Throughout the revolution, territory on the island changed hands many times, and the actual possession of land was in constant flux. Yet there was a continuous and scrupulous effort to keep track of legal ownership. Why this was deemed necessary and what was at stake in the assertion of property rights are the subject matter of this chapter.

The 1791 Slave Insurrection and the Fall of Dondon

On the night of August 22, 1791, an uprising took place on several plantations of Acul Parish, in the northern plain of Saint-Domingue. The early stages of the uprising are narrated in the report of the French parliamentary commission headed by Jean-Philippe Garran-Coulon, which worked from several eyewitness testimonies:

> At ten in the evening, the slaves of the Turpin and Flaville plantation came to look for those of the Clément plantation. The two gangs chose as their leaders Boukmans and Auguste, slaves on these two plantations. From there they went to the Trémès plantation, where they spared the life of a carpenter they shot and missed. Then they went to the Noé plantation, where they killed the manager and the head of the refinery. They spared the life of Mongès the surgeon and his wife. It was on that last plantation that the fire started around midnight.[1]

As Jacques de Cauna has shown, the path of the insurrection can be followed on eighteenth-century maps of the coastal plain of Cap-Français.[2] The Noé plantation was in a district called Les Manquets, in Acul Parish, at the southern extremity of the plain, where the road starts climbing toward Dondon and Marmelade. It is not clear where exactly the Turpin-Flaville and Clément plantations were located, but the name "Trémès" (Trémais) is already known to us.[3] In 1782, Charles de Trémais and his wife, Marie-Elizabeth Lamerenx, prosperous coffee growers in the mountainous parish of Marmelade, purchased two plantations in the neighboring Acul Parish. One plantation featured a large warehouse (50 by 20 feet) that was used to store coffee crops. When the insurrection broke out, the warehouse contained one hundred tons of coffee.[4] The location was convenient, with easy access to ships in Cap-Français via the coastal plain. This allowed the planters greater control of how and when coffee was sold. (Shipping coffee directly from Marmelade, on the other hand, required mule convoys on a bad road.) Jean Mouscardy made a similar move around the same time. He bought a small lot in the same area with a building measuring 24 by 12 feet.[5] It was on his newly acquired Acul properties that Charles de Trémais died in 1784 at sixty years of age.[6] The burial certificate was signed by a few relatives and neighbors, including Jean-Pierre Lamerenx of Dondon, whose emigration from La Bastide Clairence we discussed in chapter 3, and Monsieur de Flaville, on whose plantation the uprising started in 1791. (The co-owner of the Flaville plantation, the marquise de Turpin, was an absentee owner who lived in Paris; she had purchased a share in the property as a high-risk, high-reward investment just a few years earlier.) The Trémais warehouse was adjacent to the Noé plantation, right across the Haut-du-Cap River.[7] We can infer from these details that the uprising started on four plantations whose masters knew one another and whose slaves likewise knew one another.

From Acul the uprising spread to the neighboring parish of Limbé, and on September 10 the insurgent slaves lead by Jeannot, a slave from the Bullet plantation,[8] took the town of Dondon. The fall of Dondon was a remarkable event because the colonists made an all-out effort to defend the town and were defeated after a one-day bloody battle. In the archives of the Garran-Coulon commission there is a detailed narrative of the event by Jean Drevet, the militia commander who defended the town.[9] From this account we learn that the colonists formed six groups of twenty-five to thirty men each that they posted in strategic locations across the parish, with instructions to retreat toward the church if they were in danger of being overrun by insurgents. Jean-Pierre Lamerenx commanded one of those six groups, as captain in what had been the colonial militia and was now called the Garde nationale, or National Guard.

At nine in the morning, the insurgents were setting fire to plantations close to the town. The colonists regrouped near the church and fired on successive waves of insurgents with shotguns, two cannons, and a stone-throwing mortar. At three thirty in the afternoon, the insurgents were retreating. Drevet, the colonists' leader, shouted: "Long live the nation!" The insurgents replied: "Long live the king!"[10] The insurgents included a large group of free coloreds (some of them on horseback), who showed particular animus against Drevet. As he was reloading his shotgun, the (unnamed) leader of the free coloreds shouted several times: "My friends, we must shoot the head of the wicked Drevet!" And he added: "Drevet, this one is for you!" Hearing this, Drevet (if we are to believe his own account) showed his behind to the assailant and yelled: "Shoot, scamp!"[11] As the historian Yves Benot indicates, free coloreds had particular reason to hate Drevet, who had played a key role in the brutal repression of the rebellion led by Vincent Ogé, a free man of color and property owner from Dondon.[12] Ogé had been seeking political rights for free coloreds and was broken on the wheel in Cap-Français on February 6, 1791. The memory of that event was still fresh. The insurgents brought in reinforcements and attacked again, thousands strong. At five thirty in the afternoon the colonists abandoned their fortified post in the church and retreated toward a camp in the hills above Acul, the Camp des Mornets, headed by Nicolas Dubison, a militia captain.

The attack left 53 defenders dead and 32 wounded (out of approximately 200).[13] If one includes the wounded defenders who died in camps in the following days, the number of dead was 77, including 7 free mulattoes and 1 free black fighting on the colonists' side.[14] According to the parish priest, Guillaume Silvestre Delahaye, who had good relations with both sides, the insurgents had approximately 500 dead and 300 wounded.[15] The fall of Dondon was a wake-up call for the colonists. It showed that the slaves, who had been assumed incapable of organizing themselves, were capable of mounting and sustaining a military operation. (As a matter of fact, many of the recently arrived Africans had military experience, having been enslaved as a result of a civil war in the Kingdom of Congo.)[16] Colonists started to defend the countryside by setting up camps in strategic locations. The insurgents followed the same tactic: "They too set up camps in the districts they occupied. Their great numbers, their vigor, and their nimbleness allowed them to continuously harass the whites."[17] Holding Dondon, which was on the border with the Spanish part of the island, the insurgents were able to get supplies from the Spanish, who, despite their official neutrality, were happy to provide gunpowder and bullets in exchange for goods and cattle seized by the insurgents on the plantations. Once Jeannot had taken Dondon, he installed Fayet, a free man of color and a relative of Ogé's, as leader of the parish. The insurgents did not try to attack the neighboring town of Marmelade, which was defended by white and free-colored militias as part of a plan to contain the insurrection from the Partie du Nord (Northern Province). Marmelade did not fall until it was taken two years later by black auxiliaries of the Spanish army.[18]

According to the militia officer who led the defense of Dondon, the insurgents had pledged allegiance to "the king" (Louis XVI), while the colonists had pledged allegiance to "the nation" (the revolutionary government, which was in open conflict with the king). It was only three years later that the black slaves and the French Republic began to fight on the same side. Seen from Paris, the slave insurrection looked and felt similar to the uprising of royalist and Catholic peasants in the Vendée. Early testimonies regarding the Saint-Domingue uprising suggest that the slaves saw themselves as defenders of the king, who they believed had decreed major improvements in their working conditions but had been thwarted by colonial authorities. The manager of the Clément plantation (one of the four plantations where the insurrection started) reported a conversation he had with two insurgent slaves who held him in custody during the first night of the uprising. According to these slaves, the insurrection was a royalist plot:

> I asked them who could be the instigators of such a vast event and what their purpose was in committing so many crimes. They answered that it was the high-ranking whites of France, that their goal was to punish us for having dethroned the king, and because we no longer had either faith, or law, or religion, and because we had burned the royal decree that gave the blacks three free days a week at Port-au-Prince. The two blacks said that if they had not received orders from these important whites to revolt in order to contribute to the restoration of the king to his throne, the question that concerned them would not have driven them to such extremes, seeing that in any event they were not intelligent enough and lacked the facilities to conceive of such a vast project, which consisted of nothing less than the destruction of all the whites except some who didn't own

property, some priests, some surgeons, and some women, and of setting fire to all the plantations and making themselves masters of the country.[19]

This testimony seems to be the stuff of conspiracy theories. Royalists in high places would have engineered the slave revolt to undermine governmental authority on the island and consequently weaken the revolutionary government in Paris. There is no clear evidence that such a plot took place, but it is certain that the 1791 slave insurrection took place in the name of king and church. The other remarkable detail in this testimony is that from the beginning, insurgents expressed an intention to wage an all-out war against white rule on the island. We have a testimony by a French official named Gabriel Le Gros, who spent several weeks in Dondon as a prisoner of the insurgent slaves starting in late October 1791. It too emphasizes the pledges of loyalty to the king. Le Gros reported that he heard "the same talk among all Negroes. Everywhere it was believed that the king had been imprisoned and had ordered that they take up arms to free him. The destruction of the clergy and the nobility was not unknown to them."[20] At that point news of the arrest and suspension of the king following his flight to Varennes on June 21, 1791, had indeed reached the colony. According to François de Kerverseau, a French general who was a fierce critic of Toussaint Louverture but had a clear sense of his abilities and ambitions, Toussaint had been the mastermind of the insurgency from the very beginning, choosing the leaders behind the scenes and producing authoritative documents because in the leadership group only he could read and write. His interests had initially been aligned with those of the royalists, but one could not tell who manipulated whom.[21]

Three Widows Make a Plea

On September 18, 1793, three French women refugees wrote to the Spanish governor of Santo Domingo, Joaquín García y Moreno, to ask for assistance. They told similar stories, in slightly different language. Since the beginning of the insurrection they had been living in San Rafael, a small town of one thousand inhabitants on the Spanish side of the border, less than eight miles from Dondon. The first letter writer, Marie-Elizabeth Lamerenx, widow Trémais, speaking of herself in the third person, as was the rule in such requests, wrote that she was "the mother of six children, three of whom are currently with her, one married, and the youngest two in France to pursue their education." (The youngest two were being raised by relatives in Tours, Prudent-Jean Bruley and his wife, Marie-Valentine Loiseau, absentee owners of plantations in Dondon and Marmelade.)[22] Marie-Elizabeth had lost all her cash holdings in the great fire of Cap-Français (which began on June 20, 1793), and the warehouse where she had kept one hundred tons of coffee in stock had burned down around the same time. She had owned "four plantations, well built, and lacking nothing," all of which had burned down. "Such a picture," she concluded, "is heartbreaking for a sensitive soul who sacrificed her life for her children's happiness."[23] The second petitioner, Marguerite-Françoise Lamerenx, widow Saint-Germain, was the younger sister of the first. She explained that she had owned "one of the handsomest coffee manufactures in the La Guille District of Dondon Parish; two years ago her slaves rebelled and would have cut her throat if it had not been for the assistance of the Spanish commander, who has protected her since." "It is in San Rafael," she added, "that she has enjoyed the tranquility of which her unhappy homeland is deprived."[24] The third letter was written by the mother of the first two petitioners, Elizabeth Le Jeune, widow of Marc-Antoine Lamerenx d'Uhart, the "first emigrant" in our story. It began as follows: "Seventy years old, for more than twenty years the widow of a cavalry captain, having lost a son who was received into the king's household in 1770, how can Madame d'Uhart, through no fault of her own, after years of constant, hard, and tedious work, having overcome all obstacles and reached a brilliant fortune, be reduced to such an underserved, dreadful future?"[25]

There is a sense of bitterness in the mother's letter that is less apparent in the daughters' pleas. Elizabeth Le Jeune, who came from a family of early settlers, had known Dondon as an entirely wooded and undeveloped area and had started a coffee plantation on lots given to her by royal grant. She and her husband had started off with a small number of slaves and reinvested profits into the purchase of additional slaves to cultivate a larger and larger area. It had indeed been a slow process, and she had not made her fortune quickly. Elizabeth said twice in the same sentence that she was blameless and that her fate was undeserved. It goes without saying that for her the legitimacy of slavery was a self-evident truth. Elizabeth had been able to support herself until recently because of funds she had had in custody with an agent in Cap-Français, but she had now lost "everything she had in currency or credits" in the great fire. The letter has a slightly odd ending. Elizabeth mentioned that she could no longer count on the income from her plantation in Dondon, since the entire parish was now "but ruins and ashes." The loss was especially grave, she said, because the water mills used to process coffee had just been rebuilt with mahogany imported from the Spanish side of the island. In addition to the cost of lumber itself, she had had to pay import duties. The Spanish side was far less developed and populated than the French side, and it had become a source of wood imports for the French colonists because deforestation on the French side had reached an advanced stage. The customs duties Elizabeth had to pay cannot have been very large, and they would appear to have been a trivial amount compared with the totality of her fortune. That she chose to end on such a detail is indicative of the mind-set of a colonist who was bent on turning a penny however she could.

The Spanish governor forwarded the letters to his superior in Madrid, Pedro de Acuña, secretary of state for graces and justice. He recommended "three honorable families of merit and misfortune, a septuagenarian lady, all accustomed to wealth and comfort; they have no recourse other than the piety of the King of Spain, to whom they have sworn allegiance, submission, and eternal loyalty."[26] He indicated that the widows had been receiving a daily allowance of four reales per person. This, he said, was not sufficient to cover their living expenses according to a budget the women had submitted, which did not even include clothing, shoes, or laundry. He recommended that the assistance be doubled and set at one Spanish dollar per person per day.

The governor and the local military commander advocated chivalrously on behalf of the French widows, but at least one Spanish official expressed skepticism about the women's loyalty to Spain and the extent of their need. A few weeks earlier, on August 5, 1793, Father José Vázquez, a mixed-race parish priest who had played a key role in enlisting the insurgent leaders Jean-François and Biassou in the service of the king of Spain,[27] had written to the archbishop of Santo Domingo to report that the women were wealthy and rented the best two houses in San Rafael. They had crossed the border with a large retinue of household slaves. These black and mulatto slaves, he averred, had shown reprehensible sexual behavior because men and women lived together unmarried. Even worse, "they do not even make a pretense of being Christian, and in two years they have never been to confession, they never talk about God, and the only thing they have displayed is great joy when the French win a military engagement."[28] It is interesting that the women's household slaves would have manifested pro-French sentiments. At that point, most of the insurgent slaves, led by Jean-François, Biassou, and Toussaint Louverture, were fighting on the Spanish side against the French republican forces on the island.[29] The French had promised freedom to the slaves who fought on their side, but so had the Spanish and the English. Still, there were rumors that the French would emancipate all the slaves, which was what did happen. On August 29, 1793, Léger-Félicité Sonthonax, the French civil commissioner, issued a declaration of emancipation for all the slaves in the Northern Province.

We know what happened to the women afterwards from a letter of recommendation that Joaquín Cabrera, who had been the military commander for the border region, wrote for Marie-Elizabeth Lamerenx, widow Trémais, in 1799. He explained that because the women were ill, he had given them passports to travel to La Hincha, which they thought had a better climate. Because the climate in La Hincha did not suit them either, they had moved to Bánica, then to San Juan de la Maguana (further and further east). It was there that Marie-Elizabeth Lamerenx lost her son, her sister, and her mother, who all died of illness "amid the greatest anxiety and grief." On January 2, 1796, Marie-Elizabeth made it to Havana, Cuba, with two surviving daughters.[30] She and her daughters were still living when the Haitian government agreed to pay an indemnity to former colonists in exchange for diplomatic recognition by France in 1825.

Haitian Memories of 1791

Démesvar Delorme (1831–1901) was one of the founding fathers of Haitian literature (Fig. 4.1). He authored numerous essays and works of fiction and was minister of foreign affairs in the administration of President Salnave. He served as Haiti's first ambassador to Germany (1891–93) and later as ambassador to the Holy See. (His second wife, Antonia Hupp, whom he married in London in 1887, was a German citizen.)[31] He died in Paris in 1901. In 1876 he wrote down memories of his youth that remained unpublished until 1942, when one of his relatives published some excerpts.[32] The occasion was the one-hundredth anniversary of the earthquake that had devastated the city of Cap-Haïtien (formerly Cap-Français). Delorme had been only eleven at the time, but his recollection of the event was very specific. His narrative included many details about his background and education, as well as portraits of his relatives, including his great-uncle, who had seen great promise in him and had shown him great affection. The great-uncle was an army general named Jean-Théodat Mouscardy, who had commanded the Grande-Rivière military district. Widespread looting had taken place after the earthquake. Mouscardy's troops had helped restore order in Cap-Haïtien and given assistance to the population. As we saw in chapter 2, Jean-Théodat Mouscardy was the eldest of the six children that Jean Mouscardy, a colonist from La Bastide Clairence, had with his household manager, a free woman of color named Françoise Alzire.

In Delorme's description, Jean-Théodat Mouscardy "was passionate about everything that seemed to show distinction or honor." The general himself had never discussed his own origins, but his sister (Delorme's grandmother) said that he had inherited his proud character from his father, "one of those French colonists of noble birth who, while they lived the sumptuous existence of Saint-Domingue's great planters, never showed harshness or contempt toward the oppressed race."[33] On the other hand, like the other *grands blancs* (wealthy whites), General Mouscardy's father had shown contempt for the *petits blancs* (poor whites). According to Delorme, racism toward slaves and free coloreds was something that came mainly from the poor whites.

During colonial times Jean-Théodat Mouscardy was a free man of color. He had spent several years in France, where his father had sent him to be educated. (Vincent Ogé, the free-colored rebel from Dondon, had a similar trajectory, apprenticing as a goldsmith in Bordeaux from 1766 to 1774.)[34] Upon returning to his father's house, "he lived the life of a great lord, and shared his father's habits of colonial pride." Thus, he had "the exceptional privilege" for a man of

Fig. 4.1. Démesvar Delorme (1831–1901), undated photograph. Delorme was the great-grandson of Jean Mouscardy, a colonist from La Bastide Clairence, and Françoise Alzire, a free woman of color. Courtesy of Imprimerie Théodore, Port-au-Prince.

African origin, that of standing above "the caste of *petits blancs* who engaged in trade," and he had "a profound contempt for those who had contempt for slaves and mistreated them."[35] Jean-Théodat's father, Jean Mouscardy, decided to stay in the colony in spite of the revolutionary upheaval. Most of his friends had fled to Louisiana or Cuba. He, however, "having nothing to fear, stayed until the last moment." The last moment was the massacre of white colonists ordered by Dessalines in 1804. "He was going to be slaughtered like the others," but he was saved by his eldest son, Jean-Théodat, who carried his elderly and disabled father on his back "at night, through the woods, stopping once in a while on plantations where he had acquaintances or friends."[36] Father and son eventually reached Cap-Français, and the son put his father, along with all the money he had, on an American brig headed to Boston.

Archival evidence suggests a different chronology of events. We know from

Fig. 4.2. The Great Fire of Cap-Français, June 21, 1793 (detail). Colored engraving by Jean-Baptiste Chapuy after a 1794 painting by Pierre-Jean Boquet (1751–1817).

the file regarding Mouscardy's sequestered properties that the father left his plantation in Marmelade in 1791, after it was burned down in the early days of the insurrection. He took refuge in Cap-Français in the house of his agent and close friend Jean Larroque, who was also the guardian of his mixed-race children. On June 20, 1793, during the huge riot that destroyed large parts of the city (Fig. 4.2), looters attacked Larroque's house. Larroque was away. Mouscardy, who was inside, narrowly escaped death. The looters set fire to the house. All the money and papers that Larroque was keeping in custody for his friends and business partners disappeared, including 112,000 livres belonging to Mouscardy. The historian Jeremy Popkin estimates that between three thousand and ten thousand people died during the rioting, which he calls "the most murderous instance of urban conflict in the entire history of the Americas."[37] (As David Geggus points out, the sack of Tenochtitlán in 1521 would probably rank higher on the scale of disaster.)[38] According to Larroque's testimony, as a result of the destruction of Larroque's house, Mouscardy "had nothing left, had lost everything," and consequently lacked the funds to leave the colony. Larroque raised the necessary funds, twenty-five Portuguese gold coins, from a group of friends.[39] On July 13, 1793, as was the custom for those leaving the colony, Mouscardy published a notice in the local newspaper, *Affiches américaines*, indicating his imminent departure to the United States and his desire to settle accounts with debtors and creditors. A few weeks later he sailed to New England and continued on to Bayonne, France, where he owned a townhouse that was occupied by his nephews. He arrived in Bayonne in February 1794 and stayed there until his death three years later.

Before comparing the narrative coming from family tradition with the narrative suggested by archival evidence, it is worth mentioning another family story that bears many similarities to the story told by Démesvar Delorme. One of Jean Mouscardy's neighbors in Marmelade was a planter from Normandy named Jean-Valentin Vastey, who like Mouscardy had several mixed-race children. One of these children, Jean-Louis Vastey, became the *éminence grise* of King Christophe, who ruled the northern part of Haiti from 1811 to 1820 and made Vastey a baron. He is best known for his book *The Colonial System Unveiled*, which was arguably the first critique of slavery written from the perspective of the former slaves. (While the author had been a free man of color and a property owner, he spoke on behalf of all Haitians.) According to testimony given in 1936 by the white planter's great-grandson, a Haitian lawyer named Louis-Marie de Vastey, in 1895 a former slave of the Vastey plantation named Djebou had spoken warmly of Jean-Valentin Vastey, the white planter from Normandy. He had always been good to his slaves and had never mistreated them. The slaves had looked up to him as a father and called him *yon bon papa pitite*, a Haitian Creole expression meaning a good father to his children. When the insurrection broke out, he had had nothing to fear from his slaves, and when Dessalines ordered the massacre of white colonists, the former slaves had resolved to organize the escape of their former master. They had blackened his face, arms, and legs, pulled up his trousers in the style of plantation workers, put a blue handkerchief on his head, put him on a mule, and carried him by night on a long trip to the shores of the sea of Limbé, where he had boarded a schooner.[40] Now, of course this is hearsay about hearsay, and it is hard to believe that the person who testified in 1895 could have had firsthand knowledge of an event that supposedly took place in 1804. What is remarkable is that in both family traditions, there was a strongly idealized image of the white planter who was protected by his slaves until the end because he had been good to them.

In many ways the Mouscardy family legend as told by Delorme is idealized and fanciful. Nevertheless, several details that were handed down through oral tradition are true, and the story itself is a good indication of the kind of relationship that may have existed between Mouscardy and his mixed-race children. Contrary to what his Haitian descendants believed, Mouscardy did not stay in Saint-Domingue until the end. He escaped his plantation in the early days of the insurrection and left the colony two years later, after the great fire of Cap-Français. He sailed to Boston, as his descendants remembered many decades later. It is worth noting that Jean Larroque, his agent and the guardian of his mulatto children, did stay until the end and was killed during the April 1804 massacre of white colonists in Cap-Français.[41] Delorme, who had a classical education, gave a description of the young Jean-Théodat Mouscardy carrying his elderly father on his back. The vignette was clearly borrowed from Virgil (Aeneas fleeing the burning city of Troy with his father Anchises on his back). Yet there is no reason to doubt that Mouscardy was helped by his mixed-race children to escape his plantation and take refuge in Cap-Français in 1791.

There is no independent testimony about whether Mouscardy treated his slaves humanely. There is, however, evidence that Mouscardy wished to establish his mulatto children, even though they were not his legal heirs. As we saw in chapter 2, he arranged for them to own one large, mostly undeveloped coffee plantation in 1784. His heirs under French law were designated in a will he wrote in 1788, naming the children of his sister Marie.[42] These nephews, who lived in the townhouse he owned in Bayonne, received compensation from the Haitian government in 1829 for the plantation in Marmelade and a house in Cap-Français. There is no reason to doubt that Jean-Théodat and his siblings had warm feelings for their father and mother, the white planter and the black household manager, who, as we saw in chapter 2, lived as a couple and were known as a couple in the neighborhood. Contrary to what Delorme says, Mouscardy was not noble: he was the younger son of peasants from La Bastide Clairence. Nevertheless, his fortune was almost as brilliant as the fortune of his compatriot and neighbor Marc-Antoine Lamerenx, whose nobility was certified by the king in 1770. Back in Lower Navarre, Mouscardy and Lamerenx would have been very far apart in the social hierarchy. In Saint-Domingue, they both belonged to the class of *grands blancs*.

There is no way of knowing whether Mouscardy was in fact kind to his slaves, but Delorme's insistence that it was the case (and the same insistence we find in the Vastey family tradition) is indicative of the status of free coloreds during colonial times as well as of their position after Haitian independence. In Saint-Domingue there was stiff competition between free coloreds, who were born on the island and were often prosperous property owners, and *petits blancs*, recent immigrants from France who were often struggling economically. Until the 1760s, wealthy free coloreds were more or less accepted as members of the colonial elite, but after the Seven Years' War, following an influx of poor white immigrants who claimed racial solidarity with *grands blancs* against free coloreds, colonial administrators began to enact measures of symbolic humiliation of free people of color.[43] It was in that context that "a new ideology of white purity" began to be used as a justification for discrimination.[44] From the point of view of poor whites, slaves and free coloreds had in common the fact that they belonged to an inferior race. Conversely, from the point of view of free coloreds, *petits blancs* belonged to an inferior social class. (This is another case in which relations of superiority and inferiority "cease[d] to be transitive," to borrow the expression from Lévi-Strauss quoted in chapter 3.)[45] The relationship between free coloreds and slaves was a complicated one, ranging from mutual hatred and contempt to empathy and solidarity. The official doctrine of the Haitian Republic, as stated in the Constitution of 1805, was that all citizens were "generically black" regardless of ethnic origin or former status under colonial rule.[46] This "black" solidarity between free coloreds and slaves was retrospectively inscribed in the Mouscardy and Vastey family stories. The evils of racism were blamed entirely on poor whites, and the *grand blanc* ancestor was construed as someone who shared the same values of honor and decency as his black children.

Sequestration of Properties

Jean Mouscardy's plantation in Marmelade was sequestered by the French authorities on October 23, 1795. The two plantations that Marie-Elizabeth Lamerenx owned in the same parish, then known as *petite place* and *grande place*, were sequestered on February 5 and 8, 1795, respectively. A similar process occurred in Dondon Parish, but the records for those years have not survived. The Mouscardy plantation was handed over to two associated farmers, the citizens Alexis and Aly, who leased the property beginning on August 3, 1797. The rent, payable in kind to the government, was 1,000 pounds of coffee per year. The smaller Trémais plantation was leased beginning on July 30, 1797, for 1,067 pounds of coffee per year. The contract for the larger Trémais plantation began on October 8, 1797, and had an annual rent of 1,334 pounds of coffee.[47]

The legal rationale for these actions was given on August 27, 1793, by the civil commissioner of the French Republic, Etienne Polverel, who decreed that absent owners had forfeited their property rights. "The right to property," Polverel declared, "cannot exist without a protective force; such force can exist only as the coming together of the individual forces of all proprietors, because those who have nothing cannot be expected to sacrifice their lives for the defense of the properties of others."[48] As a consequence of this principle, "those who abandoned or betrayed the common defense"[49] would be stripped of their rights to movable and immovable property in the colony, and their properties would be distributed to the loyal republicans (most of them former slaves) who were fighting for the defense of the colony. Polverel's declaration was ambitious politically and philosophically: "The African race has been slandered for a long time; it is said that without slavery it will never develop habits of work. May the experiment that I am about to conduct belie this prejudice, which is no less absurd than the hierarchy of colors."[50] For Polverel, the distribution of property to former slaves would demonstrate that in the Antilles as in Europe the land could be cultivated by free labor. Ultimately, planters elsewhere in the British and Spanish Antilles would understand their true interests and turn their slaves into salaried workers because of the greater productivity of free labor (an economic argument put forward by Adam Smith and others, as we saw in chapter 2).

Under the new organization decreed by Polverel, the former slaves would get one-third of the net revenue of the plantation, payable to them by the farmer leasing the property or by the owner, if he or she had not left the colony. One important feature of the new organization was that former slaves were not free to leave the plantation and could be arrested for vagrancy if they did. Slavery had been abolished, but it had been replaced by a system of forced labor. The civil commissioners calculated that the wealth of the colony was based on the plantation system, and they feared that abolishing that system would bring about economic collapse.[51]

As Gabriel Debien points out, Polverel's decree was less radical than it seems, and largely respectful of property rights.[52] There was no outright expropriation followed by transfer of ownership to former slaves. The republican government sequestered the properties of planters who had left the island and leased them to private citizens, but the absent proprietor still had title. As custodian, the state was responsible for managing debts and receivables attached to the property. In addition, the sequestration of abandoned properties had been standard practice in the *ancien régime*. Originally the land had been the property of the king, who had made grants to the colonists with the understanding that they would develop it. The law mandated that if the colonists did not develop the land within a reasonable period of time, it would revert to the king. There was longstanding jurisprudence in that respect. A 1683 decree by the Council of State stipulated that land should revert to the state if it remained undeveloped for three years, and the governor of the colony had the final say in deciding the expropriation, which was called a *réunion* (return of the land to the king's domain).[53] A similar procedure of *réunion* was applied in 1688 to properties left behind by Protestants who fled France following the Revocation of the Edict of Nantes.[54]

As to Polverel's declaration that those who did not participate in the common defense of private properties had forfeited their property rights, it was consistent with the doctrine applied to émigrés in continental France. Nobles who fled the country following the Revolution were suspected to be in the service of the enemies of the nation. It was lawful to expropriate an enemy, but leaving the country was not a crime in and of itself. In addition, establishing treason required a high standard of proof and an in-depth investigation into individual cases. Yet, even if they were not engaged in active warfare against France, émigrés were civilly liable for their failure to participate in the common defense of French private properties, and their possessions could lawfully be seized to offset the consequences of such dereliction of duty. This formed the basis for the law of April 8, 1792, ordering the sequestration of émigré properties.[55] Jean-Pierre

Lamerenx, who was still a significant landowner in his hometown of La Bastide Clairence, was the target of an investigation by the municipal government in September 1794. A Saint-Domingue colonist from La Bastide Clairence named Jean Hiriart, who was back home to take care of some business, was asked about the whereabouts of Lamerenx, whom the town officials suspected of being an émigré. Hiriart testified that he had indeed known Lamerenx and his family back in the colony and that according to some reports Lamerenx had crossed over to the Spanish side of the island.[56] The information was correct. What Hiriart and the town officials could not have known is that Lamerenx was now fighting for the French Republic under the command of Toussaint Louverture (more on this later). In any case, the investigation never went any further, and Lamerenx's properties in France were not sequestered.

Debien says there is little information about the practical and economic consequences of the reorganization decreed by Polverel.[57] Regarding the commune of Marmelade, we do have a detailed table describing the state of sequestered properties at the beginning of the first lease in 1797 and as of May 20, 1798. The data regarding the Mouscardy and Trémais properties are summarized in table 4.1. We can see that from 1797 to 1798 there was a small increase in the number of *cultivateurs* (the word used to designate former slaves) working on each property and a modest effort to rehabilitate their dwellings. It also appears that the vast majority of former slaves did remain on the plantations or returned to the plantations if they left after the 1791 insurrection.

We have an itemized list of the Trémais plantation slaves in Marmelade recorded by a notary in 1788.[58] It shows 38 men and 32 women, including all adult plantation workers but excluding slaves attached to the household. The fact that 87 adult cultivators were working on the Trémais plantations in 1797 would suggest that all the plantation workers and some of the former household slaves did in fact stay on the plantation. (We know that some household slaves accompanied the owner in her flight to San Rafael.) Regarding the Mouscardy plantation, in chapter 2 we estimated that on the eve of the Revolution it had between 135 and 160 slaves (including children). This would suggest that a larger proportion left the plantation, but a significant number were still there in 1797. It is safe to assume that on both plantations from 1791 to 1797 the coffee trees were left unattended and were quickly overgrown by the natural vegetation of the island. The occupants of the land probably dedicated themselves to subsistence farming, which was a continuation of the practice under the slavery regime: slaves were expected to support themselves in part by growing their own food. Table 4.1 also shows that there was an effort to replant coffee trees or perhaps to reclaim existing coffee trees from the newly grown forest. On the Mouscardy plantation the number of coffee trees tripled from 1797 to 1798. It increased by about 50 percent during the same period on the Trémais plantations.

TABLE 4.1.
Cultivation status of Mouscardy and Trémais plantations, Marmelade

	Mouscardy Plantation		Trémais Plantations	
	1797	1798	1797	1798
Lease price (in pounds of coffee)	1,000	1,000	2,400	2,400
Property size (in *carreaux*)	100	100	140	140
Number of cultivators (adults)	56	58	82	87
Number of coffee trees	3,000	9,050	7,200	11,000
Number of buildings	16	17	23	24

Source: Based on tallies of sequestered properties in the commune of Marmelade, ANOM, Fonds ministériels, Dépôt des papiers publics des colonies, Saint-Domingue, Recensement des biens domaniaux et urbains, an III [1795]–1814, DPPC 5SUPSDOM 2.

Note: The data for the Trémais plantations have been merged into one property.

The production, however, was still only a fraction of what it had been under the slavery regime. In 1798 the Trémais plantation had 11,000 coffee trees attended by 87 workers. In 1788 the same plantation had had a comparable number of workers attending 126,900 coffee trees.[59]

A White Plantation Owner Serves under a Black General

After the fall of Dondon in September 1791, Jean-Pierre Lamerenx took refuge in the Camp des Mornets, a defense post occupied by progovernment forces that was part of a larger system called Cordon de l'Ouest, designed to prevent the insurrection from spreading from the Northern Province to the rest of the colony. We have no details about his whereabouts during that period. He may have served in the Camp des Mornets or in the neighboring town of Marmelade, which was part of the Cordon de l'Ouest, or in Cap-Français. What is known with certainty is that in November 1792 Jean-Pierre Lamerenx crossed the border with three other Garde nationale officers from Dondon and put himself under the protection of the Spanish authorities. On November 25, 1792, the Spanish governor, Joaquín García, wrote to Madrid to report that "Mr. Lamerens, military commander in Dondon before it was taken over by the Negroes," had submitted a petition for asylum to Colonel Joaquín Cabrera, the Spanish commander for the border region. Colonel Cabrera approved the request, but he did not want Lamerenx and his fellow officers to stay in San Rafael, because the town was too close to the French border. Therefore, he sent them to La Hincha. Lamerenx and his fellow officers reportedly wished "to protect their lives from the danger of proscription and the envy of their rivals, who had requested their arrest and deportation to France."[60]

Who were those rivals who wanted Lamerenx deported to France? It is highly likely that Lamerenx was caught in the conflict between royalists and republicans that erupted within the white community in the Northern Province in the fall of 1792. On October 18, the municipal government in Cap-Français decreed that leaders of the royalist faction would be deported to France, and several were put on ships the following day. Several army officers with royalist sympathies were removed from their posts and replaced by republican loyalists. According to Thomas Madiou, "The class of wealthy white landowners was dealt a mortal blow during the days of October 17, 18, and 19. The old colonial aristocracy was annihilated in the North. In this instance Polverel and Sonthonax served the interests of blacks and browns by having whites crush whites."[61] In part the case against royalist officers was based on the belief that they sympathized with the slave insurrection and coordinated secretly with its leaders. It is not known where Lamerenx's sympathies lay at that point, but clearly some believed he was not loyal to the republic. We will see that a few months later he joined the ranks of the slave army that was fighting for the king of Spain under the command of Toussaint Louverture.[62]

In early 1793 the French republican troops were having some successes against the Spanish and the insurgent slaves. On January 27, 1793, a French commander named Neuilly, serving under General Laveaux, who headed the French republican forces, retook the town of Dondon.[63] There were jealousies and infighting among the black military leaders who fought on the Spanish side. Toussaint Louverture was imprisoned by Jean-François, who feared him. He was freed by Biassou, who was Jean-François's rival. Upon his release, Toussaint Louverture put himself under the command of Matías de Armona, the Spanish officer who had succeeded Joaquín Cabrera as commander of the border region. He was given the rank of camp marshal (brigadier general). With six hundred well-trained black troops he took the town of Marmelade in the early summer of 1793. Many of the republican troops defending the town switched sides and put themselves under his command. According to Toussaint Louverture's son Isaac, following the takeover of Marmelade, "all the white landowners of the area and of Plaisance, who had taken refuge in San Rafael and other Spanish possessions, returned to Marmelade."[64]

Toussaint made several appointments: "For the civil administration of the area he appointed the white landowners Gilbin and Copet, and Jean-Baptiste Poparel for the military. For his aides-de-camp he took Dubuisson, a native of Bayonne, and Birete, a young white landowner from Marmelade."[65] These names should sound familiar, especially if one goes beyond the printed version and checks the spelling in Isaac Louverture's manuscript. Julbin and Cappé were major landowners from Marmelade: Pierre Cappé was the troublesome neighbor discussed in chapter 2, who was known for his atrocities against slaves, and Pierre-Basile Julbin de Saint-Vertry was a neighbor whose plantation bordered both the Cappé and the Trémais plantations (see Fig. 2.2). Jean-Baptiste Paparel, also a landowner, was one of the Garde nationale leaders who switched sides during the attack on Marmelade by Toussaint. Pierre Biret owned a small plantation in Marmelade that had been managed a few years earlier by Jean-Pierre Colombots, a young immigrant from La Bastide Clairence.[66] According to Isaac's account, following the takeover of Marmelade, Toussaint Louverture's reputation among white colonists was extremely high: "Everyone was happy with him; they kept talking about his high-minded genius, his courage, and his magnanimity."[67]

In the printed version of Isaac Louverture's memoirs, Jean-Pierre Lamerenx appears a few pages later as an aide-de-camp of Toussaint's who was personally saved from danger by his general during a military engagement that took place in the early summer of 1794, shortly after Toussaint decided to switch sides and put himself under the command of the French republican commander, General Laveaux: "In this campaign, on the left bank of the Artibonite River, he extracted Captain Lamérens, his aide-de-camp, who was surrounded by six Spanish troops, and he wounded one enemy soldier."[68] Toussaint's decision to switch sides was undoubtedly connected to the emancipation proclamation made by Sonthonax on August 29, 1793, but the causal chain and Toussaint's "true" motives have been a matter of speculation.[69] The emancipation was ratified by the French National Convention on February 4, 1794, and the news took at least a couple of months to reach the colony. If Isaac Louverture's account is to be trusted, by the time Toussaint Louverture decided to switch sides, Jean-Pierre Lamerenx was serving as his aide-de-camp, and the white officer and former slave owner stayed with his general when Toussaint switched to the French republican side. Here is how Isaac Louverture tells the story in the unpublished part of his manuscript: "Followed by his aides-de-camp Birette, Dubuisson, Charles Belair, and Lamérens, and by two officers of color, Lieutenant Colonel Dessalines and Captain Vène, who had escaped from Gonaïves, he departed from Marmelade, having decided to change the course of things and to deal with General Lavaux."[70]

According to Isaac, by the early summer of 1794, Toussaint had added two aides-de-camp to his staff: Charles Belair and Jean-Pierre Lamerenx. Belair was a very young black officer and Toussaint's nephew. Jean-Pierre Lamerenx is already familiar to us, but his behavior, as well as Toussaint Louverture's, may be a puzzle. In hindsight, the alignment of ideas, ideals, and interests would seem rather simple. Since the republic had declared universal human rights, we would expect the next step to have been the abolition of slavery, with the insurgent slaves rallying behind the republic. As to white planters, we would expect them to have defended their privileges and their properties by making alliances with the Spanish and/or the English against the French Republic.

What happened at the time and how the different actors calculated their interests was much more complicated. It may well be that general emancipation had been a part of Toussaint Louverture's game plan from the very beginning, but he initially made much more modest and limited demands.[71] In the first two years of the insurrection, what the French were offering in terms of emancipation of slaves who fought on their side was no more generous than Spanish or English policies. We must also recall that expropriating white planters and kicking them out of the colony does not seem to have been a part of Toussaint's plan. As we saw above, white planters who had taken refuge in San Rafael came back to Marmelade when Toussaint took the town from French republican forces. (We might note in passing that Toussaint's own wife also resided in San Rafael, where she may have befriended the three Lamerenx widows.) Toussaint calculated that the plantation system was the source of the island's wealth, and he wished to preserve it. When he became the leader of the entire colony, he retained the forced-labor system that Polverel had designed.

We might reconstruct the motivations of Jean-Pierre Lamerenx as follows. As a local militia officer and property owner, he took part in the defense of Dondon when the town was attacked by the insurgent slaves. During the following year, he fought against the insurgents on the side of French republican forces. Being a white, aristocratic landowner, he was suspected of royalist sympathies and fled to the Spanish side of the island. There he started serving under the command of Toussaint Louverture. That Toussaint picked him as an aide-de-camp seems entirely logical if we look at the names of Toussaint's staff as reported by his son Isaac: Biret was a white landowner from Marmelade; Lamerenx was a white landowner and militia officer from the neighboring town of Dondon. Toussaint chose locals whom he knew and trusted and who knew and trusted one another. Why did Lamerenx decide to stay with Toussaint Louverture when his general switched to the French republican side? He probably calculated that the emancipation of slaves was a *fait accompli* and something he could live with as long as he could resume possession of his coffee plantation. That was not an unrealistic prospect given Toussaint Louverture's record and stated plans.

After serving as Toussaint's aide-de-camp for about one year, Jean-Pierre Lamerenx was appointed battalion commander in the large army that Toussaint assembled during the summer of 1795. General Laveaux provided Toussaint with a batch of blank commissions that could be used to appoint or promote officers on the spot.[72] Lamerenx was put in charge of one battalion within the Seventh Regiment, made up of black volunteer troops, under Colonel Desrouleaux.[73] This regiment, according to Madiou, "comprised citizens of Soufrière, Grande-Rivière, Rivière Dorée, and Fond-Bleu."[74] Fond-Bleu was a district of Acul Parish. Grande-Rivière was a parish neighboring Dondon and Marmelade. Rivière Dorée and Soufrière were areas on the border between Marmelade and Acul Parishes. This means that Lamerenx's battalion was made up of soldiers who had been the slaves of his immediate neighbors. The Seventh Regiment distinguished itself in particular during the *affaire du 30 ventôse* (March 20, 1796), when Toussaint's forces had a decisive win against the English: "The following day, English troops who had survived the fury of their adversaries were completely defeated near Saint-Marc by General Toussaint Louverture, who had pursued them with his scouts and with a squad under Colonel Dessalines's command, and by Desrouleaux, colonel of the Seventh Regiment, who had attacked them from behind."[75]

It is not clear how long Jean-Pierre Lamerenx served in Toussaint Louverture's army. By 1800 he had left Saint-Domingue and was in the process of establishing a coffee plantation in Matanzas, Cuba. Unlike his cousin Marie-Elizabeth Lamerenx, who was in Cuba as well, he did not file an application to lift the sequestration of the coffee plantation he had in Dondon when plantation owners were invited to do so by Toussaint Louverture's government in the late 1790s. By that time his interests lay entirely elsewhere.

Toussaint Louverture as Guardian of Property Rights

At the beginning of the insurrection, the standard practice for the insurgents who seized a plantation was to burn down the buildings and the crops. (Often, rape and murder also took place, but apparently not systematically.)[76] As the uprising turned into a military operation, there was an effort to turn the slaves into disciplined soldiers. Jeannot, the slave leader who took Dondon, was sentenced to death and executed by another insurgent leader, Jean-François, on November 1, 1791, reportedly because of the atrocities he had committed during the first weeks of the insurrection. According to Madiou, it was Toussaint Louverture who had the most success in enforcing discipline among his troops. After Toussaint's switch to the French Republic, "many blacks who fought on behalf of the king of Spain followed his example and rallied to the republican side. He made them disciplined and forced them to respect private property."[77]

When Toussaint consolidated his rule over the colony, owners who had left their plantations were officially encouraged to file applications with the Domaines nationaux (the government body that administered sequestered properties) to have the sequestration lifted and resume possession of their plantations. The body was administered by Julien Raimond, a mixed-race property owner who was Toussaint Louverture's political ally. Of all the colonists whose trajectories we have followed in this story, three did file an application. Marc-Antoine Lamerenx's widow, Elizabeth Le Jeune, who died in Santo Domingo in 1795, did not file. Jean-Pierre Lamerenx, who owned a coffee plantation in Dondon, also did not file, because he was starting a new plantation in Cuba. Jean-Baptiste Aubert, a colonist who circulated between Havana and Cap-Français, filed applications on behalf of Marie-Elizabeth Lamerenx and on behalf of the estate of her sister, Marguerite-Françoise Lamerenx, who had died in Santo Domingo in 1795. (Aubert was Marie-Elizabeth Lamerenx's son-in-law, having recently married one of her daughters.)[78] Jean Larroque, a merchant based in Cap-Français, filed an application on behalf of the estate of his friend Jean Mouscardy, who had died in Bayonne in 1797.

The main point the applicants had to establish was that they were not émigrés in the service of the enemies of the republic: they had not left French territories, or if they had, they had done so because they had no other choice. For Mouscardy the case was easy to make: he had sailed from Cap-Français to Bayonne via Boston and had remained in France until his death in 1797. For the Lamerenx sisters the case was a lot harder to make because they had continuously resided in Spanish possessions since the beginning of the uprising. The letter of recommendation by Joaquín Cabrera, the Spanish colonel who gave them asylum in San Rafael in 1791, explained that their intention had always been to return to the French part of the island but that they had never been able to do so, "sometimes because blocked roadways were very dangerous, especially for persons of their sex, sometimes because their ill health did not allow it, and finally because there had been a great fire in Cap-Français, the city where they intended to take refuge."[79] Afterwards they were unable to cross the border because Spain and France were at war. When peace came, the lone survivor among the three Lamerenx widows meant to go to Cap-Français, but she had business in Havana and sailed there first.

Intent is always difficult to prove, but the Spanish officer's testimony seemed sufficient to the French officials in charge of sequestered properties. In any case, instructions from above were to look favorably on applications, and bribes undoubtedly accelerated the treatment of the dossiers. The applications of the Lamerenx sisters were successful. Mouscardy's application was successful as well. On July 8, 1801, the sequestration of Mouscardy's estate was lifted at the request of his agent, Jean Larroque.[80] The decree was signed by Toussaint Louverture, "general-in-chief" of the colony (Fig. 4.3). A few weeks later, Toussaint Louverture, who in the meantime had been appointed "governor of Saint-Domingue" by Napoleon Bonaparte, signed the decree lifting the sequestration of the properties of Marie-Elizabeth Lamerenx.[81] It took much longer to treat the dossier of her sister, Marguerite-Françoise, who had died, leaving only one heir, a daughter residing in the French city of Caen. The sequestration was lifted on March 6, 1803.[82] By then Toussaint Louverture was nearing the end of his life, imprisoned in a fortress on the French-Swiss border. The decree was signed by Donatien-Marie-Joseph Rochambeau, "captain general" of the colony, and cosigned by Hector Daure, "colonial prefect." Rochambeau, the son of the general who took part in the American War of Independence, had been in charge of the island after Charles Leclerc, sent by Napoleon to retake the colony from Toussaint

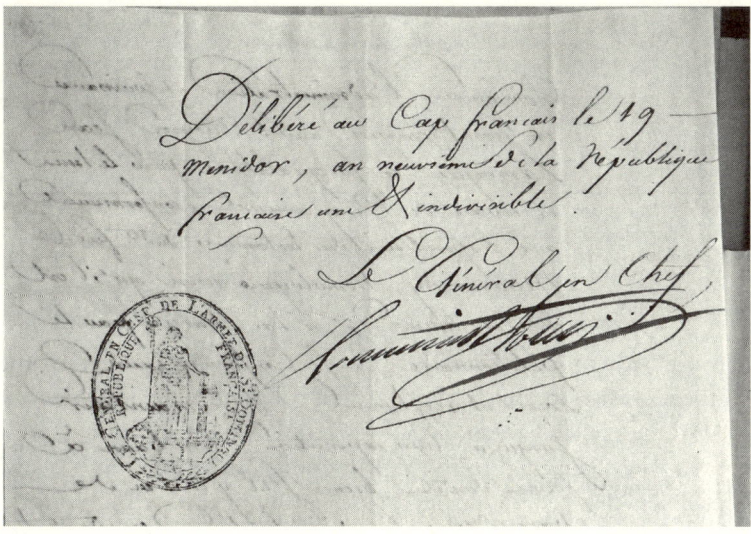

Fig. 4.3. Toussaint Louverture's signature on decree lifting the sequestration of the Mouscardy estate, 19 Messidor, Year Nine of the French Republic (July 8, 1801). ANOM, Dépôt des papiers publics des colonies, Saint-Domingue. Domaines, 1690–1828, 3SUPSDOM 40.

Louverture, died of yellow fever on November 2, 1802. Rochambeau's surrender to Dessalines six months later marked the end of French rule on the island.[83]

It is unclear what the practical effect of the decrees was in these three cases. In two cases the owner was deceased. In the case of Marie-Elizabeth Lamerenx, widow Trémais, the owner stayed in Cuba and did not take possession of her plantations in Acul and Marmelade. After Toussaint Louverture's arrest in 1802, a detailed inventory was made listing the properties he owned or leased in several areas of the island. (Toussaint acquired an impressive real estate portfolio during his years in power, seemingly at bargain prices.) The leased properties included the Trémais-Lamerenx plantation and warehouse in Acul, where the slave uprising started on August 22, 1791. (The adjacent Noé plantation, one of the four originally involved in the uprising, was also included.) After eleven years of war and revolution, the plantations where the insurrection started were still the property of their original owners, and they were being leased to Toussaint Louverture himself, who had gone from leader of the insurrection to governor of the colony. The Trémais-Lamerenx plantation was managed by a man named Jean-Baptiste (who also managed the Noé plantation). There was no furniture and no valuables. The only assets were six sacks of coffee weighing a total of 532 pounds. (As noted earlier, in 1791 the warehouse contained 100 tons of coffee.)[84]

TABLE 4.2.
Legal status of coffee plantations, Marmelade

	1798	1799	1801
Owner present and in possession of property	N/A	N/A	49
Property sequestered	66	68	47
Sequestration lifted	N/A	N/A	14

Source: Based on tallies of sequestered properties in the commune of Marmelade, ANOM, Fonds ministériels, Dépôt des papiers publics des colonies, Saint-Domingue, Recensement des biens domaniaux et urbains, an III [1795]–1814, DPPC 5SUPSDOM 2.

The Mouscardy properties and the properties of Marie-Elizabeth Lamerenx were for the most part located in the commune of Marmelade. The information contained in the French Overseas Archives is fragmentary but sufficient to give us a sense of what happened to coffee plantations in the commune as a whole. Three detailed tallies were conducted in the commune during Toussaint's rule.[85] The first took place on April 21, 1798; the second, on January 20, 1799; and the third seems to have been conducted sometime in 1801 (Table 4.2). The three tallies show us how many coffee plantations were sequestered, how many were in their owners' possession, and how many had the sequestration lifted.

The 1798 and 1799 tallies inform us only about the sequestered plantations, but we can infer from the 1801 tally that the commune had approximately 110 coffee plantations. Of those, approximately 60 percent were sequestered in the late 1790s. The rest either had been abandoned or were in their owners' possession. The detailed figures for 1801 show a surprisingly high number of properties in their owners' possession (45%). The proportion of sequestered properties was 43 percent, and the sequestration had recently been lifted on 13 percent of properties. One should add that when the 1801 tally was conducted, the Mouscardy plantation and the plantation of Marie-Elizabeth Lamerenx were still under sequestration, which suggests that the proportion of de-sequestered properties rose after that date. These figures indicate that in the commune of Marmelade at the dawn of the nineteenth century Toussaint Louverture's economic plan for the island was being implemented: plantations in the hands of their original owners, with salaried workers whose freedom of movement was severely constrained.

The Indemnity Debate

Article 6 of the Haitian Constitution of 1805 proclaimed that "property is sacred; its violation will be rigorously prosecuted."[86] Two other articles, however, were designed to enshrine the expropriation of the former colonists. Article 7 stipulated that émigrés as well as anyone who acquired the citizenship of another country would be stripped of their Haitian citizenship, and their properties would be confiscated (emigration was also punishable by death).[87] Article 12 forbade land ownership in Haiti by "white persons of any nation."[88] The point of these articles was not to make a statement about race (German and Polish soldiers who stayed in Haiti following the demise of the Leclerc expedition were granted Haitian citizenship). Articles 7 and 12 were intended, with a great deal of redundancy, to make it impossible for anyone who had left the island to reclaim his or her property.

The radical nature of these stipulations is obvious. The leaders who promulgated the constitution intended it as the foundation of a new political and social order, from which the former slave owners and property holders were entirely excluded. At the same time, there were continuities with the colonial and revolutionary periods. The dispositions against émigrés essentially continued what the French republicans had done on the island, except that sequestration of émigré property had now turned to outright confiscation. In addition, as seen above, the takeover by the state of abandoned land had been standard practice in the colonies during the *ancien régime*. In the French Overseas Archives, the dossiers regarding sequestered properties include a large register from the Direction des domaines of the Republic of Haiti listing state properties for the Partie du Nord.[89] It is not clear how such a document was acquired by the French, as the holdings of the archives are in principle limited to colonial times. It was perhaps provided by the Haitian government to help distribute the proceeds of the 1825 indemnity. What is remarkable is the bureaucratic continuity through war, revolutionary change, and change in sovereignty. It was the same Direction des domaines that managed state properties under the French Republic and under the Republic of Haiti.

The legal heirs (as defined by French law) of all the property holders whose trajectories are described in this book received a share of the indemnity the Haitian government agreed to provide in 1825 in exchange for diplomatic recognition by France. The mixed-race children of Jean Mouscardy, who stayed in Haiti, continued to own the coffee plantation in Ennery that they had received as a gift from their father in 1784. They were Haitian citizens and never left the island. Their property rights were therefore not affected by the new political order. It is hard to estimate how many property owners whose title predated the revolution remained in Haiti after it gained independence, but the number was significant. This did not escape the members of the commission in charge of allocating the proceeds of the 1825 indemnity. The indemnity was supposed to cover one-tenth of the fair market value of all real estate in Saint-Domingue as of 1789. As members of the commission noted, some of those 1789 proprietors stayed in Haiti and became Haitians. The indemnity could not go to Haitians, "because the revolution of Saint-Domingue did not dispossess them." Consequently, "it is obvious that colonists will receive more than one-tenth of the value of properties lost."[90]

Jean Mouscardy's heirs (his nephews from Bayonne) received a total of 55,280 francs for a coffee plantation in Marmelade and a house in Cap-Français. The heirs of Jean-Pierre Lamerenx (his widow and four children) received 15,275 francs for a coffee plantation in Dondon. At that point the widow and two children lived in Matanzas, Cuba; one daughter lived in France; and one son lived in France as well, even though his legal residence was in New Orleans. Marie-Elizabeth Lamerenx and her two daughters received 70,056 francs for four coffee plantations in Acul and Marmelade. The heirs of Marguerite-Françoise Lamerenx received 38,350 francs for the La Guille coffee plantation in Dondon. The value of the coffee plantation that Marc-Antoine Lamerenx and Elizabeth Le Jeune established in the Matador District of Dondon in the 1740s was estimated at 18,200 francs for indemnity purposes. The proceeds were split between Marie-Elizabeth Lamerenx and the heirs of her deceased sister. These were the official allocations. The sums actually received by the beneficiaries were less, as the payments were made over many years and the total indemnity was reduced from 150 million to 90 million francs by an agreement between the Haitian and French governments in 1838.

Haitian independence and the indemnity gave rise to a heated debate in the French Parliament.[91] The government argued that the granting of independence to a former colony was an executive act that was not subject to parliamentary scrutiny. The purpose of the bill under discussion was simply to determine how the indemnity would be allocated to its beneficiaries. Still, there was ample discussion about the political and legal implications of Haitian independence. Some parliamentarians said that the loss of Saint-Domingue by France was a catastrophe without precedent. "The law cannot have predicted such a disaster," one speaker opined, and he went on to compare the loss of the colony to a once-in-a-millennium natural cataclysm: "It is without precedent in human history. It is not hail, not a fire, not an earthquake; it is Pompeii buried under Vesuvius."[92] In a less grandiloquent style, the editors of the *Code des colons de Saint-Domingue*, two liberal lawyers who were sympathetic to Haitian independence, argued that the new laws and rules applying to the former colonists, which they compiled for French readers, were, "properly speaking, a legislation of exception, such that no analogy can help."[93]

Those supporting the government's position contended that the recognition of Haitian independence had plenty of political and legal precedent. They quoted Emer de Vattel, according to whom a king had the right to concede a portion of the state's territory to an enemy if the necessities of war required it.[94] (Vattel's treatise *Le Droit des gens* [*The Law of Nations*] was the work of reference for matters of international law.) They declined to mention precedents regarding territories in metropolitan France, because such discussions would recall "painful memories" or bring up "hypotheses carrying a bad omen."[95] They affirmed that at the very least with respect to colonial territories the government was on firm legal ground. Much more than the rest of the king's possessions, the colonies depended on the successful exercise of military force:

> Having a special status due to the nature of things and to the very purpose of their establishment, the colonies belong to a particular category in the political order and cannot be confused or assimilated with other social bodies. Because they are, in general, a result of conquest and are a set of military and commercial posts as much as a set of immovable properties, preserving them, much more so than for the rest of the State, is a function of the fortunes of war and of the ability to maintain a presence there.[96]

Ultimately, holding on to French territory in Europe was also predicated on military strength, but the exercise of that strength in faraway lands was much more precarious. This put the colonies in a special category and explained why the cession of Louisiana in 1762 and Canada in 1763 was uncontroversial. In conclusion, the government supporters quoted the precedent of sovereigns who recognized the independence of rebel provinces in Europe itself: "Isn't it the case that the sovereigns of Austria in the fourteenth century, of Spain in the seventeenth century, of England in the last century, were forced to recognize the independence of their insurgent provinces."[97] In the final analysis, Haitian independence was an outcome of the French Revolution itself. It was "the consequence of an insurrection that took place at the same time as the dreadful revolution that destroyed everything in metropolitan France, including the scepter itself."[98]

Regarding the colonist's properties, the parliamentary commission tasked with examining the bill argued, quoting Pufendorf, that the preservation of private property was indeed a duty of the sovereign with respect to the citizens, but that duty was subordinated to a higher principle, which was the common good of the state. Haitian independence and the confiscation of the colonists' properties was "a fact of war, which cannot be judged according to the rules of civil law nor governed by its principles."[99] Consequently, the French government could not be held responsible for the loss of property incurred by the colonists in Saint-Domingue. Furthermore, "if the good of France had made it necessary to recognize Haitian independence without conditions, if the king had deemed it wise not to demand an indemnity for the former colonists, one would have to bend to that necessity."[100]

In that sense the indemnity that France extracted from Haiti pertained entirely to the law of war and peace. The French offer of diplomatic recognition had been accompanied by a threat of a naval blockade made verbally by the negotiator. The indemnity was the price the Haitians agreed to pay in exchange for diplomatic relations. The French government held that individual property claims by former colonists were an entirely separate issue; it construed itself as the trustee of Haitian government funds destined to compensate private French citizens. Citizens who declined to receive their share of the indemnity could still make a lawful claim on confiscated property, and that property could be restituted to them in the (highly unlikely) event of a French reconquest of Haiti. On the other hand, accepting one's share of the indemnity meant giving up one's claims on confiscated property. This was clarified when a parliamentarian asked why the money was going to legal heirs, who were often distant relatives of the former colonists, and proposed that it should be restricted to those who had actually been harmed by the dispossession. A speaker replied that the purpose of the indemnity was not humanitarian assistance but rather the settling of claims based on property rights; this was the clear intent of the president of Haiti in granting the indemnity.[101] Regular rules of civil law applied in that instance, including inheritance by distant relatives when close relatives were deceased.

The question of property rights is debated in the classics of Haitian historiography, Thomas Madiou and Beaubrun Ardouin, who published their voluminous histories of Haiti in the 1840s and 1850s. Ardouin, discussing the Haitian declaration of independence, which excluded the French from the new society, contended that exclusion was understandable as it was the mirror image of declarations made by French politicians in the 1790s saying that blacks and mulattoes "are not, no matter what is being said, truly French, because they have never seen France, because they are islanders whose true homeland is Africa, natives who are foreign to the French nation."[102] According to Ardouin, the confiscation of colonist properties and the killing of remaining colonists in 1804 were the "necessary consequence" of that exclusion.[103] In accordance with the right of conquest, the Haitian state was the successor of the French state, and it enjoyed the same sovereign prerogatives as its predecessor, including ownership of state properties and the right to seize properties that were vacant because of the death or exclusion of the owners. Ardouin insisted that the killing of white colonists in 1804 had been an act of revenge for the atrocities committed by the French expeditionary force, not an act whose purpose was confiscation. Regarding the indemnity of 1825, Ardouin took issue with his fellow historian Madiou, who criticized President Boyer for betraying the heroes of the War of Independence by agreeing to pay 150 million francs for the recognition of an independence that had already been earned with their blood. This is Madiou quoted by Ardouin: "If the *heroes* of that time rose from their graves, how outraged would they be to learn, when they saw the French flag flying in our cities, that we had *consented, having forgotten* that they had acquired the land of Haiti thanks to their courage, to *indemnify*, with a sum that was beyond our means, the descendants of those who had tortured and maimed them?"[104] Furthermore, according to Madiou, since the wounds of 1802 and 1803 were now healed, it was important to have friendly relations with France, and paying the indemnity was a question of national honor and credibility. However, in 1825 Boyer should have insisted on unconditional recognition by France and accepted war if the French refused. "Haiti's debt toward colonists," Madiou concluded, "is just as illegitimate as the 1 billion francs that was imposed on France on behalf of émigrés when Bonaparte fell."[105]

Regarding the 1 billion francs (the famous *milliard des émigrés*), Beaubrun retorted correctly that it had not been imposed on France by the coalition that defeated Napoleon in 1815. Rather, it was an obligation that France had imposed upon itself in 1825 (the same year it recognized Haitian independence). I should add that there were many similarities between the two indemnities, starting with formal ones. The layout of the official documents listing the sums allocated to individual recipients was identical. More importantly, the purpose in each case was to accomplish a final settlement of individual property claims. During the Revolution in continental France, many émigré properties seized by the government had been sold to private citizens, often at bargain prices. (Many bourgeois fortunes of the nineteenth century started in this way, as illustrated by Balzac's novels.) The practice in that respect had been much more radical than it was in Saint-Domingue, where émigré properties remained under sequestration and were not sold off until after Haitian independence. The most important legal consequence of the *milliard des émigrés*, according to the jurisprudence expert Jean-Baptiste Duvergier, was to establish the legality of those revolutionary sales as a point that was "beyond contestation."[106]

In Ardouin's view, President Boyer's decision to indemnify the former colonists had been made for prudential reasons. If Boyer had acted in this way, it was because he had felt that he was not in a position to get a better deal, that he did not have the military and diplomatic strength to demand unconditional recognition. (One could add that he was implicitly following the Hobbesian principle underlying international law: "Covenants extorted by fear are valid.")[107] Finally, Ardouin mentioned the precedent of loyalist properties confiscated during the American War of Independence. Article 5 of the Treaty of Paris, which Ardouin quoted in English, stipulated that "Congress shall earnestly recommend to the legislatures of the respective States, to provide for the restitution of estates, rights, and properties, which have been confiscated, belonging to real British subjects, etc." Ardouin added in a footnote that "things were done as stated in this article."[108] According to Ardouin, "If the United States had denied citizenship rights or property rights to the English, as Haiti did to the colonists, there is no doubt that compensation would have been paid to those who had their properties confiscated."[109]

In making this assessment, Ardouin greatly overestimated the generosity of the newly independent American states. Things were not done as stated in article 5 of the Treaty of Paris, which was not legally binding on the states. (Most American negotiators were inclined toward generous restitution policies, but Benjamin Franklin was adamantly opposed and made sure that the language of article 5 was entirely noncommittal.) There was no blanket exclusion from property rights on the basis of nationality, but the practical consequences of property seizures in the United States and Haiti were essentially the same, because the same principles were at work: émigrés were enemies of the state who had forfeited citizenship as well as property rights. In a recent article studying confiscation in New York State, the legal historian Howard Pashman insists on its radical nature: "Forcible dispossession proved crucial in consolidating the legal authority of New York's revolutionary regime." "Such a claim," Pashman continues, "might be unsettling to someone who expected to find a greater respect for rights in America's legal past." However, "the revolutionaries who redistributed property transformed a chaotic environment into a new legal system based on popular consent."[110]

After the Treaty of Paris was signed, some loyalists who were in England, assuming they had a case under article 5 of the treaty, returned to the United States to claim restitution of their estates, but in the words of the first historian of loyalism, "Their applications were unheeded, and some of them were imprisoned, and afterwards banished."[111] Some relief was eventually provided, but the funds came from the British government, not the US government. The claimants "applied to the government which they had ruined themselves to serve."[112] Saint-Domingue colonists, on the other hand, got relief from the government they had ruined themselves to prevent coming into existence. According to Démesvar Delorme, for veterans of the Haitian War of Independence like General Mouscardy, the indemnity made sense only as a unilateral act of lordly generosity. Because obtaining diplomatic recognition by France against the payment of an indemnity had been a demeaning quid pro quo, "in a manifestation of their generous and unthinking national pride, they had wanted at least a separate act stipulating that the Republic spontaneously offered the indemnity as a gesture of benevolence toward dispossessed colonists."[113]

CHAPTER FIVE

Nation, Citizenship, and Atlantic Migrations

> *Ayer español nací,*
> *A la tarde fui francés,*
> *A la noche etíope fui,*
> *Hoy dicen que soy inglés:*
> *No sé qué será de mí.*
>
> Yesterday I was born Spanish,
> In the afternoon I was French,
> At night I was African,
> Now they say that I am English.
> I know not what will become of me.
>
> Attributed to Father José Vázquez, c. 1805

In *The Wealth of Nations*, Adam Smith argued that wealth derived from the ownership of land was much more stable than wealth generated by the use of capital. "The proprietor of land," he remarked, "is necessarily a citizen of the particular country in which his estate lies." On the other hand, "the proprietor of stock is properly a citizen of the world, and is not necessarily attached to any particular country."[1] Many of the characters in our story were landowners. Yet their behavior would seem to match Smith's description of the "proprietor of stock." Jean-Pierre Lamerenx, after serving under the command of Toussaint Louverture, did not file an application to lift the sequestration of his coffee plantation in Dondon. Instead he moved to Matanzas, Cuba, with his wife and children. There he established himself as a merchant. He used the profits to purchase land and slaves and start a new coffee plantation. He had made a fortune under the authority of the king of France. He began to make a new one under the authority of the king of Spain. Citizenship, it seems, was determined by business interests. As to the Mouscardy descendants who stayed in Haiti, their national belonging might at first sight appear unproblematic. Yet Démesvar Delorme was criticized by a Haitian essayist for his "spirit of escape,"[2] which was reportedly shared to some degree by all Haitian writers. According to this view, Delorme "chose to negate the possibility of a national literature" and instead decided "to become a

French writer."[3] Literary citizenship was determined by business interests, as selling books was much easier in Europe than in Haiti.

In the above description, the characters in our story were like Adam Smith's "merchant," who "is not necessarily the citizen of any particular country."[4] They moved across the Atlantic and reinvented themselves politically and culturally amid fast-changing political and economic circumstances. Yet it would be a mistake to say that because of shifting allegiances national belonging did not matter. It played a central role, but in a way that is not immediately obvious, because of the inchoate nature of national communities in the Atlantic world of the early nineteenth century.

Following the peregrinations of the Lamerenx and Mouscardy families will afford us a glimpse of the nation-state when it was new. In the introduction to his classic *Imagined Communities*, Benedict Anderson mentions "three paradoxes" that have long perplexed theorists of nationalism. The first is "the objective modernity of nations to the historian's eye vs. their subjective antiquity in the eyes of nationalists." The second is "the formal universality of nationality as a socio-cultural concept . . . vs. the irremediable particularity of its concrete manifestations." The third is "the 'political' power of nationalisms vs. their philosophical poverty and even incoherence."[5] Tied to the first paradox is the sense that the nation is "something to which one is naturally tied," and in that sense "something unchosen."[6] By changing the usual scale of observation and looking at these issues microhistorically, we can question some of the assumptions behind the paradoxes mentioned by Anderson. In particular, we will see that for many of the characters in this story, who dealt with incipient and relatively weak national communities, national belonging was to some extent a matter of choice.

La Bastide Clairence Joins the Kingdom of France

In the history of the Haitian Revolution, Etienne Polverel is remembered for the role he played, along with his colleague Léger-Félicité Sonthonax, in ending slavery in the French colony of Saint-Domingue (see chapter 4). Much less well known is the role he played advocating for the rights of the Kingdom of Navarre before and during the French Revolution. Polverel himself was not from Navarre. He was born in Brive-la-Gaillarde, in the Limousin region, and became a barrister with the Parliament of Paris. He developed a reputation as a talented lawyer and legal historian who knew how to make the case for local and regional privileges. The Estates General of Navarre retained Polverel to defend the interests of the Kingdom of Navarre in its dealings with the central bureaucracy of the Kingdom of France, especially in the fiscal area. He authored a memorandum arguing that there had never been any feudal property in Navarre and that all property in the kingdom was exempt from feudal taxes and obligations.[7] The Estates General of Navarre were so pleased with his work that in 1785 they voted to ennoble him.⁸ This seems to have presented the royal genealogists with an issue reminiscent of the case of Marc-Antoine Lamerenx in 1770. Endorsing the act of the Estates General of Navarre would break the king's monopoly on conferring noble rank. Polverel was told that his Navarrese nobility would be recognized as hereditary if he could prove that he was already of noble birth. With a dubious sense of timing, on the eve of the French Revolution Polverel was busy gathering documents to prove his nobility; he submitted a thick file to the Estates General of Navarre in the spring of 1789.⁹ The case was built on a creative interpretation of the documents, but the Estates General of Navarre were satisfied, issuing a certificate of nobility for Polverel on April 8, 1789.¹⁰

In July 1789, Polverel was serving as the *syndic* (secretary) of the delegation sent by the Estates General of Navarre to represent the interests of the kingdom in Paris. He tried to have the king swear that he would protect the customs and privileges of Navarre, but the request was politely deferred by the king's advisers. On August 7, 1789, Polverel wrote to the Estates General of Navarre to inform them of the momentous decisions made during the *nuit du quatre août* (the voluntary termination of their own privileges by the clergy and the nobility). The tone of his letter was not at all enthusiastic. He reported that the "national assembly of France has in a single meeting taken some large and important actions. It has ordered the freeing of serfs and the termination of every kind of mortmain."¹¹ He lamented the fact that "everything was done in a five-four meeting" and judged that it would have been preferable to make those decisions after careful deliberation. There was a rush to decide, he wrote, because of "the terror induced by arsonists and thieves who burned and pillaged castles in Alsace, Franche-Comté, and other provinces" and because the members of the clergy and the nobility were trying to outdo one another in showing generosity and "made the sacrifice of their properties."¹² Now himself a member of the Navarrese nobility, Polverel seemed to take a jaundiced view of the abolition of the privileges of his caste. He had more principled reasons for worrying, however. On August 4, 1789, there was no outright elimination of feudal taxes and duties, but rather a decision that these privileges could be bought back. Because there were no such feudal duties in Navarre anyway, the decisions of the National Assembly were moot as far as Navarre was concerned. Or rather they could be a source of complication if there were an attempt to apply those decisions to Navarre and ask Navarrese property owners to buy back feudal duties that had never existed.¹³

On October 12, 1789, the National Assembly debated the new title to be given to the king. Traditionally, the king had been called King of France and of Navarre (since Henri III of Navarre became Henry IV of France). There was a consensus that the king, as the embodiment of the nation, should now be called *roi des Français* (king of the French). However, many in the Assembly worried about dropping the title King of Navarre. During the meeting a letter by Polverel was read in which he argued that abandoning the title King of Navarre would be interpreted as forfeiting French claims to the southern part of the Kingdom of Navarre, which had been annexed by Spain in 1512. Polverel's arguments seemed to make an impression on the parliamentarians and generated significant applause. Then a representative from Corsica said that he was personally opposed to any additions to the title King of the French but that if "King of Navarre" was added, it was only fair that "King of Corsica" be added as well. Mirabeau seized this opportunity to argue that "nothing is more opposed to monarchic unity than the multiplicity of titles." He went on to ask rhetorically, "Instead of being the fusion of homogeneous parts, would this empire comprise diverse parts that would soon be divided?"[14] Either the Navarrese were a part of the French nation, Mirabeau said, or they were not. If they were not, they had no business with the French. If they were, they were subject to the same laws as the rest of the French. Mirabeau called for a vote to decide the question. The Assembly voted and decreed that nothing would be added to the title King of the French. The historian David Bell has shown how the modern idea of the nation emerged in France in *ancien régime* thinking about the monarchy.[15] Traditionally the unity of the nation existed only in the person of the king, while the kingdom was itself an assortment of corporate units of all sorts. Mirabeau was still alluding to this traditional conception when he spoke of "monarchic unity," but he gave it a new twist. The unity of the nation was now something that had to be achieved concretely and practically by having all citizens obey the same laws and develop a common love for those laws.

Polverel and the Navarrese representatives were extremely disappointed with this decision of the National Assembly, which came on top of excuses made by the king's advisers to delay the oath to protect the customs and privileges of Navarre. They decided to appeal to public opinion and published a lengthy volume, entirely authored by Polverel, that stated the position of the Navarrese delegation and included a detailed philosophical and historical discussion of the constitution of the Kingdom of Navarre.[16] At the beginning of the volume, Polverel recounted the many attempts by the Navarrese delegation to have the king take the traditional oath and the various pretexts given by the king's advisers to postpone it. He also reported that the king, yielding to Navarrese pressure, had called a meeting of the Estates General of Navarre, only to disband the Estates a few days later. The position of the Navarrese delegation could be summarized as follows: The Navarrese people might well decide to join the French nation, but they could not make this decision until the French nation gave itself a constitution. The Navarrese people had a constitution that had served them well and guaranteed their freedoms for a thousand years (what Polverel called "constitution" was a set of customs that served as the kingdom's fundamental laws). They would not give up this constitution before knowing what fundamental laws they would obey if they decided to become French. Polverel went on to compare the Navarrese constitution with the constitution of France during the reign of Charlemagne: "France had a true Constitution only during the reign of Charlemagne. This Constitution has been abundantly praised, and rightly so in many ways. But how did it compare with that of Navarre? This is what we shall now be able to judge."[17]

Polverel's discussion was probably inspired by the work of Gabriel Bonnot de Mably, who had described the constitution of Charlemagne as a model of republican liberty. In Mably's account, as Keith Baker points out, Charlemagne had "restored the principles of republican government" inherited from the Franks, but this political order had disappeared with the collapse of the Carolingian Empire, and "the very conception of the public good was dissolved by the growth of feudal government."[18] Polverel adopted Mably's premise to make his case. Under the best constitution the French had ever had, "slavery was the natural and legal status of the majority of the French"[19] and "those of free condition enjoyed only limited liberty."[20] Thus the ancient constitution of France was seriously deficient in the area of civil liberty. It was better in the area of political liberty because legislative power lay with the National Assembly. According to Polverel, the constitution of the Navarrese monarchy was better on all counts because it was a set of fundamental laws the Navarrese adopted *before* electing their first king: "The constitution of the Navarrese Monarchy is not the work of a King or of a Conqueror. It is the work of a free and brave people surrounded by powerful enemies who had no laws or tribunals and wanted a King to lead the forces of the Nation against foreign enemies and to keep civil peace inside. Before electing their first King, they dictated the laws that were meant to protect the civil and political liberty of the Navarrese forever."[21]

In conclusion, Polverel contended that "of all the constitutions of modern Europe, that of Navarre is the least faulty; it has done more than any other for civil and political liberty; and in terms of freedom and equality, it has done everything that was compatible with the distinction of Orders."[22] In that sense, the decision by the king's ministers to disband the Estates General of Navarre was "a project worthy at best of Machiavelli's Prince," and Polverel could not believe that the ministers would hope to "invite Louis XVI to attempt to enslave a people who have been free for more than a thousand years, precisely when he is giving back their freedom to a people who have been enslaved for nine hundred years."[23]

In some ways it is difficult to reconcile the two Polverels: the one who emancipated the slaves in Saint-Domingue and sequestered the properties of the colonists to hand them over to the *nouveaux libres* (newly freed citizens) and the one who spent considerable time and money to prove his noble birth and made a full display of his rhetorical powers to defend the medieval privileges of a minuscule province that was a kingdom in name only. At the same time, it can be argued that there was continuity and consistency in Polverel's views. His defense of the privileges of Navarre was conducted in the name of republican principles, and it is interesting in that respect that Polverel, like Mably, saw no middle ground between liberty and slavery: "Choose between a revolution and slavery; there is no middle point," Mably wrote in *Des droits et des devoirs du citoyen* in 1758.[24] Polverel's volume on the constitution of Navarre ended with a threat of secession and war. If their constitution were violated, Polverel warned, the Navarrese people would choose independence from France and become a republic. As to "those who doubt Navarre's ability to keep its independence," they "do not know its mountains, or the fearlessness of the Basques, or their love of freedom."[25] In her work on representations of colonization and slavery in eighteenth-century French culture, Madeleine Dobie argues that metaphorical references to slavery to designate the lack of civil liberties in metropolitan France tended to obfuscate the real and literal presence of slavery in the colonies.[26] Remarkably, in Polverel's (admittedly unusual) career, freedom from slavery extended from the metaphorical to the literal, and it was arguably the same script, borrowed from Mably, that Polverel used to conceptualize the freedom of the Navarrese people and the freedom of Saint-Domingue's enslaved Africans.

The official position of the Navarrese delegation was that any decision of the Navarrese people to join the French nation would have to wait until the French gave themselves a constitution. That constitution was adopted on September 3, 1791, but things moved much faster in Navarre itself. On December 8, 1789, the Municipal Assembly of La Bastide Clairence was convened to discuss the possible "incorporation" of La Bastide Clairence into the kingdom of France. The town was divided into eight neighborhoods. Each neighborhood would deputize about half of the heads of its "houses" to represent it at the town meeting. As a result, the Municipal Assembly had about two hundred participants. The deliberation rehearsed the story of the origins of Navarre, mixed with philosophical considerations about the origins of government: "When men unite to form a political body, their only motive is to avoid the evils resulting from anarchy and to enjoy the benefits of wise government." The first condition of such association was "the sacrifice of individual interests to the public interest," and the second was "the union of all individual forces to defend the common cause." Having gone back to first principles, the participants reminded themselves that "it was those motives that determined the Navarrese, whose origins are lost in the mists of time, to unite as a national body [*corps de nation*] near the beginning of the eighth century."[27]

The participants made a distinction between the Navarrese nation in the ethnic sense of the term, which had purportedly been in existence since time immemorial, and the Navarrese nation in the political sense, which was marked by the adoption of a constitution in the eighth century. They also reiterated the point made in Polverel's volume that the fundamental laws of Navarre predated the election of its first kings. In the final analysis, however, the constitution that was being designed by the French National Assembly offered better guarantees of freedom. Thus the Municipal Assembly decreed that "this town incorporates itself into the kingdom of France and consequently adheres with its heart and soul, purely and simply, to the current and future decrees of the National Assembly." In addition, it decided that the town would write to the National Assembly to request its agreement to the decision that had just been made and "to accept the sacrifice" La Bastide Clairence had made of its own constitution as a token of "its most perfect love for the French nation and its deepest respect for the decrees of its august representatives."[28] The motion was put to a vote after being read and explained "in the vernacular" (i.e., in Gascon).[29] It passed unanimously and by acclamation. Fifty-nine heads of houses affixed their signatures to the solemn declaration, and the meeting ended with the cry *Vivent les Français!* (Long live the French!).

This episode illustrates what David Bell has shown about the origins of French nationalism in the eighteenth century, and it does it in an especially vivid way because of the marginal and ambiguous status of Lower Navarre at the end of the *ancien régime*. Like the other Navarrese, the citizens of La Bastide Clairence clung to their customs and privileges and repeatedly refused to be treated as a French province. Yet they suddenly decided to join the French nation. It was a political decision (the constitution of the French nation would offer better guarantees for freedom) that did not presuppose a common language or culture (most inhabitants of La Bastide Clairence only spoke Gascon), and it was a decision couched in emotional and quasi-religious language (*heart and soul, sacrifice,* and *perfect love*). La Bastide Clairence was one of the first Navarrese communities to join the French nation. The following week, the town of Saint-Jean-Pied-de-Port followed suit, soon imitated by the Pays de Cize, which surrounded it. By the end of December 1789 the Kingdom of Navarre was history.

The connections between La Bastide Clairence and Saint-Domingue do appear in the records of the municipal council during the French Revolution. On November 14, 1789, Jean-Pierre Colombots *américain*, recently returned from the colony, lent a sum of 4,000 livres to the municipal government for the purchase of 1,990 *conques* (2,300 bushels) of maize in order to offset the local production deficit, which had driven up prices and triggered fears of famine.[30] (There had been food riots earlier that year, led by the town's women.) Money earned in Saint-Domingue thanks to slave labor was used to help avoid starvation and civil unrest among the peasantry in La Bastide Clairence. Colombots had sailed to Saint-Domingue as an *engagé* (i.e., without any startup capital) in

1770, but he had started to make a fortune quickly thanks to the help of his fellow Bastidot Jean Mouscardy. He worked as a plantation manager, purchased several slaves, and by the late 1780s he was the farmer of a coffee plantation. (Jean Mouscardy agreed to guarantee the lease payments due to the proprietor of the plantation.)[31] It is not clear why Colombots decided to return to his hometown. Perhaps, like many other colonists, he viewed his emigration as an opportunity to get rich quickly before returning home. He left long before the slave uprising and brought back significant earnings. He also came with a five-year-old son, François, whose mother, a slave named Marie-Claire, had remained in the colony.[32] As the illegitimate son of a local nobleman, Jean-Pierre Colombots would normally have had limited marriage opportunities, but the wealth acquired in Saint-Domingue changed the rules of the game. In 1792 he married a woman named Marie Labarthe, who was the heiress of the house of Lapeyre, an agricultural estate.[33]

Even before he contracted an advantageous marriage, Colombots *américain* (always thus designated in municipal records, to distinguish him from his half-brother, who was the legitimate heir to the Colombots estate) was entrusted with high responsibilities by his fellow citizens. On November 28, 1790, he was elected to the Municipal Council, where he served alongside his father, Jean-Pierre de Colombots. A few months later the mayor, Emmanuel de Bordus Darrieux, resigned for reasons of conscience: he was opposed to the Civil Constitution of the Clergy and supported the local parish priest, who had declined to take an oath of loyalty to the constitution. Colombots was elected as the new mayor and was sworn in on June 19, 1791.[34] He served until the end of 1792.[35] The wealth earned in Saint-Domingue and the prestige of being an *Américain* had propelled him to his hometown's highest office.

French Coffee Growers in Cuba

The massive influx of French refugees into Cuba following the demise of the Leclerc expedition is a well-known episode in Cuban history.[36] It forms the basis for Alejo Carpentier's novel *The Kingdom of This World*. The narrator in Carpentier's story is a slave named Ti Noël, who follows his master to Cuba after the collapse of French rule in Saint-Domingue in 1803. Ti Noël and his owner, Monsieur Lenormand de Mézy, arrive with thousands of other refugees in Santiago de Cuba, on the southeastern shores of the island, approximately two hundred nautical miles away from Cap-Français. In the novel, Lenormand de Mézy reacts to his new circumstances by adopting a carefree attitude and living for the moment. Upon his arrival he visits a *café chantant*, where "the best tables were occupied by old friends of his, landowners who, like himself, had fled from the machetes whetted with molasses." Paradoxically, "with their fortunes gone, ruined, half their families unaccounted for," the former colonists, "far from bemoaning their situation, seemed to have taken a new lease on life." As a result, they "reveled in their improvidence, in living from day to day, in freedom from their obligations, seeking, for the moment, to suck from everything what pleasure they could find." This stood in contrast to the behavior of "others more foresighted than they," who "had got their money out of Saint-Domingue and had gone to New Orleans, or were starting new coffee plantations in Cuba."[37]

The Lamerenx family seems to have been of the "more foresighted" kind. They left Saint-Domingue earlier and went to a different part of Cuba.[38] It is not clear when exactly Jean-Pierre Lamerenx went to Cuba. We know that in 1795 he was serving as a battalion commander in Toussaint Louverture's army. The first record of his presence in Cuba is from the baptism of the newborn son of one of his slaves in the church of San Carlos de Matanzas, on the northern shore of the island, in 1800. The family probably had arrived several years earlier, because it is known that one of Jean-Pierre's sons, Jean Lamerenx, settled in far western Cuba in 1796.[39] Emigration from Saint-Domingue to Cuba became legal for French citizens after the Treaty of Basel, signed on July 22, 1795, which ended the war between France and Spain and ceded the eastern part of Hispaniola to France. Jean Lamerenx established a small coffee plantation near Santa Cruz de los Pinos, in Pinar del Río Province, at the western tip of the island of Cuba. At the time, the area was undeveloped and had a very small population. Jean Lamerenx's coffee plantation had twelve slaves in 1810.[40]

It is not known whether Jean-Pierre Lamerenx and his family were able to "get their money out of Saint-Domingue," as Carpentier suggests some colonists did. Carrying cash was perilous, of course, especially in those chaotic circumstances. Letters of credit were an effective tool because they were immune from confiscation, but they seem to have been used mostly by merchants or by owners of large sugar plantations. In any case, the planters' assets did not consist mostly of money. Their capital was the human beings they owned, and this capital evaporated with the slave insurrection. Despite the uncertainties about the amount of starting capital the Lamerenx family may have taken with them to Cuba, we can get a clear sense of how they set out to make a new fortune. They followed the Saint-Domingue playbook. Jean-Pierre Lamerenx initially established himself in Matanzas as a *négociant*,[41] a profession that was new to him. Being a *négociant* was a standard way for newly arrived immigrants of some means to accumulate capital in Saint-Domingue (see chapter 2). It did not require a large initial investment, as their role was to sell merchandise on consignment from ship captains, with payment due to the captains within one or two years.

With money earned in commerce, Jean-Pierre Lamerenx and his wife, Françoise Silly, were able to establish a coffee plantation, the *cafetal* San Pedro, a few miles south of the city of Matanzas. Acquiring land was not a big hurdle. Land in Cuba was plentiful and cheap, and it was made even more affordable by the *censo* system. The *censo* was a perpetual mortgage that carried an interest payment of 5 percent per year. The borrower was required to pay the interest only and had the option of paying down the principal at any time.[42] As the Cuban historian Juan Pérez de la Riva wrote, "The former coffee planter from Haiti could count from the start on lots of excellent land with little or no money down."[43] We know from his last will that in 1810 Jean-Pierre Lamerenx leased a huge area near Matanzas (27 *caballerías*, equivalent to 280 Saint-Domingue *carreaux*, or 900 acres).[44] The land was valued at 250 Spanish dollars per *caballería*,[45] meaning that Jean-Pierre paid an annual lease of 337.50 Spanish dollars (assuming a payment of 5% per year). According to Juan Pérez de la Riva, in the early nineteenth century land in southeastern Cuba was sold to French immigrants in lots of ten *caballerías* at 250 Spanish dollars per *caballería*.[46] This would indicate that the price paid by Jean-Pierre was consistent with what other settlers paid in the Santiago de Cuba area, where French immigration was greatest.

Converted into French *ancien régime* currency and French area units, the price paid for land in Cuba would have been about 200 colonial livres per *carreau*. As we saw in earlier chapters, uncultivated land in Marmelade in the 1780s sold for 500 livres per *carreau*. This means that for Jean-Pierre the land in Cuba cost about two-fifths of what he would have had to pay in Saint-Domingue, and he could acquire it with no money down. Near Havana, land prices were higher. A prospectus filed in 1806 by the French investor Louis de Belle Garde reported that in the vicinity of Havana, land planted in coffee sold for up to 200 Spanish dollars per *carreau*. This was still less than prices in Saint-Domingue, which hit a maximum of 600 dollars per *carreau* (5,000 colonial livres) for the most desirable coffee plantations in the late 1780s. In the investor's opinion, "French population and industry are the sole cause of such a considerable increase."[47] In that sense, land acquisition in Cuba in the early 1800s repeated the experience of the first coffee growers in Dondon in the 1740s and 1750s, who were given land grants by the colonial authorities or purchased land from the original grantees for modest amounts of money. As in Saint-Domingue, the biggest cost was labor. Slaves could be purchased from Liverpool or Nantes traders, who typically accepted letters of credit with a maturity of eighteen to thirty-six months, with the land as collateral.[48]

The sacramental records for San Carlos Parish in Matanzas show that on November 26, 1804, twelve slaves belonging to Jean-Pierre Lamerenx were baptized.[49] They included nine men and three women, a ratio consistent with the Spanish policy of importing three men for one woman. Among the men, four were from the Mandingo nation, two were Congos, and two were Carabalí (a name given by the Spanish to slaves shipped from Calabar in modern-day southeast Nigeria). All three women were Carabalí. Jean-Pierre was the godfather for all the men. His daughter Adélaïde Charlotte was the godmother for all the women. Given Spanish customs and regulations regarding the baptism of slaves, it is likely that these slaves had been brought to Cuba very recently. (The Spanish had a policy of systematically baptizing slaves upon arrival.) This mass baptism also probably corresponds to the moment when Jean-Pierre and his wife started their coffee plantation: a dozen slaves was the minimum required to clear the forest and plant the coffee trees.

What gave Saint-Domingue refugees an edge was their know-how, and the know-how of the slaves they brought with them. According to Gabriel Debien, new coffee plantations were typically run by a slave commander from Saint-Domingue, who supervised the work of the slaves and knew all the routines involved in coffee planting. Slaves on these new coffee plantations were subject to much stricter and harsher working conditions than had previously been the rule in Cuba.[50] There is no record of the Lamerenx family bringing a slave commander from Dondon with them, but we know that they traveled from Saint-Domingue to Cuba with at least one household slave, a mixed-race woman named Thérèse, who gave birth to a son "of an unknown father" in 1800.[51] In the record she is mentioned as being a native of Guárico (the Taíno name used by the Spanish to designate the area the French called Cap-Français). The newborn, named Thomas Aquinas, who was in all likelihood the offspring of one of the Lamerenx males, was manumitted at birth by his owner, Jean-Pierre Lamerenx.

French expertise in matters of coffee cultivation was greatly appreciated in Cuba, and it was propagated in book form by the end of the first decade of the nineteenth century. Laborie's *Coffee Planter of Saint-Domingo*, originally published in London in 1798, had been intended as a handbook for those interested in applying French coffee-planting methods in Jamaica (see chapter 2). When it was translated into Spanish and published by the colonial authorities in 1809,[52] it became the standard reference for coffee planting in Cuba. The book never appeared in the language in which it originally had been written (French); the Spanish edition was a translation of the English translation. Imperial rivalries came with strongly protectionist rules for Atlantic commerce, but they did not stand in the way of technology transfers. Another manual, written in Spanish by a French coffee planter established in Cuba, Alexandre Dumont, was published in Havana in 1823.[53]

The coffee boom in Cuba in the first decades of the nineteenth century shared many characteristics with the coffee boom in Saint-Domingue in the second half of the eighteenth century. The coffee was planted on newly cleared land, and the cultivation relied on the importation of a huge number of slaves, entirely out of proportion with what had been the practice in Cuba in the eighteenth century.[54] (The twelve slaves Jean-Pierre Lamerenx purchased in 1804 had all recently been brought in from Africa.) In 1789 Saint-Domingue exported 662,000 tons of coffee. During the same year, coffee exports from Cuba were minuscule: 1,850 tons. Cuban exports rose to 12,500 tons in 1804 (the year Jean-Pierre Lamerenx and his wife started their coffee plantation in Matanzas) and to 99,900 tons in 1810 (the year Jean-Pierre died), peaking at 641,589 tons in 1833 (slightly below what had been the peak of Saint-Domingue's production). In 1840, when the Lamerenx family sold the San Pedro coffee plantation, Cuban coffee exports were 16 percent below their 1833 peak. There was a precipitous drop in 1845, and in the 1860s exports stabilized at the low level of approximately 40,000 tons per year.[55] By that time Brazil had entirely overtaken Cuba as the leading coffee exporter, and sugar had long replaced coffee as Cuba's top export.[56]

When the San Pedro coffee plantation was sold in 1840, its size had decreased from 27 to 7½ *caballerías* (250 acres), but the Lamerenx family members were by that time the full owners of the land. Even with the diminished acreage, it is likely that only a fraction of the land was planted in coffee. The sale of the *cafetal* San Pedro was probably a response to increasingly adverse market conditions. The immediate cause, however, was the death of the family matriarch, Françoise Silly, who had started a coffee plantation with her husband, Jean-Pierre Lamerenx, in Dondon in the 1770s. When she dictated her last will in 1840, she could not sign it, because she was too frail and her vision was impaired.[57] An interpreter had to be brought in to translate what she said. Although she had been living in Cuba for more than forty years, she never learned to speak Spanish.

Charles Lamerenx's Odyssey

Of the seven children of Jean-Pierre Lamerenx and Françoise Silly, Charles, the firstborn, had a particularly eventful life. On April 7, 1817, Charles Lamerenx, jailed in Cádiz and about to be transferred to the Spanish presidio of Ceuta, on the northern coast of Africa, wrote a lengthy petition to the king of Spain to justify himself and ask for clemency.[58] In the letter, now kept in the Archivo General de Indias in Seville, Charles Lamerenx explained that he was a resident of New Orleans. He had to sail to Cartagena, a city on the Atlantic coast of modern-day Colombia, to attend to some business. Because there was no regular ship headed back to New Orleans, he reluctantly boarded the privateer schooner *La Belona*. On the way, the privateer captured a Spanish brigantine named *Cupido*, with its entire crew and passengers. Charles Lamerenx insisted that he personally had had nothing to do with this act of piracy and never profited from it. He pleaded with the captain to treat the prisoners humanely, and he even helped them with his own money. Charles disembarked in Jamaica. Still unable to make his way back to New Orleans, he found another ship that took him to Trinidad and eventually to the city of Matanzas, Cuba, where he had relatives. In the meantime, the Spanish prisoners had been freed by their captors, and they had arrived in Cuba. They recognized Charles Lamerenx and denounced him as a pirate. He was tried by a Spanish court and sentenced to ten years of hard labor in a penitentiary in Africa. (According to a 1771 Spanish law, hard labor in Africa was the punishment for crimes committed with "a depraved and wicked mind.")[59] Charles Lamerenx was doubly guilty in the eyes of the Spanish. It was bad enough that the privateer had captured a Spanish vessel. The aggravating circumstance was that the pirates had flown the insurgent flag: Cartagena was a rebel city, having declared its independence from Spain in 1811. Charles Lamerenx was both a pirate and a traitor.

More details about this case can be discovered in the "Political Affairs" section of the Cuban National Archives,[60] and Charles Lamerenx's complicated trajectory can be pieced together with documents from the New Orleans Archives and the French Overseas Archives. Evidence shows that in the early 1800s Charles Lamerenx lived a somewhat peaceful life with the rest of the Lamerenx family in Matanzas, Cuba. (One piece of evidence for his presence in Matanzas is his suit against his brother-in-law over a business transaction in 1807.)[61] However, in the spring of 1809 he was in a conflict zone. On April 1, 1809, he was appointed *capitaine adjudant major* (staff captain) in a regiment of black volunteer troops commanded by Colonel Repussard.[62] The regiment helped defend a French enclave in the eastern part of Hispaniola that had resisted Haitian, English, and Spanish offensives since the proclamation of Haitian independence in 1804. The enclave was ruled by Jean-Louis Ferrand, a general who had served in the Leclerc expedition and governed a small part of Hispaniola around the city of Santo Domingo in the name of Napoleon Bonaparte and the French Empire. A Spanish insurgency against Ferrand's rule began with English support in the eastern part of Hispaniola in the fall of 1808. Ferrand committed suicide on the battlefield on November 7, 1808, when some of his troops switched sides and turned against him. He was replaced by Joseph-David Barquier, his second-in-command, who surrendered to the British on July 7, 1809, and handed them the city of Santo Domingo, an episode that marked the end of French rule in Hispaniola. Thus Charles Lamerenx's service in Santo Domingo was very short. He became a staff captain on April 1, when the city was already under siege, and his name was removed from the rolls on June 22, two weeks before the final surrender.

Why did Charles Lamerenx leave Cuba, where his family was establishing a coffee plantation and beginning to accumulate the kind of wealth it had enjoyed in Saint-Domingue, to join the losing side in a very dangerous battle? The short answer is that he may not have had a choice. Following the invasion of Spain by Napoleon's troops in 1808, Spanish colonists in Cuba proclaimed their allegiance to Ferdinand VII, the captive king of Spain, and in a wave of nationalist fervor,[63] they demanded the expulsion from Saint-Domingue of French refugees who had been living on the island since 1803, even earlier in the case of the

Lamerenx family. The Spanish colonial authorities in Cuba were generally inclined to protect the French refugees, whose presence they saw as benefitting the island's economy, but they yielded to popular pressure. A proclamation of March 12, 1809, expelled all those who had not pledged allegiance to Spain. Popular *juntas de vigilancia* (vigilance committees) were tasked with probing the refugees' loyalty to Spain. The Spanish had a long history of mass expulsions in the name of religion (the Jews in 1492 and the Moriscos in 1609). This one was done in a different spirit, even though a profession of Catholic faith was a key component in the loyalty test. Spanish popular resistance to French invasion is usually associated with the birth of modern Spanish nationalism.[64] One could say that the expulsion of the French coincided with the moment when the colonists in Cuba reinvented themselves as Spanish patriots. In the end the majority of the refugees were expelled, and most of them resettled in New Orleans, leading to a doubling of the city's population in just a few months. Charles Lamerenx was the only Lamerenx family member to be expelled. It seems that the Matanzas junta was not convinced by his plea of loyalty to Spain.

If Charles Lamerenx was expelled by a junta in March 1809, it is not clear how he managed to reach Santo Domingo, since the Spanish authorities in Cuba were formally at war with France at that time. It is also possible that his departure took place earlier and was in part voluntary. There was already pressure on the French refugees during the summer of 1808. News of the insurrection against the French in Spain reached Havana on July 17, 1808. On July 28, the Spanish captain general of the island ordered the registration of all French refugees and the expulsion of those who had not acquired Spanish citizenship. This initial expulsion order was not implemented very vigorously (unlike the expulsion that took place the following year). Besides, General Ferrand needed volunteers to defend the French enclave in Santo Domingo against British attacks. During the summer and fall of 1808, a number of young Frenchmen left Cuba, with passports provided by the Spanish governor of Santiago de Cuba Province, Sebastián Kindelán y O'Regan, to join Ferrand's troops in Santo Domingo.[65] Around the same time, apparently unbeknownst to Governor Kindelán, the Spanish governor of Puerto Rico, Toribio Montes, was beginning a campaign with British support to dislodge Ferrand and his troops from Santo Domingo. Charles Lamerenx's destiny was determined by conflicts in Europe, as well as by colonial officials who acted essentially as free agents and waged war in the name of this or that sovereign power.

Charles Lamerenx went from Santo Domingo to New Orleans, where he joined the thousands of French refugees who had just been expelled from Cuba. He tried to make a living as a merchant, probably acting as a correspondent for his relatives in Matanzas. On February 11, 1811, he bought a house from a free man of color, Charles Decoudreau. This house was located on Bayou Saint John

Road, on the left side of the road as one leaves the city, not far from the city limits, an area known today as Faubourg Tremé. For the house and two arpents of land (1.69 acres), Charles Lamerenx agreed to pay $3,660. He paid $500 in cash and the rest in the form of two promissory notes, one with a one-year term and the other with a two-year term. The notes were guaranteed by a mortgage on the house. Charles Lamerenx failed to make the promised payments. On February 9, 1813, Marc Lafitte, notary public for the parish of New Orleans, went to the Bayou Road house to notify Lamerenx of his delinquency. Lamerenx was not there. His neighbors said that he had left town and was "sailing." Charles Lamerenx being still absent and delinquent, on July 14, 1813, the parish court judge ordered the seizure of the house to settle an outstanding debt of $2,559.[66]

We know from Charles Lamerenx's letter to the king of Spain that he was absent from New Orleans because he had to attend to some business in Cartagena. The minutes of his trial for piracy and treason contain additional information about the purpose of the trip. Lamerenx said at his trial that he had sailed from New Orleans to Cartagena to collect a $1,800 debt from a merchant (money he needed desperately because his financial position in New Orleans was very precarious). Able to collect only $800, he had decided to sail back home on the privateer ship, whose captain, instead of heading to New Orleans, had dropped him off in the Haitian port of Jérémie. From there Lamerenx had sailed to Jamaica, where he learned that there was peace between France and Spain, Napoleon having abdicated on April 6, 1814. Lamerenx had therefore assumed he was no longer unwelcome in Cuba and decided to join his relatives in Matanzas instead of going to New Orleans. He had boarded the British brigantine *Alexandrine*, which was headed to Trinidad. Once in Trinidad, he had obtained a passport to sail to Matanzas and join his family.

The prosecution sought to cast doubt on the story. They said that no legitimate business could have been conducted in Cartagena at the time because the city was in a state of revolutionary upheaval. The real purpose of the trip, the prosecutor argued, had been to join a band of pirates. The fact is that the city of Cartagena, a republic that had just declared its independence from Spain, was in a state of great effervescence and acted as a magnet for revolutionaries, merchants, traffickers, and adventurers of all kinds from all across the Caribbean. During the four years it operated as an independent state, Cartagena became, according to the historian Edgardo Pérez Morales, "a truly cosmopolitan port-city."[67] The republican junta adopted very liberal immigration policies. The new constitution explicitly allowed the immigration of "foreigners of any profession that is useful to the country."[68] Shortly after the proclamation of the city's independence on November 11, 1811, emissaries were sent to New Orleans to recruit new citizens.[69] Charles Lamerenx may have heeded that call, especially given his shaky financial position in New Orleans.

One of the prerogatives of sovereignty was the ability to get into the privateering business. Since Cartagena was at war with its former colonial ruler, it reserved the right to seize the cargo of any Spanish ship. Several privateers worked for the Republic of Cartagena at the time. The most active was a Frenchman named Louis Aury, who was given letters of marque by the new state in June 1813 and operated a fleet of four vessels that seized a large number of Spanish ships in the following months.[70] Aury was known for his Jacobin republican views and is recorded in the national histories of Colombia, Venezuela, and Argentina as a hero of Latin American independence. Aury's flagship was named *La Belona*. This was the name of the privateer schooner mentioned by Lamerenx in his letter to the king of Spain, leading us to conclude that Charles Lamerenx left Cartagena on Aury's ship. As to the seizures made by *La Belona* during that trip, they were a matter of public record. On August 19, 1814, a local newspaper in Cartagena printed Aury's report to the president of the Republic of Cartagena.[71] From this document we learn that *La Belona* sailed out of Cartagena on April 2, 1814, and did indeed capture a Spanish brigantine named *Cupido*, which was armed and made some initial resistance, leaving four dead and eight wounded among the Spanish sailors. The Spanish ship, which carried two passengers and a crew of seventy-two, was en route from Jamaica to Havana when it was captured on May 12, 1814. The booty included 20,000 Spanish dollars in silver coins, as well as official letters from the Spanish viceroy of Nueva Granada to the Spanish governor of Cuba and to the Spanish governor of the province of Santa Marta, on the South American mainland.

Privateering operations had very precise rules of engagement.[72] Seizures usually took place without violence. The privateer had to respect the lives and personal property of his captives, who could pay with their own money to receive better food and accommodation on board. Charles Lamerenx's claim that he helped the captives with his own money was therefore consistent with the rules of privateering. In his report, Aury specified that the brigantine *Cupido* raised the flag of the Kingdom of Spain, after which *La Belona* raised the flag of the Republic of Cartagena. This was the signal that representatives of two sovereign powers were ready to use force against each other. The two ships exchanged fire for a while, until the *Cupido* lowered its flag, signaling its surrender. *La Belona* sent a small boat to the *Cupido* to make contact with its captain and take possession of the ship. After the booty and the prisoners were transferred from one ship to the other, Aury gave the order to sink the Spanish ship. Privateers saw themselves as business people who operated in a fully legal fashion. Louis Aury's private correspondence is revealing in that respect. In 1812 he wrote from Baltimore to his younger sister in Paris. Referring to himself in the third person, he said that she must imagine her brother the privateer "as another Barbarossa, smoking, swearing, drinking brandy, fierce and savage of face." Aury went on to protest that he did not match the stereotype: "Not at all, my dear. The gentleman has a manly face, brown, a little harsh, but that is all, not smoking at all, drinking and swearing but little."[73]

The Spanish judges in Cuba took another view of Aury's activities and of the activities of Charles Lamerenx, whom they saw as entirely complicit. After being denounced by former captives from the *Cupido* who recognized him, Lamerenx was arrested at his mother's house in Matanzas on December 10, 1814. He was still sleeping when the police arrived at dawn and seized a trunk containing all his papers and personal possessions. The judicial proceedings dragged on for several years. Lamerenx did not have the means to hire a lawyer. His counsel was a *procurador de pobres* (public defender). He was initially exonerated by a lower court, but the prosecution appealed and he was sentenced on December 4, 1815, by the Real Audiencia of the island of Cuba.[74] Lamerenx appealed the judgment and was turned down on February 9, 1816.[75] By 1817 he had exhausted all possibilities of appeal and was in a prison in Cádiz, waiting to be transferred to the penitentiary of Ceuta to serve a ten-year sentence to hard labor. His only recourse was a royal pardon, which he solicited in his letter of April 7, 1817.

During the trial before the Real Audiencia in 1815, the prosecutor agreed to drop the charges of *infidencia* (treason) because "el Francés Lamerenx" (the Frenchman Lamerenx) was not a "vassal" of the king of Spain and had not taken an oath of loyalty to him.[76] However, according to the prosecutor, Lamerenx was "a true and obstinate pirate against the Spanish."[77] Aury and his crew could not legitimately call themselves privateers, because they had broken the laws of privateering. They had killed agents of the Spanish crown who had not resisted the privateers' assault. (As we saw above, Aury claimed that the Spanish crew did initially resist.) In addition, they had sent their prey to the bottom of the ocean. This was the behavior of a pirate, "a malevolent one, and an enemy of the human race."[78] Regardless of national belonging or national loyalties, pirates broke the laws of humanity. Therefore, the Spanish court in Cuba considered itself competent to judge a French citizen for an act committed in international waters.

The Spanish witnesses testified that Lamerenx had appeared to have "the friendship and trust" of the French privateer captain,[79] suggesting a longer acquaintance between the two and aggravating the suspicion of complicity. In his own deposition, Lamerenx said that he had boarded Aury's schooner because he wanted to sail back to New Orleans and the privateer's ship was the only option. It is likely, however, that Lamerenx and Aury had met before. Aury had operated out of the French enclave of Santo Domingo in the spring of 1809,[80] precisely when Lamerenx was fighting there on the French side against the Spanish and the English. As captain and part owner of a schooner named *Le Beau Narcisse*, Aury had run the British blockade on May 5, 1809, and delivered 250 barrels of flour and some salted meat to the starving population and troops.[81] After the city's fall to the English, Aury had retreated to the French colony of Guadeloupe, and after Guadeloupe's fall a few months later, he had gone to New Orleans. We know that Lamerenx was in New Orleans in early 1811. It may be that Lamerenx fled Santo Domingo with Aury and eventually made it with him to New Orleans in 1811.

Privateers operated multipurpose ships and often carried passengers as well as commercial cargo in addition to goods seized by force. We can form a very precise idea of the makeup of Aury's crew thanks to a documented incident that took place in 1815. A black sailor named Ignace, captured by the Spanish, testified that *La Belona*'s crew under Aury's command had comprised "all kinds of sailors, including Spaniards, Frenchmen, Englishmen, Americans, and many from the colony of Guárico [Cap-Français], most of them men of color." We can see from this testimony that Aury had a multinational crew, the majority being black sailors from Haiti. The crew were indeed known and feared throughout the Spanish Caribbean as *los negros de Aury* (Aury's blacks). As we saw earlier, in the spring of 1809 Charles Lamerenx served in a regiment of volunteer black troops defending the French enclave of Santo Domingo against British and Spanish attacks. Aury's sailors and Lamerenx's soldiers had similar profiles: they were free men of color from the former French colony of Saint-Domingue who spoke French or French creole and roamed the Atlantic seeking riches or glory. When Aury's crew member Ignace was asked about his profession, he said that he was a sailor and that "if the Devil himself became a ship, he would sail on it."[82] That was an eloquent way of signaling that his primary allegiance was not to a nation or a sovereign but to a particular way of life.

The collapse of French and Spanish imperial control made room for local and individual initiatives in nation building.[83] The city of Cartagena decreed that it was a sovereign nation, and it ran its own privateer fleet for four years. General Ferrand's rule in Santo Domingo was an individual initiative at first. Ferrand managed to salvage a few hundred troops from the collapse of the Leclerc expedition, took refuge in Santo Domingo, and repelled a Haitian attempt to dislodge him. Having gained a semblance of stability, he governed the enclave on behalf of the French Empire, with all the trappings of French sovereignty, including the Etat-Civil (vital records) and French notaries to record all transactions. By most accounts, he governed wisely and was careful not to offend the feelings and the interests of the mostly Spanish-speaking population under his control. The most extreme case of individual initiative is probably the government that Louis Aury established on Galveston Island. In 1816, a group of insurgents in the province of Veracruz in New Spain gave formal powers to Aury to take possession of Galveston in the name of the Mexican Republic. Those insurgents were far from having full control of Veracruz, but no matter. Aury had full control of Galveston, where he raised the Mexican flag on September

13, 1816. He governed the island as supreme civil and military governor and used it as a base for privateering, with its own prize court to validate the seizures and record the transfer of goods to the new owners. Under Aury's rule Galveston had the beginnings of a fiduciary currency system. An uncomprehending Spanish prisoner reported that "they pay the people with drafts (*vales*) of different denominations, signed by Aury and his secretary." According to the historian Stanley Faye, "With warehouse receipts Commodore Aury created a national currency. It was his currency. It was his nation. The sea that broke in surf on the beach of his island was his sea. He commanded it."[84]

There is no record of an official response by the king of Spain to Charles Lamerenx's plea for clemency, and it is not clear whether the outcome was the result of bribes or a royal pardon (or both), but the fact is that the prisoner was released. In December 1817 Charles Lamerenx, forty-two years old, set foot in France, a country he had never seen before. He was welcomed by his sister Marguerite, whom he had not seen since they were both young children. As we saw in chapter 3, in 1785 Jean-Pierre Lamerenx, the father of Charles and Marguerite, left his coffee plantation in Dondon in the hands of his wife, Françoise Silly, and traveled to his native Lower Navarre to manage his parents' succession. He brought three children with him: Marguerite, who was eight years old, and two younger sons, Jacques and Jean-Baptiste. The eldest son, Charles, nine years old, as well as the youngest children, Marie-Adélaïde and Charles-François, remained in Saint-Domingue. Jean-Pierre Lamerenx left the two sons who accompanied him in the care of his sister Ursule, who lived in Gurs, Béarn, with her husband, Bernard Casenave. He initially left his daughter Marguerite in a convent in Bayonne, but she was reunited with her brothers two years later. The three siblings were raised by their aunt and uncle. (Sending children to be educated in France was standard practice for Saint-Domingue colonists.) In 1802, the two brothers, taking advantage of the peace between France and England, crossed the ocean to join their parents, who were in the process of starting a coffee plantation in Matanzas, Cuba. Marguerite stayed in France and married Daniel Laborde, an innkeeper, in 1804.[85] In 1812, she took possession of the Lamerenx family estate in Aïcirits. Charles Lamerenx stayed with his sister Marguerite when he arrived in France in December 1817. Brother and sister had not seen each other for exactly thirty-two years. The first thing Charles did was to sue his sister for control of the family estate.

An Atlantic Family Network and Its Discontents

When Jean-Pierre Lamerenx sailed back to Saint-Domingue in 1788, after spending two years in Lower Navarre managing his parents' succession, he named inhabitants of Saint-Palais as administrator and alternate administrator of his properties. By 1794 the proxy and the alternate were both dead. Since communications with Saint-Domingue were extremely difficult and there was no news of Jean-Pierre Lamerenx, Bernard Casenave, Jean-Pierre's brother-in-law, called a family council that appointed him custodian of the children and property of Jean-Pierre, a decision that was eventually endorsed by Jean-Pierre when communication was reestablished. Jean-Pierre renewed his brother-in-law's proxy in 1802 and 1804. In 1812, however, Jean-Pierre's daughter Marguerite obtained a judicial decision declaring her father's absence and giving her custody of all family properties in France (both in Aïcirits and in La Bastide Clairence). Thus, when Marguerite welcomed her brother Charles, recently released from a Spanish prison in 1817, she was in possession of the estate in Aïcirits, which had been the property of the Lamerenx family since the 1690s.

As we saw in chapter 3, the conflict that arose between Charles and Marguerite in 1817 was similar to the conflict that had arisen in the previous generation between Jean-Pierre and his sister Ursule. The firstborn was normally the heir and the head of the "house," but the legitimacy of that claim could be contested by a younger sibling (male or female) if the firstborn had been away for a long time and there had been no news of his whereabouts. In that case, proximity trumped primogeniture. In the 1780s, Jean-Pierre Lamerenx was able to reassert his status as heir of the Lamerenx estate because he was physically present in Lower Navarre for two years. In 1817, the issue presented itself in somewhat different terms because the law had changed in the meantime and the Civil Code was in effect. There was no longer any rule of primogeniture or a need to designate a single heir for the estate. The rule by default in successions was equal shares for all children, male or female. Yet the fight between the firstborn Charles and his sister for control of the family estate had symbolic overtones that harked back to *ancien régime* practices. Legally, Marguerite was only the custodian of the estate and administered it on behalf of her mother and her siblings. Symbolically, however, she had assumed the mantle of head of the "house." It was precisely that symbolic place that her brother Charles sought to occupy in her stead. Charles arrived in France in 1817 with a power of attorney signed two years earlier by his mother and all his Cuban siblings, giving him the authority to conduct any transactions in France on their behalf. (Oddly, the document was signed when Charles was incarcerated in Cuba, suggesting that his relatives were optimistic about his eventual release.) The court in Saint-Palais found that Marguerite Lamerenx had dissimulated the existence of the powers of attorney sent by her father Jean-Pierre to her uncle Bernard Casenave in 1802 and 1804. By law it took an absence of ten years to declare that an owner was no longer in possession of a property. Since the last manifestation of the owner's intentions had taken place in 1804, ten years had not elapsed when the court declared the owner's absence in 1812 and gave custody of his properties to his daughter Marguerite. The judge ruled that the 1812 decision had been made in error, and based on the power of attorney Charles brought with him from Cuba, gave custody of the Lamerenx family properties to Charles.

There is every indication that Charles, once he was appointed administrator of the Lamerenx estate, behaved *en maître*. He followed the same strategy his father, Jean-Pierre, had followed thirty years earlier. He sold all the assets in La Bastide Clairence that had reverted to the family since the death of his uncle the chevalier de Lamerenx (see chapter 3),[86] and he used the proceeds to pay off some creditors. This was not sufficient to cover all debts, however. When Jean-Pierre sailed back to Saint-Domingue in 1788, he borrowed a fairly large sum (4,286 livres) from a notary to cover outstanding debts, calculating that money earned in Saint-Domingue was better reinvested there. In 1818 that sum was still due. Charles Lamerenx acknowledged the thirty-year-old debt and promised to pay it back within three years with 2,000 francs in accrued interests (an implied interest rate of approximately 1.5% per year).[87] This set a pattern for the following years. The Lamerenx family was never able to repay those debts going back to the *ancien régime*. Ten years later, in 1829, they signed a new acknowledgment of debt to the same creditors, with another 2,000 francs in additional accrued interest, bringing the total debt, including interest, to 8,486 francs.[88]

When Marguerite welcomed her brother Charles in Aïcirits in 1817, she was living in the large Lamerenx house with her husband, Daniel Laborde, and their son, Jean-Pierre Laborde. It is not known how many stories from the New World Charles Lamerenx told to his guests, but news of the emerging prosperity of the Lamerenx family in Cuba must have made an impression on Daniel Laborde, who sailed to Matanzas, leaving his nine-year-old son and his pregnant wife behind. When Marguerite, aged forty-three, gave birth to a son on June 12, 1819, her husband was seeking his fortune in Cuba. It was Charles Lamerenx who declared the birth of his nephew and godson before the municipal authorities. Marguerite named her newborn son Charles. The clerk recorded in florid *ancien régime* style that the declaration had been made by "Charles de Lamerenx, esquire, godfather of the child, *rentier*, master of the noble house of Lamerenx."[89] It was as if the Revolution had not happened and Navarrese houses still had masters. Charles, born in Saint-Domingue and arrived in France as a result of unexpected circumstances, was reclaiming the symbolic place of his great-grandfather Jean Lamerenx, the first proprietor of the Uhart-Juzon estate.

Charles ran the estate and shared the Lamerenx house with his sister Marguerite and nephew Jean-Pierre (the newborn nephew Charles lived only one year). He probably felt that he had achieved through inheritance the status of wealthy landowner that would have been his if the Haitian Revolution had not happened. After a few years he even took a concubine Saint-Domingue style, not a manumitted slave but a woman considerably below his station, an illiterate seamstress who was the daughter of local farmers. Such an arrangement would have been considered normal in colonial Saint-Domingue, but it was bound to raise eyebrows in nineteenth-century France. In 1828 Charles Lamerenx's mother and siblings wrote from Cuba to remove him as administrator of the family properties and to reinstate Marguerite.⁹⁰ The scandal of Charles's private life may have been a factor in the decision, but the primary reason was probably Charles's lack of success in running the estate, although the Cuban relatives politely wrote that they had "nothing to say against" Charles's management.⁹¹ Charles had discovered that an agricultural estate in southwestern France was not nearly as profitable as a coffee plantation based on slave labor in Saint-Domingue or Cuba. Immediately after Marguerite was reinstated as administrator, she sent a bailiff to notify her brother of the new arrangement and to inform him that additional staff would be hired for the upkeep of the estate, which had been badly neglected.⁹²

Charles Lamerenx may have felt almost relieved to be in this new position. Then fifty-six years old and having never been married, he tied the knot with Madeleine Biscay, the woman who shared his life; recognized the two sons he had with her; and moved to her hometown, Arette, approximately thirty miles from Aïcirits.⁹³ In 1833, for a sum of 2,000 francs, he sold to his sister Marguerite his share of the Lamerenx estate, along with any claims he might have on family properties in Cuba.⁹⁴ At that point he was entirely without property, which made him eligible for government assistance as a refugee from Saint-Domingue. In fact he had filed a request on those grounds three years earlier. This assistance, which was entirely distinct from the indemnity for former property owners paid out from Haitian government funds, was granted for humanitarian reasons to former colonists in need.

On November 20, 1829, Charles Lamerenx sent a request to the French minister of the interior.⁹⁵ He began by mentioning his service as staff captain in the black volunteer legion, which did not entitle him to a military pension, a fact he denounced as unfair in view of his loyal service to the state and the wounds he had received defending it.⁹⁶ "I was born to enjoy a good fortune," he wrote in a separate letter, "but the fateful revolution of the island of Saint-Domingue destroyed all my hopes."⁹⁷ He continued: "Having survived the massacres perpetrated by the Negroes, I thought I could find support in the estate of my ancestors, but the infidelity or the incompetence of those agents who were entrusted with it was such that the debts outweighed the money I was owed and could not collect. I therefore have no choice but to humbly solicit the annual support granted by the King's munificence to those ill-fated colonists who survived the events."⁹⁸

The ministry initially responded that Lamerenx was indeed eligible but would not receive any money for a while because all the funds in the budget had already been committed. Lamerenx then drew on an *ancien régime* connection:

Jean-Bernard d'Uhart, a local elected official who had been a representative of the nobility at the Estates General in Versailles in 1789,[99] intervened on his behalf, and Lamerenx was granted a stipend of 300 francs per year. Every six months, the mayor of his place of residence had to certify that he was without resources. A few years later, Lamerenx wrote again to ask for a raise. The stipend was increased to 480 francs because of the petitioner's age. His only source of revenue besides the stipend was his meager income as *receveur buraliste*, a job given to indigent but politically connected veterans, who collected local excise taxes and sold tobacco products, which were subject to government monopoly.

During the first half of the nineteenth century the Lamerenx family functioned as a transatlantic network. The Cuban members of the family owned shares of the Lamerenx estate in France. In turn, the French members of the family were co-owners of the Lamerenx properties in Cuba. And there was migration in both directions. The most tangible piece of evidence for co-ownership is the large number of powers of attorney, often signed when someone was about to cross the ocean.[100] In 1842, just six years before the abolition of slavery in the French colonies, Marguerite Lamerenx signed a power of attorney to one of her brothers in Cuba to receive her share in the sale of the San Pedro coffee plantation, including the sale of slaves. The flow of emigration was mostly from France to Cuba, but not all emigration was successful, and there were some returns to France. This pattern of joint ownership was fundamentally different from the single ownership prescribed by Navarrese custom, which had been the rule during the *ancien régime*.

Marguerite Lamerenx's husband, Daniel Laborde, did not make a fortune in Cuba. He died in Matanzas in 1824, barely six years after his emigration from France.[101] The lure of American wealth was still strong in the following generation. Jean-Pierre Laborde, the only son of Marguerite Lamerenx and Daniel Laborde, emigrated to Cuba in 1837. (It is not clear whether his wife, Hélène d'Oro, and their young daughter accompanied him.)[102] It does not seem to have been a successful move, because Jean-Pierre Laborde was back in France a few years later and lived with his wife, his daughter, and his mother on the Lamerenx estate in Aïcirits. In the following twenty years, mother and son made increasingly desperate attempts to keep the Lamerenx estate afloat. In 1839, the debt contracted by Jean-Pierre Lamerenx in 1787 was transferred to a new creditor.[103] Marguerite and her son repaid their debts by borrowing from well-to-do neighbors, and they repaid those loans by borrowing more.[104] In one instance the lender was someone who had recently resettled in France after making a fortune in Cuba.[105] By the late 1850s Marguerite and her son were running out of options and put the Lamerenx estate up for sale. An advertisement appeared in a local newspaper with a flattering description of the property: the 36-hectare (89-acre) estate was said to generate 4,000 francs per year in net revenue.[106] The estate was sold on December 4, 1859, for 40,000 francs.[107] A large part of the proceeds from the sale was used to pay off creditors. Marguerite was eighty-three years old when the sale took place. She died the following summer.[108] The house of Uhart-Juzon, purchased by her ancestor Rachel de la Forcade a century and a half earlier, was no more.

Charles Lamerenx had three sons with his wife, Madeleine Biscay. The family rented an apartment in the center of Pau during the late 1840s,[109] suggesting that in spite of their limited means, they were able to send their sons to the Collège royal, which happened to have a number of students coming from New Orleans or Cuba (almost certainly descendants of Saint-Domingue colonists).[110] Charles died in Arette in 1854 at the age of seventy-nine.[111] One year before his death, on December 22, 1853, his oldest son, Eugène, boarded the *François Théodore* in Bordeaux and arrived in Havana on March 14, 1854.[112] He carried in his pocket a power of attorney from his seventy-eight-year-old aunt Marguerite Lamerenx, who was still anxious to assert her property rights in Cuba, a land she had never seen. (Born in Saint-Domingue before the Revolution, she had lived in France since 1786.) The youngest son, Adolphe, migrated to Cuba later the same year.[113] The secondborn son, Auguste, held off for a while and finally decided to emigrate as well, sailing from Bordeaux to Havana on January 6, 1858.[114] Starting in the 1860s the story of the Lamerenx family was entirely a Cuban story. When Marguerite Lamerenx died in France in 1860, the clerk in charge of recording her death erroneously indicated her birthplace as Matanzas, Cuba. She was assumed to have been born where all her relatives now lived.

Charles Lamerenx, born in colonial Saint-Domingue in 1775, set foot in France for the first time in his life in 1817, at the age of forty-two, and sold the house where his father had been born. He was only sixteen when the Haitian Revolution broke out. Between 1791 and 1817, initially following his father, Jean-Pierre, and later on his own, he was constantly on the move, fighting wars, trying to do business, or trying to secure his own freedom. In *Atlantic Creoles in the Age of Revolutions*, Jane Landers studies the trajectories of black sailors and soldiers who crisscrossed the Atlantic in the early nineteenth century, repeatedly reinventing themselves amid fast-changing political and social circumstances. She writes that "the Atlantic Creoles . . . fought variously for the King of Kongo, the King of England, the King of France, the French Jacobins, Muskogee and Seminole chiefs, the King of Spain, and sometimes for themselves. Each shift of allegiance required a reevaluation of political platforms and programs, with the possibilities of freedom that each offered."[115] A white man, Charles Lamerenx fits this definition of the Atlantic creole. Buffeted by wars and revolutions, he pledged allegiance to Louis XVI of France, then to Charles IV of Spain, then to the French Republic, then to the Emperor of the French, then to Ferdinand VII of Spain, then to Charles X of France, then to Louis Philippe of France.

In that sense Lamerenx had a lot in common with his compatriot Louis Aury, who served France, then Venezuela, then Colombia, then Mexico, then Argentina and Chile (and briefly ran his own semi-independent state on Galveston Island). Aury's crew was multiracial. So was Toussaint Louverture's army, in which Lamerenx probably served with his father, and so was the Santo-Domingo volunteer regiment in which he served as staff captain. The only stable reference point in Lamerenx's peregrinations was his family: his mother sent money to pay the courts fees when he was tried by the Spanish. In that respect Lamerenx may have shared the feelings Aury expressed in a letter to his family in Paris: "You have to have traveled around the world for ten or twelve years to treasure the ability to conjure up what is dear to you. Having met since that time almost exclusively people I did not care about, it is sweet to remember that there are still human beings who share your pleasures, who listen to your complaints, and who will feel your pain."[116] After he finally settled in France in 1818, Charles Lamerenx remained in touch with his brothers and sisters in Cuba, and the connection remained active for a long time, since his three sons sailed to Havana nearly forty years later and one of them married his Cuban first cousin. One could say that for Charles Lamerenx the family horizon was coextensive with the Atlantic horizon.

Later in this chapter we will discuss national identities more broadly, but it should be noted here that Atlantic wars and revolutions made *individual* identities uncertain. When Charles Lamerenx's sister Marguerite, born in Saint-Domingue and raised in France, was married in 1804, the clerk of the court refused to validate the marriage because the bride could not provide a valid birth certificate. That was impossible because there was no communication with Haiti.[117] An investigation had to be conducted by a magistrate, and several witnesses came forward to certify that Marguerite had been born in Saint-Domingue and had been approximately nine years old when she arrived in the town of Gurs in 1787 to live with her aunt and uncle. Marguerite herself claimed to have been born in 1778. (The sacramental records for Dondon, now available at the French Overseas Archives, show that she was born on May 19, 1776.) The marriage was eventually validated in 1806.[118] When Charles Lamerenx married Madeleine Biscay in 1831, he assumed the identity of his younger brother François-Charles, whose birth certificate was available, as his own birth record had not survived the Haitian Revolution. This made him nine years younger in the eyes of French law.

General Mouscardy's Career

As we saw in chapter 4, Jean Mouscardy left Saint-Domingue in 1793, leaving behind at least six mixed-race children and their mother, Françoise Alzire, a free woman of color. He was already in his seventies at the time. In France, he lived with his nephews in Bayonne and died in 1797. There was intense privateering activity in Bayonne during those years, and one of Jean Mouscardy's grand-nephews, Etienne Thore, enrolled as a crew member on a privateer ship named *L'Impatient* in 1799.[119] The ship's owners were the wealthy and enterprising Basterreche brothers of Bayonne. There is a detailed record of a seizure made by *L'Impatient* shortly before Etienne Thore enrolled. On October 28, 1798, a Portuguese vessel coming from Brazil and captured by *L'Impatient* entered the port of Bayonne. (Portugal was an ally of Britain in its war with France.) The Portuguese ship's cargo included sugar, tobacco, leather, cotton, ipecac, and mahogany—no treasure, simply an assortment of colonial commodities.[120] As Aury wrote to his sister, privateering was just business.[121]

Of Jean Mouscardy's six children, there is one whose life is fairly well documented. The firstborn, Jean-Théodat Mouscardy, had a military career in Haiti and became a general. As we shift the focus of this chapter from the Lamerenx family in Cuba to the Mouscardy family in Haiti, we follow the same path as the narrator in Carpentier's novel, who left his French owner in Cuba and moved back to the North of Haiti, where he had been a slave and was now a free citizen. There he was forced to join the thousands of workers who were building the Citadel La Ferrière, the fortress that King Henri Christophe, who ruled the northern part of Haiti, intended as protection against the French. (The citadel was near Dondon, just a few miles from the old Mouscardy plantation.) In the novel, the narrator, Ti Noël, describes his position as even worse in some ways than colonial slavery: "In other days, the colonists—except when they had lost their heads—had been careful not to kill their slaves, for dead slaves were money out of their pockets. Whereas here the death of a slave was no drain on the public funds."[122] At enormous human cost, "in the event of any attempt by France to retake the island, he, Henri Christophe, *God, my cause and my sword*, could hold out here, above the clouds as long as was necessary, with his whole court, his army, his chaplains, his musicians, his African pages, his jesters."[123]

Jean-Théodat Mouscardy was one of the courtiers that Carpentier describes in his novel. There are few details about his activities during the Haitian Revolution. All we have is the testimony of his grandnephew Démesvar Delorme, who says "he fought in the War of Independence and became a colonel under Christophe."[124] (We also know that before the Revolution his father sent him to be educated in France.) We have more details about his role during the reign of King Christophe, who ruled from 1811 to 1820. Jean-Théodat was one of the king's most trusted associates and served as manager of the royal household. On August 15, 1813, in the middle of the night, he received a Frenchman named Armand who came to warn the king of a conspiracy against him. He walked into the king's bedroom. King Christophe, who was still awake, told Mouscardy to let the informant in.[125] The *Almanach Royal* of Haiti for the year 1816 mentions

Jean-Théodat Mouscardy as one of two intendants of the royal household serving under one general intendant, the Baron de Chevalier.[126]

How exactly Mouscardy reached this position is not clear, but his ascension is reminiscent of that of Jean-Louis Vastey, better known as the Baron de Vastey, who became the king's *éminence grise*. Both men spent time in France during their adolescence. (Jean-Louis Vastey stayed with relatives in the Pays de Caux in Normandy, an area of important outmigration to Saint-Domingue, from 1791 to 1796.)[127] As we saw in chapter 4, Jean-Théodat Mouscardy was the coowner of a large coffee plantation in the Ennery district of Marmelade, given to his mixed-race children by their white father, Jean Mouscardy. Jean-Louis Vastey himself was the mixed-race son of Jean-Valentin Vastey, a white man from the Pays de Caux who owned a large coffee plantation in the Ennery district of Marmelade. Like Jean-Théodat Mouscardy's mother, Jean-Louis Vastey's mother was a free woman of color.[128] The Vastey plantation and the plantation of the Mouscardy children were within the same subdivision of the Ennery district, called Nouvelle Flandre. Toussaint Louverture acquired four coffee plantations in Ennery in the 1790s and paid frequent visits to the district (his wife Suzanne supervised the administration of the properties).[129] For a while, the Vastey plantation served as his military headquarters.[130] Toussaint's association with Ennery was so strong that Ennery was renamed Louverture when it seceded from Marmelade to become a separate commune. It is very likely that Mouscardy and Vastey had known each other since childhood. It is also likely that neighborly ties to Toussaint Louverture facilitated their careers at the beginning. Jean-Théodat Mouscardy and Jean-Louis Vastey were made knights in the Order of Saint-Henry on the same day, October 15, 1815. The Order of Saint-Henry was King Christophe's version of the Saint-Louis Cross, as the Legion of Honor was Napoleon's version of that *ancien régime* medal.

In Aimé Césaire's play *The Tragedy of King Christophe*, there is a scene of confrontation between the king and an agent named Franco de Medina, sent by France to try to persuade Christophe to submit to the authority of Louis XVIII.[131] Medina happens to be a traitor who cannot claim diplomatic immunity and is thrown into prison. (All these details correspond to what happened historically.) What is especially interesting for our purposes is that the attempt by France to persuade Christophe to give up the throne was the occasion for his followers to make a solemn declaration of allegiance to the king in the name of the Haitian nation. Jean-Théodat Mouscardy was one of the signatories of the declaration. The French delegation was a team of two agents whose mandate was not totally clear. (After the negotiation failed, the envoys were disavowed by the French Ministry of the Navy.) Franco de Medina was second to a retired general named Jean Joseph Dauxion Lavaysse, who attempted to open negotiations by sending letters to each of the two men in charge of the former colony, Alexandre Pétion in the South and Henri Christophe in the North. The letter to Pétion was relatively short. It started by rehearsing the common hatred French royalists and Haitian revolutionaries had of Napoleon Bonaparte and went on to portray Louis XVIII as a philosopher-king committed to constitutional government. It concluded by offering the following alternative: to pledge allegiance to the king and "share in the rights of French subjects and citizens" or "to be treated like evil savages or hunted down like runaway Negroes."[132] If you choose the former, Dauxion Lavaysse said to Pétion, you will "deserve the most honorable tokens of your sovereign's satisfaction and the gratitude of your fatherland and of the inhabitants of Haiti, whom we cannot cease to consider French."[133] Aside from the rather offensive allusion to runaway slaves, the tone of the letter was moderate.

The letter to Christophe was a toxic mix of condescension and strident threats. It too started with a denunciation of Bonaparte's tyranny and lamented the arrest and death of Toussaint Louverture, who had been a loyal supporter of the royal cause. (There was a kernel of truth in this: Toussaint had indeed been a royalist until he rallied the republic in 1794.) Then the threats: if Christophe did not step down, France would overrun the island with a slave army brought in from Africa and exterminate its rebel population. The threat had to be taken seriously, the letter said, because all European powers were now allied and ready to help one another in keeping order in their colonial possessions. Britain was in the process of retaking its former colony in North America, which should serve as a warning to the Haitians. (At that point the British had the upper hand in their war against the United States.) If Christophe and his entourage pledged allegiance to Louis XVIII, they would be rewarded with flattering titles and fat pensions, and they should not be worried about "prejudice" (meaning racial prejudice) standing against the granting of these distinctions. Commoners like Jean-de-Dieu Soult and Louis-Gabriel Suchet (former generals in Napoleon's army) had been distinguished by the Bourbon Restoration. If the restored Bourbons had honored commoners in the same way that nobles had been honored in the *ancien régime*, they could very well bestow on blacks honors that had heretofore been reserved for whites. There was in that respect the precedent of the Spanish Bourbons, who made their supporters legally white regardless of the color of their skins by issuing *lettres de blanc* (letters of whiteness). As he did in the letter to Pétion, Dauxion Lavaysse presented Christophe with a choice: to be "the illustrious servant of the great sovereign of the French" or to have "the more precarious fate of a chief of rebel slaves."[134]

For an indication of the state of mind of Christophe's entourage, it is useful to read the response that one of the king's advisers, the chevalier de Prézeau (also featured in Césaire's play), published shortly after Dauxion Lavaysse's letter was made public. The war between the United States and Britain, Prézeau wrote, was taking place fifteen hundred leagues away from Haiti and "has nothing to do with us."[135] The alliance of all European powers was a false supposition, as the British government was favorable to Haitian interests and would never support the reenslavement of the Haitians. On the conferral of whiteness, Prézeau wrote: "We do not wish to become white thanks to *lettres de blancs*: we take pride in the color that God decided to put on our faces. We ask to enjoy the natural rights of man and the political rights enjoyed by free and independent nations."[136]

On October 21, 1814, King Christophe called an extraordinary meeting of the Council General of the Nation, made up of all the dignitaries of the court and all the high-ranking civil and military officers of the kingdom. The meeting took place in the Sans-Souci Palace, five miles from Dondon. Christophe started with a short speech in which he ordered that both letters from Dauxion Lavaysse be read and asked the council to decide what response should be given. After deliberating, the council wrote a declaration stating that the letters were offensive and unacceptable. Allusions to slavery were especially intolerable, since the Haitians had won their freedom with their own blood. Dauxion Lavaysse's statement about "the inhabitants of Haiti, whom we cannot cease to consider French" generated the following response: "We have a new name, a new life, new customs; we are nothing like the French, a people who never ceased to persecute us and whom we hate."[137] The declaration ended with a pledge of allegiance to the king and to the constitution of the kingdom. After the declaration was read before the council, all the members cried, "Long Live the King! Long Live Freedom! Independence or Death!" and went to the desk to affix their signatures. This was done in hierarchical order, beginning with the royal family, followed by the barons, then the chevaliers, then the colonels, then the lieutenant colonels. Jean-Théodat Mouscardy signed with the lieutenant colonels.

The episode was reported in the British press at the time. The *Christian Observer*, an Anglican antislavery journal based in London, gave summaries of Dauxion Lavaysse's letters. The article characterized the letter to Pétion as "an attempt to allure him, in a manner, however, but ill adapted to the end it had in view, to acknowledge the authority of Louis XVIII." As to the letter to Christophe, it was "of a very different description, forming a strange mixture of stupid flattery, and still more stupid intimidation." According to the British paper, the letter to Christophe was "full of the grossest misstatements of fact, in respect to the recent events which have taken place in Europe," and it proved "the entire ignorance of M. Dauxion Lavaysse, and of his master Malouet [the French minister of the navy] as to the state of information in Haiti. Every occurrence which takes place in Europe is as fully known there as it is on the Exchange of London."[138]

Jean-Thédodat Mouscardy survived the end of King Christophe's regime and pledged allegiance to President Jean-Pierre Boyer when the northern and southern parts of the island were reunited after King Christophe's death by suicide in 1820. By then a colonel, Mouscardy was appointed deputy commander of the military garrison in Cap-Haïtien, and he purchased (in all likelihood at a bargain price) a house that came from the large stock of government property. The house stood at the corner of rue du Gouvernement and rue des Religieuses, in the center of the city.[139] His superior was Thomas Béliard, an out-of-wedlock son of King Christophe who had been appointed brigadier general by his father in 1819 and pledged allegiance to the new regime as well.[140] In 1822, General Belliard served as a witness for the declaration of birth of Marguerite Mouscardy, an out-of-wedlock daughter of Jean-Théodat.[141] A few months later Mouscardy returned the favor, serving as a witness for the declaration of birth of General Belliard's son. The newborn was named Jean-Théodat.[142]

In 1837, Jean-Théodat Mouscardy had a spectacular occasion to prove his loyalty to the Boyer government. He was ordered to arrest a rebel colonel named Isidor Gabriel, who had started a revolt on the grounds that "Boyer had sold the country to French whites." According to the Haitian historian Beaubrun Ardouin (who was pro-Boyer), this was "an old accusation borrowed from Christophe's regime." Isidor criticized the breakup of large estates in the North and promised a return to military discipline among plantation workers. Under Boyer, there was a policy of land distribution based on the idea that small proprietors would be a strong political base for the regime. (The distribution came with centrally mandated production targets, which were never enforced.) Isidor, himself a sugar plantation owner, dismissed this policy as inefficient and favored the kind of forced labor on large estates that had existed under Toussaint Louverture, Dessalines, and Christophe. He reportedly said in Creole, "Cé à present que nègres va travaillé" (It's time for Negroes to get to work). That was not exactly a popular platform, and many of Isidor's supporters defected when his plans became clearer.[143] According to a contemporary account in a government newspaper, after tracking him for several days, Mouscardy found a wounded and dying Isidor and began to lecture him on his revolt against the republic and his ingratitude to President Boyer, who had been a benefactor and a father to him. To which Isidor reportedly replied: "This is true, I am guilty. My fate is well deserved."[144]

Following this episode, Jean-Théodat Mouscardy was promoted to brigadier general and given the command of the military district of Grande-Rivière, which comprised the towns of Grande-Rivière-du-Nord and Dondon, as well as the formerly Spanish town of Saint-Raphaël. This was where the young Démesvar Delorme visited his great-uncle, who at first seemed "standoffish, intimidating, and full of aristocratic mannerisms."[145] However, Jean-Théodat Mouscardy showed great affection for his great-nephew. He "kissed me tenderly," Delorme writes, and "he loved me for the good heart he found in me and for what he called a happy disposition."¹⁴⁶

On May 7, 1842, a devastating earthquake leveled the entire city of Cap-Haïtien. Démesvar Delorme, eleven years old, was playing marbles with his brother while watching the maneuvers of a local infantry regiment. A terrifying noise began to be heard, and soldiers started to fall. The bell tower of the cathedral began to swing and then collapsed. The cathedral itself crumbled, then all the houses. A huge fire erupted, and everyone was presented with a picture of hell: "This is how one should describe the judgment day they tell us about when we are children: it lacked neither the Angel's trumpet nor the cries of despair nor the lamentations."¹⁴⁷ Delorme, his mother, and his siblings ran to the mountains—a seismic sea wave had also flooded the lowlands—and took refuge in Grande-Rivière, where Jean-Théodat Mouscardy received them "with an emotion that is hard to express."¹⁴⁸ In the meantime, widespread looting had started in the city. Victims of the earthquake were being robbed and killed. As soon as General Mouscardy heard news of civil disturbance, he dispatched troops to Cap-Haïtien in an attempt to restore order. A contemporary press report credits Mouscardy for a rapid response, comparing him favorably with the commander of the neighboring Limbé District, who sent troops much later. The earthquake took place on a Saturday, and the looting began on Sunday. By Tuesday Mouscardy's troops were in the city.¹⁴⁹

Jean-Théodat Mouscardy's career ended with the revolution of 1843, which came after a long period of political stability in Haiti. On May 29, 1843, Mouscardy was removed from his post as military commander of the Grande-Rivière District. A popular tribunal accused and convicted him of corruption and mismanagement. The list of misdeeds was a long one. He had kept in his own house property seized from looters in Cap-Haïtien and had sold it for his own benefit without holding public auctions. He had protected cattle robbers. For many years he had had a legal monopoly on the wholesale of meat in the district, holding on to it whenever it was being reauctioned by intimidating other bidders and securing a lower price at each new auction. He had not enforced sanitary regulations on the sale of meat. He had curbed dissent, had not kept order, and had not protected individual property. The tribunal ruled that "it does not fit the morality of the revolution to seek out the guilty auxiliaries of the former tyranny, yet it behooves the dignity of a sovereign people to remove from leadership positions those wicked men who have dishonored themselves because of their immoral excesses and who have forfeited the consideration and esteem of their fellow citizens."¹⁵⁰ The removal of Mouscardy took place under the direct supervision of the new strongman of Haiti, Charles Rivière-Hérard, who visited the Grande-Rivière District before the trial and made speeches before the population on the following theme: "You are the people, and as such you are the sovereign; now your leaders are only your servants."[151] Rivière-Hérard concluded his report as follows: "Hearing this, the people, whom I know because I did share their life, gathered around me and told me about their suffering; together with their committee, they denounced General Mouscardy, who had been oppressing, demeaning, and pillaging them for a long time. The general could not justify himself against accusations of extortion and abuse of power. He was therefore removed from his command in the Grande-Rivière District, and I issued a proclamation to inform the people of his guilt."[152]

For Mouscardy the outcome was humiliating but bloodless. When his great-nephew remembered him in writing in 1876, he did not mention Mouscardy's downfall, but he implicitly defended his reputation by mentioning that acting on President Boyer's orders, General Mouscardy had seized stolen items from the homes of looters and sold them at public auction to benefit the victims of the earthquake.[153] Jean-Théodat Mouscardy died not long after his forced retirement. "If General Mouscardy had lived longer," Delorme wrote, "my destiny could have been very different."[154]

Démesvar Delorme on the Haitian Nation

In 1861, Pedro Santana, the leader of the Dominican Republic, signed a pact with Spain to return the eastern part of Hispaniola to colonial status. The ostensible goal of that move was to protect the Spanish-speaking part of the island from annexation by Haiti. The Haitians were greatly alarmed to have a European colonial power on their border, especially one that kept slavery legal in its Caribbean possessions. They sent a diplomatic delegation to Britain and France to seek support against possible Spanish designs. Démesvar Delorme, thirty years old, was a junior member of the delegation. Upon his arrival he wrote to Alphonse de Lamartine, the poet-politician who was a staunch supporter of the Haitian cause. Lamartine wrote back immediately with words of support.

During the same trip to Europe, Delorme also befriended Victor Hugo and Alexandre Dumas. Delorme's main contribution to the mission was a slim volume entitled *L'Indépendance d'Haïti et la France* (Haiti's independence and France).[155] The book was published under the name of Charolais, a journalist and colonial administrator whom Delorme also befriended in Paris.[156] Its main thesis was that protecting Haitian independence was in France's best interest. And if France had colonial ambitions, it should expand its presence in Algeria, a colony whose development was incomplete. "Algeria will be another France one day," Delorme wrote, "as great, as beautiful, and as radiant as the motherland."[157] It may seem surprising that a Haitian citizen would support France's colonial ambitions, and one might suspect Delorme of pandering to French public opinion for reasons of national self-interest. However, his position was consistent with the views of liberal economists like Jean-Baptiste Say, who had argued that there was "good" and "bad" colonization. The colonial system of the eighteenth century was "bad" because it was based on slavery and monopoly and because the colonists had a mercenary spirit: they were loyal neither to the mother country nor to the land that had made them rich. The colonization of North Africa was "good" because it was based on free trade and free labor and the colonists, like those of antiquity, were loyal to their new homeland as well as to the mother country.[158] Still impersonating a French journalist, Delorme concluded with the following exhortation: "Let's love and respect the independence of Haiti. . . . Let's trade extensively with the young republic. It will return a hundred times what it earned us before. It will be another France in the Antilles, a grateful, dedicated, and faithful friend instead of a rebellious vassal."[159]

In the 1860s Delorme played a prominent but fleeting role in Haiti's political life. An opinion leader of liberal persuasion, he served briefly in three different ministerial capacities—foreign affairs, education, and religious affairs—and he was exiled twice. In exile in Paris in 1870, he published an ambitious work, *Les théoriciens au pouvoir* (Theoreticians in power). The book received a prize from the Académie française. It was a historical-philosophical meditation on great thinkers such as Pericles, Solon, Mirabeau, and Lamartine, who had taken part in politics. The book was written as a Platonic dialogue between two friends, Paul and Georges, who took long walks in the Haitian countryside. At the beginning of the second volume, the two characters decide to make a journey on horseback to the places that are familiar to the readers of this story: "They went through Plaisance, rode past Marmelade, and after many detours, which they extended on purpose, they reached the town of Dondon, sitting below the summit that bears that stone giant armed with cannons, the Citadel Laferrière, whose head is in the clouds."[160] After visiting the citadel, they make a pilgrimage to the Voûte à Minguet (Fig. 5.1). The cave was a former Taíno place of worship that had been used as a shelter by the first French settler, the freebooter André Minguet (see chapter 2). The cave's walls were still covered with "the names and the dates, written in charcoal since the end of the sixteenth century, of those Europeans who were looking for data about the extinct Caribbean race, which does not have a single descendant on this large island."[161] The extermination of the Taínos was a puzzle, because the sixteenth century had been a period of incipient enlightenment. The Spanish, however, had behaved in contrast to the new spirit of the age, and their retrograde behavior had been consistent across the Atlantic. The extermination of the natives of Hispaniola coincided with the expulsion of the Moors, "those sons of Africa who sustained Spain's prosperity." In that sense "what Spain did in America corresponds to what it was doing in Europe itself. It is the implementation of the same mind-set, the same system."[162] (Interestingly, the characters show little animus against the subsequent use of

Fig. 5.1. Minguet's Cave. Engraving by Theodore Weber (1838–1907) from a sketch by Luis Antonio. The round shapes in the foreground are Taíno statues. *Le Tour du monde. Nouveau journal des voyages* 38 (1879).

slavery by the French.) The characters spend the entire day in the cave and continue the conversation over dinner in Dondon.

Three years later, still in exile in Paris, Delorme published another book, *La misère au sein des richesses* (Poverty in the midst of wealth). Like the 1861 book on Haiti's independence and France, it was a response to immediate political-military circumstances. The United States had plans to take over the Dominican Republic, which raised the possibility of an annexation of Haiti itself. Such a prospect might appear attractive to some, Delorme wrote, because the United States had just abolished slavery and the Haitians would therefore remain free citizens. Such freedom would be illusory, however, because of the strength of racial prejudice in the United States. Delorme went on to mention an incident he personally had witnessed during a trip to the United States in 1858. While in New York, a city located in a state that did not have slavery, he had taken a ship to Boston. A white man of suspicious appearance had boarded the ship and put his hand in the pocket of a light-skinned black man who was well dressed and prosperous-looking. Realizing what was happening, the black man had protested. Instead of running away, the pickpocket had slapped the black man in the face and cried: "I have just punished this Negro, who dared to suspect me!"[163] Everyone had laughed. The black man had said nothing, lowered his head, and walked away. "How demeaning," Delorme had thought to himself, and he had reminded himself that no Haitian, not even the humblest one, would have tolerated such a slight, even if it had come from the president of the United States. If the Haitians became citizens of the United Sates, they would always have second-class status, comparable to the fate of Jews in medieval Europe or Moors in early modern Spain: "In that country the men of our race must resign themselves to live as Jews lived everywhere in the Middle Ages, tolerated but persecuted. They live like Moors in Spain after the fall of the kingdom of Granada, forced to bend and to tremble."[164]

According to Delorme, the "stupid and shameful racial exclusion" that he had witnessed in New York fortunately did not exist in Europe.[165] This adamant critique of racism in the United States was coupled with a declaration of love for the Haitian nation. Delorme declared himself "the son of those generous men who, hearing the voice of the humanitarian Revolution of 1789, won the rights of man and the citizen on this land of Saint-Domingue, where they founded a refuge for their oppressed race in the Americas."[166] (General Mouscardy, who had fought in the Haitian War of Independence, was surely one of those "generous men.") Delorme professed admiration and gratitude for the European countries that had given him asylum, but he made a pledge of eternal loyalty to the Haitian nation: "No matter how advantageous it might be to me personally, I would never agree to give up my Haitian citizenship. This land of Haiti, which I love so intimately, this land where I was born, where my parents and grandparents were born, is my only homeland. I do not have another."[167]

The same criticism of racial prejudice in the United States appeared in a slim volume Delorme published in Brussels in 1866, *La démocratie et le préjugé de couleur aux Etats-Unis d'Amérique* (Democracy and racial prejudice in the United States of America). Delorme highlighted the contradiction between the United States as "the country of freedom par excellence" and "the classic land of slavery."[168] He argued that racial prejudice in the United Sates was not a contingent fact but rather a necessary consequence of the pursuit of self-interest. According to Delorme, the Haitian people, who had been free since the beginning of the nineteenth century, bore "religiously in their hearts the sentiment of a providential mission" on the American continent: "to destroy all the sophisms that have been used until now in the world to oppress and despise the black races of Africa."[169]

Delorme's last work, *Les petits: La Hollande*, published in Brussels in 1898, was a historical-philosophical meditation on Holland. This might seem like an odd choice of topic, but it made sense from the point of view of Delorme's cosmopolitan nationalism. The history of Holland showed that a small nation could accomplish great things if it loved freedom and stuck to republican principles. This could be an inspiration for Haiti. The recurring slogan of the book was, "Small land, great nation!"[170] The account of Dutch history was interspersed with allusions to the history of Haiti and to contemporary geopolitics. In a poetic pairing, Delorme compared the end of Toussaint Louverture, who died of cold in the icy mountains of Jura, to the death of Napoleon, "who was thrown into the tropics, where the English buried him in fire."[171] He also denounced European colonialism in sub-Saharan Africa and compared it to the extermination of native peoples by the Spanish in America. He praised African resistance and mentioned the recent Ethiopian victory against Italian invaders at Adwa.[172] This, he predicted, was the beginning of the end of European colonialism in Africa.

Choosing One's Nation

At first sight, there would seem to be little in common between the republic proclaimed by Louis Aury on Galveston Island and the French nation that the inhabitants of La Bastide Clairence decided to join or the Haitian nation that Jean-Théodat Mouscardy refused to leave behind. Also, it would initially appear that nationhood mattered to some, while others were indifferent to it. According to the testimony of the crew member Ignace, Aury's ship carried all sorts of flags, raising the flag of the Republic of Cartegena only when it was about to make a seizure.[173] This is the most extreme case of national allegiance shifting according to circumstances. We saw how Charles Lamerenx pledged allegiance to successive sovereigns depending on where he was and what he needed. At the other end of the spectrum, we see passionate displays of national loyalty in Delorme's writings, in Jean-Théodat Mouscardy's allegiance to King Christophe, or in the decision by the inhabitants of La Bastide Clairence to join the kingdom of France. These are examples of the "love, and often profoundly self-sacrificing love,"[174] that nations inspire.

There is, however, a common thread in these people's behavior, which we can retrieve if we consider that for the characters in this story, the nation was, to some extent at least, not "something unchosen," as Anderson suggests,[175] but a matter of choice. As David Bell has shown, for nationalists in eighteenth-century France, national belonging was not a given but something that needed to be worked on and achieved over time, just as religious belonging had relied on the pedagogical work of Jesuit and other missionaries with the peasantry in the seventeenth century.[176] In a different context, Jeremy Adelman has argued (against Anderson) that the "creole nations" of Latin America "did not predate formal announcements of their existence."[177] For the citizens of La Bastide Clairence in 1789, there was a moment of choice. They could remain citizens of the Kingdom of Navarre, or they could join the French nation. Loyalty to the king was not an issue, since the king of Navarre was also the king of France. The citizens of La Bastide Clairence voted in favor of incorporating their town into the kingdom of France. In so doing, they abandoned the special laws and privileges that had protected them, an act of self-denial that was a manifestation of their "most perfect love" for the French nation. Similarly, in 1814 the followers of King Christophe had a choice: they could acknowledge the authority of Louis XVIII and become French citizens again or reaffirm that they were members of the new Haitian nation. Contrary to what Anderson suggests, these pledges of national belonging were not philosophically poor.[178] The declaration of the inhabitants of La Bastide Clairence drew directly on the writings of Polverel, who had a sophisticated understanding of legal, historical, and constitutional issues. The same can be said of the pledge of Christophe's followers, signed by Jean-Théodat Mouscardy, which was accompanied by a point-by-point refutation of the letters sent by the French envoys. In both cases an elaborate ritual of loyalty concluded with a solemn signing ceremony.

As Jeremy Adelman points out, "The Spanish and Portuguese domains, like so many others, crumbled less out of internal conflicts and more from the compound pressures of several centuries of rivalry between Atlantic powers. Social revolutions transpired when international pressures of competing sovereignties broke down state systems."[179] The same might be said of the French Atlantic domain. In the "big bang" thus created, there was room for all kinds of initiatives in nation-building and some degree of freedom, for some agents at least, in deciding which nation to join. There were varying degrees of difficulty in joining a nation. Becoming a citizen of the Republic of Cartagena was easy. Being accepted as a Spanish citizen in Cuba was hard, at least for French refugees. But in this case too there was a choice to be made. Charles Lamerenx and his family had to choose between, on the one hand, becoming Spanish citizens and remaining in Cuba and, on the other hand, keeping their French citizenship and leaving the island. The tests of loyalty performed by the *juntas de vigilancia*, reminiscent of the procedures of the Inquisition, crossed into the obscure territory of inner feelings and desires and were aimed at establishing whether the pledges of allegiance to Spain were sincere. A simple profession of love for the Spanish nation was not enough. Everyone but Charles passed the test. It may have helped that the family came originally from Lower Navarre, a territory to which the Spanish crown had claims. Fluency in Spanish was not an absolute requirement. Françoise Silly, the matriarch of the family, spent the rest of her life in Cuba without knowing one word of Spanish.

For two or three generations, the Lamerenxes functioned as a transnational family.[180] At one time or another, its members cultivated land or engaged in commerce in southwestern France, Saint-Domingue, Cuba, and New Orleans. They used all the legal means at their disposal, frequently including powers of attorney, to manage assets from afar and to acquire or preserve wealth across national boundaries, languages, and legal systems. Family ties made up for the lack of trust that distance usually generates, but intrafamily trust was not a given: siblings sued one another over the control of family assets.[181] As Atlantic creoles, they cultivated a capacity for intercultural negotiation, and they were able to succeed in different national contexts. What made the circulation possible was the fact that they moved between coastal enclaves where they dealt with other migrants, including their own relatives, who shared "a way of life that transcended particular venues."[182] There were significant political, legal, and cultural differences between Cap-Français and Matanzas, for example, but also enough similarities to make for a relatively quick adjustment. And in that sense Bayonne and its Basque hinterland can also be thought of as an Atlantic creole enclave. During the French Revolutionary and Napoleonic Wars, Bayonne was a hub of privateering,[183] just like Cartagena de Indias and Santiago de Cuba. And well into the nineteenth century, notaries in the rural towns of Saint-Palais and La Bastide Clairence drafted powers of attorney that included language regarding the sale and purchase of slaves. For many years there was circulation between the French and Cuban branches of the Lamerenx family, but national belonging became increasingly "sticky," and the flow was more and more in one direction, from France to Cuba, where the opportunities lay. By 1860 the Lamerenxes had become a Cuban family, no longer attracting relatives from France, because everyone eligible had already crossed the ocean. Nevertheless, they held on to a "French" identity through cousin marriages (a behavior typical of what the historian Philip Curtin calls "trading diasporas").[184] Eugène Lamerenx sailed from Bordeaux to Havana in 1854. Once in Matanzas, he met his first cousin Rosa de Lamerens Pérez and married her, having received a dispensation from the local bishop for consanguinity. One of their sons, Carlos Alejo de Lamerens y Lamerens (1860–1925), married his first cousin Emeteria Dolores de Lamerens y Vallenilla in 1889.[185] In the following generation, Carlos Lamerens, son of Carlos and Emeteria, served as editor of a local daily newspaper, *La Aurora del Yumurí*, near the end of World War I.[186] He is also mentioned in the *Dictionary of Cuban Literature* as the cofounder of the *Revista Azul*, a short-lived periodical that appeared in Matanzas in 1921.[187]

CHAPTER SIX

Conclusion

—*Je suis comme la plupart des gens qui passent leur vie à attendre le bonheur comme on attend un héritage. Quelque chose qui vous est dû. L'héritage d'un oncle d'Amérique.*
—*L'Amérique, ça n'existe pas. Je sais, j'y ai vécu.*

—I am like the majority of people, who spend their lives waiting for happiness as one waits for an inheritance. Something one is entitled to: the inheritance of an American uncle.
—It doesn't exist, America. I know: I used to live there.

Alain Resnais, *Mon Oncle d'Amérique*, 1980

The capital, however, that is acquired to any country by commerce and manufactures, is all a very precarious and uncertain possession. . . . No vestige now remains of the great wealth, said to have been possessed by the greater part of the Hans towns, except in the obscure histories of the thirteenth and fourteenth centuries.

Adam Smith, *The Wealth of Nations*, 1776

In Alain Resnais's film *Mon Oncle d'Amérique* (My American Uncle), released in 1980, the somewhat mysterious title is explained near the end, when three allusions are made by the characters to the proverbial phrase *oncle d'Amérique*. The most developed is in a conversation between a media executive and his former lover while visiting an islet near the coast of Brittany that belongs to the executive. As they walk past a particular location on the islet, the executive remembers that when he was a child, he was convinced a treasure was buried there, and he spent entire days digging for it. He had heard about a great-uncle, a brother of his grandmother's, who had gone to America. He was sure the uncle, whom he called "the King of Gold," would come back to tell him where the treasure was. "My American uncle," the executive exclaims, "I am still looking for him!" The former lover replies, "You are five years old!" To which the executive retorts, "But the treasure exists, it is proven! All of these islands used to be hiding places for corsairs and freebooters. Do you know I have not shared these awesome secrets with anyone else?"

Here the American uncle is tied to a childhood memory and to an image of America as the mythical land of gold. "The King of Gold" is an allusion to an illustrated novel for children published in 1920 whose protagonist, named Samuel Knight, is an eighteen-year-old American citizen of French origin who owns a gold-bar factory in the United States and decides to enroll in the French army in World War I.[1] In this instance the image of American wealth is an over-the-top fantasy that is playfully invoked by the character to describe a basic human longing for happiness. This scene is preceded and followed by allusions to the American uncle that seem to convey the exact opposite image. In a conversation with his wife about the wisdom of accepting an attractive but risky promotion, a character mentions a great-uncle who migrated to America with hopes of becoming rich but reportedly became a homeless person in Chicago. Also, after her conversation with the executive, the former lover brings up the image of the American uncle in a conversation with a colleague, who quips: "It doesn't exist, America. I know: I used to live there." The film ends with images of the South Bronx in the late 1970s, a desolate urban landscape in ruins. Here, the American uncle is tied to a darkly dystopian image of America as a land of poverty and destruction.

This book's argument has been that in the French context the highly ambivalent image of the "American uncle" that appears, for instance, in Resnais's film can be traced to a specific historical experience. Originally at least, it had little to do with emigration to the United States and a lot to do with fortunes made and lost in the Caribbean in the eighteenth century. In Resnais's film a character's allusion to "corsairs and freebooters" could be heard as a faint echo of that historical experience. One may also consider the fact that the author of *The King of Gold*, Alice Pujo (1869–1953), happened to be the granddaughter of a man named Alexis-Solange Pujo (1798–1886),[2] who appears in the *Indemnité de Saint-Domingue* as the recipient of Haitian government funds for the Pujo coffee plantation in the Haut-du-Trou District of Dondon, not far from Jean Mouscardy's plantation.[3] The property was formerly owned by an uncle, Jean-Baptiste Pujo (1717–after 1791), who hailed from the western Pyrenees (Labatut in Bigorre).[4] The author of *The King of Gold*, a fantasy for children about wealth in the United States, probably knew about Saint-Domingue wealth (and ruin) from family tradition.

The dystopian version of the image of the "American uncle" was tied not only to the loss of colonists' properties following the Haitian Revolution but to the colonial experience itself, in which the acquisition of wealth felt eminently fragile and tainted by its reliance on slave labor. In the opinion of Stanislas de Wimpffen, who visited Saint-Domingue in the late 1780s, "If you calculate the deprivations of all kinds, the vicissitudes of trade, the never-ending fears, the abhorrent details of the slavery regime, the state of depression or anxiety in which he stagnates between a steely sky and an earth that is always ready to engulf him, there is no European farmer or day laborer whose existence is not preferable to that of a Saint-Domingue colonist."[5] On the other hand, we have seen that fortunes made in Saint-Domingue did make a strong impression on popular imagination when emigrants returned to the rural areas of the western Pyrenees they had departed years before. When Marguerite Lamerenx, born in Saint-Domingue and brought to France by her father in 1786, wanted to get married in 1806, several neighbors came forward to testify that the arrival of her father, Jean-Pierre Lamerenx, in 1786 "made a big splash and attracted a number of people who were curious to see him."[6] Twenty years after the fact, the memory of conspicuous displays of wealth by "Americans" was still vivid.

It seems that these memories faded fairly quickly as historical memories once Haiti became independent, and the image of the American uncle was disconnected in popular consciousness from its historical origins. Paradoxically, it was in Haiti that an idealized image of colonial wealth and luxury took hold, helped in part by the fact that Haitians had won their independence thanks to their own military efforts, resulting in surprisingly little bitterness regarding slavery and colonial oppression.[7] Démesvar Delorme painted a picture of Cap-Français in colonial times as a city with "habits of luxury, a taste for celebrations, traditions of bourgeois aristocracy, a passion for music, an enthusiastic temperament." He reported that "from everywhere in the country, even from the neighboring islands, people came to the Cape for Carnival. It was no less rowdy or splendid than that of Venice or Rome." The Cape, Delorme concluded, was "a city of good company, a city of luxury, of concerts, of spectacles."[8]

Throughout the nineteenth century, how colonial wealth could have suddenly vanished was a puzzle to Haitian thinkers like Démesvar Delorme. In his book *La misère au sein des richesses*, Delorme began by giving statistics about the "stunning" wealth of the colony.[9] He estimated that the gross value of Saint-Domingue's exports, including illegal trade with the United States, was half a billion francs near the end of the colonial period and that the overall net value of agricultural properties was 1.5 billion francs. In 1873, however, Haiti's only valuable export was coffee (sugar production had almost entirely disappeared), and production levels were only a fraction of what they had been in colonial times: "Haiti now produces about 60 million pounds of a coffee that is badly grown, badly harvested, of lower quality compared with all other producing countries, worth approximately 50 million francs, or one-tenth of the value the country used to produce."[10] Since taxes on coffee exports were the main source of government revenue, public finances were squeezed between a low level of agricultural exports and an indemnity to former colonists that was still being paid out and was beyond the country's means.[11] The tone of Delorme's comments was not dark or dystopian, however. Other countries in the hemisphere, he argued, had shown that agriculture could be productive under a free-labor regime. He blamed previous governments for a lack of focus on agriculture and expressed the hope that greater productivity could be achieved through the diffusion of best practices and the mechanization of coffee growing.

The obvious difference between 1873 and colonial times was that slavery had been abolished. Delorme mentioned that "it was under a forced labor regime that Saint-Domingue's colonists had achieved the incredible opulence mentioned above," but he argued that "liberal means" could achieve the same results.[12] A change that had taken place between colonial times and 1873 that he did not mention was the shift away from colonial monopoly to free trade. As we saw in chapter 2, economists like Jean-Baptiste Say ascribed the spectacular wealth creation in the colonies to two causes: not only the exploitation of slave labor but also the monopolistic trade between the colony and the mother country, which raised the prices of colonial commodities above their "natural" levels and concentrated wealth in the hands of a few merchants and planters. Following the demise of the French and Spanish colonial empires in the Americas, the British navy was in full control of Atlantic sea lanes, and the old system of exclusive trade between the colony and the mother country was abolished. As a result, the price of colonial commodities fell. Haitian coffee in the French port of Le Havre, which was 2.11 francs per kilogram in 1821, was only 0.73 franc in 1844.[13] Haitian producers had to compete with coffee produced in Cuba and, later, in Brazil. The coffee produced by the Mouscardy family in Ennery, Haiti, had to compete with the coffee produced by their former neighbors the Lamerenxes, who were now coffee growers in Matanzas, Cuba. The combination of superior expertise, cheap land values, and cheap slave labor made the Cuban producers unbeatable on the world market. Cuba in turn was overtaken by Brazil, which relied on slave labor as well, in the 1840s. Haiti's share of the global coffee trade remained very small throughout.

The coffee trade between Haiti and France was already active in the early 1820s, well before the 1825 recognition of Haitian independence by Charles X. It was conducted through third parties with the full knowledge of both governments. Throughout the nineteenth century, France was by far the largest buyer of Haitian coffee. The economic historian Benoît Joachim estimates that between 30 percent and 55 percent of coffee produced in Haiti was shipped to France. (On the other hand, France was only the third largest source of Haitian imports.)[14] As a result of this "dependency" the French government had considerable influence in Haiti's affairs. In his 1945 book *National Power and the Structure of Foreign Trade*, Albert Hirschman argues that when a small and poor country conducts a large part of its trade with a large and rich country, the trade is economically beneficial to both sides, but the large country enjoys disproportionate political clout with the smaller one because an interruption of trade would be comparatively much more harmful to the smaller country. A threat, whether implicit or explicit, to halt trade relations is a powerful means of pressure. In Haitian-French relations those circumstances were in place at the very beginning. It was under the threat of a naval blockade by France that President Boyer decided to grant an indemnity to former colonists in exchange for the recognition of Haiti's independence and the establishment of direct trade relations. Boyer calculated that Haiti had much more to lose than France did if the coffee trade came to a halt.

In the preface to the 1980 expanded edition of his book, Hirschman criticizes the proponents of "dependency theory" for simply wishing away the unpleasant reality of dependency instead of "scrutinizing it further for some possibly built-in modifier or remedy." He asks: "How solid or stable is the resulting relation of domination and dependency?"[15] In response, he suggests that the very asymmetry that characterizes "dependency" can be turned to the advantage of the smaller country:

> A country whose trade and investment is dominated by ties to a large and rich country is, at some point, likely to devote its attention with single-minded concentration to this uncomfortable situation and to attempt to loosen or cut ties. But the large rich country which carries on only a small portion of its international economic relations with the country that dominates it is normally preoccupied with its more vital other interests, for instance its relations with the other large powers. Hence our basic economic disparity generates a disparity of attention, or at least of high-level attention to use the language of bureaucratic politics, and this disparity now favors the dependent country: that country is likely to pursue its escape more actively and energetically than the dominant country will work on preventing this escape.[16]

Because the dependent country has comparatively much more at stake, it will dedicate much more energy to cutting or loosening ties with the dominant country. The dominant country will work to keep ties, but its leadership may eventually lose interest because these ties are not vital. This is a pretty good description of what happened in the Haitian War of Independence. Napoleon made an energetic attempt to retake control of Saint-Domingue by sending Leclerc in 1802. After Leclerc's expeditionary force was soundly defeated by the Haitians, he lost interest, moved on, and with the subsequent sale of Louisiana to the United States signed away one-third of the North American continent.[17] As Hirschman puts it, "The British Empire is said to have been acquired in a fit of absent-mindedness. However that may be, it seems a more convincing proposition that empires, formal or informal, tend to crumble that way."[18] This insight can be generalized to the colonial relations described in this book. As Hirschman suggests, they were inherently unstable. The asymmetry of the relationship between the colony and the mother country made the relationship unstable. And the system of colonial commerce as a whole was unstable. The accumulation of wealth was predicated on monopolistic trade, which had to be defended militarily. Monopolistic profits funded large armies and navies, but those profits vanished in case of open war, which slowed trade or stopped it altogether. The same causes that produced colonial wealth also made it very fragile. This is why the emigrants in this book had such chaotic lives and why their story was one of wealth and disaster.

APPENDIX A
Genealogical Table: House of Uhart-Juzon

Name	Spouse	Birth rank	Date and place of birth	Date and place of death	Date of emigration	Occupation	Notes
				GENERATION 1			
Isaac Lamerenx	Rachel de la Forcade Gouze	—	—	Before 1697	Did not emigrate	Barrister with Parliament of Navarre	Calvinist; purchased Domec de Précilhon house in Béarn (1663); received as member of the nobility in Estates General of Navarre the same year
				GENERATION 2			
Pierre Lamerenx	Unmarried	1	Circa 1660, Oloron (Béarn)	1700, Batavia (Dutch East Indies)	1684 (Holland, then Batavia)	Officer in Dutch East India Company	Protestant emigrant to Holland
Anne	Jean de Bonine	2	After 1660, Oloron (Béarn)	—	1684 (England)		Protestant emigrant to England
Marthe	Unmarried	3	Circa 1665, Oloron (Béarn)	After 1728, Ireland (?)	1684 (Holland, then England)		Protestant emigrant to Holland
Jean Lamerenx, master of Uhart-Juzon house	Suzanne de Lespade	4	Circa 1670, Oloron (Béarn)	1750, Aïcirits	Did not emigrate	Landowner	Converted to Catholicism circa 1685; received Domec de Précilhon house following emigration of older brother, which was exchanged for the Uhart-Juzon house in Lower Navarre; town bailiff of Saint-Palais (1726)
Jeanne	Jacques de Roux	5	Circa 1680, Oloron (Béarn)	—	Did not emigrate		

continued

Name	Birth rank	Date and place of birth	Date and place of death	Date of emigration	Occupation	Spouse	Notes
Anne (Jeanne)	6	1682, Oloron (Béarn)	1758, Celle (Lower Saxony)	1684 (Holland, then Germany)		Gabriel Migault	Protestant emigrant to Holland
GENERATION 3 (children of Jean Lamerenx and Suzanne de Lespade)							
Mathieu Lamerenx, master of Uhart-Juzon house	1	Circa 1706, Aïcirits (Lower Navarre)	1783, Aïcirits	Did not emigrate	Landowner; infantry captain	Anne de Marmont (1724–1781), heiress of Berrio house (La Bastide Clairence)	Master of Uhart-Juzon; introduced to Estates General of Navarre by father, Jean Lamerenx. as eldest son and presumptive heir (1730); *jurat* of La Bastide Clairence (1752)
Françoise	2	Circa 1707, Aïcirits	1785, Aïcirits	Did not emigrate		Unmarried	
Marc Antoine	3	1710, Aïcirits	Circa 1771, Saint-Domingue	1729	Coffee planter; colonial militia captain	Elizabeth Le Jeune (c.1723–1795), daughter of Vincent Le Jeune and Marguerite Robert, colonists from Sainte-Rose de la Grande-Rivière (Saint-Domingue)	Owner of Duhart coffee plantation in Matador District of Dondon, overtaken by slaves in 1791; certificate of nobility issued by d'Hozier (1769), signed by Choiseul in the king's name on August 4, 1770
Jacques	4	Aïcirits	—	Did not emigrate	Parish priest	Unmarried	Pastor of Arbouet-Sussaute (1764)
Marie-Ursule	5	Circa 1720, Aïcirits	1787, Aïcirits	Did not emigrate		Unmarried	

Name	#	Birth	Death/Emigration	Occupation	Notes
Henri	6	Circa 1721, Aïcirits	1791, Hélette (Lower Navarre)	Did not emigrate	Employee of state tobacco agency
Louis	7	After 1721, Aïcirits	Before 1769	1755	Captain in Cantabres Volunteer Regiment, Bayonne	a.k.a. Chevalier de Lamerenx

GENERATION 4 (children of Mathieu Lamerenx and Anne de Marmont)

Name	#	Birth	Death/Emigration	Occupation	Notes
Jean-Pierre Lamerenx, master of Uhart-Juzon house	1	1742, La Bastide Clairence	1810, Matanzas (Cuba)	1764	Coffee planter; colonial militia captain	Owner of Lamerenx coffee plantation in Matador District of Dondon; in France 1786–88; received at Estates General of Navarre as master of Uhart-Juzon (1787); aide-de-camp to Toussaint Louverture (1794)
Marie-Ursule	2	After 1742, La Bastide Clairence	—	Did not emigrate		Had inventory of Uhart-Juzon drawn up after death of father, Mathieu Lamerenx (1783)
Arnaud Jean-Pierre	4	1752, La Bastide Clairence	—	After 1764		a.k.a. Chevalier de Lamerenx
Claire	6	1754, La Bastide Clairence	1757, La Bastide Clairence	Did not emigrate		Buried at Aïcirits (1760)

Françoise Silly (d. 1840), daughter of François Silly and Elizabeth Fleury, coffee planters

Bernard Casenave, merchant

Unmarried

Died in infancy

continued

Name	Spouse	Birth rank	Date and place of birth	Date and place of death	Date of emigration	Occupation	Notes
GENERATION 4 (children of Marc-Antoine Lamerenx and Elizabeth Le Jeune)							
Marie-Elizabeth Lamerenx	Charles Pichot de Kerdisien Trémais (1724–1784), subdelegate general of intendant of Saint-Domingue	1	Before 1752, Dondon (Saint-Domingue)	After 1831	Born in Saint-Domingue	Coffee planter	Owner of L'Hermitage coffee plantation, Marmelade, overtaken by slaves in 1791
Margue-rite-Françoise	Charles de Saint-Germain (1740–1787), captain in Agenois Regiment	2	Before 1752, Dondon (Saint-Domingue)	1795, San Juan de la Maguana (Santo Domingo)	Born in Saint-Domingue	Coffee planter	Owner of La Guille coffee plantation, Dondon, overtaken by slaves in 1791
Jean-François	Unmarried	3	1752, Dondon (Saint-Domingue)	Before 1793	Born in Saint-Domingue	Cavalry officer	Joined light cavalry of King's Guards (1770)
GENERATION 5 (children of Jean-Pierre Lamerenx and Françoise Silly)							
Charles François Lamerenx Duhart	Madeleine Biscay (1807–1876), seamstress	1	1775, Dondon (Saint-Domingue)	1854 Arette (Basses-Pyrénées)	Born in Saint-Domingue	Staff captain in black volunteer troops; tobacconist	Property owner in New Orleans (1811–13); imprisoned in Cuba for piracy (1815–17); administrator of family properties in France, 1818–28
Jean	Raphaëlle Chappotin	2	1775, Dondon	Cuba	Born in Saint-Domingue	Coffee planter in Pinar del Río (Cuba)	

Marguerite	Daniel Laborde (1782–1824), property owner	3	1776, Dondon	1860, Sorde l'Abbaye (Landes)	Born in Saint-Domingue	Landowner	In France after 1786; administrator of family properties in France, 1812–18 and after 1828
Jean-Baptiste		4	1777, Dondon	Cuba	Born in Saint-Domingue		
Jean-Jacques Théodat		5	1779, Dondon	Cuba	Born in Saint-Domingue		
Marie-Adélaïde	Mathieu Grout (d. before 1829)	6	1781, Dondon	Cuba	Born in Saint-Domingue		Godmother of three female slaves of San Pedro coffee plantation in Matanzas (1804)
Charles François	Léocadie Rousselot (d. before 1830), then Rita Pérez	7	1784, Dondon	Cuba	Born in Saint-Domingue	Coffee planter in Matanzas (Cuba)	Part owner and manager of San Pedro coffee plantation in Matanzas

APPENDIX B
Genealogical Table: House of Berrio

Name	Spouse	Birth rank	Date and place of birth	Date and place of death	Date of emigration	Profession	Notes
GENERATION 1							
Marie de Lombart, mistress of Berrio, daughter of Bernard de Lombart, master of Berrio, substitute prosecutor general, and Jeanne de Colombots	Jean de Marmont (1652–1718), younger son of the Lay Abbey of Marmont (Béarn); Calvinist, converted to Catholicism circa 1685; purchased office of Mayor of La Bastide Clairence (1693)	1	La Bastide Clairence	1721, La Bastide Clairence	Did not emigrate	Landowner	
GENERATION 2							
Bernard de Marmont, master of Berrio, son of Marie de Lombart and Jean de Marmont	Anne de Moirie, daughter of Michel de Moirie, Bayonne financier, and Antoinette Petit	1	1686, La Bastide Clairence	1739, La Bastide Clairence	Did not emigrate	Landowner	
GENERATION 3							
Anne Antoinette de Marmont, mistress of Berrio, daughter of Bernard de Marmont and Anne de Moirie,	Mathieu Lamerenx, master of Uhart-Juzon	1	1724, La Bastide Clairence	1781, La Bastide Clairence	Did not emigrate	Landowner	Legal dispute with husband regarding sale of land belonging to the Berrio house (1763)

Marie Anne de Marmont	Jean Labat (born 1733), ship owner	2	La Bastide Clairence	After 1793	Did not emigrate	Settled with her husband in Sainte-Marie-de-Gosse (Dax diocese)
Jean-Pierre de Marmont	Marie, heiress of Alsurrun house at Saint-Martin d'Arberoue, Lower Navarre	3	La Bastide Clairence	—	Before 1764	Notary	Went to Saint-Domingue but returned to settle as notary in Saint-Martin-d'Arberoue
Paul Auguste de Marmont	Dominique Etchevers, heiress of Tartarive	4	La Bastide Clairence	La Bastide Clairence, 1787	Did not emigrate	Master surgeon	Jurat (town official) of La Bastide Clairence

GENERATION 4

Jean-Pierre Lamerenx, master of Berrio, son of Anne Antoinette de Marmont and Mathieu Lamerenx,	Françoise Silly (d. 1840), daughter of François Silly and Elizabeth Fleury, coffee planters	1	1742, La Bastide Clairence	1810, Matanzas (Cuba)	1764	Coffee planter; colonial militia captain,	Owner of Lamerenx coffee plantation in Matador District of Dondon (Saint-Domingue); in France 1786–1788; aide-de-camp to Toussaint Louverture (1794)
Arnaud Jean Pierre Lamerenx	Unmarried	4	1752, La Bastide Clairence	—	After 1764		a.k.a. Chevalier de Lamerenx; received the Berrio house in payment of his legitime (1787); died without heirs

continued

167

Name	Spouse	Birth rank	Date and place of birth	Date and place of death	Date of emigration	Profession	Notes
			GENERATION 5				
François Charles Lamerenx	Madeleine Biscay (1807–1876), seamstress	1	1775, Dondon (Saint-Domingue)	1854, Arette (Basses-Pyrénées)	Born in Saint-Domingue	Staff captain in black volunteer troops; tobacconist	Sold the Berrio house to Bayonne merchant Jacob Gomès (1818)
Marguerite Lamerenx	Daniel Laborde (1782–1824), property owner	3	1776, Dondon (Saint-Domingue)	1860, Sorde l'Abbaye (Landes)	Born in Saint-Domingue	Landowner	In France after 1786; administrator of the Berrio house from 1812–1818

APPENDIX C
Genealogical Table: House of Mouscardy

Name	Spouse	Birth rank	Date and place of birth	Date and place of death	Date of emigration	Occupation	Notes
GENERATION 1							
Augé de Mouscardits, master of the Mouscardits house	Marie Labache, younger daughter of the Montory house in Arancou (Lower Navarre)	1	1686, La Bastide Clairence	1740, La Bastide Clairence	Did not emigrate	Landowning farmer	
GENERATION 2							
Jeanne de Mouscardits, mistress of the Mouscardits house	Jean Bordenave, carpenter, adventitious master of the Mouscardits house	1	Circa 1715, La Bastide Clairence	1795, La Bastide Clairence	Did not emigrate	Landowning farmer	
Jean Mouscardy, younger son of the Mouscardits house	Françoise Alzire, free woman of color	2	Circa 1720, La Bastide Clairence	1797, Bayonne (Basses-Pyrénées)	Before 1750	Coffee planter	Established coffee plantation in Marmelade circa 1750, overtaken by slaves in 1791
Marie Mouscardits, younger daughter of the Mouscardits house	Jean Thore, master cooper	3	Circa 1725, La Bastide Clairence	Circa 1780, Bayonne (Basses-Pyrénées)	Did not emigrate	Governess	
Jean Mouscardits, younger son of the Mouscardits house	Jeanne Padouen, day laborer	4	Circa 1726, La Bastide Clairence	1808, La Bastide Clairence	Did not emigrate	Day laborer, then landowning farmer	Became master of the Guillebert house in 1797

continued

169

Name	Spouse	Birth rank	Date and place of birth	Date and place of death	Date of emigration	Occupation	Notes
GENERATION 3 (children of Jeanne de Mouscardits and Jean Bordenave)							
Jean Bordenave, master of the Mouscardits house	Etiennette Darrieux	1	Circa 1737, La Bastide Clairence	1795, La Bastide Clairence	Did not emigrate	Carpenter, landowning farmer	
Jean Bordenave, younger son of the Mouscardits house	Unmarried	2	1748, La Bastide Clairence	—	1768	Cooper	Joined his uncle Jean Mouscardy, coffee planter in Marmelade
Jean, a.k.a. Pierre Bordenave, younger son of the Mouscardits house	Unmarried	5	1757, La Bastide Clairence	—	1776	Carpenter	Joined his uncle Jean Mouscardy, coffee planter in Marmelade
GENERATION 3 (children of Jean Mouscardy and Françoise Alzire)							
Jean-Théodat Mouscardy	—	1	Before 1784, Marmelade (Saint-Domingue)	After 1843	Born in Saint-Domingue	Coffee plantation owner; general in the Haitian Army	aide to King Christophe (1811–1820); co-owner of coffee plantation in Nouvelle Flandre district of Marmelade
Bonne Mouscardy	Pierre Lagroue	—	Before 1784, Marmelade (Saint-Domingue)	Before 1861	Born in Saint-Domingue	Coffee plantation owner	Grandmother of Démesvar Delorme (1831–1901), Haitian writer and statesman
Pierre Mouscardy	—	—	Before 1784, Marmelade (Saint-Domingue)		Born in Saint-Domingue	Coffee plantation owner; colonel in the Haitian Army	

		GENERATION 4		
Laurent Bordenave, son of Jean Bordenave and Etiennette Darrieux, master of the Mouscardits house	Jeanne Léglise	1	1770, La Bastide Clairence	La Bastide Clairence	Did not emigrate	Carpenter, landowning farmer

Preface

1. "BONNICHON: Oui, ma belle enfant. Je suis propriétaire en Amérique, à Saint-Domingue. C'est loin, n'est-ce pas? On n'y va pas en poste.
Air de Partie carrée
Négociant des plus intègres,
J'y suis fameux par mes plantations
J'ai là des champs, des maisons et des nègres
A peu près pour deux millions.
LOUISE: Eh quoi, des noirs?
BONNICHON: Un produit magnifique!
Va, la couleur n'y fait rien mon enfant:
Qu'il soit venu d'Europe ou d'Amérique,
L'argent est toujours blanc."

Scribe, *L'oncle d'Amérique*, 32. See Little, "Date for L'oncle d'Amérique."

2. "Il est si bien établi, et chez les habitants de la métropole surtout, qu'il ne faut que respirer l'air des colonies pour devenir un Crésus, que sans s'embarrasser de ce que sont devenus ceux qui sont morts à la peine, il suffit de voir, de temps à autre, revenir quelqu'un qui, particulièrement favorisé par les circonstances, aura fait fortune, pour donner à ce préjugé la consistance d'une démonstration mathématique." Wimpffen, *Voyage à Saint-Domingue*, 136.

3. "Un Américain et un millionnaire seront encore longtemps synonymes en France." Ibid.

4. "Ne vous en laissez donc pas imposer par le faste puéril et ridicule que certains habitants étalent passagèrement à Paris, ou dans les villes maritimes. J'ai le secret de ces charlatans. Ce carrosse dans lequel Monsieur l'Américain se pavane si gauchement, cette garde-robe du marquis de Mascarille, ces brillants qui étincellent sur sa main noire, sont le prix de plusieurs récoltes et de la vente d'une partie de son atelier." Ibid., 139.

5. "Je n'ai jamais rencontré d'Américain en France qui ne m'ait énuméré, avec plus d'emphase que d'exactitude, les charmes du séjour de Saint-Domingue. Depuis que j'y suis, je n'en ai pas encore trouvé un, pas un seul auquel je n'aie entendu maudire et Saint-Domingue, et les obstacles toujours renaissants qui, d'une année à l'autre, prolongeaient son séjour dans cet enfer." Ibid., 140.

6. For a theoretical reflection on case studies in historical scholarship, see Passeron and Revel, "Penser par cas."

7. Cauna, *L'Eldorado des Aquitains*, 104–8. See also Dubesset and Cauna, *Dynamiques caribéennes*.

8. "Bayonne. Passagers allant aux colonies depuis 1749, jusques et compris 1777," ANOM, Fonds ministériels, Premier empire colonial, Documents divers, Passagers, 1744–1886, COL

F 5B 30. The total number of departures for the period, including returns to Saint-Domingue and departures to other colonies, was approximately eighteen hundred.

9. Le Play, *Les ouvriers européens*, 4:445–510.

10. Bourdieu, *Bachelors' Ball*.

11. Lefebvre, *Les communautés paysannes pyrénéennes*. See also Lefebvre, *La vallée de Campan*.

12. Lévi-Strauss, "Histoire et ethnologie."

13. Both sociologists grew up in rural areas of the Pyrénées-Atlantiques department, Bourdieu in Denguin and Lasseube, Lefebvre in Navarrenx.

14. Bailyn, *Atlantic History*, 95.

15. Ibid., 84.

16. In a letter to Andreas Holt in October 1780, Adam Smith wrote of "the very violent attack I had made upon the whole commercial system of Great Britain." Smith, *Correspondence*, 251.

17. Hont, *Jealousy of Trade*, 185–266.

18. See Cheney, *Revolutionary Commerce*, 11–12.

19. Heckscher, *Mercantilism*. See also Findlay, *Eli Heckscher*. For an attempt to reappraise mercantilism on fresh grounds, see Stern and Wennerlind, *Mercantilism Reimagined*.

20. Pares, *War and Trade in the West Indies*.

21. Hirschman, *National Power*.

22. Thomas Jefferson to James Monroe, 14 July 1793, Thomas Jefferson Papers, Library of Congress, Manuscript Division, www.loc.gov/item/mtjbib007732/.

23. Thomas Jefferson to Martha Jefferson, 26 May 1793, ibid., www.loc.gov/item/mtjbib007461/.

24. Carpentier, *Kingdom of This World*.

25. Bourdieu, *Bachelors' Ball*, 153.

26. Geggus, "Gabriel Debien (1906–1990)"; Bouche, "Gabriel Debien (1906–1990)."

27. Rothschild, *Inner Life of Empires*.

28. Colley, *Ordeal of Elizabeth Marsh*.

29. Scott and Hébrard, *Freedom Papers*.

30. See "Liste des immeubles protégés au titre des monuments historiques en 2011," accessed 19 June 2015, legifrance.gouv.fr/eli/liste/2012/4/6/MCCC1208454K/jo/texte.

Chapter 1 · *Origins of a Migration Network*

1. Lévi-Strauss, "Histoire et ethnologie."

2. Ibid., 1224.

3. Jenkins, *Life of Property*.

4. See Jenkins, "Bourdieu's Béarnais Ethnography."

5. Le Play, *Les ouvriers européens*, 4:445–510.

6. For a press dossier about the film, see download.pro.arte.tv/archives/fichiers/01783617.pdf, accessed 25 October 2014. For a critical discussion of Le Play and of the concept of Pyrenean rural communities, see Lefebvre, *Les communautés paysannes pyrénéennes*, 11–68.

7. Cauna, *L'Eldorado des Aquitains*, 23–50.

8. See ibid., 143–49; and Rey Castelao, "Inheritance, Marital Strategies, and the Formation of Households."

9. Bourdieu, *Bachelors' Ball*, 25n16.

10. Arrizabalaga, "Family Structures, Inheritance Practices and Migration Networks"; Arrizabalaga, "Famille, succession, émigration."
11. Blázquez Garbajosa, *L'émigration basco-béarnaise*, 21.
12. Viret, "Coutumes et migrations vers la Nouvelle France." See also Viret, *Le sol et le sang*.
13. Lévi-Strauss, "Histoire et ethnologie," 1231.
14. Ibid.
15. Hägerstrand, "Migration and Area." For an account and discussion of Hägerstrand's arguments, see Rosental, *Les sentiers invisibles*, 92–106.
16. Hägerstrand, "Migration and Area," 80–81.
17. MacDonald and MacDonald, "Chain Migration."
18. Marc-Antoine Lamerenx, Lamerens Duhart-Juzon file, ANOM, Fonds ministériels, Premier empire colonial, Personnel colonial ancien, COL E 251, dossier titled "Duhart-Juzon, gentilhomme navarrais."
19. "Les États protestent contre la qualité de province appliquée à la Navarre, ils rappellent que c'est un royaume; qu'ils n'ont jamais consenti à l'union de la Navarre à la France." ADPA, Administrations provinciales, Etats de Navarre, 1789, C 1540.
20. Bourdieu, *Bachelors' Ball*, 11.
21. Biancalana, *Fee Tail and the Common Recovery*.
22. Clavero, *Mayorazgo*.
23. Karl Marx, quoted in Bourdieu, *Bachelors' Ball*, 133.
24. Bourdieu, *Bachelors' Ball*, 141 (my translation).
25. See Desplat, "Une 'fort bizarre' noblesse."
26. Acknowledgment of debt agreement between Rachel de la Forcade, widow of Isaac Lamerenx, and Gabriel de Sarrabere, mayor of Lagor, 17 August 1696, Casenave, notary in Saint-Palais, ADPA, Minutes notariales, 3E 1212.
27. "Pour avoir acquis purement et simplement la noble salle d'Uhart-Juzon située au lieu d'Aïcirits." Deliberations of the Estates General of Navarre, 25–29 August 1704, ADPA, Administrations provinciales, Etats de Navarre, C 1533.
28. BnF, Nouveau d'Hozier 201–4482.
29. Ibid.
30. Magdeleine Lamerenx, "natural daughter" of Marc-Antoine Lamerenx and Marie Lacoin, born in Arhansus, Lower Navarre, 27 September 1741, *Généalogie et histoire des familles Pays basque / Adour maritime*, www.ghfpbam.org/.
31. Marriage contract signed on 24 November 1742, Richard, notary in Cap-Français, BnF, Chérin 115–2381.
32. The land was granted on 13 August 1740. Its area was 64 *carreaux* (approximately 200 acres). See *Mémoire pour Dame Elizabeth Lejeune, veuve commune en biens de M. Antoine de Lamerenx-Duhart, écuyer . . . contre Demoiselle Person . . . veuve commune en biens de Jean-Baptiste Perrodin* (Cap-Français: Imprimerie royale, April 1782), ANOM, Dépôt des papiers publics des colonies, Saint-Domingue, Domaines, 1690–1828, DPPC 3SUPSDOM 71.
33. Origin of property sold by Charles Pichot de Kerdisien de Trémais and Marie-Elizabeth Lamerenx Duhart-Juzon (Marc-Antoine's daughter) to Jean Mouscardy, 21 October 1778, Bordier *jeune*, notary in Cap-Français, ANOM, Dépôt des papiers publics des colonies, Saint-Domingue, Notariat, DPPC NOT SDOM 175.
34. "Le S. Duhart n'a pu accepter plus tôt le grade d'officier quoiqu'on le lui eut offert en

arrivant dans la colonie, et même plusieurs fois, mais il n'était pas en état d'en soutenir la dépense et d'aider à la subsistance nécessaire à de simples soldats dont plusieurs se trouvent dépourvus lorsqu'on est obligé de marcher en détachement, ou monter la garde." Lamerens Duhart-Juzon file, ANOM, Fonds ministériels, Premier empire colonial, Personnel colonial ancien, COL E 251.

35. "Car il est important d'observer ici que chaque habitant quoiqu'enrôlé est sans solde et sert à ses frais dans la colonie." Ibid.

36. See the account of these efforts to defend the area in Moreau de Saint-Méry, *Description de la partie française*, 1:266–67.

37. On the attempt to colonize Kourou, see Rothschild, "Horrible Tragedy in the French Atlantic."

38. Moreau de Saint-Méry, *Description de la partie française*, 1:266–67.

39. Pares, *War and Trade in the West Indies*, 180–81.

40. Truxes, *Defying Empire*.

41. Pares, *War and Trade in the West Indies*, 387–88.

42. *Affiches américaines* (Cap-Français), 1 January 1766, 1.

43. ANOM, Fonds ministériels, Premier empire colonial, Troupes et personnel civil, Matricules et revues, 1650–1901, COL D2C 116.

44. BnF, Chérin 115–2381.

45. "Recueil de notes, extraits et pièces concernant les chevau-légers de la garde du Roi, avec un état de ceux qui ont été admis de 1738 à 1787," BnF, Clairambault 812.

46. Elizabeth Le Jeune, widow Duhart, to Joaquín García y Moreno, captain general of Santo Domingo, 18 September 1793, AGS, Secretaría del Despacho de Guerra, Santo Domingo, SGU LEG 7158.

47. Diderot and d'Alembert, *Encyclopédie*, s.v. "Chevaux-Legers."

48. Le Blant, "Un officier béarnais à Saint Domingue"; Cauna, *L'Eldorado des Aquitains*, 85–89.

49. Cauna, *L'Eldorado des Aquitains*, 34–38.

50. *Le grand dictionnaire historique*, s.v. "Irumberry de Salaberry." According to this entry, Charles de Salaberry was called to the Estates General of Navarre as a member of the nobility in 1692 and 1704. See also Aubert de la Chesnaye-Desbois, *Dictionnaire de la noblesse*, s.v. "Irumberry de Salaberry."

51. Salaberry was a distant relative of Jean-Baptiste Colbert. His ancestors were commoners from Champagne. See Vergé-Franceschi, *Les officiers généraux de la marine royale*, 410–23.

52. *Etat sommaire des archives de la Marine*, xxxviii. See also La Roque de Roquebrune, "La direction de la Nouvelle-France," 475. The Ponant bureau, which was directed by La Touche, was responsible for the ports of Bordeaux, Rochefort, Brest, Dunkerque, and Le Havre, the trading companies of Senegal, Guinea, and the East Indies, as well as Canada.

53. "J'ai profité de l'occasion qui s'est présentée par une faute faite par le S. de la Salle, qu'il aurait été juste autrement de placer devant vous pour proposer au Roi de vous accorder une des compagnies vacantes dans l'île de Saint-Domingue." Charles de Salaberry to Pierre-Gédéon de Nolivos, 31 August 1707, ANOM, Fonds ministériel, Premier empire colonial, Correspondance au départ, 1654–1816, COL B28.

54. "J'ai proposé au Roi de vous donner dès à présent une commission de capitaine en pied quoique vous ne dussiez être que réformé pour vous marquer l'attention que sa Majesté a fait de la diligence avec laquelle vous avez rempli votre recrue, et parce que j'espère que cette

grâce vous engagera à servir avec plus d'application et à donner tous les soins nécessaires pour maintenir votre compagnie et en bien dresser les soldats." Salaberry to Nolivos, 21 September 1707, ibid.

55. Service historique de la défense, Toulon, Var, Prises, 2Q1. See also Bromley, "Les prêts de vaisseaux de la marine française," 82.

56. "Si elle se trouve assez bonne pour faire usage, je proposerai volontiers au Roi de vous donner un privilège pour la culture; vous en aurez un naturel pour le débit en France parce que vous pourrez l'établir à beaucoup meilleur marché que le thé de la Chine, et qu'il n'y aura point de droits." Salaberry to Jean-Pierre Casamajor de Charitte, 28 January 1705, ANOM, Fonds ministériel, Premier empire colonial, Correspondance au départ, 1654–1816, COL B26.

57. "J'approuve beaucoup le soin que vous avez continué de prendre de cultiver la plante qui vous a paru être du thé, et je veux bien croire que la vue du bien public y est entrée outre celle de votre intérêt particulier." Salaberry to Charitte, 14 April 1706, ibid., B28.

58. On the French system of colonial commerce, see Tarrade, *Le commerce colonial de la France*.

59. "Sa Majesté étant informée que rien n'est plus capable de faire fleurir le commerce dans un pays et d'y attirer nombre de vaisseaux que la diversité des manufactures qui y sont établies et des marchandises qui s'y fabriquent, nous a très expressément ordonné d'exciter les habitants de Saint-Domingue à rétablir la culture des tabacs." André Bourreau-Deslandes to Salaberry, 7 February 1707, ANOM, Fonds ministériel, Correspondance à l'arrivée, Saint-Domingue et Îles-sous-le-vent, 1664–1792, C9 A8.

60. "Les plus riches d'entre eux pourront y employer une partie de leurs nègres et . . . les garçons et les petits habitants trouveront par cette culture les moyens de subsister et de se procurer dans la suite de bons établissements." Ibid.

61. Jacques Mithon de Senneville, "Mémoire sur le commerce en général et surtout sur celui qui a rapport à St. Domingue, fait par ordre du Conseil," 20 September 1717, BnF, Mémoires sur le commerce et les colonies, NAF 22762.

62. Pritchard, *In Search of Empire*, 414.

63. "Ces vaisseaux servent à manifester la puissance de sa Majesté dans des pays aussi éloignés, la font respecter des étrangers, et font connaître aux peuples une attention présente à les protéger qui les maintient dans une parfaite obéissance et dans le respect dû à l'autorité des chefs. Déshabitués d'en voir paraître aucuns que de loin en loin . . . ils se sont regardés comme abandonnés, ils perdent peu à peu cette haute impression de la grandeur de notre souverain maître, et l'audace prend la place du respect et de la crainte qu'ils avaient conçues." Ibid.

64. BnF, Nouveau d'Hozier 201–4482.

65. "Il est malheureusement impossible au Sr Marc-Antoine de Lamérenx d'Uhart-Juson de donner une filiation exacte de sa famille parce qu'il se trouve dépourvu des titres et actes nécessaires pour la former. Comme tous ses ancêtres ont été de la Religion Prétendue Réformée la plupart se sont réfugiés en Hollande du temps de la révocation de l'Edit de Nantes, et son oncle paternel, fils aîné d'Isaac de Lamerenx, aïeul de l'exposant, mourut à Batavia dans le service militaire des Etats-Généraux, ayant emporté avec lui les principaux papiers de la famille, lesquels on n'a pu retirer de Hollande après son décès des mains des deux sœurs dudit oncle mortes elles-mêmes dans ce pays-là." Ibid.

66. "Deux filles mortes en Hollande; mais l'une mariée en ce pays-là, sans qu'on sache ni le nom de son mari ni si elle a eu des enfants." Ibid.

67. Inventory of the estate of Mathieu Lamerenx, Baïhaut, notary in Saint-Palais, 18 March 1783, ADPA, Minutes notariales, 3E 2468.

68. ADPA, Cours et juridictions, Chambres des comptes de Pau et de Nérac, 1446–1690, B 3665.

69. BnF, Nouveau d'Hozier 201–4482.

70. Nicolas-Joseph Foucault to Charles Colbert de Croissy, 7 June 1685, in Soulice, "Documents pour l'histoire du protestantisme en Béarn" 85.

71. ADPA, Cours et juridictions, Parlement de Navarre, 1299–1799, B 4539, quoted in Soulice, "Documents pour l'histoire du protestantisme en Béarn," 100–101.

72. "Étant beaucoup plus attachés à leur bien qu'à leur religion." Foucault to Colbert de Croissy, 7 June 1685,

73. "Il n'est pas à craindre qu'ils passent en Espagne." Ibid.

74. ADPA, Administrations provinciales, Etats de Béarn, Délibérations, 1687–1704, C 741, quoted in Soulice, "Documents pour l'histoire du protestantisme en Béarn," 52.

75. ADPA, Cours et juridictions, Parlement de Navarre, 1299–1799, B 4539, quoted in ibid., 105–6.

76. "Pieter Lamorenx uit Oleron," *VOC Sea Voyagers Database*, accessed 18 October 2014.

77. Foucault, *Mémoires*, 107.

78. Donation by Rachel de la Fourcade to her daughter Jeanne de Lamerenx, 19 June 1698, Casenave, notary in Saint-Palais, ADPA, Minutes notariales, 3E 1212.

79. *Etat de la distribution de la somme de douze mille livres sterling*, 22.

80. *Etat de la distribution de la somme de vingt et quatre mille livres*, 2.

81. Jeanne (Anne) Lamerenx was born in Oloron (Béarn) on 14 October 1682 and died in Celle (Lower Saxony) on 2 February 1758. She married Gabriel Migault, from the town of Mougon in Poitou, in Amsterdam on 8 July 1704. See Migault, *Journal de Jean Migault*, 31, 250n1. The editors mistakenly indicate Jeanne Lamerenx's family name as "Laffont."

82. Anne Lamerenx and Jean de Bonine, marriage contract signed 27 March 1681, Forcade, notary. See inventory of the estate of Mathieu Lamerenx, Baïhaut, notary in Saint-Palais, 18 March 1783, ADPA, Minutes notariales, 3E 2468. Anne and Jean's son Peter Abadie de Bonine was naturalized by an act of the British Parliament on 16 July 1713. See Agnew, *Protestant Exiles from France*, 80.

83. Jeanne Lamerenx and Jacques de Roux, marriage contract signed 4 July 1702, Casenave, notary in Saint-Palais, ADPA, Minutes notariales, 3E 1213.

84. Marriage celebrated in Saint-Palais, 28 January 1706; marriage contract signed 11 November 1705, Sorhouet, notary in Saint-Palais, BnF, Chérin 115–2381.

85. De Haan, "Uit oude notaris papieren," 304; Kalff, "Isaac de St. Martin."

86. Foucault, *Mémoires*, 107.

87. ADPA, Seigneuries et familles, Titres de la famille royale de Navarre et d'autres familles nobles, E 1018.

88. Le Blant, "A Ceylan."

89. *VOC Sea Voyagers Database*, accessed 18 October 2014.

90. Donation by Rachel de la Forcade to her son Jean de Lamerenx, 13 February 1710, Casenave, notary in Saint-Palais, ADPA, Minutes notariales, 3E 1214. The sum was 1,002 guilders and 19 stuivers. In exchange for the gift, Jean promised to pay his mother a lifetime annuity worth 5 percent of two-thirds of the capital.

91. "Je m'étonne fort que vous qui me pressés de me retirer pour beaucoup de raisons

laissiés faire des résolutions aux nostres de me venir trouver icy, vous ne sçavés pas la difficulté de ce voyage et combien cella m'embarasseroit, c'est pourquoy ie m'attens que cette intention aura esté divertie et si le contraire arrive ie n'en pourray estre que très fasché: s'il y en a a quelcun que les armes chatouillent, il n'y en a point de plus avantageuses ny de plus glorieuses que celles de nostre Roy au service duquel ils peuvent s'adonner pour y cercher (sic) leur fortune ou une fin glorieuse." Isaac Lostal de Saint-Martin to his brother, Gratian, 18 January 1668, in Le Blant, "A Ceylan," 114.

92. Soulice, "Documents pour l'histoire du protestantisme en Béarn," 2.

93. Donation by Rachel de la Fourcade to her daughter Jeanne de Lamerenx, 19 June 1698, Casenave, notary in Saint-Palais, ADPA, Minutes notariales, 3E 1212.

94. Sharecropping contract (*contrat de colonage*) for the estate of Duhart-Juzon between Rachel de la Forcade and Arnaud de Pourtau of Mont in Béarn, a.k.a. Master Isaac, 8 August 1696, Casenave, notary in Saint-Palais, ibid.

95. Molhuysen and Blok, *Nieuw Nederlandsch biografisch woordenboek*, 255–59. Caron was granted French citizenship (*lettre de naturalité et droit de bourgeoisie*) in 1665 without converting to Catholicism. See Sahlins, "Fictions of a Catholic France," 92.

96. *Dictionnaire béarnais ancien et moderne*, s.v. "capdèt."

97. Courtilz de Sandras, *Memoirs of Monsieur d'Artagnan*, 2.

98. "Cadet de Gascogne, qui n'avait rien, quoique de bonne maison." Saint-Simon, *Mémoires*, 17:74.

99. "Pour se faire riche en cadet de Normandie fort pauvre." Ibid., 3:67.

100. See Reiss, *Black Count*.

101. BnF, Chérin 115–2381.

102. Ibid.

103. Hardÿ de Périni, *Batailles françaises*, 345.

104. "Se tienne content et payé de ses droits légitimes paternels et maternels, ce qui est d'autant plus raisonnable que le testateur a dépensé considérablement pour parvenir à faire promouvoir Jacques à l'ordre de la prêtrise." Will of Jean Lamerenx, 22 July 1749, ADPA, Minutes notariales, 3E 2436.

105. "À ce qui est revenu au testateur, dans un état de fortune honnête, et comme il lui a coûté pour l'équiper et pour les frais de deux voyages, il veut qu'il se contente de la somme de 800 livres pour tous ses droits de légitime paternels et maternels." Ibid.

106. Zink, *L'héritier de la maison*; Derouet, "Les pratiques familiales."

107. Le Play, *L'organisation du travail*, 465–74.

108. Choquette, *Frenchmen into Peasants*.

109. Wegge, "Migration Decisions in Mid-Nineteenth-Century Germany."

110. Derouet, "Les pratiques familiales," 378.

111. "Mes si loditz fils & filhas despux los primogenitz nascutz son maridats & son estatz dotatz per loditz pays & mays, aquetz no poiran demandà auguna parcelle ni supplement de legitime deus beés avitins & de papoadge." *Los fors e costumas deu Royaume de Navarre deça ports*, chap. 27, art. 7.

112. Zink, *L'héritier de la maison*, 134.

113. "Et lodit dot sera emplegat per loditz pays & mays proprietaris a racheptâ las pesses alienades de las aportenences de lors maisons, pagà los deutes, maridà lors filhs e filhas . . . & deu restan deudit dot losditz pays & mays proprietaris poyran disposâ en bon pays de familha." *Los fors e costumas deu Royaume de Navarre deça ports*, chap. 24, art. 9.

114. "Le chevalier de Lamerenx, capitaine au Régiment des Cantabres," passenger for Saint-Domingue on the ship *La Société*, Pierre Doucy captain, outfitted in Bayonne on 15 February 1755, in "Bayonne. Passagers allant aux colonies depuis 1749 jusques et compris 1777," ANOM, Fonds ministériels, Premier empire colonial, Documents divers, Passagers, 1744–1886, COL F 5B 30.

115. Petition to the Estates General of Navarre by Mathieu Lamerenx, 1763, ADPA, Administrations provinciales, Etats de Navarre, C 1602.

116. Zink, *L'héritier de la maison*, 269.

117. Ibid., 262.

Chapter 2 · *The Coffee Boom and the Jealousy of Trade*

1. *Etat détaillé des liquidations opérées à l'époque du 1er janvier 1828–1832*, referred to hereafter in text and notes as *Indemnité de Saint-Domingue*. The total indemnity was 126,608.40 francs. The fair-market value of the property was estimated to be ten times the amount of the indemnity. See below.

2. Adam Smith, *Wealth of Nations*; Smith, *Correspondence*.

3. Say, *Treatise on Political Economy*.

4. Adam Smith, *Wealth of Nations*, IV.vii.b.

5. Pierre Joseph Laborie, *Coffee Planter of Saint Domingo*.

6. Coeurjoly, *Manuel des habitants de Saint-Domingue*.

7. Ibid., cxliv.

8. Topik, "World Coffee Market in the Eighteenth and Nineteenth Centuries."

9. Pierre Joseph Laborie, *Coffee Planter of Saint Domingo*, 1.

10. Moreau de Saint-Méry, *Description de la partie française*, 1:173.

11. Ibid., 2:1117. See also *Journal de Saint-Domingue* 3 (January 1766), quoted in Le Fortia, *L'art de vérifier les dates*, 34.

12. "C'est au Dondon que les premiers caféiers portés des îles du vent à Saint-Domingue, ont été plantés, et il y a eu de grandes fortunes créées dans cette paroisse par le succès de ces premières manufactures, dont on fixe l'époque à 1738." Moreau de Saint-Méry, *Description de la partie française*, 1:264.

13. "Il n'y a peut-être dans nul lieu de la Colonie un site plus pittoresque que celui de cette paroisse. D'énormes montagnes dont les sommets sont quelquefois escarpés, présentent des rochers inclinés, souvent même renversés les uns sur les autres, et le désordre de ces masses offrent presque partout des témoignages des grandes agitations terrestres." Ibid., 1:256.

14. "Tout prouve que le Dondon était fort peuplé par les Indiens. On y trouve continuellement des débris de leurs vases, et des figures qui rappellent leurs idées superstitieuses." Ibid., 1:264.

15. Pané, *Relación de Fray Ramón*. See also Rouse, *Tainos*.

16. "Ces hommes nus et ignorants affectaient les idées les plus orgueilleuses ... et ce million de fils aînés de la nature ... une poignée d'Espagnols l'a anéanti pour jamais et à peine quelques-unes de ses erreurs et le souvenir de sa cruelle destinée, surnagent-ils sur l'océan des siècles." Moreau de Saint-Méry, *Description de la partie française*, 1:266.

17. Adam Smith, *Wealth of Nations*, IV.vii.b.

18. "Dans le cas où vous vous détermineriez à y aller, souvenez-vous qu'avec une bonne conduite, on peut aisément y faire fortune." Coeurjoly, *Manuel des habitants de Saint-Domingue*, 2:85.

19. Pierre Joseph Laborie, *Coffee Planter of Saint Domingo*, 14.

20. See *Mémoire pour Dame Elizabeth Lejeune, veuve commune en biens de M. Antoine de Lamerenx-Duhart, écuyer . . . contre Demoiselle Person . . . veuve commune en biens de Jean-Baptiste Perrodin* (Cap-Français: Imprimerie royale, April 1782), ANOM, Dépôt des papiers publics des colonies, Saint-Domingue, Domaines, 1690–1828, DPPC 3SUPSDOM 71. The dispute began in 1766 and was ultimately decided in favor of Elizabeth Le Jeune in 1782.

21. Moreau de Saint-Méry, *Description de la partie française*, 1:255.

22. "Duhart: Habitation située dans la section rurale de Matador, commune de Dondon." Rouzier, *Dictionnaire géographique et administratif universel d'Haïti*.

23. Origin of property sold by Charles Pichot de Kerdisien de Trémais and Marie-Elizabeth Lamerenx Duhart-Juzon (Marc-Antoine's daughter) to Jean Mouscardy, 21 October 1778, Bordier *jeune*, notary in Cap-Français, ANOM, Dépôt des papiers publics des colonies, Saint-Domingue. Notariat, DPPC NOT SDOM 175.

24. On coffee planting, see Michel-Rolph Trouillot, "Coffee Planters and Coffee Slaves in the Antilles"; Geggus, "Sugar and Coffee Cultivation in Saint-Domingue"; and Debien, "Le plan et les débuts d'une caféière à Saint-Domingue."

25. Adam Smith, *Wealth of Nations*, IV.vii.b.

26. Ibid. For a critical discussion of Smith's assessment, see Pares, *Merchants and Planters*, 47–48; and S. D. Smith, *Slavery, Family, and Gentry Capitalism*, 139–76.

27. Adam Smith, *Wealth of Nations*, III.i.9. On the "retrograde" path to economic development, see Hont, *Jealousy of Trade*, 104–11.

28. Adam Smith, *Wealth of Nations*, III.iv.19.

29. Marriage contract between Marguerite-Françoise Lamerenx Duhart Juzon and Charles de Saint-Germain, Grimperel, notary in Cap-Français, 12 November 1777, ANOM, Dépôt des papiers publics des colonies, Saint-Domingue, Notariat, DPPC NOT SDOM, 853.

30. "L'éclat de sa fortune a attiré à Saint-Domingue quantité de Basques ses compatriotes, et comme il est naturellement magnifique, généreux, bienfaisant, ils n'ont pas perdu leurs pas, non plus que quantité d'autres qu'il a avancés, et mis en état de pouvoir faire plaisir à d'autres, pourvu qu'ils suivent les exemples qu'il leur a donnés." Labat, *Nouveau voyage aux îles d'Amérique*, 166.

31. Cauna, *L'Eldorado des Aquitains*, 27–31.

32. "La Gascogne est le pays des inventions, plutôt que des lettres de change." Labat, *Nouveau voyage aux îles d'Amérique*, 171.

33. "Diable voulez-vous il fallait bien se marier, pour obliger ce Gascon à sortir de la case: car il avait juré de n'en pas sortir sans cela." Ibid., 179.

34. Charles de Cadignan, colonel of the Agenois regiment, to Antoine de Sartine, secretary of the navy, 30 March 1778, ANOM, Fonds ministériels, Premier empire colonial, Personnel colonial ancien, COL E 362bis.

35. Cadignan to Sartine, 10 May 1779, ibid.

36. Sartine to Cadignan, 31 July 1779, ibid.

37. *Rochambeau: A Commemoration*, 577–78.

38. Marguerite-Françoise Lamerenx, widow Saint-Germain, to the captain general of Santo Domingo, 18 September 1793, AGS, Secretaría del Despacho de Guerra, Santo Domingo, SGU LEG 7158.

39. "Nous sommes vous et moi deux hommes parvenus." Pierre Cappé to Charles Pichot

de Kerdisien de Trémais, December 1783, BnF, Papiers du maréchal de Bellecombe et de sa famille, NAF 24349(1), fol. 423.

40. "Ma femme ne m'a rien apporté en mariage, ou bien peu: le peu que j'ai je crois l'avoir bien gagné à la sueur de mon front sans faire de tort à personne." Ibid.

41. Pierre Joseph Laborie, *Coffee Planter of Saint Domingo*, appendix, 20.

42. Adam Smith, *Wealth of Nations*, IV.vii.b.

43. Ibid., III.iv.

44. See Dauvergne, "Les anciens plans ruraux dans les colonies françaises."

45. Ibid.

46. Derouet, "Dot et héritage."

47. Adam Smith mentioned this feature of the Custom of Paris as a potential hindrance (*Wealth of Nations*, IV.vii.b.19). According to another observer, this clause was largely ignored. See Hilliard d'Auberteuil, *Considérations sur l'état présent*, 333.

48. Sale by Charles Pichot de Kerdisien de Trémais and Marie-Elizabeth Lamerenx Duhart-Juzon to Jean Mouscardy, 21 October 1778, Bordier *jeune*, notary in Cap-Français, ANOM, Dépôt des papiers publics des colonies, Saint-Domingue, Notariat, DPPC NOT SDOM 175.

49. Sale by Jean Mouscardy to François Fauquet, 13 January 1780, Baratte, notary in Marmelade, ibid., DPPC NOT SDOM 53.

50. Adam Smith, *Wealth of Nations*, III.iv.

51. Evaluation of the property of Marie-Elizabeth Lamerenx, 2 September 1788, Riberon, notary in Marmelade, ANOM, Dépôt des papiers publics des colonies, Saint-Domingue, Notariat, DPPC NOT SDOM 1544.

52. Locke, *Second Treatise of Government*.

53. Ibid. According to James Tully, this theory was itself a reflection of the interests of the first settlers, as it negated any claims on the land made by the natives. See Tully, *Approach to Political Philosophy*, 137–76.

54. Mouscardy dossier, ANOM, Dépôt des papiers publics des colonies, Saint-Domingue, Domaines, 1690–1828, DPPC 3SUPSDOM 40.

55. Marriage contract between Marie Mouscardy and Jean Thore, 30 January 1750, Lesseps, notary in Bayonne, ADPA, Minutes notariales, 3E 3847.

56. Sale by Anne Soubercase, widow Saphore, to Jean Mouscardy, 29 August 1769, Delage, notary in Bayonne, ibid., 3E 1769.

57. Inventory of the Mouscardy house, 14 December 1789, Dhiriart, notary in Bayonne, ibid., 3E 4516.

58. ADG, Amirauté de Guyenne, Certificats d'identité et de catholicité, 1713–87, 6B 53.

59. Purchase of notes receivable by Jean Mouscardy, 3 June 1772, Lambert, notary in La Bastide Clairence, ADPA, Minutes notariales, 3E 2414.

60. See Hoffman, Postel-Vinay, and Rosenthal, "Entry, Information, and Financial Development."

61. The coffee plantations were estimated at 480,000 livres. The estimation for the house was 72,000 livres. The coffee plantations are listed under the Dondon Parish, even though they were located in Marmelade, suggesting that Jean Mouscardy kept telling his relatives in Lower Navarre that his properties were in Dondon even after Marmelade Parish was established.

62. Marriage contract between Jean Thore and Jeanne Mouscardy, Lesseps, notary in Bayonne, 30 January 1750, ADPA, Minutes notariales, 3E 3847.

63. The average price of a slave in the 1740s was 1,000 livres. It was more than 2,000 livres in the 1780s. See "Etat des progressions qu'il y a eu à St. Domingue depuis l'année 1744 jusqu'en 1785 sur le prix des terres propres aux sucreries, des sucres, des nègres, des mulets, et sur celui des divers objets de consommation à St. Domingue, ANOM, Dépôt des fortifications des colonies, 1636–1913, 15 DFC 3.

64. Sale by Charles de Trémais and Marie-Elizabeth Lamerenx to Jean Mouscardy, 21 October 1778, Bordier *jeune*, notary in Cap-Francais, ANOM, Dépôt des papiers publics des colonies, Saint-Domingue, Notariat, DPPC NOT SDOM 175.

65. Sale by Jean Artaud to Jean Mouscardy, 27 September 1784, Cassanet, notary in Cap-Français, ibid., DPPC NOT SDOM 368.

66. ANOM, Fonds ministériels, Premier empire colonial, Documents divers, Passagers, 1744–1886, COL F 5B 30.

67. See Debien, *Les engagés pour les Antilles*.

68. ANOM, Fonds ministériels, Premier empire colonial, Documents divers, Passagers, 1744–1886, COL F 5B 30.

69. Revel de Grandcourt, notary in Marmelade, March 1778, ANOM, Dépôt des papiers publics des colonies, Saint-Domingue, Notariat, NOT SDOM 1542.

70. "Ceux qui sont charpentiers, menuisiers, maçons, tonneliers, serruriers, charrons, selliers, carrossiers, horlogers, orfèvres, bijoutiers, tailleurs, perruquiers, y trouvent aisément de l'emploi. La main-d'œuvre s'y paie très-cher." Coeurjoly, *Manuel des habitants de Saint-Domingue*, 2:63.

71. The ship was *Le Cheval marin*, sailing to Cap-Français, with André Tauzin as captain. It was outfitted for departure from Bayonne on 2 March 1770. ANOM, Fonds ministériels, Premier empire colonial, Documents divers, Passagers, 1744–1886, COL F 5B 30.

72. Leasing agreement between Jean-Pierre Colombots, manager of the Biret plantation, and Pierre Bos, master carpenter, 18 March 1779, Revel de Grandcourt, notary in Marmelade, ANOM, Dépôt des papiers publics des colonies, Saint-Domingue, Notariat, DPPC NOT SDOM 1542. According to the *Indemnité de Saint-Domingue*, the Biret family owned two coffee plantations worth 36,840 francs each, located in Le Basin in Marmelade. Pierre Biret, a merchant in Cap-Français, purchased a coffee plantation of six *carreaux* in Marmelade from Françoise Perrodin and her husband J. Dureau for 24,000 livres on 19 March 1774. Carmaux de La Chapelle, notary, 12 July 1778, ibid., DPPC NOT SDOM 405.

73. Leasing agreement between Jean-Pierre Colombots, manager of the Biret plantation, and Pierre Bos, master carpenter, 18 March 1779, Revel de Grandcourt, notary in Marmelade, ibid., DPPC NOT SDOM 1542.

74. "Si l'on a du goût pour la culture, on peut faire alors un apprentissage dans cette partie; cela vous conduit à être Econome, ensuite Gérant; et la confiance que vous pouvez acquérir dans cet état, vous procure souvent des procurations *ad negotia*." Coeurjoly, *Manuel des habitants de Saint-Domingue*, 2:62.

75. Sale by Bernard Bonnemaison to Jean Larroque, representing the following mulatto children: Jean-Théodat; François, a.k.a. Fortuné; Elizabeth-Hortense; Elizabeth-Louise-Justine; Elizabeth Hortense, a.k.a. Bonne; and an unnamed mulatto called Pierre for the purposes of the deed, 10 April 1784, Baratte, notary in Marmelade, ANOM, Dépôt des papiers publics des colonies, Saint-Domingue, Notariat, DPPC NOT SDOM 53.

76. Mouscardy dossier, ANOM, Dépôt des papiers publics des colonies, Saint-Domingue, Domaines, 1690–1828, DPPC 3SUPSDOM 40.

77. Delorme, *1842 au Cap*, 27–30.

78. Baptism of Pierre Mouscarditz, La Bastide Clairence, 11 May 1748, AMLBC, Baptêmes, mariages, sépultures: registres paroissiaux, 1628–1793, GG8.

79. On *Alzire* as an (indirect) representation of the slave trade, see Miller, *French Atlantic Triangle*, 71–74; and Dobie, *Trading Places*, 160–62.

80. Miller, *French Atlantic Triangle*, 79. See also *Afro-Louisiana History and Genealogy Database, 1719–1820*.

81. Garrigus, *Before Haiti*, 56. See also King, *Blue Coat or Powdered Wig*.

82. Coeurjoly, *Manuel des habitants de Saint-Domingue*, 2:4–5.

83. Garrigus, *Before Haiti*, 171–94.

84. Delorme, *1842 au Cap*, 29.

85. "Si vous entreprenez le commerce, il faut que vous soyez surveillant à la rentrée de vos fonds, et ne pas trop vous livrer au crédit avec le premier venu; car, dans ce pays, chacun est fort avide d'acheter; mais aussi beaucoup de personnes sont peu jalouses de payer." Coeurjoly, *Manuel des habitants de Saint-Domingue*, 2:63.

86. Martin Hiriart, born in La Bastide Clairence, 13 March 1771, AMLBC, Baptêmes, mariages, sépultures: registres paroissiaux, 1628–1793, GG10.

87. Inventory of the estate of Jean Hiriart, a.k.a. Jean Bastidot, 26 October 1808, Leroy, notary in Santo Domingo, ANOM, Dépôt des papiers publics des colonies, Saint-Domingue, Notariat, DPPC NOT SDOM 1302.

88. Charles Lamerenx of Dondon, son of Jean-Pierre Lamerenx of La Bastide Clairence, appeared as a witness on the death certificate of Pierre Silly, also of Dondon, in Santo Domingo on 14 April 1809. Archives nationales d'outre-mer, Instruments de recherche en ligne, anom.archivesnationales.culture.gouv.fr/.

89. Deliberations of the municipal council of La Bastide Clairence, 25 September 1794, AMLBC, Conseil municipal: registres des délibérations, 1790–1950, 1D2.

90. Pierre Cappé was from Labatut, a town in the Pyrenean foothills. See Massio, "La Bigorre et Saint-Domingue au XVIIIe siècle," 28.

91. Report on Charles de Trémais by Jean-François Vincent de Montarcher, intendant of Saint-Domingue, 24 June 1771, ANOM, Fonds ministériels, Premier empire colonial, Personnel colonial ancien, COL E 324.

92. Moreau de Saint-Méry, *Description de la partie française*, 1:272.

93. "La politique admise dans ce genre de police voulant que satisfaction soit donnée à tout Blanc qui se plaint d'un Nègre, les préparatifs pour le châtiment étaient déjà faits." ANOM, Fonds ministériels, Premier empire colonial, Personnel colonial ancien, COL E 62.

94. Pierre Joseph Laborie, *Coffee Planter of Saint Domingo*, 164–65.

95. "Cependant ne vous reposez pas trop sur sa prétendue fidélité; il vaut souvent moins que tous les autres, et on a intérêt de le choisir de même, parce qu'étant plus méchant, il se fait mieux craindre . . . il affectera d'avoir pour vous un parfait dévouement qui n'aboutira qu'à vous tromper." Coeurjoly, *Manuel des habitants de Saint-Domingue*, 1:59.

96. "Ce M. Cappé en sa qualité de militaire vit dans les liaisons les plus intimes avec M. de Cockburn, dont il a adopté les principes sanguinaires sur la police des Nègres, et je les ai l'un et l'autre pour voisins. Ils font la désolation du quartier." ANOM, Fonds ministériels, Premier empire colonial, Personnel colonial ancien, COL E 62.

97. Baron de Vastey, *Le système colonial dévoilé*, 46.

98. ANOM, Fonds ministériels, Premier empire colonial, Personnel colonial ancien, COL E 62.

99. Ghachem, *Old Regime and the Haitian Revolution*, 136–89.

100. Adam Smith, *Wealth of Nations*, IV.vii.b.

101. Say, *Treatise on Political Economy*, bk. 1, chap. 14, para. 7.

102. "Vous ne vivez avec personne dans le quartier." Cappé to Trémais, December 1783, BnF, Papiers du maréchal de Bellecombe et de sa famille, NAF 24349(1), fol. 423.

103. Pierre Joseph Laborie, *Coffee Planter of Saint Domingo*, appendix, 55.

104. *Affiches américaines* (Cap-Français), 19 January 1785. On runaway slaves, see Geggus, "On the Eve of the Haitian Revolution."

105. "Est partie marronne avec un carcan à trois branches, n'étant pas encore guérie des coups de fouet qu'elle a reçus depuis peu." *Affiches américaines* (Cap-Français), 11 July 1770.

106. Moreau de Saint-Méry, *Description de la partie française*, 1:275–76.

107. Debien, "Assemblées nocturnes d'esclaves à Saint-Domingue."

108. Adam Smith, *Wealth of Nations*, III.ii.10n.

109. Say, *Treatise on Political Economy*, bk. 1, chap. 19, para. 17. Jean-Baptiste Say had knowledge of the sugar plantation system through his brother Louis Say, who established a sugar refinery in Nantes in 1812. The Béghin-Say sugar company is still in existence today, a subsidiary of the Tereos Group.

110. "Créole aussi entendue qu'intelligente." Memoirs of Prudent-Jean Bruley (1759–1847), quoted in Bruley, *Généalogie de la famille Bruley*, 94.

111.

"L'Européen. Les habitants de ce pays doivent être très-riches?
L'Américain. Une grande partie des habitants de St.-Domingue sont fort riches en apparence; mais ils doivent beaucoup aux négocians, parce qu'ils ne savent point se modérer dans leur dépense. Il y a des habitants qui possèdent plusieurs habitations, et qui ont jusqu'à sept à huit cents nègres à eux appartenant."

Coeurjoly, *Manuel des habitants de Saint-Domingue*, 2:84.

112. On merchants, planters, and slaves in the British context, see Pares, *Merchants and Planters*; Galenson, *Traders, Planters, and Slaves*; and S. D. Smith, *Slavery, Family, and Gentry Capitalism*, 139–225. On the French slave trade, see Pétré-Grenouilleau, *L'argent de la traite*.

113. "Notre café continue de se vendre 21 sols le beau; il y a lieu de croire que ce prix se soutiendra, vu la mauvaise récolte que tout le monde fait, cette année, généralement parlant; il y a presque une diminution des deux tiers à la Marmelade et au Dondon. D'après cela il est inconcevable de voir augmenter le prix des Nègres au point de les voir vendre à bord jusqu'à 2500#." Marie-Elizabeth Lamerenx, widow Trémais, to Guillaume Léonard de Bellecombe, December 1787, BnF, Papiers du maréchal de Bellecombe et de sa famille, NAF 24349 (1), fols. 131–32.

114. Pierre Joseph Laborie, *Coffee Planter of Saint Domingo*, appendix, 87. See also Pares, *Merchants and Planters*, 38–50.

115. Adam Smith, *Wealth of Nations*, IV.vii.b.

116. Pierre Joseph Laborie, *Coffee Planter of Saint Domingo*, appendix, 88.

117. Adam Smith, *Wealth of Nations*, III.ii.10.

118. "L'esclave travaille pour un besoin illimité: la cupidité de son maître; et l'indolence

de celui-ci, son amour pour les plaisirs ne font qu'aggraver son labeur." Say, *Traité d'économie politique*, bk. 1, chap. 28.

119. Ibid. Say qualified his assessment in subsequent editions. See Steiner, "L'esclavage chez les économistes français."

120. "Les colons seraient-ils si invinciblement attachés à cet ordre de choses, si l'expérience, si l'instinct ne leur disaient pas que leurs profits diminueraient et que leurs dépenses augmenteraient à les changer?" Say, *Traité d'économie politique*, bk. 1, chap. 28.

121. "Nous ne calculons nos revenus que sur le nombre de nègres, de l'un ou de l'autre sexe, qui sont employés dans nos manufactures." Coeurjoly, *Manuel des habitants de Saint-Domingue*, 1:57.

122. Discussion of the bill regarding the distribution of the indemnity of 150 million to former Saint-Domingue colonists, in Vanufel and Champion de Villeneuve, *Code des colons de Saint-Domingue*, 83–92.

123. Beauvois, "Monnayer l'incalculable?," 626.

124. Report of the commission of the Chamber of Deputies, in Vanufel and Champion de Villeneuve, *Code des colons de Saint-Domingue*, 110–11.

125. Analysis of the report to the king, in ibid., 345–46.

126. "Puisqu'ils sont reconnus libres." Diary of Jean Joseph Dauxion Lavaysse (1814–15), ANOM, Fonds ministériels, Premier empire colonial, Correspondance à l'arrivée, Saint-Domingue, 1789–1850, COL CC9A 48, 216 MIOM 34, quoted in Beauvois, "Monnayer l'incalculable?," 614.

127. Elizabeth Le Jeune, widow Lamerenx; Marie-Elizabeth Lamerenx, widow Trémais; and Marguerite-Françoise Lamerenx, widow Saint-Germain, to the captain general of Santo Domingo, 18 September 1793, AGS, Secretaría del Despacho de Guerra, Santo Domingo, SGU LEG 7158.

128. Beauvois, "Monnayer l'incalculable?," 614.

129. Bailyn, *Atlantic History*, 83.

130. Hont, *Jealousy of Trade*, 185–266.

131. Cheney, *Revolutionary Commerce*, 11–12.

132. Pares, *War and Trade in the West Indies*, 410.

133. See Butel, "L'essor antillais au XVIIIe siècle," 120.

134. Pares, *War and Trade in the West Indies*, 265–325; Pares, *Colonial Blockade and Neutral Rights*.

135. Butel, "L'essor antillais au XVIIIe siècle," 125.

136. Cheney, "Colonial Cul de Sac."

137. Ibid., 49.

138. *Dictionary of Canadian Biography*, s.v. "Pichot (Pichon) de Querdisien (Kerdisien de) Trémais, Charles-François," accessed 2 December 2014, www.biographi.ca/en/bio/pichot_de_querdisien_tremais_charles_francois_4E.html.

139. Susane, *Histoire de l'infanterie française*, 70–104.

140. "L'économie qui résulte du travail de l'esclave, entre dans la poche du planteur en vertu du privilège à peu près exclusif qu'il a de vendre à la métropole. Le consommateur n'en profite pas, et il aurait les mêmes denrées à meilleur marché, dût-il les tirer de plus loin, si le commerce en était libre." Say, *Traité d'économie politique*, bk. 1, chap. 28.

141. Say, *Treatise on Political Economy*, bk. 1, chap. 19, para. 25. See also Shovlin, "War and Peace."

Chapter 3 · House-Based Societies and Emigration

1. Dufourcq, "La Bastide Clairence à la veille et au début de la période révolutionnaire."
2. AMLBC, Assemblées capitulaires: délibérations, 1750–63, FF2 (1763).
3. Jean-Pierre de Colombots had an illegitimate son, also named Jean-Pierre, who migrated to Saint-Domingue in 1770 (see chapter 2).
4. Deliberation of the town council, AMLBC, Conseil de ville: registres des délibérations, 1680–1790, BB14, 1 January 1752.
5. "Triste situation . . . bien roturier . . . bien noble." AMLBC, Assemblées capitulaires: délibérations, 1750–63, FF2 (1763).
6. BnF, Chérin 115–2381 and Nouveau d'Hozier 201–4482.
7. "Il n'est que trop vrai que la situation des affaires du sieur de Lamerenx et des siennes est des plus tristes, c'est du su public . . . [Lamerenx] s'est approprié l'argent et le bétail . . . refusant jusqu'au nécessaire à sa famille . . . il a disposé en maître . . . il a fait des coupes et des dégradations dont il a eu le seul profit . . . le bien du sieur de Lamerenx fut expressément dotalisé dans le contrat de mariage de ses père et mère." AMLBC, Assemblées capitulaires: délibérations, 1750–63, FF2 (1763).
8. Zink, *L'héritier de la maison*, 219.
9. "[Anne de Marmont] doit tranquillement jouir de son bien propre . . . une somme de deux mille livres en habits, en pacotille . . . imaginaire . . . entièrement démantelé, vendu et fondu ensuite . . . se verrait, si cela était, sans bien et sans secours . . . résiste à la vente de son bien pour le confondre dans celui de Lamerenx." AMLBC, Assemblées capitulaires: délibérations, 1750–63, FF2 (1763).
10. "Moins pour critiquer la conduite de sa femme que pour faire connaître à nous les commissaires et proches la situation triste de la famille . . . elle vendit mes grains en mon absence. . . . [Anne de Marmont] a dû se servir de la récolte de cette année et s'est même défait de certains meubles pour fournir à sa subsistance et à celle de son fils aîné. Si le sieur de Lamerenx se fût comporté en mari et père elle n'en serait pas venue à ces extrémités . . . par rapport aux dots dont ils sont responsables et qui s'élèvent à 18 000 livres. . . . N'importe que les biens du sieur de Lamerenx soient nobles, leur qualité ne diminue point le mérite de ceux de la dame exposante, celle-ci chérit ses biens quoique ruraux autant et plus que ceux du sieur Lamerenx puisqu'en les possédant elle vivra tranquillement et suivant son dessein." Ibid.
11. Gratacos, *Femmes pyrénéennes*. For a discussion of women and inheritance rights in the Basque country in the nineteenth century, see Arrizabalaga, "Destins de femmes dans les Pyrénées au XIXe siècle."
12. Bourdieu, *Bachelors' Ball*, 145, translation modified. See also Lefebvre, *Les communautés paysannes pyrénéennes*, 13–16.
13. "Nous sommes d'avis que la dame de Lamerenx rejoigne le sieur son époux pour faire leur habitation dans la maison du sieur de Lamerenx pour y vivre selon les règles de la raison et du bon sens, ledit sieur de Lamerenx ayant les égards convenables pour ladite dame. Et s'ils ne peuvent compatir ensemble, nous sommes d'avis que la dame soit mise dans le couvent Sainte-Marie d'Oloron en Béarn pour y demeurer cloîtrée jusqu'à ce qu'il plaise à Dieu de lui inspirer de rejoindre le sieur son époux et sa famille sans que sous aucun autre prétexte elle puisse sortir du couvent." AMLBC, Assemblées capitulaires: délibérations, 1750–63, FF2 (1763).
14. "Les motifs qui nous ont déterminés à consentir la vente du bien Marmont, pour du produit liquider les dettes de ladite maison et celles du bien Lamerenx, n'ont but que de

conserver au moins ce dernier, que nous regardons comme le patrimoine inaliénable des enfants du sieur et dame de Lamerenx." Ibid.

15. "De contracter dette, hypothéquer ni aliéner lesdits biens sans la permission de la justice." Ibid.

16. Bourdieu and Lamaison, "From Rules to Strategies," 111.

17. Ibid., 112.

18. Ibid., 113.

19. "Est advenu l'une heure de relevée du jour quinze décembre 1763, nous dits commissaire et proches assistés dudit sieur de Lamerenx nous étant transportés en ladite maison de Berrio il a été procédé à la publication de l'avis des proches ci-dessus en présence des sieur et dame de Lamerenx, auquel avis le sieur de Lamerenx a dit acquiescer. Ladite dame a dit ne point acquiescer et a refusé de signer de ce interpellée tant par nous dit commissaire que proches." AMLBC, Assemblées capitulaires: délibérations, 1750–63, FF2 (1763).

20. Opinion of the Parliament of Navarre, 1 August 1771, ADPA, Cours et juridictions, Parlement de Navarre, B 4953.

21. Sale by Anne de Marmont to Daniel Mendès, Campagne, notary in La Bastide Clairence, 27 October 1779, ADPA, Minutes notariales, 3E 2889.

22. Sale by Anne de Marmont to Jean Lestelle, Campagne, notary in La Bastide Clairence, 16 November 1780, ibid., 3E 2890.

23. Marriage between Pierre Lamerenx and Jeanne de Mocoro, Aïcirits, Lower Navarre, 22 April 1761, *Généalogie et histoire des familles Pays basque / Adour maritime*, www.ghfpbam.org/.

24. Baptism of Marie Lamerenx, daughter of Pierre Lamerenx and Jeanne de Mocoro, Aïcirits, Lower Navarre, 19 November 1762, ibid.

25. Marriage between Mathieu Lamerenx and Marie Larraburu, Aïcirits, Lower Navarre, 27 February 1770, ibid.

26. Bourdieu, *Bachelors' Ball*, 155n34.

27. "Aucun des deux époux ne voulait quitter sa maison pour aller retrouver l'autre ... sont persuadés que le mariage d'un héritier avec une héritière ne peut que porter malheur aux deux époux." Cordier, *Le droit de famille aux Pyrénées*, 49.

28. Bourdieu, *Bachelors' Ball*, 152n29.

29. Nassiet, "Parenté et successions dynastiques," 640–41.

30. Lévi-Strauss, "Histoire et ethnologie," 1225.

31. Bourdieu, *Bachelors' Ball*, 152.

32. "La vente de son bien pour le confondre dans celui de Lamerenx." AMLBC, Assemblées capitulaires: délibérations, 1750–63, FF2 (1763).

33. Bourdieu, *Bachelors' Ball*, 153.

34. Darrieux-Juson family papers.

35. "Lamerenx fils aîné." Ibid.

36. See Cauna and Graff, *La traite bayonnaise au XVIIIe siècle*.

37. ANOM, Fonds ministériels, Premier empire colonial, Documents divers, Passagers, 1744–1886, COL F 5B 30.

38. Coeurjoly, *Manuel des habitants de Saint-Domingue*, 2:56.

39. *État détaillé des liquidations opérées à l'époque du 1er janvier 1828–1832*.

40. On the value of the Nolivos (232,750 livres and 77 slaves) and Dupoy (130,000 livres and 40 slaves) coffee plantations, see Cauna, *L'Eldorado des Aquitains*, 268–77.

41. Moreau de Saint-Méry, *Description de la partie française*, 1:259.

42. Donation by Elizabeth Fleury to Françoise Silly and Jean-Pierre Lamerenx, 18 July 1777, Revel de Grandcourt, notary in Marmelade, ANOM, Dépôt des papiers publics des colonies, Saint-Domingue, Notariat, DPPC NOT SDOM 1542.

43. Derouet, "Dot et héritage," 291.

44. Settlement between Brice Silly and Jean-Pierre Lamerenx, Cassanet, notary in Cap-Français, 5 April 1785, ANOM, Dépôt des papiers publics des colonies, Saint-Domingue, Notariat, DPPC NOT SDOM 369.

45. Colonial militia rolls, ANOM, Fonds ministériels, Premier empire colonial, Troupes et personnel civil, Matricules et revues, 1650–1901, COL D2C 115 (1769).

46. Ibid., D2C 93 (1772) and D2C 116 (1772).

47. "L'arrivée de M. Lamerenx fit beaucoup d'éclat . . . et attira nombre de curieux pour le voir." ADPA, Fonds privés, Fonds Batcave, 2 J 503, Hyppolite Dabbadie, justice of the peace of the canton of Navarrenx, 13 August 1806.

48. See Passeron and Revel, "Penser par cas."

49. "Il est essentiel de faciliter à Jean-Pierre Lamerenx leur fils aîné un passage aux Îles de l'Amérique où il témoigne vouloir aller." AMLBC, Assemblées capitulaires: délibérations, 1750–63, FF2 (1763).

50. Lévi-Strauss, "Histoire et ethnologie," 1225.

51. BnF, Chérin 115–2381 and Nouveau d'Hozier 201–4482.

52. "La famille de Lamerens se trouve hantée [*sic*] sur celle d'Uhart Juzon." Lamerens Duhart-Juzon file, ANOM, Fonds ministériels, Premier empire colonial, Personnel colonial ancien, COL E 251.

53. The genealogist, who came from a family of Bordeaux merchants and financiers, had himself been ennobled by the king just a few years earlier. His older brother purchased what later became the Elysée Palace in 1773. See Marzagalli, "De Grateloup à l'Elysée en passant par Bordeaux," 21. See also Grell and Da Vinha, "Les généalogistes, le roi et la cour de France."

54. Marriage of Marguerite Lamerenx and Daniel Laborde, Gurs, Basses-Pyrénées, 20 September 1804, Archives départementales des Pyrénées-Atlantiques, E-archives, earchives.le64.fr/.

55. Lamerens Duhart-Juzon file, ANOM, Fonds ministériels, Premier empire colonial, Personnel colonial ancien, COL E 251.

56. Sale of the Lamarque farm by Jean-Pierre Lamerenx to Antoine Charles d'Abbadie, 8 September 1787, Baïhaut, notary in Saint-Palais, ADPA, Minutes notariales, 3E 2472.

57. Renewal of mortgage contract, 16 October 1818, Dilor, notary in Saint-Palais, ibid., 3E 1274.

58. Opinion of the Parliament of Navarre, 16 June 1787, ADPA, Cours et juridictions, Parlement de Navarre, B 5022.

59. Settlement of the succession of Anne de Marmont, 7 September 1787, Baïhaut, notary in Saint-Palais, ADPA, Minutes notariales, 3E 2472.

60. Settlement of the succession of Anne de Marmont, 26 October 1787, ibid.

61. ADG, Amirauté de Guyenne, Certificats d'identité et de catholicité, 1713–87, 6B 58.

62. "D'une ruine prochaine et qu'en tombant elle pourrait occasionner du mal aux habitants qui sont obligés de passer dans la rue où est cette maison." Deliberation of the Municipal Council, 8 September 1790, AMLBC, Conseil municipal: registres des délibérations, 1790–1950, 1D1. Thanks to Geneviève Sallaberry for this reference.

63. 1800 Census, AMLBC, Registre des dénombrements de la population de la commune, 1F1.

64. Judgment by the Court of First Instance, Saint-Palais, 5 May 1818, ADPA, Justice, Tribunaux de première instance, 3U 5 190.

65. See Force, "House on Bayou Road."

66. Sale of the Berrio house and two tenant farms (Betbeder and Trivailly) by Charles Lamerenx and his co-inheritors to Jacob Gomès, merchant in Saint-Esprit near Bayonne, Damborgez, notary in Bayonne, recorded at Bureau des hypothèques de Bayonne on 29 June 1818, ADPA, Registres de formalités et hypothèques, 312 Q 35.

67. Sale of the Garchot house from Jacob Gomès to Pierre Cornu, a.k.a. Galant, 14 August 1823, Haramboure, notary in La Bastide Clairence, ADPA, Minutes notariales, 3E 2909.

68. Sale of the Garchot house to Bernardin Hapette, recorded on 1 December 1899, in Bureau des hypothèques de Bayonne, vol. 528, no. 24, Service de publicité foncière, Muret, Haute-Garonne.

69. Arrizabalaga, "Family Structures, Inheritance Practices and Migration Networks"; Arrizabalaga, "Famille, succession, émigration." See also Arrizabalaga, "Basque Migration and Inheritance in the Nineteenth Century"; and Arrizabalaga, "Stratégies de l'indivision et rapport."

70. Etcheverry, "L'émigration des Basses-Pyrénées vers l'Amérique."

71. Le Play, *Les ouvriers européens*, 5:493.

72. Zink, *L'héritier de la maison*, 269.

73. Ibid.

74. Nassiet, "Parenté et successions dynastiques," 640.

75. Zink, *L'héritier de la maison*, 262.

76. 1800 Census, AMLBC, Registre des dénombrements de la population de la commune, 1F1.

77. Derouet, "Territoire et parenté."

78. "La dame exposante se trouvant la plus habile à s'immiscer dans l'administration des biens du feu sieur son père." Inventory of the estate of Mathieu Lamerenx, 18 March 1783, Baïhaut, notary in Saint-Palais, ADPA, Minutes notariales, 3E 2468.

79. Grant of power of attorney by Jean-Pierre Lamerenx to Paul Auguste de Marmont, maternal uncle of the declarant, Legrand, notary in Dondon, 28 August 1782, ANOM, Dépôt des papiers publics des colonies, Saint-Domingue, Notariat, DPPC NOT SDOM 1254.

80. Grant of power of attorney by Jean-Pierre Lamerenx to Ursule Lamerenx, spinster, paternal aunt of the declarant, Legrand, notary in Dondon, 3 January 1784, ibid.

81. Grant of power of attorney by Jean-Pierre Lamerenx to Paul Auguste de Marmont, Legrand, notary in Dondon, 20 September 1784, ibid., 1256.

82. "Presque dévastés." Inventory of the estate of Mathieu Lamerenx, 18 March 1783, Baïhaut, notary in Saint-Palais, ADPA, Minutes notariales, 3E 2468.

83. Marriage contract between Bernard de Marmont and Anne de Moirie, 1 September 1722, Lesseps, notary in Bayonne, ibid., 3E 3801.

84. Bourdieu and Lamaison, "From Rules to Strategies," 115.

85. Arrizabalaga, "Famille, succession, émigration," 198–224.

Chapter 4 · War and Property Rights

1. "Les esclaves de l'habitation Turpin et Flaville vinrent chercher à 10 heures du soir ceux de l'habitation Clément. Les deux ateliers choisirent pour chefs Boukmans et Auguste, esclaves sur ces deux habitations. De là ils allèrent sur l'habitation Trémès où ils firent grâce à un charpentier qu'ils avaient manqué d'un coup de fusil; puis sur celle de Noé dont ils tuèrent le procureur et le raffineur. Ils donnèrent la vie au chirurgien Mongès et à son épouse. C'est sur cette dernière habitation que l'incendie commença vers minuit." Garran, *Rapport sur les troubles de Saint-Domingue*, 2:261. On the Haitian Revolution as a whole, see Geggus, *Haitian Revolution*; Geggus, *Haitian Revolutionary Studies*; and Dubois, *Avengers of the New World*.

2. Cauna, *Toussaint Louverture: Le grand précurseur*, 151–56.

3. Jacques de Cauna is the first historian to have identified "Trémès" as the Trémais plantation, owned by Marie-Elizebeth Lamerenx, widow Trémais. See Cauna, "Toussaint Louverture et le déclenchement," 147.

4. Marie-Elizabeth Lamerenx, widow Trémais, to Joaquín García y Moreno, captain general of Santo Domingo, 18 September 1793, AGS, Secretaría del Despacho de Guerra, Santo Domingo, SGU LEG 7158.

5. Purchase by Jean Mouscardy of half a *carreau* in the Périgourdins District of Acul, Bordier, notary in Cap-Français, November 1777, ANOM, Dépôt des papiers publics des colonies, Saint-Domingue, Notariat, DPPC NOT SDOM 173.

6. Trémais sequestered-properties file, ANOM, Dépôt des papiers publics des colonies, Saint-Domingue, Domaines, 1690–1828, DPPC 3SUPSDOM 60.

7. The plantation featuring the warehouse appears as the Joly plantation on the map of the Cap-Français plain. See Phelipeau, *Plan de la plaine*. It was purchased by Charles Kerdisien de Tremais in November 1782. Grimperel, notary in Cap-Français, ANOM, Dépôt des papiers publics des colonies, Saint-Domingue, Notariat, DPPC NOT SDOM 542.

8. Cauna, *Toussaint Louverture: Le grand précurseur*, 168–69.

9. Benot, "Un épisode décisif de l'insurrection." This article includes a full transcription and analysis of the account of the takeover of Dondon from the papers of the Garran-Coulon commission. ANF, Missions des représentants du peuple et comités des assemblées révolutionnaires, Comité des colonies, D-XXV, 78–79. Benot does not identify the author of the report. It seems highly likely that Drevet himself was the author. The fact that the account switches constantly between the first and the third persons and is presented as the colonists' leader's report is a strong indication. See also Benot, "Insurgents of 1791."

10. "Je me mis à crier: Vive la nation! Et ces coquins me répliquèrent: Vive le roi!" Benot, "Un épisode décisif de l'insurrection," 107.

11. "Le commandant de leur secte cria plusieurs fois: Il faut, mes amis, avoir la tête de ce drôle de Drevet, et en chargeant son fusil, il lui dit: Tiens, Drevet, voilà pour toi, ce que voyant le sieur Drevet, il lui présenta son derrière en disant: Tire, coquin!" Ibid.

12. Ibid., 111.

13. ANF, Missions des représentants du peuple et comités des assemblées révolutionnaires, Comité des colonies, D-XXV, 79.

14. "Note des personnes mortes au Dondon depuis le 23 août 1791 tant dans les combats que dans les camps," ibid., 78.

15. Ibid., 79.

16. See Thornton, "I Am the Subject of the King of Congo."

17. "Les insurgés suivirent le même plan. Ils formèrent aussi des camps dans les quartiers qu'ils occupaient. Leur grand nombre, leur vigueur et leur agilité, leur permettaient de harceler perpétuellement les blancs." Garran, *Rapport sur les troubles de Saint-Domingue*, 2:261.

18. Dalmas, *Histoire de la Révolution de Saint-Domingue*, 167.

19. Testimony of the manager of the Clément plantation in Popkin, *Facing Racial Revolution*, 53.

20. "Là, comme ailleurs, j'ai entendu un langage uniforme chez tous les nègres; partout on croyait à l'emprisonnement du roi et aux ordres qu'il leur avait fait parvenir pour s'armer et lui redonner la liberté. La destruction du clergé et de la noblesse ne leur était pas inconnue." Gros, *Isle St.-Domingue*, 13.

21. Report by General de Kerverseau to the minister of the navy (7 September 1801, ANOM, Fonds ministériels, Premier empire colonial, Correspondance à l'arrivée, Saint-Domingue, premier supplément, 1796–1810, COL CC9B 23), transcribed and annotated by Pierre Pluchon in *Toussaint Louverture d'après le général de Kerverseau*, 15–74, 20.

22. Bruley, *Généalogie de la famille Bruley*, 126–28.

23. "Quatre habitations solidement bâties ne manquant de rien et qui toutes ont été réduites en cendres sans avoir pu rien sauver, un pareil tableau, comme vous voyez, est bien déchirant pour une âme sensible qui a sacrifié sa vie voulant faire le bonheur de ses malheureux enfants." Marie-Elizabeth Lamerenx, widow Trémais, to Joaquín García y Moreno, captain general of Santo Domingo, 17 September 1793, AGS, Secretaría del Despacho de Guerra, Santo Domingo, SGU LEG 7158.

24. "Propriétaire d'une des plus belles manufactures à café, située au quartier de la Guille, paroisse du Dondon, ses nègres il y a deux ans passés se sont révoltés et l'auraient égorgée sans l'heureuse assistance du commandant espagnol près duquel elle s'est réfugiée depuis ce temps. C'est à St. Raphaël qu'elle jouit de cette tranquillité dont sa malheureuse patrie est privée." Marguerite-Françoise Lamerenx, widow Saint-Germain, to Joaquín García y Moreno, captain general of Santo Domingo, 18 September 1793, ibid.

25. "Soixante-dix ans, veuve depuis vingt ans passés d'un capitaine de dragons et ayant perdu un fils reçu en 1770 dans la maison du roi, faut-il que Madame Duhart sans aucun reproche à se faire, après un travail constant, pénible, laborieux, et avoir vaincu enfin toute difficulté à une fortune brillante se trouve réduite aujourd'hui sans l'avoir mérité à un avenir aussi effrayant." Elizabeth Le Jeune, widow Lamerenx, to Joaquín García y Moreno, captain general of Santo Domingo, 18 September 1793, ibid.

26. "Recomiendo a Ud. estas tres honradas familias de mérito y desgracia, una señora septuagenaria, acostumbradas todas a la opulencia, y comodidad, y unas personas sin otro arbitrio que la piedad del Rey de España a quien han jurado vasallaje, sumisión y eterna fidelidad." Joaquín García y Moreno, captain general of Santo Domingo, to Pedro de Acuña, secretary of state for graces and justice, 18 October 1793, ibid.

27. José Vázquez was the parish priest of Dajabón. He was appointed chaplain of the black auxiliary army in the service of the king of Spain the following year (June 1794). See Ojeda, *Tendencias monárquicas en la revolución haitiana*, 28–30, 70–72. See also Ferrer, *Freedom's Mirror*, 88.

28. "No tienen ni aun visos de cristianos y en dos años no se han confesado ni hablan de Dios ni les he notado otra cosa que una grande complacencia cuando los franceses ganan una función." Father Vázquez to Archbishop Portillo of Santo Domingo, 5 August 1793, AGI, Santo Domingo 1110, quoted in Deive, *Los refugiados franceses en Santo Domingo*, 162.

29. For an account of the war from the Spanish point of view, see Ferrer, *Freedom's Mirror*, 96–158.

30. "En medio de los mayores sustos y quebrantos." Affidavit by Joaquín Cabrera, 24 October 1799, Trémais file, ANOM, Dépôt des papiers publics des colonies, Saint-Domingue, Domaines, 1690–1828, DPPC 3SUPSDOM 60.

31. See Ernst Trouillot, *Démesvar Delorme*; and Hénock Trouillot, *Démesvar Delorme*.

32. Delorme, *1842 au Cap*.

33. "Il se passionnait pour tout ce qui lui faisait l'effet de la distinction ou de l'honneur. Il tenait cela de son père, comme je l'ai entendu dire à sa sœur, ma grand-mère maternelle. Son père, un de ces colons français de haut parage, qui tout en vivant de la somptueuse existence des grands planteurs de Saint-Domingue, n'avaient jamais eu ni dureté ni mépris pour la race opprimée. Mais ils tenaient à distance ce qu'on appelait dans la colonie les petits blancs. Ce sont ces derniers surtout qui ont été cruels pour les esclaves et les affranchis." Ibid., 28.

34. See Garrigus, "Vincent Ogé *jeune*."

35. "Mais, chéri de son père, qui l'avait fait élever en France, il avait partagé à son retour sa vie de grand Seigneur, ses habitudes de fierté coloniale, et avait eu le privilège exceptionnel, parmi les hommes de son origine, de vivre, ainsi que ma grand-mère, son autre sœur et son frère Pierre, au-dessus de la caste des petits blancs faisant le négoce, dans un dédain profond pour ceux qui dédaignaient les malheureux et les maltraitaient." Delorme, *1842 au Cap*, 29.

36. "Lui, n'ayant rien à craindre, était resté jusqu'au dernier moment. Ce dernier moment avait été le temps des dernières proscriptions sous Dessalines. Il allait être égorgé comme les autres. Son fils aîné, le grand oncle dont je parle ici, le sauva, portant son père malade, infirme, sur ses épaules, la nuit, à travers les bois, s'arrêtant de distance en distance, dans les habitations, chez des personnes de sa connaissance, chez des amis. Furtivement il gagna ainsi le Cap et embarqua le vieillard avec tout ce qu'il avait d'argent sur un brick américain allant à Boston." Ibid.

37. Popkin, *You Are All Free*, 2.

38. Geggus, "Haiti and its Revolution," 200.

39. "Le citoyen Mouscardy qui n'ayant plus rien, ayant tout perdu, ne pouvait passer à la Nouvelle Angleterre où il voulait se rendre, faute de moyens pécuniaires, le déclarant parvint, avec le secours de ses amis, à lui procurer une somme de 25 portugaises, pour lui faciliter son voyage." ANOM, Dépôt des papiers publics des colonies, Saint-Domingue, Domaines, 1690–1828, DPPC 3SUPSDOM 40.

40. L.-M. Vastey, "Un souvenir de l'esclavage." See also Quevilly, *Le baron de Vastey*, 266–69.

41. "Jean Larroque, ancien négociant au Cap-Français, dont le sort a demeuré longtemps incertain et ignoré, y avait péri lui et tout son avoir vers le neuf avril de l'année 1804." Affidavit by Jeanne Laugar of Sauveterre, Basses-Pyrénées, 23 July 1829, Casadavant, notary in Sauveterre-de-Béarn, ADPA, Minutes notariales, 3E 7153.

42. The will, recorded on 4 October 1787 by Baratte, notary in Marmelade, is mentioned in the Mouscardy sequestered-properties file, ANOM, Dépôt des papiers publics des colonies, Saint-Domingue, Domaines, 1690–1828, DPPC 3SUPSDOM 40. The document itself is not available because the notary's records for that year have not been preserved.

43. See Garrigus, *Before Haiti*, 141–70.

44. Ibid., 161.

45. Lévi-Strauss, "Histoire et ethnologie," 1225.

46. "Les Haïtiens ne seront désormais connus que sous la nomination générique de noirs." Haitian Constitution of 1805, article 14.

47. ANOM, Dépôt des papiers publics des colonies, Saint-Domingue, Recensement des biens domaniaux et urbains, an III [1795]–1814, DPPC 5SUPSDOM 2.

48. "Le droit de propriété ne peut exister sans force protectrice; cette force ne peut exister que par la réunion des forces individuelles de tous les propriétaires; car ce n'est pas à ceux qui n'ont rien, à sacrifier leurs vies pour la défense des propriétés d'autrui." Etienne Polverel, quoted in Debien, "Aux origines de l'abolition de l'esclavage," 43. Polverel's declaration applied officially to the West and South of the island. Its principles were subsequently endorsed by Sonthonax, who was in charge of the North. See Debien, "Aux origines de l'abolition de l'esclavage," 26.

49. "Tous ceux qui avaient abandonné ou trahi, qui abandonneraient ou trahiraient la défense commune." Debien, "Aux origines de l'abolition de l'esclavage," 26.

50. "Depuis longtemps on calomnie la race africaine, on dit que sans l'esclavage on ne l'accoutumera jamais au travail. Puisse l'essai que je vais faire, démentir ce préjugé, non moins absurde que celui de l'aristocratie des couleurs." Ibid., 47.

51. Ibid., 26–27.

52. Ibid., 29–30.

53. Decree of the Council of State regarding land grants, 12 October 1683, in Moreau de Saint-Méry, *Lois et constitutions des colonies françaises*, 392–93.

54. *Edit du roi.*

55. Vialay, *La vente des biens nationaux*, 21–37.

56. Deliberations of the municipal council of La Bastide Clairence, 25 September 1794, AMLBC, Conseil municipal: registres des délibérations, 1790–1950, 1D2.

57. Debien, "Aux origines de l'abolition de l'esclavage," 27–28.

58. Inventory of the Trémais plantations located in the parish of Marmelade, 2 September 1788, Riberon, notary in Marmelade, ANOM, Dépôt des papiers publics des colonies, Saint-Domingue, Notariat, DPPC NOT SDOM 1544.

59. Ibid.

60. "Mr. Lamerens comandante militar del Dondon antes de su toma por los negros . . . libertar sus vidas del peligro que les amenazaba la proscripción, el encono de sus émulos quienes han pedido su arresto y despacho para Francia." Joaquín García to Pedro de Acuña, Santo Domingo, 25 November 1792, AGS, Secretaría del Despacho de Guerra, Santo Domingo, SGU LEG 7158.

61. "La classe des riches propriétaires blancs reçut un coup mortel par les journées du 17, du 18, et 19 octobre. La vieille aristocratie coloniale fut anéantie dans le Nord. Polvérel et Sonthonax servirent dans cette circonstance les intérêts des noirs et des jaunes en écrasant les blancs par les blancs." Madiou, *Histoire d'Haïti*, vol. 1 (1847), 118.

62. On slave armies, see Brown and Morgan, *Arming Slaves*.

63. Garran, *Rapport sur les troubles de Saint-Domingue*, 3:247.

64. "Tous les propriétaires blancs de ce pays et de Plaisance, qui s'étaient réfugiés à Saint-Raphaël et dans les autres possessions espagnoles retournèrent à la Marmelade." Louverture, *Notes sur la vie de Toussaint Louverture*, 330.

65. Ibid.

66. Sale by Jacques Deschez, Marie-Catherine Biret, Pierre Biret, and Marianne Biret of

three-quarter *carreaux* of land to Jean Carbonnel, Riberon, notary in Marmelade, 22 February 1788, ANOM, Dépôt des papiers publics des colonies, Saint-Domingue, Notariat, DPPC NOT SDOM 1544.

67. "Tout le monde était content de lui, on ne parlait que de l'élévation de son génie, de son courage et de sa magnanimité." Louverture, *Notes sur la vie de Toussaint Louverture*, 330.

68. "Dans cette campagne il dégagea sur la rive gauche de l'Artibonite, le capitaine Lamérens, son aide-de-camp, qui était entouré par six Espagnols, et blessa un soldat ennemi." Ibid., 334.

69. On Toussaint Louverture's decision to switch sides, see Geggus, "From His Most Catholic Majesty to the Godless Republic."

70. "Suivi de ses aides-de-camp Birette, Dubuisson, Charles Bélair et Lamérens, et de deux officiers de couleur, le lieutenant-colonel Dessalines et le capitaine Vène qui s'étaient échappés des Gonaïves, il partit de la Marmelade, décidé de changer la face des choses et de traiter avec le général Lavaux." Isaac Louverture, "Notes historiques sur Toussaint Louverture," BnF, NAF 12409, fol. 58. Jacques de Cauna does mention Lamerenx as an aide-de-camp to Toussaint. His source is the printed version of Isaac's memoirs. See Cauna, *Toussaint Louverture et l'indépendance d'Haïti*, 200. In a 2013 article (Force, "House on Bayou Road") I indicated that the person named Lamerens who was recorded by Isaac Louverture as Toussaint's aide-de-camp could have been either Jean-Pierre Lamerenx or his son Charles Lamerenx. Based on new evidence, in particular the appointment of "Pierre Lamérince" as battalion commander (see n. 73 below), it seems highly likely that the aide-de-camp was the father.

71. A delegation headed by Toussaint initially sought amnesty for the rebels and freedom for some fifty plantation commanders in exchange for a commitment to return to work on the plantations. See report by General de Kerverseau in Pluchon, *Toussaint Louverture d'après le général de Kerverseau*, 21.

72. Madiou, *Histoire d'Haïti*, vol. 1 (1847), 223.

73. "Pierre Lamérince a été nommé chef de bataillon au 7e régiment des troupes [franches] de la colonie en date du 9 thermidor l'an 3e [27 July 1795] donné au Port-de-Paix enregistré au bureau. [Signed]: Freyssinet." ANOM, Fonds ministériels, Premier empire colonial, Troupes et personnel civil, Matricules et revues, 1650–1901, COL D2C 360. See also Madiou, *Histoire d'Haïti*, vol. 1 (1847), 224.

74. Madiou, *Histoire d'Haïti*, vol. 1 (1847), 224.

75. "Le lendemain les troupes anglaises échappées dans ce combat à la furie de leurs adversaires furent complètement défaites près de Saint-Marc par le général Toussaint Louverture qui les avait poursuivies à la tête de ses guides et d'un escadron que commandait le colonel Dessalines et par Desrouleaux colonel du 7e régiment qui les avait prises à dos." Isaac Louverture, "Notes historiques sur Toussaint Louverture," BnF, NAF 12409.

76. Popkin, *Facing Racial Revolution*, 17–18.

77. "Son exemple rallia au parti républicain de nombreux noirs qui combattaient pour le roi d'Espagne. Il les disciplina, les contraignit à respecter les propriétés." Madiou, *Histoire d'Haïti*, vol. 1 (1847), 196.

78. Aubert file, ANF, Commerce et industrie, Secours aux réfugiés et colons spoliés, F/12/2742.

79. "Unas veces por hallarse interceptados o muy expuestos para las de su sexo los caminos; otras para impedirlo la mucha falta de salud que sufrían, y últimamente por el incendio

ocurrido en la misma Ciudad del Cabo, donde preferían retirarse como paraje considerado más seguro." Affidavit by Joaquín Cabrera, 24 October 1799, Trémais file, ANOM, Dépôt des papiers publics des colonies, Saint-Domingue, Domaines, 1690–1828, DPPC 3SUPSDOM 60.

80. Mouscardy file, ibid., DPPC 3SUPSDOM 40.

81. Trémais file, ibid., DPPC 3SUPSDOM 60.

82. Saint-Germain file, ibid., DPPC 3SUPSDOM 58.

83. On the Leclerc expedition, see Girard, *Slaves Who Defeated Napoléon*.

84. Debien, "Les biens de Toussaint Louverture (documents)," 17.

85. ANOM, Dépôt des papiers publics des colonies, Saint-Domingue, Recensement des biens domaniaux et urbains, an III [1795]–1814, DPPC 5SUPSDOM 2.

86. "La propriété est sacrée, sa violation sera rigoureusement poursuivie."

87. "La qualité de citoyen d'Haïti se perd par l'émigration et par la naturalisation en pays étranger, et par la condamnation à des peines afflictives et infamantes. Le premier cas emporte la peine de mort et la confiscation des propriétés."

88. "Aucun blanc, quelle que soit sa nation, ne mettra le pied sur ce territoire, à titre de maître ou de propriétaire et ne pourra à l'avenir y acquérir aucune propriété."

89. ANOM, Dépôt des papiers publics des colonies, Saint-Domingue, Recensement des biens domaniaux et urbains, an III [1795]–1814, DPPC 5SUPSDOM 2.

90. "Le fonds destiné aux colons ne peut, ni d'après le droit, ni d'après l'esprit de l'ordonnance du 17 avril, être accordé aux Haïtiens, puisque la révolution de Saint-Domingue ne les a pas dépouillés; il est évident que les colons recevront au-delà du dixième de la valeur capitale de leurs propriétés perdues." Analysis of the Indemnity Commission's report to the king, in Vanufel and Champion de Villeneuve, *Code des colons de Saint-Domingue*, 333.

91. See Brière, "La France et la reconnaissance de l'indépendance haïtienne."

92. "La loi n'a pu prévoir un tel désastre. Il est sans exemple dans l'histoire des peuples. Ce n'est point une grêle, un incendie, un tremblement de terre, c'est Pompéia engloutie sous le Vésuve." Louis-Humbert de Sesmaisons, member of the Chamber of Deputies, in Vanufel and Champion de Villeneuve, *Code des colons de Saint-Domingue*, 235.

93. "Elles constituent, à proprement parler, un droit exceptionnel, où nulle analogie ne peut aider." Vanufel and Champion de Villeneuve, *Code des colons de Saint-Domingue*, vij.

94. "Les publicistes reconnaissent que le droit de céder des portions de l'état, à l'ennemi qui les a envahies, lorsque la nécessité de terminer la guerre commande ces sacrifices, appartient à la couronne dans un gouvernement monarchique* [* Wattel, *Droit des Gens*, liv. iv, §11 in finem]." Jean-Marie Pardessus, rapporteur of the commission of the Chamber of Deputies, in ibid., 96.

95. "Cet examen ne pourrait être attaché qu'à des souvenirs pénibles ou à des hypothèses de triste présage." Vanufel and Champion de Villeneuve, *Code des colons de Saint-Domingue*, 96.

96. "Placées par la nature des choses et l'objet même de leur établissement, dans une situation toute spéciale, les colonies forment, dans l'ordre politique, une classe particulière qu'il n'est ni possible de confondre avec les autres corps sociaux, ni permis de leur assimiler; parce qu'étant, en général, un résultat de la conquête et considérées comme des postes militaires et des établissements commerciaux, non moins que comme des propriétés foncières, leur conservation dépend bien plus que celle des autres parties de l'Etat, du sort des armes et de la possibilité de s'y maintenir." Ibid.

97. "Les souverains d'Autriche, au quatorzième siècle, d'Espagne au dix-septième siècle,

d'Angleterre, au siècle dernier, n'ont-ils pas été forcés de reconnaître l'indépendance de leurs provinces insurgées." Ibid., 97.

98. "La suite d'une insurrection survenue au temps même de la terrible révolution qui, dans la métropole, a tout brisé, jusqu'au sceptre lui-même." Ibid.

99. "C'est un fait de guerre qui ne saurait être apprécié par les règles du droit civil, ni régi par ses principes." Jean-Marie Pardessus, rapporteur of the commission of the Chamber of Deputies, in ibid., 106.

100. "Si le bien de la France avait nécessité de reconnaître l'indépendance de Saint-Domingue sans condition; si le roi avait jugé à propos de n'exiger aucun dédommagement pour les anciens colons, il faudrait se soumettre à cette nécessité." Ibid.

101. "Ceux à qui vous donnez des secours ne seront pas dépouillés de leurs droits de propriété par l'ordonnance royale ni par la loi; et s'ils restent propriétaires, il en résulte que l'ordonnance et la loi seront inutiles. Cependant il est bien constant que le président d'Haïti n'a entendu donner les 150 millions que comme une indemnité représentative des propriétés appartenant aux anciens colons." Jacques Mestadier, member of the Chamber of Deputies, in ibid., 183.

102. "Que les nègres et les mulâtres ne sont pas, quoi qu'on en dise, de véritables Français, puisqu'ils n'ont pas même vu la France; qu'ils sont des insulaires dont l'Afrique est la véritable patrie, des indigènes étrangers à la nation française." Ardouin, *Etudes sur l'histoire d'Haïti*, 6:38.

103. Ibid.

104. "Si les *héros* de l'époque sortaient de leurs tombeaux, avec quelle indignation n'apprendraient-ils pas, en voyant le drapeau français flotter au sein de nos villes, que *nous avons consenti, oubliant* qu'ils avaient acquis la terre d'Haïti par leur courage, à *indemniser* d'une somme au-dessus de nos ressources, les descendants de ceux qui les avaient torturés, mutilés?" Ibid., 6:39, quoting Madiou, *Histoire d'Haïti*, vol. 3 (1848), 113.

105. "La dette d'Haïti envers les colons est aussi illégitime que le milliard qui fut imposé à la France en faveur des émigrés, à la chute de Bonaparte." Ibid., 6:40, quoting Madiou, *Histoire d'Haïti*, vol. 3 (1848), 113.

106. "La légalité des ventes nationales est donc désormais un point hors de toute contestation." Discussion of the law of 27 April 1825, in Duvergier, *Collection complète des lois, décrets, ordonnances, règlements, et avis du Conseil d'Etat*, 156.

107. Hobbes, *Leviathan* 1.14.

108. "Il fut fait comme il est dit dans cet article." Ardouin, *Etudes sur l'histoire d'Haïti*, 6:41n.

109. "Or, si les Etats-Unis avaient exclu les Anglais du droit de cité et de propriété sur leur sol, comme Haïti a agi à l'égard des colons, il n'y a aucun doute qu'ils auraient indemnisé également ceux dont les propriétés avaient été confisquées." Ibid.

110. Pashman, "People's Property Law," 594.

111. Sabine, *Biographical Sketches of Loyalists*, 103. See also Jasanoff, *Liberty's Exiles*.

112. Sabine, *Biographical Sketches of Loyalists*, 104.

113. "[Le Cap] Ville puissante ... pleine encore de ces combattants de l'Indépendance, soldats, officiers généraux influents qui n'avaient accepté qu'à grand-peine le Traité de Boyer avec Charles X et qui avaient voulu en 1825 dans la généreuse irréflexion de leur orgueil national qu'on stipulât au moins dans un acte à part que la République offrait d'elle-même l'indemnité dans sa bienveillance aux colons dépossédés." Delorme, *1842 au Cap*, 22.

Chapter 5 · *Nation, Citizenship, and Atlantic Migrations*

1. Adam Smith, *Wealth of Nations*, V.ii.f.
2. "Esprit d'évasion." Hénock Trouillot, *Démesvar Delorme*, 5.
3. "Lui, a choisi de nier toute possibilité d'une littérature nationale et a préféré ... devenir un écrivain français." Ibid.
4. Adam Smith, *Wealth of Nations*, III.iv.24.
5. Anderson, *Imagined Communities*, 5.
6. Ibid., 143.
7. Polverel, *Mémoire*.
8. Ennobling of Etienne Polverel by the Estates General of Navarre, 11 May 1785, ADPA, Administrations provinciales, Etats de Navarre, C 1539.
9. Proofs of nobility for Etienne Polverel, ibid., C 1602.
10. Certificate of nobility for Etienne Polverel, 8 April 1789, ibid., C 1540. On Polverel's career prior to his Saint-Domingue assignment, see Clément-Simon, "Etienne de Polverel"; and Morbieu, "Le Royaume de Navarre et la Révolution française."
11. "L'assemblée nationale de France vient de faire dans une seule séance de grandes et importantes opérations. Elle a ordonné l'affranchissement des serfs et la suppression de toute espèce de mainmorte." Etienne Polverel to the Estates General of Navarre, 7 August 1789, ADPA, Administrations provinciales, Etats de Navarre, C 1601.
12. "Tout cela a été fait dans une séance de cinq heures. Il eût été à désirer que de si grandes réformes eussent pu être délibérées de sang-froid et librement discutées. L'assentiment général a été entraîné par la terreur qu'avaient répandue les incendiaires et les brigands qui brûlaient et pillaient les châteaux de l'Alsace, de la Franche-Comté, et de quelques autres provinces, et par la générosité des membres du clergé et de la noblesse qui, à l'envi les uns des autres, ont fait le sacrifice de leurs propriétés." Ibid.
13. See Jacquemin, "Etienne Polverel et l'abolition de l'esclavage," 158.
14. "Rien n'est plus contraire à l'unité monarchique que la variété des titres; au lieu d'être une véritable fusion de parties homogènes, cet empire serait donc composé de parties diverses, qui ne tarderaient pas à être divisées?" Honoré Gabriel Riqueti, comte de Mirabeau, National Assembly session of 12 October 1789, in *Réimpression de l'Ancien Moniteur*, 48.
15. Bell, *Cult of the Nation in France*.
16. Polverel, *Tableau de la constitution du Royaume de Navarre*.
17. "La France n'a eu une véritable Constitution que sous le règne de Charlemagne. On a beaucoup vanté cette Constitution, et l'on a eu raison à beaucoup d'égards. Mais valait-elle celle de la Navarre? On pourra en juger par la comparaison." Ibid., xxvj.
18. Baker, *Inventing the French Revolution*, 48.
19. "La servitude était l'état naturel et légal du plus grand nombre des Français." Polverel, *Tableau de la constitution du Royaume de Navarre*, xxvj.
20. "Ceux qui étaient d'une condition libre n'avaient eux-mêmes qu'une liberté précaire." Ibid., xxvij.
21. "La constitution de la Monarchie Navarraise, n'est l'ouvrage ni d'un Roi ni d'un Conquérant. C'est un peuple libre et courageux, entouré de puissants ennemis, n'ayant ni lois ni tribunaux, qui a voulu avoir un Roi pour diriger les forces de la Nation contre les ennemis du dehors pour maintenir au dedans la paix publique, et qui, avant d'élire son premier Roi, a dicté les lois qui devaient protéger à jamais la liberté civile et politique des Navarrais." Ibid., xiij.

22. "Osons le dire, de toutes les constitutions de notre Europe moderne, celle de la Navarre est la moins défectueuse; elle a plus fait qu'aucune autre pour la liberté civile et politique; elle a fait, pour la liberté et pour l'égalité, tout ce qu'il était possible de concilier avec la distinction des Ordres." Ibid., xxxvij.

23. "Quoi, ce projet, digne tout au plus du Prince de Machiavel, aurait été conçu sous le meilleur, sous le plus juste des Rois! Quoi, l'on aurait espéré d'engager Louis XVI à tenter d'asservir un peuple qui fut libre pendant plus de mille ans, au même instant où il rend la liberté à un peuple qui a été esclave pendant neuf cents ans!" Ibid., lix.

24. Mably, *Des droits et des devoirs du citoyen*, quoted in Baker, *Inventing the French Revolution*, 95.

25. Polverel, *Tableau de la constitution du Royaume de Navarre*, lxxviij.

26. Dobie, *Trading Places*.

27. "L'assemblée considérant que, lorsque les hommes se sont réunis pour former un corps politique, ils n'ont d'autres motifs que d'éviter les maux qui accompagnent l'anarchie pour jouir des avantages que procure un sage gouvernement; que la première condition de leur association est le sacrifice de leur intérêt particulier à l'intérêt général et que la seconde est l'assemblage de toutes les forces individuelles pour défendre la cause commune; que ce furent ces motifs qui déterminèrent les Navarrais, dont l'origine se perd dans la nuit des temps, à se réunir en corps de nation vers le commencement du huitième siècle." Deliberation of the Municipal Assembly, 8 December 1789, AMLBC, Conseil de ville: registres des délibérations, 1680–1790, BB22. See also Dufourcq, "La Bastide Clairence à la veille et au début de la période révolutionnaire."

28. "Lecture et explication ayant été faites, la présente assemblée, après avoir déclaré qu'elle a saisi et bien compris tout leur contenu, a arrêté d'une voix unanime et par acclamation:

1) que cette ville s'incorpore au royaume de France, qu'en conséquence elle adhère de cœur et d'âme, purement et simplement, aux décrets faits et à faire par l'assemblée nationale. . . .

2) qu'il sera fait une adresse à l'assemblée nationale pour la prier d'agréer l'incorporation de la présente ville au royaume de France, et d'accepter le sacrifice qu'elle fait de sa constitution comme un témoignage de l'amour le plus parfait pour la nation française et le respect le plus profond pour les décrets de ses augustes représentants."

AMLBC, Conseil de ville: registres des délibérations, 1680–1790, BB22.

29. "En langue vulgaire." Ibid. In La Bastide Clairence, a chartered town that was originally populated with immigrants from a wide area in what is now southwestern France, the vernacular language was Gascon. In the rest of Lower Navarre the vernacular was Basque.

30. Financial report of 8 February 1790, ibid.

31. ANOM, Dépôt des papiers publics des colonies, Saint-Domingue, Domaines, 1690–1828, DPPC 3SUPSDOM 40.

32. François Colombots, son of Jean-Pierre Colombots *américain* and "Marie-Claire of Saint-Domingue in America," died in La Bastide Clairence on 10 November 1799, at the age of fifteen. AMLBC, Etat-Civil, 1792–1952, E30.

33. Marriage of Jean-Pierre Colombots *américain* and Marie Labarthe, La Bastide Clairence, 1 May 1792, ibid., E16.

34. Deliberation of the Municipal Council, 19 June 1791, AMLBC, Conseil municipal: registres des délibérations, 1790–1950, 1D1.

35. Deliberation of the Municipal Council, 16 December 1792, ibid.

36. On the impact of the Haitian Revolution on Cuban history, see Ferrer, *Freedom's Mirror*.

37. Carpentier, *Kingdom of This World*, 76.

38. On migration from Saint-Domingue to Cuba, see Debien, "Les colons de Saint-Domingue réfugiés à Cuba."

39. See Yacou, "La présence française dans la partie occidentale," 152. See also Ramírez Pérez, *Francia en Cuba*; and Tabío and Payarés, *Sobre los cafetales coloniales*.

40. Yacou, "La présence française dans la partie occidentale," 179.

41. Jean-Pierre Lamerenx was mentioned as a *négociant* in a declaration his daughter Marguerite made in France in 1806. See affidavits by several citizens of Gurs, Basses-Pyrénées, 13 August 1806, ADPA, Fonds privés, Fonds Batcave, 2 J 503, Hyppolite Dabbadie, justice of the peace of the canton of Navarrenx.

42. See Juan Pérez de la Riva, "La implantación francesa en la cuenca superior del Cauto," 386–88.

43. Ibid., 387.

44. Last will of Jean-Pierre Lamerenx, Matanzas, Cuba, 18 January 1810, translated into French in Saint-Palais, France, on 13 December 1817, attached to contract recorded on 16 October 1818 by Dilor, notary in Saint-Palais, ADPA, Minutes notariales, 3E 1274.

45. Sale of the San Pedro coffee plantation, ANC, Protocoles notariales, Matanzas, Notario o escribano: Santiago Luis López Villavicencio, Año 1840, 849–56.

46. Ibid.

47. "La population et l'industrie française ont seules occasionné une hausse aussi considérable." Concession in the province of Guantanamo, Cuba, 15 October 1806, Service historique de la défense, Toulon, Var, Guyane et autres colonies, 5R1 20, quoted in Francisco Pérez de la Riva, *El café*, 318.

48. Juan Pérez de la Riva, "La implantación francesa en la cuenca superior del Cauto," 387.

49. Parish of San Carlos de Matanzas, sacramental records, 26 November 1804, Baptism of Blacks and Mulattoes, Book 5, 1801–1805, in *Ecclesiastical and Secular Sources for Slave Societies*.

50. Debien, "Les colons de Saint-Domingue réfugiés à Cuba," 14:32.

51. Parish of San Carlos de Matanzas, sacramental records, 10 March 1800, Baptism of Blacks and Mulattoes, Book 4, 1796–1801, in *Ecclesiastical and Secular Sources for Slave Societies*.

52. M. J. Laborie, *Cultivo del cafeto o árbol que produce el café*. See Jean Lamore, "Le *Manuel du planteur de café* de Pierre-Joseph Laborie."

53. Dumont, *Consideraciones sobre el cultivo del café en esta isla*.

54. On the massive increase in the African population in Matanzas in the nineteenth century, see Landers, *Atlantic Creoles in the Age of Revolutions*, 204–9.

55. Francisco Pérez de la Riva, *El café*, 51, 74.

56. See Guerra y Sánchez, *Sugar and Society in the Caribbean*.

57. Last will of Françoise Silly, ANC, Protocoles notariales, Matanzas, Notario o escribano: Santiago Luis López Villavicencio, Año 1840, 589–92.

58. Carlos de Lamerenx Duhart to the king of Spain, 7 April 1817, AGI, Ultramar 155, 51.

59. *Institutes of the Civil Law of Spain*, 283.

60. ANC, Asuntos políticos, Cuaderno de los autos contra D. Carlos Lamerens por infidencia, 31 August 1815, Legajo 15, Número 36.

61. ANC, Autos, Don Carlos Lamerens contra Don Mateo Grout sobre pesos (1807), Legajo 685, Número 5.

62. Officer rolls for Santo Domingo, appointments and promotions since 1 April 1808, ANOM, Fonds ministériels, Premier empire colonial, Troupes et personnel civil, Matricules et revues, 1650–1901, COL D2C 367. The record mentions that he was "rayé des contrôles," the standard expression for the termination of noncareer military personnel. The regiment was known as the Légion coloniale or Chasseurs volontaires coloniaux. According to a contemporary witness, Repussard's black troops were "fearless." See Guillermin, *Précis historique des derniers événements de la partie de l'est de Saint-Domingue*, 189.

63. See Ferrer, *Freedom's Mirror*, 249–65.

64. See Álvarez-Junco, *Spanish Identity in the Age of Nations*, 91–114.

65. See Debien, "Réfugiés de Saint-Domingue expulsés de La Havane en 1809," 3.

66. Estate of Françoise Dubrauil [*sic*], alias Franchonette [*sic*] Decoudreau, vs. Charles Lamerenx, NOPL, parish court records, Orleans Parish, 020-187 (1813). See Force, "House on Bayou Road." On Saint-Domingue refugees in New Orleans, see Dessens, *From Saint-Domingue to New Orleans*.

67. Pérez Morales, *El gran diablo hecho barco*, 31.

68. "Admisión y establecimiento de extranjeros que profesen algún género de industria útil al país." Article 30 of the Constitution of the Republic of Cartagena, quoted in ibid., 96.

69. See Cossé Bell, *Revolution, Romanticism*, 47.

70. See Cacua Prada, *El corsario Louis Aury*, 24. See also Ferro, *Vida de Luis Aury*.

71. Report by Louis Aury to the president of the Republic of Cartagena, August 1814, printed in *El mensajero de Cartagena de Indias*, 19 August 1814, in Pérez Morales, *El gran diablo hecho barco*, 229–33.

72. For an overview of the legal aspects of privateering, see Kert, *Privateering*, 38–56.

73. Louis Aury to his sister, Victorine Aury, 1812, in Danbey, "Louis Aury," 110.

74. AGI, Ultramar 28, 3, fol. 52r.

75. AGI, Ultramar 97, 5, fol. 19v.

76. "El fiscal dice que el Francés Lamerens no es desde luego infidente porque . . . no ser vasallo de nuestro rey." ANC, Asuntos políticos, Cuaderno de los autos contra D. Carlos Lamerens por infidencia, Legajo 15, Número 36.

77. "Pero es un verdadero y obstinado pirata de los Españoles." Ibid.

78. "Malévolo y enemigo del género humano." Ibid.

79. "Amistad y confianza con el capitán francés." Ibid.

80. Agreement between Louis Aury and the owner of the privateer schooner *Le Beau Narcisse*, 27 April 1809, Leroy, notary in Santo Domingo, ANOM, Dépôt des papiers publics des colonies, Saint-Domingue, Notariat, DPPC NOT SDOM 1701.

81. Guillermin, *Précis historique des derniers événements de la partie de l'est de Saint-Domingue*, 279.

82. "Toda clase de marineros como Españoles, Franceses, Ingleses, Americanos, y muchos de la colonia del Guárico; que los más eran de color: que como su oficio es de marinero, si el gran Diablo se hace barco, en él Navegaría; y responde." Testimony of the "French Negro" Ignacio, crew member of *La Belona*, before the Spanish authorities of Real Mineral de Veragua, in Pérez Morales, *El gran diablo hecho barco*, 235.

83. Jeremy Adelman argues that the rise of independent nations in Latin America re-

sulted primarily from a collapse at the imperial center. Adelman, *Sovereignty and Revolution in the Iberian Atlantic.*

84. Faye, "Commodore Aury," 639.

85. Marriage of Marguerite Lamerenx and Daniel Laborde, Gurs, Basses-Pyrénées, 20 September 1804, Archives départementales des Pyrénées-Atlantiques, E-archives, earchives.le64.fr.

86. Sale of the Marmont family house and two tenant farms (Betbeder and Trivailly) in La Bastide Clairence to Jacob Gomès, merchant in Saint-Esprit, near Bayonne, Damborgez, notary in Bayonne, recorded at Bureau des hypothèques de Bayonne on 29 June 1818, ADPA, Registres de formalités et hypothèques, 312 Q 35. The total price of sale was 4,000 francs.

87. Renewal of mortgage contract, 16 October 1818, Dilor, notary in Saint-Palais, ADPA, Minutes notariales, 3E 1274. The original debt (4,286 livres) had been contracted by Jean-Pierre Lamerenx on 17 October 1787. The original creditor was Jean-Claude Pommé, notary in Arudy, Béarn, and the current creditor was Pommé's son Jean-François Pommé. The debt was guaranteed by a mortgage on Lamerenx house and land in Aïcirits.

88. Acknowledgement of debt, 9 February 1829, Dilor, notary in Saint-Palais, ibid., 3E 8755.

89. "Noble Charles de Lamerens, parrain de l'enfant, rentier, maître de la noble maison de Lamerens." The child died on 13 September 1820.

90. Power of attorney signed in Matanzas, Cuba, on 28 April 1828, recorded in Saint-Palais, France, on 15 July 1828, Dilor, notary in Saint-Palais, ADPA, Minutes notariales, 3E 8755.

91. "Quoiqu'ils n'aient d'ailleurs rien à redire sur son compte." Ibid.

92. Bailiff notification, 16 July 1828, Dilor, notary in Saint-Palais, ibid.

93. Charles Lamerenx married Madeleine Biscay in Arette, Basses-Pyrénées, on 5 July 1831. On that occasion he legitimized his son Jean-Pierre Eugène Lamerenx, born in Saint-Palais on 24 January 1830. His son Auguste was born in Arette three days after the wedding, on 8 July 1831.

94. Agreement between Charles Lamerenx and his sister Marguerite, 11 October 1833, Dilor, notary in Saint-Palais, ADPA, Minutes notariales, 3E 8759.

95. Lamerens Duhart file, ANF, Commerce et industrie, Secours aux réfugiés et colons spoliés, F/12/2821.

96. "A l'honneur de vous exposer de Lamerenx Duhart (Charles) ex-capitaine d'état-major dans la légion colonial [*sic*] de Saint-Domingue que n'ayant pu à ce titre obtenir ni retrait ni pension du gouvernement, ce qu'il croyait avoir justement mérité par ses longs services à déffendre [*sic*] les droits de l'état que ses blessures attestent hautement; il se trouve dans la nécessité de supplier votre Excellence." Ibid.

97. "J'étais né pour jouir d'une belle fortune et la funeste révolution de l'île de Saint-Domingue vint détruire toutes mes espérances." Ibid.

98. "Echappé aux massacres exercés par les nègres, j'ai cru trouver quelques ressources dans le patrimoine de mes ancêtres; l'infidélité ou l'incurie de leurs agents en avait absorbé la valeur par des dettes que n'ont pu compenser des créances irrécouvrables. Me voilà donc réduit à implorer un secours annuel annoncé par la munificence Royale aux malheureux colons qui ont survécu aux événements." Ibid.

99. Jean-Bernard, marquis d'Uhart, had become interim governor of the Basque province

of Soule in 1787 and had been elected to represent the nobility for the province on 1 July 1789. See Robert, Bourloton, and Cougny, *Dictionnaire des parlementaires français*, s.v. "Uhart (d'), Jean-Bernard."

100. Power of attorney from Marguerite Lamerenx, widow Laborde, to "X," to receive succession of her husband, Daniel Laborde, who died in Matanzas, Cuba, 21 July 1828, Dilor, notary in Saint-Palais, ADPA, Minutes notariales, 3E 8754; translation into Spanish of power of attorney given by Marguerite Lamerenx to her son, Jean-Pierre Laborde, on 5 December 1837, ANC, Bienes de difuntos, Matanzas, Año 1838, Legajo 15, Número 319 (original in Diriart, notary in Saint-Palais, ADPA, Minutes notariales, 3E 8812); power of attorney from Marguerite Lamerenx (widow Laborde) to her brother Jean-Baptiste to receive in her name her share of the sale of the San Pedro coffee plantation (including slaves) and any other sums she is owed, 16 October 1842, Diriart, notary in Saint-Palais, ADPA, Minutes notariales, 3E 8822; power of attorney from Marguerite Lamerenx to Pierre Etchavarria, vice-consul of France in Matanzas, to recover money from the successors of Jean-Baptiste Lamerenx, her deceased brother, 28 May 1844, Diriart, notary in Saint-Palais, ibid., 3E 8825; power of attorney from Marguerite Lamerenx, widow Laborde, to her nephew Jean-Pierre Eugène Lamerenx of Arette, Basses-Pyrénées, son of Charles Lamerenx, 2 December 1853, Diriart, notary in Saint-Palais, ibid., 3E 18066 (the document does not appear in the minutes but is listed in the index).

101. Death of Daniel Laborde, 3 October 1824, Parish of San Carlos de Matanzas, sacramental records.

102. Marriage of Jean-Pierre Laborde and Hélène d'Oro, Pontonx-sur-l'Adour, Landes, 18 September 1834, Archives départementales des Pyrénées-Atlantiques, E-archives, earchives.le64.fr.

103. Mortgage agreement, 24 February 1839, Ganderats, notary in Saint-Palais, ADPA, Minutes notariales, 3E 18015.

104. Mortgage agreement, 4 April 1857, Sunhary, notary in Saint-Palais, ibid., 3E 18139; mortgage agreement, 2 March 1859, Ganderats, notary in Saint-Palais, ibid., 3E 18144.

105. Mortgage agreement, 24 October 1845, Ganderats, notary in Saint-Palais, ibid., 3E 18017. Marguerite Lamerenx and her son borrowed 5,000 francs, due in five years, and mortgaged the Lamerenx estate. The lender was Jean Elizalde.

106. *Mémorial des Pyrénées*, 7 April 1857, 6.

107. Sale of the Lamerenx estate by Marguerite Lamerenx, widow Laborde, and her son, Pierre Laborde, to Henry Lagouardette, 4 December 1859, Ganderats, notary in Saint-Palais, ADPA, Minutes notariales, 3E 18144.

108. Death of Marguerite Françoise Lamerenx, Sorde-L'Abbaye, Landes, 3 August 1860, Archives départementales des Pyrénées-Atlantiques, E-archives, earchives.le64.fr.

109. The Lamerenx family lived at 35, rue Gassies (now rue Carnot) in Pau from 1847 to 1851. Lamerens Duhart file, ANF, Commerce et industrie, Secours aux réfugiés et colons spoliés, F/12/2821.

110. Delfour, *Histoire du lycée de Pau*.

111. Death of Charles Lamerenx, Arette, Basses-Pyrénées, 25 November 1854, Archives départementales des Pyrénées-Atlantiques, E-archives, earchives.le64.fr.

112. *Les visas en Bordelais*, visasenbordelais.fr. Original visa record in ADG, Police, 1790–1941, 4M 666; ship departure record in ADG, Commerce, 1760–1942, 8M 237.

113. Adolphe's visa was granted in Bordeaux on 12 December 1854. He sailed to Havana

on the *Ferdinand*. *Les visas en Bordelais*, visasenbordelais.fr. Original visa record in ADG, Police, 1790–1941, 4M 668 2064.

114. Auguste's visa was granted in Bordeaux on 6 January 1858, and he sailed to Havana on the *Joachino Victoire*. *Les visas en Bordelais*, visasenbordelais.fr. Original visa record in ADG, Police, 1790–1941, 4M 668 20.

115. Landers, *Atlantic Creoles in the Age of Revolutions*, 7. The phrase *Atlantic creoles* was coined by Ira Berlin. See Berlin, *Many Thousands Gone*; and Berlin, "From Creole to African."

116. "Ah! Il faut avoir parcouru le monde pendant 10 ou 12 ans pour connaître le prix que l'on donne à la résurrection de ce qui vous est cher. Depuis cette époque, n'ayant trouvé presque que des indifférents combien il est doux de se rappeler qu'il y a encore des êtres qui partagent vos plaisirs, qui écoutent vos plaintes et prendront part à vos douleurs." Louis Aury to his sister, aunt, and uncle, Baltimore, 10 October 1812, Luis Aury Papers, Library of Congress, Manuscript Division, box 1, folder 6.

117. Hippolyte Dabadie, justice of the peace of the canton of Navarrenx, 1806, ADPA, Fonds privés, Fonds Batcave, 2 J 503.

118. Ibid.

119. On 11 April 1799 Etienne Thore gave powers of attorney to his father, Bertrand Thore, before embarking on *L'Impatient*, whose captain was named Bailly. Dhiriart, notary in Bayonne, ADPA, Minutes notariales, 3E 4527.

120. See Ducéré, *Les corsaires basques et bayonnais*, 329.

121. Louis Aury to his sister, Victorine Aury, 1812, in Danbey, "Louis Aury," 110.

122. Carpentier, *Kingdom of This World*, 117.

123. Ibid., 118.

124. "Il avait fait la guerre de l'Indépendance et était devenu colonel sous Christophe." Delorme, *1842 au Cap*, 29.

125. Mollien, *Haïti ou Saint-Domingue*, 117.

126. *Almanach royal d'Hayti pour l'année 1816*.

127. Quevilly, *Le baron de Vastey*, 159–67.

128. Mouscardy's parents were not married. Vastey's parents were married in Marmelade on 3 July 1777. The mother was Elisabeth, a.k.a. Mimy, "quarteronne libre" (free quadroon). See ibid., 83.

129. Debien, "Les biens de Toussaint Louverture (documents)."

130. Quevilly, *Le baron de Vastey*, 222–23.

131. Césaire, *La tragédie du roi Christophe*, act 2, scene 5.

132. "Il nous fera partager les droits de sujets et de citoyens français, ce qui, certes, est préférable au sort d'être traité comme des sauvages malfaisants, ou traqués comme des nègres marrons." Dauxion Lavaysse to Alexandre Pétion, in *Procès-verbal des séances*, 11.

133. "Vous mériterez les marques les plus honorables de la satisfaction de votre souverain et la reconnaissance de votre patrie et des habitants d'Haïti, que nous ne pouvons cesser de considérer comme français." Ibid.

134. Dauxion Lavaysse to Henri Christophe, in ibid., 7.

135. Prézeau, *Réfutation de la lettre*, 13.

136. "Nous ne désirons pas devenir blancs par des lettres de blancs: nous nous glorifions de la couleur qu'il a plu à la divinité de couvrir nos fronts. Nous demandons à jouir des droits naturels de l'homme et des droits politiques que jouissent les nations libres et indépendantes." Ibid., 21.

137. "Nous avons changé de nom, de vie, de mœurs, nous ne ressemblons en rien aux Français; à ce people qui n'a cessé de nous persécuter et que nous abhorrons." Council General of the Nation to King Henry, in *Procès-verbal des séances*, 15.

138. *Christian Observer* (London), January 1815, 66–67.

139. *Le Télégraphe. Gazette Officielle* (Port-au-Prince), 7 October 1821.

140. Madiou, *Histoire d'Haïti*, vol. 6 (1988), 42.

141. Birth of Marguerite Mouscardy, daughter of Jean-Théodat Mouscardy, colonel, and Victoire Philippe Mandrut, hat maker, Cap-Haïtien, 16 May 1822, *Association de Généalogie d'Haïti*.

142. Birth of Jean-Théodat Belliard, son of Thomas Belliard, brigadier general, and of Françoise Etienne Albert, Cap-Haïtien, 17 October 1822, ibid.

143. Ardouin, *Etudes sur l'histoire d'Haïti*, 10:281–82. See also Madiou, *Histoire d'Haïti*, vol. 7 (1987), 180–81. On the history of land ownership in Haiti, see Renaud, *Le régime foncier en Haïti*.

144. "A cette vue, le colonel MOUSCARDY s'élance vers ISIDOR et lui reproche en termes énergiques sa révolte contre la République, et son ingratitude envers le Président d'Haïti qui avait été son bienfaiteur et son père. C'est vrai, répondit ISIDOR, je suis coupable, je mérite bien mon sort." *Le Télégraphe. Gazette Officielle*, 12 February 1837, quoted in *Recueil général des lois et actes du gouvernement d'Haïti*, 6:329.

145. "Il était en outre, d'un abord difficile, imposant, tout plein de façons aristocratiques." Delorme, *1842 au Cap*, 27.

146. "Il m'aimait pour tout ce qu'il trouvait en moi de naturel aimant et de ce qu'il appelait d'heureuses dispositions." Ibid., 28.

147. "C'est ainsi qu'il faudrait décrire ce jour du jugement dernier dont on nous parle dans notre enfance. La trompette de l'Ange n'y manquait pas ni les cris de détresse ni les lamentations." Ibid., 3.

148. 'Mon oncle me reçut avec une émotion difficile à dire." Ibid., 10.

149. "L'on ne peut que s'applaudir de l'empressement du général Mouscardi [sic] commandant l'arrondissement de la Grande Rivière, qui a dépêché aussitôt qu'il a pu le mardi deux détachements du 26e et du 3e régiment pour aider à rétablir l'ordre et arrêter autant que possible le désordre, le brigandage et le pillage exercés dans cette malheureuse ville dès le dimanche." *Feuille du commerce*, 15 May 1842, 3. See also Madiou, *Histoire d'Haïti*, vol. 7 (1987), 401.

150. "Considérant que si la moralité de la révolution est de ne point rechercher les coupables auxiliaires de la tyrannie abattue, il n'est pas moins de la dignité du peuple souverain d'exclure de la direction de ses affaires ces hommes tarés dont les excès immoraux ont flétri l'honneur en les déshéritant de la considération et de l'estime de leurs concitoyens." Judgment against General Jean-Théodat Mouscardy, *Feuille du commerce*, 6 August 1843, 3–4.

151. "Vous êtes peuple; et, comme tel, vous êtes souverain, vos chefs maintenant ne sont que vos serviteurs." Report by Charles Hérard *aîné* to the members of the provisional government, May 1843, in *Recueil général des lois et actes du Gouvernement d'Haïti*, 7:310.

152. "A ces mots, le peuple que je connais, parce que j'ai vécu de sa vie, s'est pressé autour de moi, m'a fait connaitre ses souffrances; uni à son comité, il m'a dénoncé le général Mouscardy qui depuis longtemps l'opprimait, l'avilissait, le pillait. Ce général, ne pouvant se justifier de ses exactions et de ses abus d'autorité, fut dépouillé du commandement de l'arrondissement

de la Grande-Rivière, et, par un ordre du jour, j'ai fait connaître au peuple les fautes dont il s'était rendu coupable." Ibid.

153. Delorme, *1842 au Cap*, 15.

154. "Si le Général Mouscardy avait vécu, ma destinée eût pu être bien autre." Ibid., 28.

155. Delorme, *L'indépendance d'Haïti et la France*.

156. See Brisson and Ribeyre, *Les grands journaux de France*, 135–37.

157. "L'Algérie sera un jour une autre France, aussi grande, aussi belle, aussi radieuse que la mère-patrie." Delorme, *L'indépendance d'Haïti et la France*, 31.

158. Say, *Treatise on Political Economy*, bk. 1, chap. 19.

159. "Mais aimons et respectons l'indépendance d'Haïti. . . . Entrons en relations commerciales suivies avec la jeune république; elle nous rendra au centuple ce qu'elle nous donnait naguère: ce sera une autre France dans l'archipel des Antilles, une amie reconnaissante, dévouée et fidèle, au lieu d'être une vassale indisciplinée." Delorme, *L'indépendance d'Haïti et la France*, 32.

160. "Ils traversèrent Plaisance, passèrent par Marmelade, et après de longs détours, allongés à dessein, ils atteignirent le bourg de Dondon, assis au pied du sommet qui porte le géant de pierre armé de canons, la citadelle Laferrière, la tête dans les nuages." Delorme, *Les théoriciens au pouvoir*, 385.

161. "Des dates et des noms, charbonnés depuis la fin du seizième siècle, par les Européens qui cherchaient des données sur cette race des Caraïbes entièrement disparue, et dont il ne reste pas un seul descendant dans toute cette grande île." Ibid., 389.

162. "Avec une égale fureur, dans le même moment, tu viens de le dire, ils exterminaient chez eux ces fils de l'Afrique qui faisaient leur prospérité. . . Ce que l'Espagne faisait en Amérique répond ainsi à ce qu'elle faisait en Europe même. C'est la mise en œuvre d'un même ordre d'idées, d'un même système." Ibid., 393.

163. "C'est moi qui viens de châtier ce nègre, qui a osé me suspecter." Delorme, *La misère au sein des richesses*, 125.

164. "Les hommes de notre race sont obligés de se résigner à vivre dans ce pays-là comme vivaient partout les Juifs dans le moyen âge, tolérés mais persécutés. Ils y vivent comme vivaient les Maures en Espagne après la chute du royaume de Grenade, réduits à courber le dos et à trembler." Ibid., 127.

165. "Ces stupides et honteuses proscriptions de races." Ibid., 126.

166. "Le fils de ces hommes généreux qui, à la voix de la Révolution humanitaire de 1789, ont conquis sur cette terre de Saint-Domingue les droits de l'homme et du citoyen, et y ont fondé un asile à leur race opprimée dans les Amériques." Ibid., 109.

167. "Je ne consentirais jamais, pour quelque avantage que ce fût, à aliéner ma qualité de citoyen haïtien. Cette terre d'Haïti, que j'aime si intimement, cette terre où je suis né, où sont nés mon père et ma mère, mes grands-pères et mes grand'mères, est mon unique patrie: je n'en ai pas deux." Ibid.

168. "Ce n'est point dans des causes fortuites qu'il faut chercher l'explication de ce nonsens qui entachait la grande république américaine, et par lequel le pays de la liberté par excellence s'est trouvé en même temps la terre classique de l'esclavage, de l'exploitation brutale d'une race d'hommes par une autre." Delorme, *La démocratie et le préjugé de couleur*, 10.

169. "Ce peuple, qui porte religieusement au fond du cœur le sentiment d'une mission providentielle, suffit, à lui seul, pour détruire tous les sophismes qui ont jusqu'ici servi dans le monde à opprimer et à mépriser les races noires de l'Afrique." Ibid., 20.

170. "PETIT TERRITOIRE, GRANDE NATION!" Delorme, *Les petits*, 234.

171. "Louverture . . . mort de froid dans les glaces du Jura, quand, lui a été jeté au milieu des tropiques où les Anglais l'ont enseveli dans le feu." Ibid., 208.

172. "Le bel usage qu'on fait de nos jours pour s'emparer du pays des Africains sans armes, en les tuant, comme au XVIe siècle on a massacré, détruit les indigènes de l'Amérique, aura sa fin. Ménélick a commencé cette fin." Ibid., 179.

173. "Que cargaban toda clase de banderas, pero para hacer las presas enarbolaban la de los insurgentes de Cartagena." Testimony of the "French Negro" Ignacio, in Pérez Morales, *El gran diablo hecho barco*, 235.

174. Anderson, *Imagined Communities*, 141.

175. Ibid., 143.

176. Bell, *Cult of the Nation in France*, 140–68.

177. Adelman, *Sovereignty and Revolution in the Iberian Atlantic*, 9.

178. Anderson, *Imagined Communities*, 5.

179. Adelman, *Sovereignty and Revolution in the Iberian Atlantic*, 5.

180. See Johnson et al., *Transregional and Transnational Families in Europe and Beyond*.

181. For a critical discussion of trust in transnational family networks, see Trivellato, *Familiarity of Strangers*, xxv–xxxi. See also Johnson and Sabean, *Sibling Relations*.

182. Berlin, *Many Thousands Gone*, 23.

183. See Ducéré, *Les corsaires basques et bayonnais*; and Rectoran, *Corsaires basques et bayonnais*.

184. Curtin, *Cross-Cultural Trade in World History*. See also Trivellato, "Marriage, Commercial Capital, and Business Agency."

185. Marriage of Carlos Alejo de Lamerens y Lamerens and Emeteria Dolores (a.k.a. Yoya) de Lamerens y Vallenilla, 29 June 1889, Parish of San Carlos de Matanzas, sacramental records.

186. *American Newspaper Annual and Directory*, 1182.

187. *Diccionario de la literatura cubana*. See also *El Mundo* (Havana), 4 June 1921, 9.

Chapter 6 • Conclusion

1. Pujo, *Le roi de l'or*.

2. http://gw.geneanet.org/jlrobert2001?lang=en&p=marie+louise+alice&n=pujo, accessed 18 September 2015. I thank Christophe Dariel for sharing the results of his genealogical research.

3. *Etat détaillé des liquidations opérées à l'époque du 1er janvier 1828–1832*, 4:88.

4. On Jean-Baptiste Pujo, see Massio, "La Bigorre et Saint-Domingue au XVIIIe siècle," 26–27.

5. "Si l'on veut calculer les privations de tous genres, les vicissitudes commerciales, les perpétuelles appréhensions, les détails dégoûtants du régime de l'esclavage, l'état de langueur ou d'anxiété dans lequel il végète entre un ciel d'airain et une terre toujours prête à l'engloutir, il n'y a pas de paysan, pas de journalier européen dont l'existence ne soit préférable à celle du colon de Saint-Domingue." Wimpffen, *Voyage à Saint-Domingue*, 138.

6. "L'arrivée de M. Lamerenx fit beaucoup d'éclat . . . et attira nombre de curieux pour le voir." Hyppolite Dabbadie, justice of the peace of the canton of Navarrenx, 13 August 1806, ADPA, Fonds privés, Fonds Batcave, 2 J 503.

7. See Hoffmann, *Littérature d'Haïti*, 73–74.

8. "Des habitudes de luxe, des goûts de fêtes, des traditions d'aristocratie bourgeoise, la passion de la musique, le tempérament enthousiaste. De toutes les parties du pays et même des îles voisines, on venait au Carnaval du Cap. Celui de Venise ou du Corso n'était pas plus bruyant assurément ni plus brillant. Ville de bonne compagnie, ville de luxe, de concerts, des spectacles." Delorme, *1842 au Cap*, 20.

9. "Les richesses *étonnantes* de cette terre de Saint-Domingue." Delorme, *La misère au sein des richesses*, 3.

10. "Aujourd'hui Haïti ne produit plus, bon an, mal an, qu'environ 60 millions de livres d'un café mal soigné, mal récolté, inférieur en raison de cela à celui de toutes les autres provenances; ce qui fait une valeur d'à peu près 50 millions de francs, à la place des 500 millions que donnait précédemment le pays." Ibid., 6.

11. For an overall analysis of Haiti in the nineteenth century, see Dubois, *Haiti*.

12. "On sait bien que c'est sous le régime du travail forcé que les colons de Saint-Domingue avaient réalisé cette opulence incroyable chiffrée plus haut. On sait bien de même que ce ne pouvait être par la contrainte que l'administration haïtienne aurait pu accomplir la tâche qui lui était imposée. Mais on sait bien aussi qu'elle pouvait la remplir par ces moyens libéraux et ces procédés si puissamment efficaces qui créent dans le siècle où nous sommes la prospérité des nations libres." Delorme, *La misère au sein des richesses*, 6.

13. Joachim, "Commerce et décolonisation."

14. Ibid.

15. Hirschman, preface to *National Power*, expanded ed., viii.

16. Ibid., ix.

17. See Geggus, "Louisiana Purchase and the Haitian Revolution."

18. Hirschman, preface to *National Power*, expanded ed., ix.

Primary Sources (Archival)
CUBA
Archivo Nacional, Havana (ANC)
Asuntos políticos. Cuaderno de los autos contra D. Carlos Lamerens por infidencia. Legajo 15, Número 36.
Autos. Don Carlos Lamerens contra Don Mateo Grout sobre pesos. Legajo 685, Número 5.
Bienes de difuntos, Matanzas. Año 1838.
Protocoles notariales, Matanzas. Notario o escribano: Santiago Luis López Villavicencio. Años 1840–43.

Parish of San Carlos de Matanzas
Sacramental records.

FRANCE
Archives départementales de la Gironde, Bordeaux (ADG)
Amirauté de Guyenne. Certificats d'identité et de catholicité, 1713–87. 6B 45–58.
Commerce, 1760–1942. 8M 1–320.
Police, 1790–1941. 4M 1–974.

Archives départementales des Pyrénées-Atlantiques, Pau and Bayonne (ADPA)
Administrations provinciales. Etats de Navarre, 1317-XVIIIe siècle. C 1526–1613.
Cours et juridictions. Chambres des comptes de Pau et de Nérac, 1446–1690. B 2061–4000.
Cours et juridictions. Parlement de Navarre, 1299–1799. B 4538–6797, 7958–94.
Fonds privés. Fonds Batcave. 2 J 503.
Justice. Tribunaux de première instance, an VIII [1800]–1969. 3U.
Minutes notariales. 3E.
Registres de formalités et hypothèques. 21–318 Q.
Seigneuries et familles. Titres de la famille royale de Navarre et d'autres familles nobles. E 1–1095.

Archives municipales, La Bastide Clairence, Pyrénées-Atlantiques (AMLBC)
Assemblées capitulaires: délibérations, 1750–63. FF2.
Baptêmes, mariages, sépultures: registres paroissiaux, 1628–1793. GG1–17.
Conseil de ville: registres des délibérations, 1680–1790. BB1–22.
Conseil municipal: registres des délibérations, 1790–1950. 1D1–8.
Etat-Civil, 1792–1952. E1–48.
Registre des dénombrements de la population de la commune (1800 [an VIII], 1804, 1806, 1809, 1817, 1820). 1F1.

Archives nationales, Pierrefitte-sur-Seine, Seine-Saint-Denis (ANF)
Commerce et industrie. Secours aux réfugiés et colons spoliés. F/12/2740–2883.
Missions des représentants du peuple et comités des assemblées révolutionnaires. Comité des colonies. D-XXV.

Archives nationales d'outre-mer, Aix-en-Provence, Bouches-du-Rhône (ANOM).
Fonds ministériels.
Dépôt des fortifications des colonies, 1636–1913. DFC.

Dépôt des papiers publics des colonies. Saint-Domingue.
Domaines, 1690–1828. DPPC 3SUPSDOM 1–82.
Etat-Civil. 1DPPC.
Notariat. DPPC NOT SDOM.
Recensement des biens domaniaux et urbains, an III [1795]–1814. DPPC 5SUPSDOM 1–7.

Premier empire colonial.
Correspondance à l'arrivée. Saint-Domingue, 1789–1850. COL CC9A 4–54.
Correspondance à l'arrivée. Saint-Domingue, premier supplément, 1796–1810. COL CC9B 1–29.
Correspondance à l'arrivée. Saint-Domingue et Îles-sous-le-vent, 1664–1792. COL C9A 1–168.
Correspondance au départ, 1654–1816. COL B1–277.
Documents divers. Passagers, 1744–1886. COL F 5B 1–144.
Personnel colonial ancien. COL E1–397.
Troupes et personnel civil. Matricules et revues, 1650–1901. COL D2C 1–387.

Bibliothèque nationale de France, Paris (BnF)
Chérin 115-2381. Lamerens file.
Clairambault 812.
Louverture, Isaac. "Notes historiques sur Toussaint Louverture. Notes intéressantes sur Banica, Etc. Etc. L'entrée de Toussaint Louverture à Santo Domingo. Vallée de Constance." NAF 12409, fols. 54–72.
Mémoires sur le commerce et les colonies. NAF 22762.
Nouveau d'Hozier 201-4482. De Lamerenx file.
Papiers du maréchal de Bellecombe et de sa famille. NAF 24349(1).

Darrieux-Juson family papers. La Bastide Clairence. Courtesy of Denis Dufourcq.

Registres de la Confrérie de Saint Nicolas. La Bastide Clairence (1356–1962). Courtesy of Denis Dufourcq.

Service de publicité foncière, Muret, Haute-Garonne
Service historique de la défense, Toulon, Var
Guyane et autres colonies. 5R1.
Prises. 2Q1.

SPAIN
Archivo General de Indias, Seville (AGI)
Santo Domingo 1110 (Cartas y Expedientes del Arzobispo de Santo Domingo).
Ultramar 28 (Expedientes seculares de Cuba, vistos por el Consejo de Indias).
Ultramar 97 (Expedientes de la Audiencia de Cuba).
Ultramar 155 (Expedientes e instancias de partes de la isla de Cuba).

Archivo General de Simancas (AGS)
Secretaría del Despacho de Guerra, Santo Domingo. SGU LEG 7150–65.

UNITED STATES
New Orleans Public Library (NOPL)
Parish Court Records, Orleans Parish.

Library of Congress, Washington, DC, Manuscript Division.
Luis Aury Papers.
Thomas Jefferson Papers.

Primary Sources (Databases)

Afro-Louisiana History and Genealogy Database, 1719–1820. Edited by Gwendolyn Midlo Hall. www.ibiblio.org/laslave/.
Archives départementales des Pyrénées-Atlantiques. E-archives. earchives.le64.fr/.
Archives nationales. Salle des inventaires virtuelle. www.archives-nationales.culture.gouv.fr/.
Archives nationales d'outre-mer. Instruments de recherche en ligne. anom.archivesnationales.culture.gouv.fr/.
Association de Généalogie d'Haïti. www.agh.qc.ca/.
Bibliothèque nationale de France. Archives et manuscrits. archivesetmanuscrits.bnf.fr/.
Dictionary of Canadian Biography. www.biographi.ca.
Ecclesiastical and Secular Sources for Slave Societies. Edited by Jane Landers. www.vanderbilt.edu/esss/.
Généalogie et histoire des familles Pays basque / Adour maritime. www.ghfpbam.org/.
Geneanet. en.geneanet.org/.
Legifrance: Le service public de la diffusion du droit. legifrance.gouv.fr.
Les visas en bordelais. L'émigration au départ de Bordeaux au cours du 19ᵉ siècle. visasenbordelais.fr/.
Portada de archivos españoles. pares.mcu.es/.
VOC Sea Voyagers Database. Dutch National Archives. vocseavoyagers.nationaalarchief.nl/.

Primary Sources (Print)

Affiches américaines (Cap-Français). 1766–91.
Almanach royal d'Hayti pour l'année 1816. Cap-Henry: Roux, 1816.
American Newspaper Annual and Directory. Philadelphia: N. W. Ayer & Son, 1918.
Aubert de la Chesnaye-Desbois, François-Alexandre. *Dictionnaire de la noblesse.* 2nd ed. 15 vols. Paris: Boudet, 1770–84.
Bruley, Georges-Prudent. *Généalogie de la famille Bruley.* Tours: Mazerau, 1879.
Carpentier, Alejo. *The Kingdom of This World.* Translated by Harriet de Onís. New York: Farrar, Straus & Giroux, 1989. Originally published as *El reino de este mundo* (Mexico City: E.D.I.A.P.S.A., 1949).
Césaire, Aimé. *La tragédie du roi Christophe.* Paris: Présence africaine, 1963.
Christian Observer (London). 1802–74.
Coeurjoly, S. J. du. *Manuel des habitants de Saint-Domingue.* 2 vols. Paris: Lenoir, 1802.
Courtilz de Sandras, Gatien de. *Memoirs of Monsieur d'Artagnan, Captain-Lieutenant of the First Company of the King's Musketeers.* Translated by Ralph Nevill. Vol. 1, *The Cadet.* Boston: Little, Brown, 1903.
Dalmas, Antoine. *Histoire de la Révolution de Saint-Domingue.* Vol. 1. Paris: Mame, 1814.
Delorme, Démesvar. *1842 au Cap: Tremblement de terre.* Edited by Jean M. Lambert. Cap-Haïtien: Imprimerie du progrès, 1942.
———. *La démocratie et le préjugé de couleur aux Etats-Unis d'Amérique: Les nationalités américaines et le système Monroë.* Brussels: Thiry, Van Buggenhoudt, 1866.

———. *L'indépendance d'Haïti et la France*. Paris: Dentu, 1861.
———. *La misère au sein des richesses: Réflexions diverses sur Haïti*. Paris: Dentu, 1873.
———. *Les petits: La Hollande*. Brussels: Société belge de librairie, 1898.
———. *Les théoriciens au pouvoir: Causeries historiques*. Paris: Plon, 1870.
Diccionario de la literatura cubana. 2 vols. Havana: Academia de Ciencias de Cuba, 1980.
Dictionnaire béarnais ancien et moderne. Montpellier: Hamelin frères, 1887.
Diderot, Denis, and Jean le Rond d'Alembert, eds. *Encyclopédie, ou dictionnaire raisonné des sciences, des arts et des métiers*. Paris, 1751–72.
Dumont, A. B. C. *Consideraciones sobre el cultivo del café en esta isla*. Havana: Imprenta Fraternal, 1823.
Duvergier, Jean-Baptiste, ed. *Collection complète des lois, décrets, ordonnances, règlements, et avis du Conseil d'Etat*. Vol. 25. Paris: Guyot & Scribe, 1827.
Edit du roi, pour la réunion au domaine des biens des consistoires et de ceux de la R.P.R. qui sont sortis du royaume, registré en Parlement le 6 février 1688. Paris, 1688.
El Mundo (Havana). 1911–24.
Etat de la distribution de la somme de douze mille livres sterling accordée par la reine aux pauvres Protestants français réfugiés. London, 1707.
Etat de la distribution de la somme de vingt et quatre mille livres accordée par Sa Majesté le feu roi, de glorieuse mémoire, aux pauvres Protestants français réfugiés. London, 1728.
Etat détaillé des liquidations opérées à l'époque du 1er janvier 1828–1832 et les six premiers mois de 1833, par la commission chargée de répartir l'indemnité attribuée aux anciens colons de Saint-Domingue, en exécution de la loi du 30 avril 1826 et conformément aux dispositions de l'ordonnance du 9 mai suivant. 6 vols. Paris: Imprimerie royale, 1828–33.
Feuille du commerce: Petites affiches et annonces du Port-au-Prince (Port-au-Prince). 1827–60.
Los fors e costumas deu Royaume de Navarre deça ports, avec l'estil et aranzel deudit royaume. Pau: Dupoux, 1722.
Foucault, Nicolas-Joseph. *Mémoires*. Edited by F. Baudry. Paris: Imprimerie impériale, 1862.
Garran, Jean-Philippe. *Rapport sur les troubles de Saint-Domingue*. 4 vols. Paris: Imprimerie nationale, 1798.
Le grand dictionnaire historique, ou le mélange curieux de l'histoire sacrée et profane. 10 vols. Paris: Libraires associés, 1759.
Gros, [Gabriel Le]. *Isle St.-Domingue: Province du Nord; Précis historique*. Paris: Potier de Lille, 1793.
Guillermin, Gilbert. *Précis historique des derniers événements de la partie de l'est de Saint-Domingue depuis le 10 août 1808 jusqu'à la capitulation de Santo-Domingo*. Paris: Arthus-Bertrand, 1811.
Haitian Constitution of 1805. haiti-reference.com/pages/plan/histoire-et-societe/documents-historiques/constitutions/constitution-imperiale-1805/.
Hilliard d'Auberteuil, Michel René. *Considérations sur l'état présent de la colonie française de Saint-Domingue*. Vol. 2. Paris: Grangé, 1777.
Institutes of the Civil Law of Spain. London: Strahan, 1825.
Labat, Jean-Baptiste. *Nouveau voyage aux îles d'Amérique*. Vol. 5. Paris: Cavelier, 1722.
Laborie, M. J. *Cultivo del cafeto o árbol que produce el café, y modo de beneficiar este fruto*. Translated by D. P. B. [Don Pablo Boloix]. Havana: Imprenta del Gobierno, 1809.
Laborie, Pierre Joseph. *The Coffee Planter of Saint Domingo*. London: Cadell & Davies, 1798.
Le Fortia, Paul Antoine. *L'art de vérifier les dates*. Vol. 16. Paris, 1837.

Locke, John. *Second Treatise of Government*. Edited by C. B. Macpherson. Indianapolis: Hackett, 1980.
Louverture, Isaac. *Notes sur la vie de Toussaint Louverture*. In *Histoire de l'expédition des Français à Saint-Domingue*, by Antoine Métral. Paris: Fanjat aîné, 1825.
Mémorial des Pyrénées (Pau). 1830–1920.
El mensajero de Cartagena de Indias (Cartagena de Indias). 1814.
Métral, Antoine. *Histoire de l'expédition des Français à Saint-Domingue*. Paris: Fanjat aîné, 1825.
Mollien, Gaspard Théodore. *Haïti ou Saint-Domingue*. Vol. 1. Paris: L'Harmattan, 2006.
Moreau de Saint-Méry, Louis Élie. *Description de la partie française de l'île de Saint-Domingue*. Philadelphia: chez l'auteur, 1797. 2 vols. in 3. Paris: Société de l'histoire des colonies françaises, 1958.
———. *Lois et constitutions des colonies françaises de l'Amérique sous le vent*. Vol. 1. Paris: chez l'auteur, 1784,
Pané, Ramón. *Relación de Fray Ramón acerca de las antigüedades de los indios*. Mexico City: Letras de México, 1932.
Phelipeau, René. *Plan de la plaine du Cap François en l'Isle de St. Domingue*. Paris, 1786. Library of Congress, Geography and Map Division. hdl.loc.gov/loc.gmd/g4944c.ar188100.
Polverel, Etienne de. *Mémoire à consulter et consultation sur le franc-alleu du Royaume de Navarre*. Paris: Knapen, 1784.
———. *Tableau de la constitution du Royaume de Navarre et de ses rapports avec la France, imprimé par ordre des Etats-Généraux de Navarre*. Paris: Desaint, 1789.
Prézeau, Chevalier de. *Réfutation de la lettre du général français Dauxion Lavaysse*. Cap-Henry: Roux, imprimeur du roi, 1814.
Procès-verbal des séances du Conseil général de la Nation. Cap-Henry: Roux, 1814.
Pujo, Alice. *Le roi de l'or*. Paris: Bonne presse, 1920.
Recueil général des lois et actes du gouvernement d'Haïti. Vol. 6, *1834–1839*. Paris: Durand, 1881.
Recueil général des lois et actes du gouvernement d'Haïti. Vol. 7, *1840–1843*. Paris: Pedone-Lauriel, 1888.
Réimpression de l'Ancien Moniteur depuis la réunion des Etats-Généraux jusqu'au Consulat. Vol. 2. Paris: Bureau central, 1840.
Robert, Adolphe, Edgar Bourloton, and Gaston Cougny, eds. *Dictionnaire des parlementaires français*. 5 vols. Paris: Bourloton, 1889–91.
Rochambeau: A Commemoration by the Congress of the United States of America of the Service of the French Auxiliary Forces in the War of Independence. Washington, DC: Government Printing Office, 1907.
Rouzier, Sémextant. *Dictionnaire géographique et administratif universel d'Haïti*. Vol. 1. Paris: Blot, 1892.
Saint-Simon, Louis de Rouvroy, duc de. *Mémoires*. 20 vols. Paris: Hachette, 1856–58.
Say, Jean-Baptiste. *Traité d'économie politique*. Paris: Deterville, 1803.
———. *A Treatise on Political Economy, or on the Production, Consumption and Distribution of Wealth, Translated from the Fourth Edition of the French*. Philadelphia: Lippincott, Grambo, 1850. Originally published as *Traité d'économie politique*, 4th ed. (Paris: Deterville, 1819).
Scribe, Eugène. *L'oncle d'Amérique, comédie-vaudeville*. Paris: Baudoin frères, Pollet, Barba, 1828.

Smith, Adam. *Correspondence of Adam Smith*. The Glasgow Edition of the Works and Correspondence of Adam Smith. Oxford: Oxford University Press, 1977.

———. *An Inquiry into the Nature and Causes of the Wealth of Nations*. The Glasgow Edition of the Works and Correspondence of Adam Smith. Oxford: Oxford University Press, 1976. First published in 1776 by Strahan & Cadell, London.

Le Télégraphe. Gazette Officielle (Port-au-Prince). 1821–39.

Vanufel, Ch., and A. Champion de Villeneuve, eds. *Code des colons de Saint-Domingue*. Paris: Vergne, 1826.

Vastey, Baron de. *Le système colonial dévoilé*. Cap-Henry: Roux, Imprimeur du roi, 1814. Translated into English as *The Colonial System Unveiled*, edited and translated by Chris Bongie (Liverpool: Liverpool University Press, 2014).

Vastey, L.-M. "Un souvenir de l'esclavage: Lettre d'Haïti." *Revue d'histoire des colonies* 24:1 (1936), 1–4.

Wimpffen, Alexandre-Stanislas de. *Voyage à Saint-Domingue pendant les années 1788, 1789 et 1790*. Vol. 2. Paris: Cocheris, 1797.

Secondary Sources

Adelman, Jeremy. *Sovereignty and Revolution in the Iberian Atlantic*. Princeton, NJ: Princeton University Press, 2006.

Agnew, David C. A. *Protestant Exiles from France, Chiefly in the Reign of Louis XIV*. 3rd ed. Vol. 3. London: Reeves & Turner, 1886.

Álvarez-Junco, José. *Spanish Identity in the Age of Nations*. Manchester: Manchester University Press, 2012.

Anderson, Benedict. *Imagined Communities: Reflections on the Origin and Spread of Nationalism*. Rev. ed. London: Verso, 2006.

Ardouin, Beaubrun. *Etudes sur l'histoire d'Haïti*. 11 vols. Paris: Dezobry & Magdeleine, 1853–60.

Arrizabalaga, Marie-Pierre. "Basque Migration and Inheritance in the Nineteenth Century." In *European Mobility: Internal, International, and Transatlantic Moves in the 19th and Early 20th Centuries*, edited by Annemarie Steidl, Josef Ehmer, Stan Nadel, and Hermann Zeitlhofer, 135–50. Göttingen: V&R Unipress, 2009.

———. "Destins de femmes dans les Pyrénées au XIXe siècle: Le cas basque." *Annales de démographie historique* 2:112 (2006), 135–70.

———. "Famille, succession, émigration au Pays basque au XIXᵉ siècle: Étude des pratiques héréditaires et des comportements migratoires au sein des familles basques." Doctoral diss., EHESS, Paris, 1998.

———. "Family Structures, Inheritance Practices and Migration Networks in the Basses-Pyrénées in the Nineteenth Century: Sare." PhD diss., University of California Davis, 1994.

———. "Stratégies de l'indivision et rapport à la terre après le Code civil: Le cas basque au XIXe siècle." In *Familles, terre, marchés: Logiques économiques et stratégies dans les milieux ruraux (XVIIe–XXe siècles)*, edited by Gérard Béaur, Christian Dessureault, and Joseph Goy, 171–83. Rennes: Presses Universitaires de Rennes, 2004.

Bailyn, Bernard. *Atlantic History: Concept and Contours*. Cambridge, MA: Harvard University Press, 2005.

Baker, Keith. *Inventing the French Revolution.* Cambridge: Cambridge University Press, 1990.
Beauvois, Frédérique. "Monnayer l'incalculable? L'indemnité de Saint-Domingue entre approximations et bricolage." *Revue historique* 3:655 (2010), 609–36.
Bell, David. *The Cult of the Nation in France: Inventing Nationalism, 1680–1800.* Cambridge, MA: Harvard University Press, 2001.
Benot, Yves. "Un épisode décisif de l'insurrection: La prise du Dondon (10 septembre 1791)." *Chemins critiques* 2:3 (1992), 97–111.
———. "The Insurgents of 1791, Their Leaders, and the Concept of Independence." In *The World of the Haitian Revolution*, edited by David Geggus and Norman Fiering, 99–110. Bloomington: Indiana University Press, 2009.
Berlin, Ira. "From Creole to African: Atlantic Creoles and the Origin of African-American Society in Mainland North America." *William and Mary Quarterly* 53:2 (1996), 251–88.
———. *Many Thousands Gone: The First Two Centuries of Slavery in North America.* Cambridge, MA: Harvard University Press, 1998.
Biancalana, Joseph. *The Fee Tail and the Common Recovery in Medieval England, 1176–1502.* Cambridge: Cambridge University Press, 2001.
Blázquez Garbajosa, Adrián, ed. *Emigration de masse et émigration d'élite vers les Amériques au XIXe siècle: Le cas des Pyrénées basco-béarnaises.* Orthez: Gascogne, 2010.
———. *L'émigration basco-béarnaise aux Amériques au XIXe siècle: Regards interdisciplinaires.* Orthez: Gascogne, 2006.
Bouche, Denise. "Gabriel Debien (1906–1990)." *Revue d'histoire d'outre-mer* 77:287 (1990), 213–15.
Bourdieu, Pierre. *The Bachelors' Ball: The Crisis of Peasant Society in Bearn.* Translated by Richard Nice. Chicago: University of Chicago Press, 2008. Originally published as *Le bal des célibataires: Crise de la société paysanne en Béarn* (Paris: Seuil, 2002).
Bourdieu, Pierre, and Pierre Lamaison. "From Rules to Strategies: An Interview with Pierre Bourdieu." *Cultural Anthropology* 1:1 (1986), 110–20.
Brière, Jean-François. "La France et la reconnaissance de l'indépendance haïtienne: Le débat sur l'Ordonnance de 1825." *French Colonial History* 5 (2004), 125–38.
Brisson, Jules, and Félix Ribeyre. *Les grands journaux de France.* Paris: Jouaust, 1862.
Bromley, John Selwyn. "Les prêts de vaisseaux de la marine française aux corsaires (1688–1713)." In *Les marines de guerre européennes, XVIIe–XVIIIe siècles*, edited by M. Acerra, J. Merino, and J. Meyer, 65–90. Paris: Presses de l'université de Paris-Sorbonne, 1985.
Brown, Christopher Leslie, and Philip D. Morgan, eds. *Arming Slaves: From Classical Times to the Modern Age.* New Haven, CT: Yale University Press, 2006.
Butel, Paul. "L'essor antillais au XVIIIe siècle." In *Histoire des Antilles*, edited by Pierre Pluchon, 109–39. Toulouse: Privat 1982.
Cacua Prada, Antonio. *El corsario Louis Aury, intimidades de la independencia.* Bogotá: Editora Guadalupe, 2001.
Cauna, Jacques de. *L'Eldorado des Aquitains: Gascons, Basques et Béarnais aux Iles d'Amérique (XVIIe–XVIIIe siècles).* Biarritz: Atlantica, 1998.
———. "Toussaint Louverture et le déclenchement de l'insurrection des esclaves du Nord en 1791: Un retour aux sources." In *Saint-Domingue espagnol et la révolution nègre d'Haïti*, edited by Alain Yacou, 135–55. Paris: Karthala, 2007.
———, ed. *Toussaint Louverture et l'indépendance d'Haïti.* Paris: Karthala, 2004.

———. *Toussaint Louverture: Le grand précurseur*. Bordeaux: Sud-Ouest, 2012.
Cauna, Jacques de, and Marion Graff. *La traite bayonnaise au XVIIIe siècle: Instructions, journal de bord, projets d'armement*. Pau: Cairn, 2009.
Cheney, Paul. "A Colonial Cul de Sac: Plantation Life in Wartime Saint-Domingue, 1775–1782." *Radical History Review* 115 (2013), 45–64.
———. *Revolutionary Commerce: Globalization and the French Monarchy*. Cambridge, MA: Harvard University Press, 2010.
Choquette, Leslie. *Frenchmen into Peasants: Modernity and Tradition in the Peopling of French Canada*. Cambridge, MA: Harvard University Press, 1997.
Clavero, Bartolomé. *Mayorazgo: Propiedad feudal en Castilla, 1369–1836*. Madrid: Siglo Veintiuno, 1974.
Clément-Simon, Gustave. "Etienne de Polverel, Commissaire civil de Saint-Domingue." *Bulletin de la Société scientifique, historique et archéologique de la Corrèze* 14 (1892), 607–11.
Colley, Linda. *The Ordeal of Elizabeth Marsh: A Woman in World History*. New York: Pantheon Books, 2007.
Cordier, Eugène. *Le droit de famille aux Pyrénées: Barège, Lavedan, Béarn et Pays basque*. Paris: A. Durand, 1859.
Cossé Bell, Caryn. *Revolution, Romanticism, and the Afro-Creole Protest Tradition in Louisiana, 1718–1868*. Baton Rouge: Louisiana State University Press, 1997.
Curtin, Philip. *Cross-Cultural Trade in World History*. Cambridge: Cambridge University Press, 1984.
Danbey, Lancaster E. "Louis Aury: The First Governor of Texas under the Mexican Republic." *Southwestern Historical Quarterly* 42:2 (1938), 108–16.
Dauvergne, Robert. "Les anciens plans ruraux dans les colonies françaises." *Revue d'histoire des colonies* 35:123–24 (1948), 231–69.
Debien, Gabriel. "Assemblées nocturnes d'esclaves à Saint-Domingue (La Marmelade, 1786)." *Annales historiques de la Révolution française* 44:208 (1972), 273–84.
———. "Aux origines de l'abolition de l'esclavage." *Revue d'histoire des colonies* 36:125 (1949), 24–55.
———. "Les biens de Toussaint Louverture (documents)." *Revue de la Société haïtienne d'histoire et de géographie* 139 (1983), 5–75.
———. "Les colons de Saint-Domingue réfugiés à Cuba (1793–1815)." *Revista de Indias* 13–14 (1953–54), 559–605, 11–36.
———. *Les engagés pour les Antilles (1634–1715)*. Abbeville: Paillart, 1951.
———. "Le plan et les débuts d'une caféière à Saint-Domingue." *Revue de la Société d'histoire et de géographie d'Haïti* 14:51 (1943), 12–32.
———. "Réfugiés de Saint-Domingue expulsés de La Havane en 1809." *Anuario de Estudios Americanos* 35 (1978), 1–54.
De Haan, F. "Uit oude notaris papieren." *Tijdschrift voor Indische Taal-, Land- en Volkenkunde* 42 (1900), 297–308.
Deive, Carlos Esteban. *Los refugiados franceses en Santo Domingo (1789–1801)*. Santo Domingo: Universidad Nacional Pedro Henríquez Ureña, 1984.
Delfour, J. *Histoire du lycée de Pau*. Pau: Garet, 1890.
Derouet, Bernard. "Dot et héritage: Les enjeux de la chronologie de la transmission." In

L'histoire grande ouverte: Hommages à Emmanuel Le Roy Ladurie, edited by André Burguière, Joseph Goy, and Marie-Jeanne Tits-Dieuaide, 282–92. Paris: Fayard, 1997.

———. "Les pratiques familiales, le droit et la construction des différences (15ᵉ–19ᵉ siècles)." *Annales HSS* 52:2 (1997), 369–91.

———. "Territoire et parenté: Pour une mise en perspective de la communauté rurale et des formes de reproduction familiale." *Annales HSS* 50:3 (1995), 645–86.

Desplat, Christian. "Une 'fort bizarre' noblesse: La noblesse réelle dans les pays d'Etats pyrénéens." *Bulletin de la Société des Amis du château de Pau* 153 (2006), 21–50.

Dessens, Nathalie. *From Saint-Domingue to New Orleans: Migration and Influences*. Gainesville: University Press of Florida, 2007.

Dobie, Madeleine. *Trading Places: Colonization and Slavery in Eighteenth-Century French Culture*. Ithaca, NY: Cornell University Press, 2010.

Dubesset, Eric, and Jacques de Cauna, eds. *Dynamiques caribéennes: Pour une histoire des circulations dans l'espace atlantique (XVIIIe–XIXe siècles)*. Bordeaux: Presses Universitaires de Bordeaux, 2014.

Dubois, Laurent. *Avengers of the New World: The Story of the Haitian Revolution*. Cambridge, MA: Harvard University Press, 2005.

———. *Haiti: The Aftershocks of History*. New York: Henry Holt, 2012.

Ducéré, Edouard. *Les corsaires basques et bayonnais sous la République et l'Empire*. Bayonne: Lamaignière, 1898.

Dufourcq, Pierre. "La Bastide Clairence à la veille et au début de la période révolutionnaire, 1780–1790." *Revue d'histoire de Bayonne, du Pays basque et du Bas-Adour* 146 (1990), 161–200.

Etat sommaire des archives de la Marine antérieures à la Révolution. Paris: Baudoin, 1898.

Etcheverry, Louis. "L'émigration des Basses-Pyrénées vers l'Amérique." *Réforme sociale*, 2nd ser., 1 (1886), 490–514.

Faye, Stanley. "Commodore Aury." *Louisiana Historical Quarterly* 24:3 (1941), 612–97.

Ferrer, Ada. *Freedom's Mirror: Cuba and Haiti in the Age of Revolution*, Cambridge: Cambridge University Press, 2014.

Ferro, Carlos A. *Vida de Luis Aury, corsario de Buenos Aires en las luchas por la independencia de Venezuela, Colombia, y Centroamérica*. Buenos Aires: Cuarto Poder, 1976.

Findlay, Ronald, ed. *Eli Heckscher, International Trade, and Economic History*. Cambridge, MA: MIT Press, 2006.

Force, Pierre. "Eighteenth-Century Matrimonial Strategies and Emigration to the Americas: The House of Berrio in La Bastide Clairence." Translated by John Angell. *Annales: Histoire, Sciences Sociales* (English ed.) 68:1 (2013), 75–106.

———. "The House on Bayou Road: Atlantic Creole Networks in the Eighteenth and Nineteenth Centuries." *Journal of American History* 100:1 (2013), 21–45.

Galenson, David W. *Traders, Planters, and Slaves: Market Behavior in Early English America*. Cambridge: Cambridge University Press, 1986.

Garrigus, John D. *Before Haiti: Race and Citizenship in French Saint-Domingue*. New York: Palgrave Macmillan, 2006.

———. "Vincent Ogé *jeune*: Social Class and Free Colored Mobilization on the Eve of the Haitian Revolution." *The Americas* 68:1 (2011), 33–62.

Geggus, David P. "From His Most Catholic Majesty to the Godless Republic: The Volte-Face of Toussaint Louverture and the Ending of Slavery in Saint Domingue." *Revue française d'histoire d'Outre-Mer* 65:241 (1978), 481–99.

———. "Gabriel Debien (1906–1990)." *Hispanic American Historical Review* 71:1 (1991), 140–42.

———. "Haiti and its Revolution: Four Recent Books." *Radical History Review* 115 (2013), 195–202.

———. *The Haitian Revolution: A Documentary History*, Cambridge, MA: Hackett, 2014.

———. *Haitian Revolutionary Studies*. Bloomington: Indiana University Press, 2002.

———. "The Louisiana Purchase and the Haitian Revolution." In *The Haitian Revolution and the Early United States: Histories, Textualities, Geographies*, edited by Elizabeth Dillon and Michael Drexler, 127–202. Philadelphia: University of Pennsylvania Press, 2016.

———. "On the Eve of the Haitian Revolution: Slave Runaways in Saint-Domingue in the Year 1790." In *Out of the House of Bondage: Runaways, Resistance and Marronage in Africa and the New World*, edited by Gad Heuman, 112–28. London: Frank Cass, 1986.

———. "Sugar and Coffee Cultivation in Saint-Domingue and the Shaping of the Slave Labor Force." In *Cultivation and Culture: Labor and the Shaping of Slave Life in the Americas*, edited by Ira Berlin and Philip D. Morgan, 73–100. Charlottesville: University of Virginia Press, 1993.

———, ed. *The World of the Haitian Revolution*. Bloomington: Indiana University Press, 2009.

Ghachem, Malick W. *The Old Regime and the Haitian Revolution*. Cambridge: Cambridge University Press, 2012.

Girard, Philippe R. *The Slaves Who Defeated Napoléon: Toussaint Louverture and the Haitian War of Independence, 1801–1804*. Tuscaloosa: University of Alabama Press, 2011.

Gratacos, Isaure. *Femmes pyrénéennes: Un statut social exceptionnel en Europe*. Toulouse: Privat, 2008.

Grell, Chantal, and Da Vinha, Mathieu. "Les généalogistes, le roi et la cour de France, XVIIe–XVIIIe siècles." In *Historiographie an europäischen Höfen (17.–18. Jahrhundert): Studien zum Hof als Produktionsort von Geschichtsschreibung und historischer Repräsentation*, edited by Markus Völkel and Arno Strohmeyer, 255–74. Berlin: Duncker & Humblot, 2009.

Guerra y Sánchez, Ramiro. *Sugar and Society in the Caribbean: An Economic History of Cuban Agriculture*. New Haven, CT: Yale University Press, 1964.

Hägerstrand, Torsten. "Migration and Area: Survey of a Sample of Swedish Migration Fields and Hypothetical Considerations on their Genesis." in *Migrations in Sweden: A Symposium*, edited by David Hannenberg, Torsten Hägerstrand, and Bruno Odeving, 27–158. Lund: Gleerup, 1957.

Hardÿ de Périni, Général. *Batailles françaises*. Vol. 6. Paris: Flammarion, 1900.

Heckscher, Eli F. *Mercantilism*. Translated by Mendel Shapiro. 2 vols. London: Allen & Unwin, 1935.

Hirschman, Albert O. *National Power and the Structure of Foreign Trade*. Berkeley: University of California Press, 1945.

———. Preface to *National Power and the Structure of Foreign Trade*. Expanded ed. Berkeley: University of California Press, 1980.

Hoffmann, Léon-François. *Littérature d'Haïti*. Paris: EDICEF/AUPELP, 1995.

Hoffman, Philip T., Gilles Postel-Vinay, and Jean-Laurent Rosenthal. "Entry, Information, and Financial Development: A Century of Competition between French Banks and Notaries." *Explorations in Economic History* 55 (2015), 39–57.

Hont, István. *Jealousy of Trade: International Competition and the Nation-State in Historical Perspective*. Cambridge, MA: Harvard University Press, 2005.

Jacquemin, Magali. "Etienne Polverel et l'abolition de l'esclavage (1792–1794), ou le lien entre la liberté et l'égalité." *Cahiers de l'histoire et des mémoires de la traite négrière, de l'esclavage et de leurs abolitions en Normandie* 2 (2009), 157–76.

Jasanoff, Maya. *Liberty's Exiles: American Loyalists in the Revolutionary World*. New York: Knopf, 2011.

Jenkins, Timothy. "Bourdieu's Béarnais Ethnography." *Theory, Culture & Society* 23:6 (2006), 45–72.

———. *The Life of Property: House, Family and Inheritance in Bearn, South-West France*. New York: Berghahn Books, 2010.

Joachim, Benoît. "Commerce et décolonisation: L'expérience franco-haïtienne au XIXe siècle." *Annales ESC* 27:6 (1972), 1497–1525.

Johnson, Christopher H., and David Warren Sabean, eds. *Sibling Relations and the Transformations of European Kinship, 1300–1900*. New York: Berghahn Books, 2011.

Johnson, Christopher H., David Warren Sabean, Simon Teuscher, and Francesca Trivellato, eds. *Transregional and Transnational Families in Europe and Beyond: Experiences since the Middle-Ages*. New York: Berghahn Books, 2011.

Kalff, S. "Isaac de St. Martin: Een verdienstelijk compagniesdienaar." *Bijdragen voor Vaderlandsche Geschiedenis en Oudheidkunde* 5:7 (1920), 37–50.

Kert, Faye M. *Privateering: Patriots and Profits in the War of 1812*. Baltimore: Johns Hopkins University Press, 2015.

King, Stewart R. *Blue Coat or Powdered Wig: Free People of Color in Pre-Revolutionary Saint-Domingue*. Athens: University of Georgia Press, 2001.

Lamore, Jean. "Le *Manuel du planteur de café* de Pierre-Joseph Laborie (Jamaïque, 1798) et ses versions cubaines (1810–1820)." In *Dynamiques caribéennes: Pour une histoire des circulations dans l'espace atlantique (XVIIIe–XIXe siècles)*, edited by Eric Dubesset and Jacques de Cauna, 169–81. Bordeaux: Presses Universitaires de Bordeaux, 2014.

Landers, Jane G. *Atlantic Creoles in the Age of Revolutions*. Cambridge, MA: Harvard University Press, 2010.

La Roque de Roquebrune, Robert. "La direction de la Nouvelle-France par le ministère de la Marine." *Revue d'histoire de l'Amérique française* 6:4 (1953), 470–88.

Le Blant, Robert. "A Ceylan, au service des États de Hollande, lettres inédites d'Isaac de Lostal, dit de Saint-Martin, mort gouverneur à Batavia, 1664–1668." *Revue d'histoire des colonies* 45:158 (1958), 109–16.

———. "Un officier béarnais à Saint Domingue: Pierre-Gédéon Ier de Nolivos." *Revue historique et archéologique du Béarn et du Pays basque*, 2nd ser., 14 (1931), 20–41.

Lefebvre, Henri. *Les communautés paysannes pyrénéennes*. Orthez: Société Ramond / Cercle historique de l'Arribère, 2014.

———. *La vallée de Campan: Etude de sociologie rurale*. Paris: PUF, 1963.

Le Play, Frédéric. *L'organisation du travail, selon la coutume des ateliers et la loi du Décalogue*. Tours: Mame, 1870.

———. *Les ouvriers européens: Étude sur les travaux, la vie domestique et la condition morale des populations ouvrières de l'Europe*. 2nd ed. 6 vols. Tours: Mame, 1877–79.

Lévi-Strauss, Claude. "Histoire et ethnologie." *Annales ESC* 38:6 (1983), 1217–31.

Little, Roger. "A Date for L'oncle d'Amérique." *French Studies Bulletin* 22:80 (2001), 14–16.

MacDonald, John S., and Leatrice D. MacDonald. "Chain Migration, Ethnic Neighborhood Formation, and Social Networks." *Milbank Memorial Fund Quarterly* 42:1 (1964), 82–97.

Madiou, Thomas. *Histoire d'Haïti*. Vols. 1–3, Port-au-Prince: Courtois, 1847–48; vols. 1–8, Port-au-Prince: Deschamps, 1987–91.

Marzagalli, Silvia. "De Grateloup à l'Elysée en passant par Bordeaux: Ascension sociale et mobilité de la famille Beaujon aux XVIIe–XVIIIe siècles." In *Négoce, ports et océans, XVIe–XXe siècles: Mélanges offerts à Paul Butel*, edited by Silvia Marzagalli and Hubert Bonin, 15–28. Bordeaux: Presses universitaires de Bordeaux, 2000.

Massio, R. "La Bigorre et Saint-Domingue au XVIIIe siècle." *Annales du Midi: Revue archéologique, historique et philologique de la France méridionale* 66:25 (1954), 21–46.

Migault, Jean. *Journal de Jean Migault*. Edited by N. Weiss and H. Clouzot. Paris: Société de l'histoire du protestantisme français, 1910.

Miller, Christopher. *The French Atlantic Triangle: Literature and Culture of the Slave Trade*. Durham, NC: Duke University Press, 2008.

Molhuysen, Philipp Christiaan, and Petrus Johannes Blok, eds. *Nieuw Nederlandsch biografisch woordenboek*. Vol. 8. Leiden: Sijthoff, 1930.

Morbieu, Georges-Émile. "Le Royaume de Navarre et la Révolution française." *Revue historique et archéologique du Béarn et du Pays basque* 2 (1911), 44–64 and 97–108.

Nassiet, Michel. "Parenté et successions dynastiques aux 14e et 15e siècles." *Annales HSS* 50:3 (1995), 621–44.

Ojeda, Jorge Victoria. *Tendencias monárquicas en la revolución haitiana: El negro Francisco Petecou bajo las banderas francesas y españolas*. Mexico City: Siglo veintiuno, 2005.

Pares, Richard. *Colonial Blockade and Neutral Rights, 1739–1763*. Oxford: Clarendon, 1938.

———. *Merchants and Planters*. Cambridge: Cambridge University Press, 1960.

———. *War and Trade in the West Indies, 1739–1763*. Oxford: Clarendon, 1936.

Pashman, Howard. "The People's Property Law: A Step toward Building a New Legal Order in Revolutionary New York." *Law and History Review* 31:3 (2013), 587–626.

Passeron, Jean-Claude, and Jacques Revel. "Penser par cas: Raisonner à partir de singularités." In *Penser par cas*, edited by Jean-Claude Passeron and Jacques Revel, 9–44. Paris: EHESS, 2005.

Pérez de la Riva, Francisco. *El café: Historia de su cultivo y explotación en Cuba*. Havana: Montero, 1944.

Pérez de la Riva, Juan. "La implantación francesa en la cuenca superior del Cauto." In *El Barracón, y otros ensayos*, 360–433. Havana: Editorial de Ciencias Sociales, 1975.

Pérez Morales, Edgardo. *El gran diablo hecho barco: Corsarios, esclavos y revolución en Cartagena y el Gran Caribe, 1791–1817*. Bucaramanga, Colombia: Universidad Industrial de Santander, 2012.

Pétré-Grenouilleau, Olivier. *L'argent de la traite: Milieu négrier, capitalisme et développement; un modèle*. Paris: Aubier, 1996.

Pluchon, Pierre. *Toussaint Louverture d'après le général de Kerverseau*. Port-au-Prince: Le Natal, 1991.

Popkin, Jeremy D. *Facing Racial Revolution: Eyewitness Accounts of the Haitian Insurrection*. Cambridge: Cambridge University Press, 2007.

———. *You Are All Free: The Haitian Revolution and the Abolition of Slavery*. Cambridge: Cambridge University Press, 2010.

Pritchard, James. *In Search of Empire: The French in the Americas, 1670–1730*. Cambridge: Cambridge University Press, 2004.

Quevilly, Laurent. *Le baron de Vastey: La voix des esclaves, ou la révolution haïtienne vécue par une famille normande*. Paris: Books on Demand, 2014.

Ramírez Pérez, Jorge Freddy. *Francia en Cuba: Los cafetales de la Sierra del Rosario*. Havana: Ediciones Unión, 2004.

Rectoran, Pierre. *Corsaires basques et bayonnais du XVe au XIXe siècle*. Bayonne: Plumon, 1946.

Reiss, Tom. *The Black Count: Glory, Revolution, Betrayal, and the Real Count of Monte Cristo*. New York: Crown, 2012.

Renaud, Raymond. *Le régime foncier en Haïti*. Paris: Domat-Montchrestien, 1934.

Rey Castelao, Ofelia. "Inheritance, Marital Strategies, and the Formation of Households in Rural North-Western Spain in the Eighteenth and Nineteenth Centuries: An Overview." In *Inheritance Practices, Marriage Strategies and Household Formation in European Rural Societies*, edited by Anne-Lise Head-Köning, 75–99. Turnhout, Belgium: Brepols, 2012.

Rosental, Paul-André. *Les sentiers invisibles: Espace, familles et migrations dans la France du XIXe siècle*. Paris: EHESS, 1999.

Rothschild, Emma. "A Horrible Tragedy in the French Atlantic." *Past and Present* 192 (2006), 67–108.

———. *The Inner Life of Empires: An Eighteenth-Century History*. Princeton, NJ: Princeton University Press, 2011.

Rouse, Irving. *The Tainos: Rise and Decline of the People Who Greeted Columbus*. New Haven, CT: Yale University Press, 1992.

Sabine, Lorenzo. *Biographical Sketches of Loyalists of the American Revolution, with an Historical Essay*. Boston: Little, Brown, 1864.

Sahlins, Peter. "Fictions of a Catholic France: The Naturalization of Foreigners, 1685–1787." *Representations* 47 (1994), 85–110.

Scott, Rebecca, and Jean Hébrard. *Freedom Papers: An Atlantic Odyssey in the Age of Emancipation*. Cambridge, MA: Harvard University Press, 2012.

Shovlin, John. "War and Peace." In *Mercantilism Reimagined: Political Economy in Early Modern Britain and Its Empire*, edited by Philip J. Stern and Carl Wennerlind, 305–20. Cambridge, MA: Harvard University Press, 2015.

Smith, S. D. *Slavery, Family, and Gentry Capitalism in the British Atlantic: The World of the Lascelles, 1648–1834*. Cambridge: Cambridge University Press, 2006.

Soulice, M. L. "Documents pour l'histoire du protestantisme en Béarn: L'intendant Foucault et la Révocation 1684–1685." *Bulletin de la Société des sciences, lettres et arts de Pau*, 2nd ser., 14 (1885), 1–151.

Steiner, Philippe. "L'esclavage chez les économistes français (1750–1803)." in *Les abolitions de l'esclavage: De L. F. Sonthonx à V. Schoelcher*, edited by Marcel Dorigny, 165–78. Saint-Denis: Presses Universitaires de Vincennes, 1995.

Stern, Philip J., and Carl Wennerlind. *Mercantilism Reimagined: Political Economy in Early Modern Britain and Its Empire*. Cambridge, MA: Harvard University Press, 2015.

Susane, Général. *Histoire de l'infanterie française*. Vol. 3. Paris: Librairie militaire J. Dumaine, 1876.

Tabío, E., and R. Payarés. *Sobre los cafetales coloniales de la Sierra del Rosario*. Serie Pinar del Río No. 17. Havana: Academia de Ciencias de Cuba, 1968.

Tarrade, Jean. *Le commerce colonial de la France à la fin de l'ancien régime: L'évolution du régime de "l'Exclusif" de 1763 à 1789.* Paris: PUF, 1972.

Thornton, John K. "'I Am the Subject of the King of Congo': African Political Ideology and the Haitian Revolution." *Journal of World History* 4:2 (1993), 181–214.

Topik, Steven. "The World Coffee Market in the Eighteenth and Nineteenth Centuries, from Colonial to National Regimes." London School of Economics Working Paper 04/04 (May 2004). www.lse.ac.uk/economicHistory/Research/GEHN/GEHNPDF/Working Paper04ST.pdf.

Trivellato, Francesca. *The Familiarity of Strangers: The Sephardic Diaspora, Livorno, and Cross-Cultural Trade in the Early Modern Period.* New Haven, CT: Yale University Press, 2009.

———. "Marriage, Commercial Capital, and Business Agency: Transregional Sephardic (and Armenian) Families in the Seventeenth- and Eighteenth-Century Mediterranean." In *Transregional and Transnational Families in Europe and Beyond: Experiences since the Middle-Ages,* edited by Christopher H. Johnson, David Warren Sabean, Simon Teuscher, and Francesca Trivellato, 107–30. New York: Berghahn Books, 2011.

Trouillot, Ernst. *Démesvar Delorme, le journaliste, le diplomate.* Port-au-Prince: Théodore, 1958.

Trouillot, Hénock. *Démesvar Delorme, ou Introduction à une sociologie de la littérature haïtienne.* Port-au-Prince: Imprimerie des Antilles, 1968.

Trouillot, Michel-Rolph. "Coffee Planters and Coffee Slaves in the Antilles: The Impact of a Secondary Crop." In *Cultivation and Culture: Labor and the Shaping of Slave Life in the Americas,* edited by Ira Berlin and Philip D. Morgan, 124–37. Charlottesville: University of Virginia Press, 1993.

Truxes, Thomas M. *Defying Empire: Trading with the Enemy in Colonial New York.* New Haven, CT: Yale University Press, 2008.

Tully, James. *An Approach to Political Philosophy. Locke in Contexts.* Cambridge: Cambridge University Press, 1993.

Vergé-Franceschi, Michel. *Les officiers généraux de la marine royale, 1715–1774: Origines, condition, services.* Vol. 2. Paris: Librairie de l'Inde, 1990.

Vialay, Amédée. *La vente des biens nationaux pendant la Révolution française.* Paris: Perrin, 1908.

Viret, Jérôme Luther. "Coutumes et migrations vers la Nouvelle France: Position du problème." In *Madeleine de La Peltrie et les pionnières de la Nouvelle-France,* edited by J.-M. Constant, 83–89. Le Mans: LHAMANS, Université du Mans/CRHQ; Caen: Université de Caen, 2004.

———. *Le sol et le sang: La famille et la reproduction sociale en France du Moyen Âge au XIXe siècle.* Paris: CNRS, 2014.

Wegge, Simone. "Migration Decisions in Mid-Nineteenth-Century Germany." *Journal of Economic History* 58:2 (1998), 532–35.

Yacou, Alain "La présence française dans la partie occidentale de l'île de Cuba au lendemain de la révolution de Saint-Domingue." *Revue française d'histoire d'outre-mer* 74:275 (1987), 149–88.

Zink, Anne. *L'héritier de la maison: Géographie coutumière du Sud-Ouest de la France sous l'ancien régime.* Paris: EHESS, 1993.

INDEX

Page numbers in italics signify graphics.

Acuña, Pedro de, 94
Adelman, Jeremy, 153, 201–2n83
Alzire, Françoise, 47, 48, 49, 141
Alzire ou les Américains (Voltaire), 48
American War of Independence, 40, 60, 115
Anderson, Benedict, 118, 178
Ardouin, Beaubrun, 114–16, 146
Arrizabalaga, Marie-Pierre, 2, 83, 87
Atlantic Creoles in the Age of Revolutions (Landers), 140
Aubert, Jean-Baptiste, 107–8
Aury, Louis, 132–34, 141, 152

Bachelors' Ball, The (Bourdieu), 1–2
Bacon, Francis, 29
Bailyn, Bernard, xii, 59
Baker, Keith, 121
Balzac, Honoré de, 6, 115
Barbaste, François, 81–82
Barquier, Joseph-David, 129
Bath, Daniel, 73
Bayonne, 44, 63, *76,* 81, 135; departures from port of, xi, 43, 46, 73; Jean Mouscardy property in, 45, 84, 98, 99; privateering activity in, 142, 154
Beaujon, Jean-Nicolas, 80
Belair, Charles, 105
Béliard (Belliard) Thomas, 146
Bell, David, 120, 123, 152–53
Bellecombe, Guillaume de, 56
Belle Garde, Louis de, 126
Belzunce, Armand de, 9, 10
Berrio house, 79, 80, 81, 86, 87; dissolution and dismantling of, 72, 81–82, 83, 84; Mathieu Lamerenx / Anne de Marmont dispute over, 64, 66–69, 71, 72
Biassou (insurgent leader), 94, 104
Biret, Pierre, 104, 105
Biret plantation, 46, 105, 183n72
Biscay, Madeleine, 138, 140, 202n93

Blázquez, Adrián, 2
Bordenave, Jean (generation 2), 44, 169
Bordenave, Jean (generation 3), 45–46, 170
Bordenave, Pierre (Jean), 46, 47, 170
Bordus Darrieux, Arnaud de, 67, 73
Bordus Darrieux, Emmanuel de, 124
Bourbon, Raymond and Jean-Pierre, 73
Bourdieu, Emmanuel, 2
Bourdieu, Pierre, xii, 67, 68, 70, 87; on house-based systems, 1–2, 5, 72; on inheritance, xiv, 5, 6
Bourreau-Deslandes, André, 14
Boyer, Jean-Pierre, 114, 115, 145–46, 150
Britain, 60, 116, 144–45, 158; Caribbean colonies of, 29, 35, 38, 53, 55, 116; in Seven Years' War, 9–10, 60–61; troops in Hispaniola from, 50, 129, 130, 134
Bruley, Prudent-Jean, 55, 92

Cabrera, Joaquín, 94, 103, 108
Cadets de Gascogne, 2
Cadignan, Charles de, 40
Calvinism, 15–16, 19
Cap-Haïtien/Cap-Français, 45, 51, *77,* 89, 99, 104, 112, 146, 154; cultural scene in, 157; earthquake of 1842 in, 95, 147; fire of 1793 in, 92–93, *97,* 108
capital accumulation, 33–43
Cappé, Pierre, 51–53, 55, 104
Caron, François, 20
Carpentier, Alejo, xiii, 124–25, 142
Cartagena de Indias, 131–32, 152, 153
Casenave, Bernard, 136
Catherine of Navarre, 71
Catholicism, 130; conversion to, 4, 7, 12, 16, 17, 18–19
Cauna, Jacques de, xi, 12, 89, 191n3; *L'Eldorado des Aquitains,* xiv–xv
Césaire, Aimé, 143
chain migrations, 3–4, 50

Charitte, Jean-Pierre Casamajor de, 13
Charlemagne, 121
Charles X, 76
Chateaubriand, François-René de, ix
Cheney, Paul, 59–60
Choiseul, Gabriel de, 11
Christian Observer, 145
Christophe, King Henri, 98, 142, 143–44, 145–46, 153
citizenship, 117–18
Civil Code, 48, 50, 82; egalitarianism of, 5–6, 40, 83; inheritance under, 87, 136
Cockburn (slave owner), 53
Code des colons de Saint-Domingue, 112
Code Noir, 53, 58
Coeurjoly, S. J. du, 45; *Manuel des habitants de Saint-Domingue,* 30, 33, 47, 49–50, 55, 57–58
coffee: Cuba and, 127–28; prices of, 55–56, 60; profitability of, 55, 59; Saint-Domingue/Haiti and, 30–33, 157, 158
coffee plantations, 37, 49; capital needed for, 35, 78; in Cuba, 124–28; land values of, 45, 182n61; and slavery, 50–55, 58–59, 76, 102–3
Coffee Planter of Saint Domingo, The (Laborie), 29–30, 31, 33, 37, 41, 54, 56, 127
Colbert, Jean-Baptiste, 20
Colbert de Croissy, Charles, 16
Colley, Linda, xv
Colombots, Jean-Pierre, 46–47, 63, 123–24, 183n72
Colonial System Unveiled, The (Vastey), 98
colonial trading system, xii, 59–60, 157; as asymmetric, 13–14, 38, 55, 61, 159–60; privateering in, 14; role of merchants in, 55–56; and slavery, 38. *See also* trade
Cordier, Eugène, 70–71
Cordon de l'Ouest, 103
corn (wheat), 56–57
Courtilz de Sandras, Gatien de, 20–21
Cuba, 124–28, 129–30, 158
Curtin, Philip, 154
Custom of Navarre, 6, 22–23, 24, 25, 26, 44, 59
Custom of Paris, 40–41, 42, 78, 182n47
Cyrano de Bergerac (Rostand), 2

Daure, Hector, 108
Dauxion Lavaysse, Jean Joseph, 143, 144–45
Davy de la Pailleterie, Antoine, 21
Debien, Gabriel, xiv, 101, 102, 127
Delahaye, Guillaume Silvestre, 90
Delorme, Démesvar, 47–48, 49, 116; on events of 1791, 95–96, 99; on Haitian nation, 117–18, 148–52; on Jean-Théodat Mouscardy, 142, 146–47, 151; photo of, 96; works: *La démocratie et le préjugé de couleur aux Etats-Unis d'Amérique,* 151–52; *L'Indépendance d'Haïti et la France,* 148; *La misère au sein des richesses,* 150–51, 157; *Les petits: La Hollande,* 152; *Les théoriciens au pouvoir,* 149–50
dependency theory, 158–59
Derouet, Bernard, 22, 23, 24, 42, 78, 85
Des droits et des devoirs du citoyen (Mably), 122
Despassailler, Etienne, 73
Desrouleaux, Colonel, 106, 107
Dessalines, Jean-Jacques, 9, 96, 98, 105, 107, 146
Diesse, Jean-Baptiste, 73
Doat, Jean-Bernard de, 7–8, 11
Dobie, Madeleine, 122
Dominican Republic, 148, 150
Dondon, Saint-Martin-du, 31, 78, 104, 149; about, 31–32; coffee production in, 31, 56, 78, 93, 112; geographic location of, 8, 9; Matador district of, 34–35, 76, 112, 162; insurgents' capture of, 89–92, 103; land grants in, 34–35, 126; sequestration of properties in, 100, 107, 117
dowry, 24, 33, 78; in house-based systems, 25–27, 42; inalienability of, 65, 67
Doyle, William, 50
Drevet, Jean, 90, 191n9
Dubison, Nicolas, 90
Ducamp, Jacques, 63
Ducasse, Jean-Baptiste, 32, 39
Dumas, Alexandre, 1, 2, 20–21, 24, 148
Dumont, Alexandre, 127
Duvergier, Jean-Baptiste, 15

Edict of Nantes, Revocation of, 4, 12, 15, 16, 101
Eldorado des Aquitains, L' (Cauna), xiv–xv

emigration. *See* migration
Ennery, 49, 111, 143, 158
Etchegorry, Noël, 72–73
Etcheverry, Louis, 83
Etcheverry, Martin d', 73

Ferdinand VII, 129, 140
Ferdinand of Aragon, 71
Ferrand, Jean-Louis, 129, 130, 134
"first emigrant" concept, 3–4
Flaville plantation, 89
Fleury, Elizabeth, 78
Forcade, Jean de la, 6, 16
Forcade, Marthe de la, 6, 8
Forcade, Rachel de la, 6, 7–8, 15, 16, 17, 20, 140
Foucault, Nicolas-Joseph, 16, 18
Franklin, Benjamin, 116
free people of color, 49, 90, 99, 100
free trade, xii–xiii, 149, 158
France, Empire of: enclave in Santo Domingo, 134; invasion of Spain by, 129–30
France, Kingdom of: debate over indemnity in, 112–15; and Kingdom of Navarre, 5, 63, 118–24, 152, 153; and Seven Years' War, 10–11; and trade with Haiti, 158
France, Republic of: constitution of 1791 of, 122; and Haitian Revolution, 88, 94, 102, 105, 158, 159; sequestering of properties by, 100–102

Galan, Pierre Cornu, 83
Galveston Island, 134–35
García y Moreno, Joaquín, 92, 103
Garran-Coulon, Jean-Philippe, 89
Garrigus, John, 48, 49
Geggus, David, 97
Ghachem, Malick, 53
Gomès, Jacob, 83
Greciet, Jean, 44, 84
Guárico, 127, 134. *See also* Cap-Haïtien/Cap-Français

Hägerstrand, Torsten, 3–4
Haitian Constitution (1805), 100, 110–11
Haitian nation: Delorme on, 148–52; Henri Christophe rule in, 143–46; indemnity debate in, 110–16; independence proclamation of, 88; United States and, 150–51. *See also* Saint-Domingue
Haitian Revolution: French military forces during, 88, 94, 102, 105, 158; Jean-Pierre Lamerenx during, 103–7; pleas by refugees during, 92–95; and property rights, 88, 107–10; refugees from, xiii, 101–2, 124–30; royalist forces during, 103–4; sequestration of properties during, 100–103; slave insurrection of 1791 during, 89–92, 95–100
Hapette, Bernardin, 83
Heckscher, Eli, xii
Henry IV of France (Henry III of Navarre), 5, 11, 12, 63, 119–20
Hiriart, Jean, 50, 102
Hirschman, Albert O., xii–xiii, 158–60
"History and Ethnology" (Lévi-Strauss), 1, 3
Hont, István, xii, xiii, 59
house-based systems, 5, 80, 85; dowry in, 25–27, 42; emigration and, 19, 79, 84, 86–87; inalienability of property in, 27, 65, 67–68; Lévi-Strauss on, xii, 1, 3, 6, 72, 87; non-multiplication of houses in, 83–84
Hozier, Charles-René d', 3, 8, 12
Hozier de Sérigny d', Antoine-Marie, 11
Hugo, Victor, 88, 148
Hume, David, xiii, 59

Imagined Communities (Anderson), 118, 178
indebtedness, 55, 65–68, 79, 81, 137–38, 139
indemnity, 29, 45, 59, 76, 159; debate over, 110–16; for slaves, 58–59
inheritance customs: Bourdieu on, xiv, 5, 6; Civil Code and, 87, 136; conflicts over, 63–70, 71–72, 80–81, 82, 136–37; emigration and, 2–3, 20–28, 83–84; in house-based societies, 5–6, 41, 65, 67–68, 83–84; and legitimacy, 85; in Lower Navarre, 41–42; and payment of debts, 81–82. *See also* primogeniture
Inner Life of Empires, The (Rothschild), xv
Iron, Jeanne d', 50
Isabella of Castile, 71
Isidor Gabriel (rebel colonel), 146

Jean d'Albret, 71
Jean-François (insurgent leader), 94, 107

Jeanne III d'Albret, 15–16
Jeannot (insurgent leader), 90, 91, 107
Jefferson, Thomas, xiii
Jenkins, Timothy, 1, 5
Jesuits, 16, 31, 153
Joachim, Benoît, 158
Julbin (Gilbin), Pierre-Basile, 104

Kerverseau, François de, 92
Kindelán y O'Regan, Sebastián, 130
Kingdom of This World, The (Carpentier), xiii, 124–25, 142
King of Gold, The, 156
kinship, xi, 1–2. *See also* house-based systems

Labache, Marie, 43–44, 169
Labarthe, Marie, 124
La Bastide Clairence: about, 62–63; geographic location of, xi, 43, 63, *77*; joins Kingdom of France, 63, 118–24, 152, 153; nobility in, 86–87; Saint-Domingue ties to, xi, 43–50, 81, 123–24; town officials of, 63, 82, 154
Labat, Jean-Baptiste, 39
Laborde, Daniel, 82, 137, 139
Laborde, Jean-Pierre, 139
Laborie, Pierre Joseph, 35; *The Coffee Planter of Saint Domingo,* 29–30, 31, 33, *37*, 41, 54, 56, *127*
Lafitte, Marc, 131
Lamartine, Alphonse de, 148
Lambert, Jean-Roch, 44
Lamerens, Carlos, 154
Lamerens Pérez, Rosa de, 154
Lamerens y Lamerens, Carlos Alejo de, 154
Lamerens y Vallenilla, Emeteria Dolores de, 154
Lamerenx, Adélaïde Charlotte, 126–27
Lamerenx, Adolphe, 140, 203–4n113
Lamerenx, Auguste, 140, 202n93
Lamerenx, Charles, 138–39, 140, 141, 164, 168; as estate owner, 86, 136–39; marriage and children of, 138, 140, 202n93; nation choosing by, 152, 153–54; in New Orleans, 130–31; privateering imprisonment of, 82, 128–30, 135
Lamerenx, Charles-François, 135, 141
Lamerenx, Eugène, 140, 154

Lamerenx, Françoise, 21, 22, 23, 162
Lamerenx, Henri, 21, 22, 23, 63, 163
Lamerenx, Isaac, 6–7, 11, 16, 20, 65, 161
Lamerenx, Jacques, 21, 69, 162
Lamerenx, Jean, 12, 22, 69–70, 125, 161, 164; inheritance of, 15, 22; and Marc-Antoine, 4, 5, 17, 26; as master of Uhart-Juzon estate, 6, 8
Lamerenx, Jean-François, 4, 164
Lamerenx, Jeanne, 17, 161
Lamerenx, Jean-Pierre, 62, 78, 89, 90, 103, 163, 167; becomes master of Lamerenx house, 79–82, 85–86, 135, 136; coffee plantation of, 73, 76, 112; in Cuba, 125–26, 127; emigration to Saint-Domingue by, 46, 62, 66, 73, 79, 84; as militia leader, 11, 78–79; as officer in slave army, 104, 105–7; return to Saint-Domingue by, 135–36, 157; sequestration of plantation of, 101–2, 107, 117; slaves owned by, 76, 126, 127
Lamerenx, Louis, 22, 23, 26, 163
Lamerenx, Marc-Antoine, 5, 43, 45, 60, 73, 76, 78, 84; capital accumulation by, 33, 35, 38, 39–40, 41–42; emigration to Saint-Domingue by, 3–11, 12, 15, *23*, 24–25, 29, 79; inheritance of, 22; marriage of, 26, 31, 38, 39; profile of, 21, 162
Lamerenx, Marguerite, 81, 86, 135, 139–40, 141, 157, 165, 168; conflict with brother Charles, 82, 136–37
Lamerenx, Marguerite-Françoise, 38, 40, 61, 93, 112, 164; and sequestration of property, 107–8, 110
Lamerenx, Marie-Adélaïde, 135, 165
Lamerenx, Marie-Elizabeth, 38, 40, 54, 56, 164; and Haitian Revolution, 92–93, 94–95; plantation ownership by, 42–43, 80, 100, 112
Lamerenx, Marie-Ursule (generation 3), 23, 81; inheritance of, 22; profile of, 21, 162
Lamerenx, Marie-Ursule (generation 4), 85, 135, 136; profile of, 163
Lamerenx, Marthe, 17, 161
Lamerenx, Mathieu, 26–27, 62; conflict with wife, 63–70, 71–72; inheritance of, 5, 23, 79; marriage of, 26, 43, 46; profile of, 21, 162

Lamerenx, Pierre, 12, 15, 16–17, 19, 69, 161
Lamerenx estate, 135, 136–38, 139–40, 203n105
Lamerenx family, xi, 80, 84; in Cuba, 125–28, 129–30, 140; emigration history of, 3–11, 12, 15–20, 23, 24–25, 29, 79; family name of, xiv; indebtedness of, 65–68, 137–39; paths to capital accumulation of, 33–43; as transatlantic network, 139, 154
Landers, Jane, 140
land grants, 33–35
land surveying, 34–35, 41
land value, 42–43, 45, 49, 58–59, 182n61
Larradé, Mr. (town crier), 72–73
Larroque, Jean, 47, 48, 49, 108; during Haitian Revolution, 97, 99
Laveaux, Étienne, 105, 106
lawyers, 46
Leclerc, Charles, 108–9, 111, 124, 129, 134, 159
Lefebvre, Henri, ix, xii
Le Gros, Gabriel, 92
Le Jeune, Elizabeth, 34–35, 42, 93, 112; Marc-Antoine Lamerenx marriage to, 8, 24, 31, 33–34, 38, 39; and sequestration of property, 107–8, 109–10; slaves of, 54, 59
Le Play, Frédéric, xii, 1–2, 5, 23, 83
Lespade, Marc-Antoine de, 11–12
Lespade, Suzanne de, 5, 17, 62
Lévi-Strauss, Claude, 80; on house-based systems, xii, 1, 3, 6, 72, 87
Lhande, Pierre, 62
Locke, John, 43
Loiseau, Marie-Valentine, 92
Lombart, Jean-Pierre, 62
Lombart, Marie de, 86–87, 166
Lostal, Gratian, 17
Lostal, Pierre, 18
Lostal de Saint-Martin, Isaac, 17, *18*, 19
Louis I of Navarre, 63
Louis X le Hutin, 63
Louis XIII, 5
Louis XIV, 4, 13, 19
Louis XV, 5
Louis XVI, 121
Louis XVIII, 144, 145, 153
Louverture, Isaac, 104–5

Louverture, Toussaint. *See* Toussaint Louverture
Lower Navarre, xix, *xx*, 16, 62, 71, 123, 154; dowry in, 78, 84; nobility in, 65, 80, 87; primogeniture in, 6, 41–42. *See also* Navarre, Kingdom of

Mably, Gabriel Bonnot de, 121, 122
MacDonald, John S., 4
MacDonald, Leatrice D., 4
Madiou, Thomas, 104, 106, 107, 114–15
maize, 123
Manuel des habitants de Saint-Domingue (Saint Domingue Planters' Handbook) (Coeurjoly), 30, 33, 47, 49–50, 55, 57–58
Marmelade: coffee plantations in, 38, 42, 45, 47, 51, 56, 78, 89, 103, 112, 182n61; Ennery district of, 49, 143; during Haitian Revolution, 91, 97, 104–5, 106, 110; about parish of, 35; sequestration of properties in, 100, 102, 110; slaves in, 54–55, 102; Soufrière district of, *36*, 43, 47
Marmont, Anne de, 46, 62, 73–74, 86, 166; conflict with husband Mathieu Lamerenx, 63–70, 71–72
Marmont, Jean de, 64, 86
Marmont, Jean-Pierre de, 46, 167
Marmont, Paul Auguste de, 85, 167
marriage: and capital accumulation, 39–41; and dowry, 24, 25–27, 33, 42, 65, 67, 78; between heirs, 70–72
Marriage Contract, The (Balzac), 6
Marx, Karl, 6, 68
Matanzas, 82, 107, 112, 117, 125, 126, 128–31, 133, 135, 137, 139, 140, 154, 158
Medina, Franco de, 143
Mendès, Daniel, 69
mercantilism, xii–xiii, 59–60, 174n16
merchants: and citizenship, 118; role of, in colonial system, 49–50, 55–56. *See also* colonial trading system
Mexico, 134–35
migration: annual timing of, 73; funding of, 27, 73; government-sponsored, 11–15; and house-based systems, 19, 79, 84, 86–87; and inheritance system, 2–3, 20–28, 83–84; of Lamerenx family, 15–20; by Protestants, 12, 15–17, 19

Miller, Christopher, 48
Minguet, André, 32, 149
Mithon de Senneville, Jean-Jacques, 14
Moirie, Anne de, 86
Moirie, Michel de, 86
Mon Oncle d'Amérique, 155–56
Monroe, James, xiii
Montes, Toribio, 130
Mora, Jean-Pierre, 73
Moreau de Saint-Méry, Louis Élie, 31–32, 35, 54
Mouscardy, Augé, 43–44
Mouscardy, Bonne, 47–48, 170
Mouscardy, Jean, 48–49, 60, 89, 112, 141, 169; emigration of, 43–46, 47, 84–85; during Haitian Revolution, 96, 97–98; sequestration of estate of, 100, 108; slaves owned by, 59, 76, 99
Mouscardy, Jeanne, 44, 45
Mouscardy, Jean-Théodat, 47–48, 170; career in Haitian army, 95–96, 142, 145–48, 152
Mouscardy, Marguerite, 146
Mouscardy, Marie, 44, 45, 99
Mouscardy family, xi, xiii, 44, 49, 84, 158; emigration history of, 43–50, 84–85; idealization of legend of, 98–99
Mouscardy plantation: coffee production on, 102–3; sequestration of, 100, 108, *109*, *110*

Napoleon Bonaparte, 41, 108, 129, 131, 144, 152, 159
Nassiet, Michel, 71, 84
nation: and belonging, 118, 120, 123, 152–57; in Latin America, 201–2n83; and nation-building initiatives, 134, 153
nationalism, 118, 123, 130, 152
National Power and the Structure of Foreign Trade (Hirschman), xii–xiii, 158–60
Navarre, Kingdom of, 5, 71, 81–82; and Kingdom of France, 63, 118–24, 153; nobility in, 8, 80; Protestants in, 15–16, 17
Neuilly (French commander), 104
New Orleans, 130–31, 140, 154
nobility, 8, 66, 80, 86–87, 101
Noé plantation, 89, 109
Nolivos, Pierre-Gédéon de (father), 8, 11–12, 31

Nolivos, Pierre-Gédéon de (son), 11–12
notaries, 58, 134, 154; role of, 44–45

Ogé, Vincent, 90, 95
oncle d'Amérique, L' (Scribe), ix–x
Ordeal of Elizabeth Marsh, The (Colley), xv

Padouen, Jeanne, 44
Pané, Ramón, 32
Paparel (Poparel), Jean-Baptiste, 104–5
Pares, Richard, 60
Pashman, Howard, 116
patronage system, 4, 11, 17
Pérez de la Riva, Juan, 126
Pérez Morales, Edgardo, 131
Pétion, Alexandre, 58–59, 143–44
plantation manager, 45, 46–47
Polverel, Etienne, 100–101, 104; and Kingdom of Navarre, 118–23
Popkin, Jeremy, 97
Portantin, Marie, 48
prejudice of color, 95, 100, 144, 151
Prézeau, Chevalier de, 144–45
primogeniture, 6, 41, 44, 66–67, 79; and emigration, 2, 83, 86; weakening of, 87. *See also* inheritance customs
privateering, 13, 14, 132–34, 142, 154
property: Haitian Constitution and, 110–11; Haitian historiographical debate over, 114–15; Haitian Revolution's defense of rights to, 88, 107–10; inalienable character of entailed, 5, 27, 65, 66, 67–68, 79; indemnity for lost, 29, 45, 58–59, 76, 110–16, 159; noble vs. non-noble, 66, 80; sequestration of, 100–103, 107–8, 109–10
Protestants, 12, 15–17, 19
Pufendorf, Samuel von, 113
Pujo, Alexis-Solange, 156
Pujo, Alice, 156
Pujo, Jean-Baptiste, 156

racism. *See* prejudice of color
Raimond, Julien, 107
reason-of-state theory, 59
refugees: French government assistance for, 138–39; from Haitian Revolution, xiii, 101–2, 124–30
Repussard, Colonel, 129, 201n62

residency, 85, 86
Resnais, Alain, 155–56
Rivière-Hérard, Charles, 147–48
Rochambeau, Donatien-Marie-Joseph, 108–9
Roman law, 22, 23, 24, 65
Rostand, Edmond, 2
Rothschild, Emma, xv

Saint-Domingue: abolition of slavery in, 94, 101, 105, 158; capital accumulation in, 33, 35, 38, 39–42; coffee production in, 30–33, 55–56, 59, 60, 157, 158; emigration to, 3–15, 15–20, 23, 24–25, 29, 46, 62, 66, 73, 79, 84; free people of color in, 49, 85, 90, 99, 100; as "hell on earth," x–xi; image of wealth in, x, 61, 157; and international trade, 55, 56, 157, 158; La Bastide Clairence connections with, 123–24; land surveying in, 41; land values in, 42–43, 45, 49, 182n61; map of northern, 9; massacre of white colonists in, 96, 98, 99; refugees from, xiii, 101–2, 124–30, 138–39; and Seven Years' War, 10–11; and Spain, 60, 93–94, 104–5; sugar production in, 29, 35, 38, 55–56, 57, 60, 61, 76; white population in, xi. *See also* Haitian nation
Saint-Domingue Planters' Handbook. See Manuel des habitants de Saint-Domingue (Saint Domingue Planters' Handbook)
Saint-Germain du Houlme, Charles de, 38, 40, 61
Saint-Palais, 82, 136, 154
Saint-Simon, Henri de, 3, 21
Salaberry, Charles de, 12–14
San Rafael (Saint-Raphaël), 92, 103, 104, 106, 108
Santana, Pedro, 148
Santo Domingo, 50, 129, 130, 133–34
Say, Jean-Baptiste, 149, 185n109; on colonial wealth and profits, 29, 55, 61, 158; on slavery, 53–54, 57, 61
Scribe, Eugène, ix–x
Seven Years' War, 9–11, 60–61, 99
Silly, Françoise, 76–78, 125, 128, 154
slavery: abolition of, 94, 101, 105, 158; and commerce, 38, 60–61; in Cuba, 158; and liberty, 122; master-slave relations under, 51–55; profitability of, 61, 78; Say on, 53–54, 57, 61; Adam Smith on, 53–54, 56–57, 101; support for legitimacy of, 93; violence of, 53, 54
slaves: African origins of, 126–27; cost of, 45, 183n63; emancipation of, 94, 105, 106; and free coloreds, 100; as housekeepers, 48; number of in coffee plantations, 76, 102–3; and plantation value, 47, 57–59; treatment of, 50–55; working and living conditions of, 35, 127
Smith, Adam, 30, 32–33, 41, 42, 43, 155; on colonies' commerce, 35, 38, 56; on mercantilism, xii, 174n16; on slavery, 53–54, 56–57, 101; on source of colonial wealth, 29, 55; on wealth and citizenship, 117, 118
Sonthonax, Léger-Félicité, 94, 104
Soult, Jean-de-Dieu, 144
Spain, 60; and Haitian Revolution, 93–94, 104–5; Napoleon's invasion of, 129–30
stem-family concept, xii, 1–2, 70, 83
Suchet, Louis-Gabriel, 144
sugar, 29; capital-intensive nature of producing, 35, 38, 76; price of, 55–56, 60; profitability of, 55, 57, 61; and slavery, 56

tea, 13–14
Thore, Etienne, 142
Thore, Jean, 44, 45
Three Musketeers, The (Dumas), 2, 20–21
tobacco, 56–57
Topik, Steven, 30
Toussaint Louverture, 104–5, 144, 152; and French republican forces, 88, 102, 105; as guardian of property rights, 107–10; initial demands of, 106, 195n71; as insurgent leader, 9, 92, 107; and large estates, 143, 146; and Spanish royalist forces, 94, 104–5
trade: in coffee, 158; and colonial system, 49–50, 55–56, 59–60; and slavery, 38, 60–61. *See also* colonial trading system
Tragedy of King Christophe, The (Césaire), 143
Treatise on Political Economy (Say), 29
Treaty of Basel, 125
Treaty of Paris, 115, 116
Trémais, Charles François Pichot de Kerdisien, 38, 42, 51–53, 54, 89

Trémais plantation, 42, 51, 109; and Haitian Revolution, 89, 191n3; sequestration of, 100, 102–3; slaves on, 54–55, 102
Tully, James, 182n53

Uhart, Jean-Bernard d', 139
Uhart-Juzon estate, 5, 19, 20, 65, 79, 136, 140; genealogical chart of, 6–8; Mathieu Lamerenx inheriting of, 5, 26, 64, 79; and Lower Navarre, 16, 80
United States, 150–51; War of Independence by, 40, 60, 115

Vastey, Jean-Louis (Pompée Valentin, Baron de Vastey), 53, 98, 143

Vastey, Jean-Valentin (white planter), 98
Vastey, Louis-Marie de (Haitian lawyer), 98
Vattel, Emer de, *Le Droit des gens*, 112–13
Vázquez, Father José, 94, 117, 192n27
Vène, Captain, 105
Viret, Jérôme Luther, 2, 24
Voltaire, 48

Wealth of Nations, The (Smith), xii, 29, 38, 53–54, 117, 118, 155
Weber, Theodore, *150*
Wegge, Simone, 24
Wimpffen, Stanislas de, x, 156

Zink, Anne, 22, 25–26, 65, 83–84